Yearbook of Cultural Property Law
2008

YEARBOOK OF CULTURAL PROPERTY LAW

***Series Editor:* Sherry Hutt**

Sponsored by the Lawyers' Committee for Cultural Heritage Preservation

The *Yearbook* provides those in the heritage-management world with summaries of notable court cases, settlements and other dispositions, legislation, government regulations, policies, and agency decisions that affect their work. Interviews with key figures, refereed research articles, think pieces, and a substantial resources section round out each volume. Thoughtful analyses and useful information from leading practitioners in the diverse field of cultural property law will assist government land managers; state, tribal, and museum officials; attorneys; anthropologists; archaeologists; public historians; and others to better preserve, protect, and manage cultural property in domestic and international venues. All royalties go directly to the Lawyers' Committee for Cultural Heritage Preservation.

Yearbook of Cultural Property Law

2008

Sherry Hutt
Editor

David Tarler
Assistant Editor

ROUTLEDGE Routledge
Taylor & Francis Group
LONDON AND NEW YORK

First published 2008 by Left Coast Press, Inc.

Published 2016 by Routledge
2 Park Square, Milton Park, Abingdon, Oxon OX14 4RN
605 Third Avenue, New York, NY 10017

Routledge is an imprint of the Taylor & Francis Group, an informa business

ISSN 1931-5627
ISBN 978-1-59874-080-6 (hbk)
LCCN 2006213755

Contents

Preface

Welcome to a review of the year 2007 in the vibrant field of cultural property law. It has been an active year as measured by the number of news articles, court actions, and journal articles that were generated and are noted in this volume. The *Yearbook* seeks to bring together thoughtful pieces that explain these issues, inform and educate, and assemble source materials useful to those who will seek to represent clients and use the law as a means to protect cultural property.

At the core of the *Yearbook* are the Practice Area sections, each with a section editor who is a practitioner and scholar in his or her respective area of the genre of law that is cultural property law. If you the reader feel that there is something that should be covered in the coming year, the editors would be pleased to receive your comments. In some instances, cases are not reported even though there was litigation during the year, as the sentencing or culminating event had not occurred by year's end.

The articles in the *Yearbook* are peer reviewed and the topics are chosen to add further depth to the Practice Areas, to give the reader insight into major events, and to provide source data that are not published elsewhere. The *Yearbook* is intended as an ongoing aid to legal practice, ranging from scholarly analysis of emerging issues to practical aids for practitioners and educators. This year two articles tackle at some length topics of interest to those who produce archaeological reports or manage CRM firms, and those who govern tribal cultural property. Kelly Yasaitis Fanizzo, who works with federal agency compliance at the Advisory Council for Historic Preservation, has researched the legal rights to the content of archaeological reports and provides pertinent insight to the layers of property interests in the tangible and intangible aspects of such research. Trinidad Contreras seeks to offer a model code for tribal cultural property by placing such code into cultural context. Holding a graduate degree in American Indian Studies and completing law school at the University of Arizona, Rogers College of Law, Contreras has spent years studying the intersection of tribal and U. S. law. He began his research for the *Yearbook* by analyzing existing codes, which appear to be modeled on federal protection and compliance laws, written in the vein of archaeological resources management. To better serve tribal governments from the perspective of the tribe, he offers a comprehensive model.

The *Yearbook* is also pleased to publish the winning submission of the 2007 Lawyers Committee for Cultural Heritage Preservation (LCCHP) Law School Writing Competition, now generously sponsored by the law firm of Andrews Kirth. The winning article by James Wawrzyniak, a graduate of Harvard Law School, provides a thoughtful analysis of the enforcement of judgments against foreign nations by attaching cultural assets.

The *Yearbook* strives to provide substantive information on current topics of interest. This year George Washington University Museum Law Professor Ildikó DeAngelis traveled to Rome to interview Paolo Ferri, the prosecutor in the trial of Getty Museum curator Marion True. It is notable that Mr. Ferri does not usually give press interviews, preferring to try his cases in court, but in this instance he was impressed by Professor DeAngelis and her ability to transcend the spectacle of the trial and focus upon a legal and ethical lesson for museum professionals.

The *Yearbook* editors are pleased to recognize those practitioners who inspire us and who have made a positive impact on the field. This year the focus is on museums and two directors of substantial note. Donny George Youkhanna earned the esteem of museum directors around the world as he sought to protect the treasures of Iraq in the midst of war and to keep museums intact. Richard West retired this year as founding director of the National Museum of the American Indian. West not only raised the funds that helped to open the museum, but his philosophy of a portrayal of American Indians, as bearers of living, vibrant and talented cultures, has shaped the museum and given it worldwide prominence in the short term. In coming years, the

Yearbook will focus on the accomplishments of those in other practice areas. Nominations are welcome.

In a continuing effort to meet the needs of practitioners and law professors, the *Yearbook* includes a section on law schools and one of published resources. This year, Michael Scherzer interviewed several law professors and gives tips from four on how they develop their courses, including two complete course outlines. Gary Nurkin has joined the editors this year and has compiled a long list of recent published items and electronic resources. It is notable that each year the list of published items is longer than the last, a reflection of the growing attention by scholars to the importance of cultural property law as an identified area of practice.

Once again this year, the *Yearbook* has been produced as a project of the LCCHP, the nonprofit organization of lawyers, which is dedicated to scholarship, education, and cultural heritage preservation, and which receives the proceeds from the sale of this volume. The regular contributors to the *Yearbook* are members of LCCHP. For more information on the benefits of membership please visit www.culturalheritagelaw.org or email the LCCHP at LCCHP@yahoogroups.com. The editors, editorial board, the LCCHP, and authors who contributed to this volume also offer their appreciation to Mitch Allen and the staff at Left Coast Press, our publisher, for their continued efforts to seek out and promote scholarship to benefit cultural resource preservation, protection, and education.

The *Yearbook* editors continue to seek information for the next edition, particularly state, local, and tribal actions that may not have been published or may have been resolved without a final judgment. Expression of interest to publish articles that meet the mission of the *Yearbook* are also welcome. Articles are desired that address topics of current interest in a scholarly and complete manner, that are of assistance to practitioners, but that leave advocacy to them. Please send information or inquiries to: Hutt_Sherry@yahoo.com. Thank you.

The information in the Yearbook *is drawn from public records. The views expressed in the* Yearbook *are those of the LCCHP members and the authors and do not necessarily reflect the view or policies of the federal agencies or the public or private firms whose employees contributed to this volume.*

Italian Prosecutor Paolo Ferri in Rome, Italy, March 2007

• • •

by Ildikó P. DeAngelis[1]

Collecting is an important museum activity that furthers the mission of museums to educate and to preserve the expressions of our human heritage. Over the past 35+ years, American museums and museum professional organizations have adopted ethical codes and guidelines in keeping with the goals enunciated in the UNESCO Convention of 1970 to preserve the world's cultural heritage through international cooperation. Twelve years of public debate on implementation of this convention in the United States[2] did much to bring to the attention of the museum community the problems inherent in the international art market and how important it is to avoid encouraging illicit trade. The delay afforded plenty of opportunity to adopt and implement sound museum acquisition policies. However, recent revelations on acquisitions of antiquities and archaeological materials by major art museums over the last three decades lead one to question whether our acquisition standards and/or their implementation have been too lax. Such inquiry is not out of line, given that (1) a former American antiquities curator has been indicted in Italy for conspiracy for allegedly trafficking in looted antiquities; (2) several of our largest and most prestigious art museums have returned significant collection objects that were allegedly looted and removed illegally from their countries of origin; and (3) several more American museums are now negotiating restitution agreements with Italian and Greek authorities.

A fortuitous discovery triggered these results. In 1994 Italian authorities, following leads in the investigation of antiquities smuggling, raided the Swiss warehouse facility of an Italian dealer named Giacomo Medici. Written records and over 4,000 Polaroid snapshots found during this and subsequent raids made it possible to trace suspect antiquities numbering in the thousands.[3] Unfortunately for some major art museums, the path of the documentation led to their own display cases.[4] Convictions of dealers and middle-men followed. For the U.S. museum community, the unprecedented step that caused uproar was the indictment of Dr. Marion True, the Getty's former antiquities curator, in an Italian court for handling or receiving thirty-five smuggled objects and for conspiracy for her alleged role in the smuggling business run by Robert Hecht and Giacomo Medici. This was the first time an American curator was held to account in a foreign court for museum collecting activities. Robert Hecht, the American-born antiquities dealer living in France, had been the major contact for many American art museums and was the source of the Getty's purchases over several decades. Giacomo Medici was allegedly Hecht's supplier.[5]

Under the Italian criminal system, hearings for a criminal trial are held one day at a time and are scheduled about once a month. Thus trials can drag on for years. At his request, Giacomo Medici was tried in Rome under a speedier option provided under Italian criminal procedure, and was subsequently found guilty. Medici is currently appealing his conviction. The trial of Marion True and Robert Hecht, the other two alleged co-conspirators, began on November 16, 2005 and is still ongoing. Both Marion True and Robert Hecht deny any wrongdoing. Dr. True, in a statement submitted as evidence in her trial, maintains that she followed Getty policies and procedures in her acquisition practices and that indeed when she first became curator in the mid 1980s she helped draft a memo to the Getty board to explore whether it was possible to continue to collect antiquities in a tainted market.[6]

A civil suit for restitution in Rome that paralleled the criminal prosecution was also filed. This suit was dismissed in 2007 as other strategies for recovery proved fruitful. For the past several years, the Italian authorities have been aggressively pursuing restitution by directly negotiating with individual museums in the United States and elsewhere based in part on evidence recovered from the Swiss raid. The agreements signed require major art museums in the United States to return objects, to agree not to acquire antiquities in the art market and to engage with Italian archaeologists and scholars in joint excavations and other educational projects. In return, the Italians are willing to loan back items for exhibition.[7] The old system of "*partage*" whereby archaeologists from a foreign country were allowed to carry away a certain portion of the finds has seemingly been updated. The new "*partage*" is loan-based. This is a sea-change in how our art museums deal with antiquities. At the same time, the museum community awaits the outcome of the criminal trial in Rome and for news of whether further indictments are forthcoming.

In fall 2006, I contacted Paolo Ferri, the chief Italian prosecutor of the case against Dr. True, and requested a meeting. He answered my e-mail almost immediately, and in March 2007 I found myself in front of the Giudizia Ufficio building in Rome waiting for his assistant to help pass me through security. The building is a modern structure of grey concrete with little to recommend it. Paolo Ferri has a small office, modestly furnished, only big enough for his desk and two chairs. He speaks English well and has a quick smile. The following is a summary of my interview with Paolo Ferri. It is not a word-for-word transcription, as the interview was not recorded. Rather it is a written summary that he later approved. After this summary, a brief history of acquisition practices of American museums is provided to shed light on how art museums came to be embroiled in this controversy. Finally, reforms of museum ethical codes are proposed for consideration by the museum community.

Summary of Interview with Prosecutor Paolo Ferri, Rome, March 7, 2007

Ildikó DeAngelis (ID): Looted undocumented cultural property became documented and traceable in significant numbers for the first time as a result of your investigations over the past decade or more. The uncovering of the extent of illicit trade in the international art market for antiquities and the role of our major museums in that market will change how museums in all the major 'art market' countries conduct their collecting in the future. Would you comment on these significant developments?

Paolo Ferri (PF): In Europe and in Italy in particular we take trafficking in stolen art objects very seriously, equivalent to trafficking in drugs in terms of its consequences and the money involved. Under the U.S. legal system, one can choose to prosecute or not. Under the Italian system, one must prosecute when there is evidence of a crime.

The Getty Museum claims to be in the avant-garde with respect to policies governing the acquisition of antiquities, but if that is so, you can imagine how bad other museums must be. I wonder what the other museums had to say about the Getty's claim.

In my view, donating art objects is often a vehicle for transferring illegally obtained items. Dealers usually group objects together to sell in order to hide the illegal ones. Collectors buy and then donate collections to museums to gain a tax advantage. An item may be offered as a gift for $100,000 tax deduction that was bought for only $1,000.

In the case of the Getty's agreement for part purchase/part donation of the Fleischman Collection,[8] the amounts of monies involved were $20 million paid and $40 million donated.

ID: I think it is fair to say that museum acquisitions of antiquities in the United States have come to a "dead halt"; and the museum world is in a crisis mode preparing for possible forthcoming claims and even indictments for alleged past misdeeds. Do these results come as a surprise to you?

PF: My trial pushed the situation forward, but it was already ripe for action. We were very lucky in 1994–1995 because we had the opportunity to accomplish a lot in Switzerland. We found documents from a virgin source [referring to the raid on Medici's "Corridor 17" Swiss storage and showroom facility]. Now it would be more difficult because people are aware of the potential consequences. It was a moment in time, one not likely to reoccur.

I was very tenacious, but it was an organized effort, not my work alone. Our work was done in a pooling of efforts. I worked on the penal side, others worked on the civil side. Archaeologists also were involved in analyzing the objects that we found, and there were experts to read the documents and photos that we obtained. Good work was also done by journalists and by public opinion. Archaeologists are in complete accord with our work. Many from the United States e-mailed me expressing agreement with what I was doing and suggesting additional questions that I should ask of Marion True and others.

This has been an interesting movement. When we started, we were not completely aware of where it would lead.

Currently new progress is happening as shown by recent agreements with the Metropolitan Museum, the Boston Museum, and Princeton University that will have impact on future archaeology. We are seeking agreements with museums in other countries as well. For example, we are getting ready for a new agreement with a museum in Copenhagen. If museums agree not to buy antiquities from either the black or green[9] markets the whole corrupt system will come falling down. Instead, we will have agreements to mutually excavate archaeological sites.

Our work has had its effect. Because of our actions, the prices for illicit objects have fallen, and the black market has slowed as demand is down:

1. One month ago a *tombarolo* [tomb robber] in possession of items from a major tomb told us that the items had been excavated four to five years ago. Prior to 1995, such items would have been sold within two months on the market. Now, it is taking four to five years due to our prosecutions.
2. Through investigations and telephone taps of other *tombaroli*, we heard them speak of a group of 15 signed vases. The whole set was up for sale for 15,000 Euros. In the past, *each* item would have sold for 15,000 Euros.

This is the most important objective of our investigations. It is not to have Marion True on trial per se but to stop the illegal market.

In my view, before 1995–1998, museums relied primarily on the statements of the dealers regarding the provenance of items. Otherwise, they turned a blind eye to where the objects came from.

Recently Marion True admitted in a written statement that the antiquities market was corrupt. In other words, the Getty had acquired items knowing that they were dirty. Her statements, however, are of a general nature, without specifics. Under Italian law, if she claims that others share in the liability she must come forward and specify her allegations and explain why these others are culpable. She has not yet done so.

I suspect that later transactions were indeed very fishy as very high prices were paid and perhaps profits in some cases split 50/50. These are my suspicions as there is no great evidence to prove this.

ID: Do you have evidence that others were involved?

PF: She [Marion True] said in a written statement that all of the trustees knew that they were acquiring items with possible origins in the black market. But this was generally-accepted practice. We did not get any specifics about this, only a general statement. We are not sure therefore that this is accurate.

ID: Why did you focus on Marion True and not other museum curators who had been active in the market?

PF: Because the evidence against her was the strongest. We focused on the Getty for several reasons. First, the Getty specifically collected Roman and Greek antiquities which directly affected us. Second, the Getty was spending so much more money than other museums. There are many reasons why the focus was on Marion True herself:

1. The number of her dealings was so great that they were impossible to ignore.
2. In the Italian system, penal action is mandatory when evidence of a crime is uncovered, as I noted before.

ID: Will you have to bring actions against others?

PF: I can't say. But, something may happen. We see that museums have begun firing curators who they know were involved in these kinds of dealings—preventive actions perhaps. If the problem is finished, perhaps there will be no need to pursue them. Also, much time has elapsed. But, I don't think we are finished yet. I do want to retire to enjoy my two grandchildren, which won't be in all that long a time as I am now near 60.

ID: How much longer will this trial take?

PF: I don't know. Many things have to be considered. We possibly may reach agreement with the defense counsel to abridge the evidence that needs to be presented, which we hope to do. Then we may be finished by the end of this year [2007].

ID: Why did you decide to combine the trial hearings for Marion True and Robert Hecht?

PF: It was not that they were combined but that they were very interrelated and heard at the same time. You will note that I am usually harder on Marion True than on Robert Hecht during the trial. Sometimes we focused more on Marion True than on Hecht simply because the existing evidence against Hecht was so overwhelming that it did not require further investigation.

ID: One might say that they appear to have been very arrogant in the way they went about their business—leaving a trail behind them.

PF: It wasn't simply arrogance but rather a certain "*legerezza*" or nonchalance because no one ever stopped them. They may have also felt that they were saving cultural patrimony, but the evidence shows otherwise. For example, the issue of collecting pottery fragments and then reconstructing the pots—that was not saving the pots, but encouraging dealers to break pots and use them to blackmail curators. The dealers were blackmailing the curators by selling the first fragment for less and then raising prices on the additional fragments as more were "found." Also, the dealers do not want the "orphans" to be on the market for long because fragments may help the carabinieri for identification purposes. Dealers also used the fragments as bargaining chips to encourage other sales (as indicated in a letter from Marion True to Medici in evidence referring to the Berlin Painter fragments). We are even aware of previous litigation between two collectors arguing who would be entitled to buy the next fragment of a broken vase that came on the market.

ID: In a recent article it is stated that at some point in 1990 Marion True "replaced the Met as the Fleischman's consultant, handpicking objects from antiquities dealers who were well known to her through her dealings at the Getty and Boston's Museum of Fine Arts" and thus they "became close friends."[10] One of the allegations you have made is that many of the objects in the Fleischman Collection were purchased on behalf of and indirectly for the Getty. Yet, Mrs. Fleischman writes that there was no agreement to sell or donate to the Getty before 1996.[11]

PF: I do not believe that this is true.

ID: What is the basis for your belief?

PF: Many curators formerly worked for dealers. Marion True worked for a dealer early in her career; others such as Arielle Kozlov left a museum and went to work for a commercial gallery. The trustees of museums employ these people because of their knowledge of important dealers. Also, in my opinion, only 10 percent of collectors are interested primarily in the art. The other 90 percent are primarily in it for the money. So the collectors have very close relationships with dealers, especially with the worst dealers.

The Fleischman Collection was put together in the 1980s but was greatly amplified in the early 1990s when it was to be sold. We have copies of invoices that are fake. I can prove this. The entire collection was built in order to be sold to a museum.

For example, I understand the *Menade and Silen* was obtained from Robin Symes [a convicted dealer who was based in the U.K.] at supposedly the same price that he had paid for it three years earlier at auction. Then, it was sold to the Getty for the same price. We have seen that often undocumented objects were placed on sale by dealers in public auctions and purchased back by them for the purpose of creating a sale history for the object, thus facilitating a subsequent sale.

Frida Tschakos [a convicted dealer] said that Marion True suggested to her and other dealers that rather than sell something directly to the Getty, she should sell it to the Fleischmans.

The Getty agreed to do a major exhibition and catalogue dedicated to the Fleischman Collection in 1994–1995. Why would they go to that considerable expense if they did not have a chance of getting the collection in the future? The exhibit and the catalogue increased the value of the collection.

The Getty didn't ask any questions about the origins of these objects when the catalogue of the Fleischman Collection was published. In fact, the Getty's own publication manufactured the provenance needed for acquisition under its new policy. Conveniently, the Getty's new [1995] acquisition policy required a previous publication as evidence of legitimacy for acquisition.

Recently Getty authorities wrote to the Italian Ministry of Culture that they would discuss things orally that they could not put into writing. They stress in America that penal action is not mandatory and that is why they made such a proposal. Can you imagine what they may have to say?

ID: It would appear that the revised 1995 Getty policy was passed to accommodate the Fleischman Collection acquisition in 1996.

PF: The Getty went through with the deal [the acquisition of the Fleischman Collection] even though they knew we had raided the Medici facility in Switzerland in the previous year. They knew the risk they were taking, but they couldn't turn back. Perhaps they hoped that the Swiss would not surrender documentation or that attitudes would be softened by their willingness to repatriate some items in 1999.

ID: What penalty may be given to Marion True if she is found guilty?

PF: I don't know what penalty I will request. There are many things to consider. My sentiments are to consider the scope of the defense. If the defense shows some willingness to cooperate, then perhaps three years. If the defense fully contests everything and it becomes a fully adversarial contest, then I am inclined to be less lenient and ask for five to six years.

ID: Can you extradite her to bring her to Italy to carry out the sentence?

PF: She is now married to a French citizen and lives in Paris. French law would allow arrest and extradition as the EU considers illegal trafficking in antiquities a serious crime. U.S. law on extradition differs. This is a peculiar situation as she is an American citizen living abroad. It will be interesting to see.

ID: Have you heard that the Getty reportedly has prepared a "loss sheet" of objects they may have to return?

PF: That is not part of my responsibility but rather of the civil claims lawyer. He is meeting with the Getty director on this case to discuss what items to surrender in future. We are especially interested in two items:

1. *Lysippos* [(Bronze of a Victorious Youth) purchased in 1977] and the
2. *Morgantina Venus/Aphrodite* [(Marble and Limestone) purchased in 1988 for $18 million from Robin Symes].[12]

The Getty's attitude is not very correct. The Met director's attitude was smarter because he agreed to surrender the *calyx krater* and the Morgantina Silver and other things without asking for anything in particular in return. He left that up to the Italian side. The Getty based its attitude on juridical conditions. The Getty needs to be more scientific and more considerate of our side. We are not so interested in the actual items, as such, nor greedy to have them back at any cost. For example, the Aphrodite is probably a pastiche. Rather we want to stop the past practices of looting and would like to see acknowledgment that they were very wrong. The Getty must surrender its best items so that future illegal purchases may stop. The Met also agreed to finance international cooperative scientific excavations in the future (in conjunction with Italian archaeologists). This will lead to more scientific excavations and preservation of our heritage. This is very good. But the Getty is greedy. The Getty asked for specific objects on loan in return. Going at this in this way is a mistake. I think that the future can be better for cultural relations, but only if the Getty changes its current attitudes.[13]

ID: General Conforti [former head of the Italian police, who testified in March 2006] is quoted as saying that the Italian rules on international loans were too restrictive and that they should be loosened. What is your opinion?

PF: The fault for this unfortunate situation lies also with the Italian side because in the past the loan regulations for archaeological material were so stupid. Also it was a fault of the former Italian government which said that it was too risky to loan such items. This forced others to go into the black or green markets including the Americans, the Australians, the Europeans and the Japanese.

The new attitude in museums globally is not to establish comprehensive museums but to have thematic shows that interpret the objects, which, in turn, require loans of objects from around the world. We must build for the future. The future mode of reaching accord includes agreement to cease acquiring all archaeological material and to loosen loan policies.

ID: In your opinion, would it be possible also to create a legitimate market?

PF: Impossible. Side by side there is always the black market that exploits honest dealers. They forge documents.

Epilogue

As I was leaving his office for the last time, Paolo Ferri remarked that ordinarily he tells his junior prosecutors not to give interviews and to try their cases in the courtroom, not in the press. However, in this case, given the importance of public opinion for bringing change, he sees informing the public as important and justified. Judging by the amount of attention his cases have received in the United States, he has certainly been successful.

For anyone keenly interested in museum collecting, reading the art news section of daily newspapers over these past few years has not been an enjoyable experience. Rather, it has been a time of open-mouthed incredulity, anger and fear that apparent abuses unveiled by the press will invite attention from lawmakers and regulators, thus further complicating the acquisition practices for all museums. As noted author Stephen Weil wrote, "no museum is an island"—one museum's reported wrongdoing will reflect on and come back to haunt all museums. Aside from further restrictive regulation, the bigger issue for the museum profession is public confidence or, simply put, *trust*. If public trust in museums is eroded, museums stand to lose support from those on whom they must rely. As public charities, museums receive a majority of their donations of both funds and collection objects from the very people they are potentially alienating.

Prosecutor Ferri impressed me as a man on a mission. Time will tell whether his allegations are proven under Italian law. No matter what the outcome, past museum acquisition policies and practices have led us to a Rome courtroom and to the loss of many millions of dollars of museum acquisition funds spent on objects that are being returned to countries of origin. The remainder of this paper will attempt to reach an understanding of how these past policies and practices went wrong and then to propose the development of new profession-wide ethical standards intended to avoid such outcomes in the future. Meaningful self-regulation informed by past missteps is the key to repairing damage done to the public trust.

How We Got Here: Critical Analysis of American Art Museum Acquisition Standards

Aside from a handful of U.S. art-collecting institutions (such as the Smithsonian in 1973, the Harvard museums in 1972),[14] most major art museums did not publish ethical codes or acquisition policies specifically for their museums in line with the UNESCO Convention of 1970. Those that did obligated themselves to make good faith inquiries into the provenance of objects offered for acquisition, professed intent to greatly limit acquisition of unprovenanced[15] objects, and declared that they would not collect objects suspected to be stolen or illegally exported from their countries of origin. By contrast, art museums, especially those that were active in the art market, moved slowly and cautiously in this regard. This was in spite of a resolution on museum acquisitions issued in January 1973 by the American Association of Art Museum Directors (AAMD), whose membership includes the directors of our major art museums, urging its members to cooperate fully with foreign countries to prevent the illicit traffic in works of art.[16] This resolution confirmed the belief of the AAMD that art museums can best implement such goals by refusing to acquire objects in violation of the relevant laws "obtaining in the countries of origin" and specifically recommending to boards of art museums that they promulgate "an appropriate acquisition policy statement." By 1981 the AAMD also included a provision in its Code of Ethics declaring it to be unprofessional for (directors of art museums) to:

> knowingly acquire . . . any art objects which have been stolen . . . in contravention of the applicable laws of its country of origin or any exporting countries and/or contravention of international treaties and international conventions.[17]

In other words, if an object considered for acquisition is determined to have been "stolen" (presumably stolen in the traditional sense of being taken wrongfully from a known rightful owner or in the broader sense of being removed from a country in violation of so-called "patrimony laws" that declared cultural property state-owned), an art museum director was instructed not to acquire it for the museum's collections. Note, however, that nothing in this 1981 AAMD provision expressly required an art museum director to abide by *export controls* of foreign nations. Absent such a prohibition, objects lacking legitimate export permits from their countries of origin could be acquired for art museum collections. Foreign export regulations attempt to control the removal of cultural property located within the country's borders, and as urged by archaeologists, typically smuggled objects are looted material headed for the international art market. By limiting acquisition to objects *known* to have been stolen, the AAMD 1981 code left the door open for art museum acquisition of objects without traceable documentation or scientifically excavated "find-spots." The AAMD mirrored a "presumption of innocence" approach: assuming objects available for acquisition in the art market were innocent until proven stolen. Underlying this approach is the belief that antiquities without provenance in the permanent collections of museums can still provide important aesthetic, cultural and educational value.[18] Also justifying lack of compliance to foreign export controls is the belief that export regulations of source countries are in effect an embargo on trade as export permits are rarely, if ever, issued. As implemented, such foreign export controls are contrary to U.S. policies that support free trade in cultural goods.

By the time the 1992 revision of the AAMD code was published, the indirect reference to compliance with foreign patrimony ownership laws was removed. Instead, the new acquisition guidelines looked essentially to what U.S. law directed. If the object was legally in the United States (as judged under U.S. law, including the Convention on Cultural Property Implementation Act (CPIA) that limited implementation of the UNESCO Convention), presumably art museum directors were free to acquire it.[19] A district court case that was decided three years before the AAMD issued this revised policy may have influenced this change. The 1989 *Peru v. Johnson* decision was often cited for the proposition that broad foreign patrimony laws declaring all cultural property to be state owned would not necessarily be recognized as valid proof of ownership by U.S. courts.[20] By relying on this case regarding Peruvian law as precedent, museum decision-makers may have concluded (with some risk) that foreign patrimony laws generally could be ignored after an object had entered the United States and came under U.S. jurisdiction. In other words, the object need not be considered "stolen" if taken in violation of a foreign patrimony law because U.S. courts would probably not define theft in that way.[21] Apparently, in the 1990s, no one considered the risk of being prosecuted in a foreign court. Even if someone had considered this possibility, the risk may have been viewed as negligible as proof required to track the movement of objects from foreign jurisdictions to the museum's display cases was highly unlikely to surface. Foreign courts may have also seemed remote to stay-at-home curators buying locally from international dealers. In sum, the 1992 AAMD code was not really an ethical policy as its aim was to avoid criminal penalties, not to set higher standards by which to earn public confidence.

In addition, neither the 1981 nor the 1992 AAMD codes specifically addressed the following key points:

(i) what steps should be taken to investigate the origins of objects proposed for acquisition

(ii) what types of documentation of clean title should be required; and

(iii) whether undocumented objects without provenance should be collected at all, and if so, under what limitations?

Neither version of the AAMD code demanded any independent inquiry about objects considered for acquisition during the very years that museums were purchasing in the art market where the "don't ask, don't tell" practice was firmly in place. Given that object histories are easily forged, requiring inquiries by those who were aware of the inner workings of the international art market would have been an prudent step.

Under both the 1981 and the 1992 versions of the AAMD code, the absence of information about an object would not work to prevent its acquisition, as only "actual knowledge" of theft would suffice. Such a standard invites a blind eye which in turn leaves no margin for error. American art museums were seemingly content to protect themselves from financial damage when buying unprovenanced objects (as did the Getty in its 1987 policy discussed below) by requiring written warranties from "reputable dealers" who could be found later to pay up if it should prove to be necessary to invoke warranties, although the AAMD codes did not specifically require warrranties. Note that in the event any director member of AAMD violated these guidelines on professional conduct, he or she could be reprimanded or dismissed from the organization and the director's museum could have been subject to sanctions such as suspension of loans of works or of shared exhibitions. No reprimands or expulsions have been reported to my knowledge for errant acquisition practices.[22]

The Getty Museum's Acquisition Standards

Ironically, the much maligned J. Paul Getty Museum under Dr. Marion True's tenure was the first large art museum actively buying in the art market that departed from following the AAMD's Code of Ethics and published its own museum-specific acquisition policy for antiquities in 1987. From 1987 to 1995, the Getty policy required warranties from dealers[23] that included warranties of clean title, of legal export, and that all other customs and patrimony laws, regulations and requirements of all relevant countries had been met. As long as a dealer was willing to sign the museum's warranty, only two additional inquiries were prescribed. Getty staff was directed to notify potential countries of origin about proposed acquisition and also to run a check through a stolen art database.[24]

Looted undocumented objects without owners to report the theft do not appear on stolen art databases and the step to check databases was abandoned in the subsequent 1995 revision of Getty's policy.[25] Similarly, the provision on contacting countries of origin for information was also removed. Asking foreign authorities about undocumented objects was placing the burden on foreign governments to investigate provenance for objects heretofore unknown. Dr. True admitted that this step had also proved ineffective for uncovering significant new information.[26] A more cynical view may note that by 1995, the date of the revised Getty policy, Italian authorities were conducting rigorous investigations of looting and smuggling activities both within and outside of Italy and thus inquiries to Italian authorities on potential acquisitions were likely to be reviewed in earnest and such reviews would inevitably cause significant delays in the acquisition process.

What about the museum's own diligence to inquire further about the history of ownership? The 1995 Getty policy appeared to set a standard in this regard. The revised policy restricted acquisitions to "known collections" by requiring a so-called provenance-by-publication.[27] In other words, the Getty would not acquire any object of antiquity after November 1995 unless the object's existence was known and documented in a publication dating before November 1995. On its face, this policy seems to go far. It tries to break the chain leading back to contemporary looting activity. Getty acquisitions could no longer fuel contemporary illicit looting as the museum would not acquire any object not known and published as of November 1995. But again, a more cynical view may note that by mid-1995, a year after a fruitful raid of an Italian dealer's warehouse in Switzerland that yielded a treasure trove of documentation of past looting, the Getty was not sacrificing much. By giving up the possibility of acquiring unpublished antiquities, the museum may have been practicing prudent risk management. In addition, past publications of suspect objects would trigger statues of limitations and under Getty policy, if a country of origin claimed an object for which the statue of limitations had expired, the country had to pay the Getty just compensation for the returned object.

The Getty's acquisition of a major collection under the terms of this new 1995 policy revealed a gaping loophole. This loophole proved very convenient, if unintended, as it facilitated the Getty's acquisition of the Fleischman Collection in the following year. Provenance-by-publication requirement of the new policy was met in this instance by a catalogue published by Getty itself for a dedicated exhibition of the Fleischman Collection which opened in Los Angeles on October 13, 1994. The close timing of the publication, the new acquisition policy, and the acquisition by the Getty of the Fleischman

Collection raised more than a few eyebrows as the collection allegedly contains undocumented objects, thirteen of which are now being returned to Italy.[28] Marion True has publicly stated that the timing of the new policy and the Fleischman acquisition were coincidental, and moreover that the new policy was never intended to prevent the acquisition of unprovenanced objects, only objects that remain unpublished as of 1995. [29] The Italian prosecutor sees it differently. He charges that the Fleischman Collection was used by Marion True to launder suspect acquisitions for the Getty.[30]

A major flaw in the practice of acquiring objects with little or no provenance is explained in part by the term "undocumented" used often to describe them. If an object cannot be traced because there are no documents describing its origin or history of ownership, there would be no evidence to prove theft, illegal export or looting. But what if documentation is later found? This is exactly what happened that brought the "house of cards" down around the knees of the antiquities art market and, in turn, our major art museums that were active in it.

Where We Should Be Heading: Proposals for Reform

First, it is clear to me now that acquisition by museums of all undocumented antiquities should cease. Often the justifications for acquiring such material have included the following:

- *There is no evidence that undocumented property has been looted. Why should we assume every object is guilty until proven innocent?* In my opinion, based on the history that Paolo Ferri and his investigators uncovered, the strong links between illegal looting and subsequent museum acquisitions of antiquities cannot be denied. Undocumented objects should be assumed suspect, until proven otherwise in spite of their potential for aesthetic, cultural and educational value.
- *Museums are saving cultural heritage by acquiring undocumented property, conserving it and exhibiting it, thus making it visible to whoever may have a claim to it.* This idea of saving heritage cannot be justified given the recent evidence uncovered of unscientific excavation of major works acquired for our art museum collections. The looting of archaeological sites results in decontextualization, the resultant irretrievable loss of the history of mankind, and the destruction of neighboring objects within those sites. "Saving" any object at this cost, no matter how aesthetically pleasing the object, seems hardly justifiable.[31]

I propose that the museum community develop new ethical standards that require all museums in the United States to establish clear and specific acquisition policies of archaeological materials and antiquities in keeping with the broad spirit of the UNESCO Convention of 1970, including provisions that

- respect other nations' laws, including patrimony laws and foreign export regulations;
- require proof of scientific excavation; and
- require active investigation and documentation of every acquisition, including procuring export documentation and proof of scientific excavation.

These mandatory provenance documents should be waived only for those objects that were known through reputable published sources to be outside of their country of origin before 1970, the date of the UNESCO Convention. To ensure compliance and transparency, all museum acquisition documentation should be a matter of public record and all acquisitions should be promptly publicized. Several of our major museums, as noted earlier, passed policies in the early 1970s that required investigations, honored foreign export restrictions, and greatly limited the acquisition of unprovenanced objects. The newly published 2006 Getty Policy Statement on Acquisitions includes such provisions. It is time for the remaining museums to follow suit.[32]

Second, the special relationship reported in the press between Dr. Marion True and the Fleischmans is troublesome from several conflict-of-interest standpoints. Dr. True is reported to have furnished assistance (as a part of her official duties) to the Fleischmans for purposes of building their private collection over a number of years. She helped organize a dedicated exhibition of their private collection and publish an accompanying catalog at the museum's expense. It was further revealed that Dr. True received a personal loan from Mr. Fleischman only three days after the Fleischman Collection was acquired by the Getty in 1996 and that she allegedly failed to report this at the time. The acceptance of the personal loan and failure to disclose the same in a timely manner constituted a breach of established ethical standards that reportedly led to her departure in 2005.

However, the consulting services she provided to the Fleischmans on the Getty's dime have not been questioned with equal ardour. Not surprisingly and according to published accounts, collectors/donors (who may also be trustees) in other U.S. museums routinely benefit from museum resources with special services not otherwise available to the general public.[33] It is time that the museum community re-examine closely the relationships with private collectors in the realm of museum collecting activities.

The charge of collection laundering by the Italian prosecutor speaks volumes on the "appearance of impropriety" evident in some museum/collector relationships. Specifically, he alleges that antiquities with faulty provenance that were available in the antiquities market were directed by Dr. True to be purchased by the Fleischmans with the understanding that these objects would be later acquired from them by the Getty. The allegation is that this interim step of ownership in a large domestic private collection would help to cleanse the provenance of these objects, especially if the suspect objects were later published in the museum's catalogue. In Prosecutor Ferri's view, a museum curator would not agree to do special favors for a private collector (consulting on acquisitions, organizing a dedicated exhibit and publishing a catalogue) unless a prior agreement for the donation/purchase of the collection had been in place. It would be difficult to explain to Paolo Ferri or indeed anyone looking at this issue why American museums in fact may provide such favors to private collectors based on a mere hope for a future donation.

Many of our professional ethical guidelines seek to avoid even the "appearance of impropriety" in order to maintain public confidence in how we go about doing our day-to-day activities. The museum community should look at the museum/collector relationships by focusing on the following questions and then establish clear and specific written ethical guidelines:

- Should museum staff be restricted from serving as "consultants" to private collectors (including trustees, donors, and others) or otherwise try to win their favor by providing services to them that are not otherwise available to the general public?
- Should museums refuse to organize dedicated exhibits of single private collections and publish catalogs of such dedicated single-collector exhibitions?
- Should anyone who actively collects or deals in objects in the same area as the museum's scope of collecting be disqualified from serving on the museum's board of trustees?
- Should a trustee who is a past or potential future donor/seller of objects to the museum's collections recuse himself or herself from any role in the development, approval or amendment of a museum's acquisition or collecting policies, or from participating in decisions on claims regarding restitution or return of collection objects?

I would answer all of these questions with a resounding "yes." The museum community is invited to debate these points. The devil will be in the details, but it is too late to look the other way.

Notes

1. B.A., M.A., J.D., Associate Professor and Director of Museum Studies, The George Washington University, Washington D.C.
2. From 1970 to late 1982 the debate continued until Congress passed The Convention on Cultural Property Implementation Act in December 1982 as Title II, Pub. L. 97-446, 19 U.S.C. Secs. 2601–2613) ("CPIA") Convention on Cultural Property Implementation Act (CPIA).
3. Watson, Peter & Todeschini, Cecelia (2006) The Medici Conspiracy (New York: Public Affairs) 54–55.
4. Silver, Vernon 2005 Lost Art. Bloomberg Markets Dec: 125–132. The Getty allegedly has 42 objects handled by Medici that match photographs found in the raid of his Swiss warehouse. The Metropolitan Museum of Art allegedly has six objects that match Medici's photos.
5. Silver, 2005.
6. Silver, Vernon. 2006 Getty Curator Says Antiquities Trade 'Corrupt,' Art Smuggled. Bloomberg.com Nov. 10, 2006.
7. The Metropolitan Museum of Art and Republic of Italy Agreement with like provisions was signed Feb. 21, 2006. The Getty signed a similar agreement in August 2007 agreeing to return 40 works to Italy. Four of these works, insured for about $425 million, were already returned in early October 2007 and will be distributed to Italian museums. But first the works will be put on exhibit at the Qurinale Palace in Rome at the end of December 2007. Associated Press (2007) Italy's presidential palace to host 40 artifacts returned from Getty Museum. Oct. 3, 2007. Los Angeles Times Oct. 3, 2007.
8. The Fleischman Collection of antiquities was acquired by the Getty through a partial gift/partial sale transaction in 1996. See discussion of the controversy surrounding its acquisition below at page 13–14.
9. "Green market" presumingly refers to the legitimate art market that in Dr. Ferri's view is replete with forged documentation.
10. Darraby, 2006, p.24.
11. Fleischman, Barbara G. 2006 The Fleischman Collection and the Getty: In response to "The Medici Conspiracy": An Exchange, New York Review of Books, New York: 53(14) Sept. 21.
12. Since this interview was taken, agreement has been reached for the Morgantina Venus. This object will be returned in 2010 in accordance with the August 2007

agreement signed by the Getty with Italy for return of 40 artifacts that Italy claims as looted. The Getty denies having knowingly bought illegally obtained objects, and Italy's deal with the museum includes no admission of guilt. In exchange, Italy will lend the Getty other artifacts for up to four years each. The agreement also provides for cultural cooperation, including research projects and exhibitions.

13. As the Getty subsequently in August 2007 has reached agreement with Italy to return 40 antiquities, it is assumed that this will satisfy the Italian side and will improve cultural relations.
14. See the Harvard University Statement on Acquisitions (January 1972) and Smithsonian Institution Policy on Museum Acquisitions (May 1973) reproduced in Malaro, Marie C. 1998 A Legal Primer on Managing Museum Collections, 2nd ed. Smithsonian Press, Washington D.C. Figures IV.1 and IV.2. The first museum to announce an acquisition policy of this nature was the University of Pennsylvania Museum on April 1, 1970. Others included the California State University at Long Beach; The Field Museum; Southern Illinois University; Washington State Museum in Seattle; Peabody Museum in Salem, Massachusetts; Arizona State Museum in Tucson; and the Utah Museum of Natural History. See Bator, Paul M. 1988 The International Trade in Art. Chicago: University of Chicago Press (Midway reprint) note 144. Notably absent from this original list are major private art museums. To my knowledge, there have been no studies to evaluate the implementation of these policies.
15. The term "provenance" refers to information on the history of an object. This includes its creation, the trail of ownership, exhibition, and publication. "Provenience" is a term used to define a work's archaeological find-spot. An object's provenience is a part of its provenance. Urice, Stephen K. (2007) Antiquities as Cultural Property: Dealing with the Past, Looking to the Future—An Introduction, ALI/ABA Legal Issues of Museum Administration Coursebook (Philadelphia: ALI/ABA) 25, n2. "Unprovenanced" objects are those that come with no information about their history.
16. The AAMD resolution was adoped on January 23, 1973 and published in an article, The AAMD Takes a Stand, Museum News (May 1973) 49. A close version of the same resolution appeared as a Joint Professional Policy on Museum Acquisitions published in Museum News (September 1973) 46, which was signed by representatives of the AAMD, American Association of Museums, the College Arts Association, the International Council of Museums, the Archeological Institute of America, the American Anthropological Association and the Society of American Anthropology.
17. Association of Art Museum Directors, 1981 A Code of Ethics for Art Museum Directors As Adopted by the Association of Art Museum Directors, published in Professional Practices in Art Museums: Report of the Ethics and Standards Committee. New York: Association of Art Museum Directors. ("1981 AAMD Code").

18. By contrast, the position of archaeologists shared by source nations is that an unprovenanced antiquity of museum quality can be presumed to be the product of illicit looting. Acquisition by museums of unprovenanced objects fuels such activity that leads to the irretrievable loss of knowledge and destruction of sites (including other less market-desirable objects) resulting from unscientific excavation. Urice (2007) 26.
19. Association of Art Museum Directors, 1992 A Code of Ethics for Art Museum Directors As Adopted by the Association of Art Museum Directors, published in Professional Practices in Art Museums: Report of the Ethics and Standards Committee. New York: Association of Art Museum Directors. ("1992 AAMD Code"). The 1992 AAMD Code declared that it is unprofessional for art museum director members: "(C) To acquire knowingly or allow to be recommended for acquisition any object that has been stolen, removed in contravention of treaties and international conventions to which the United States is a signatory, or illegally imported into the United States)." Note that this provision refers to U.S. laws and treaties and conventions as limited by U.S. laws only.
20. See, *Peru v. Johnson,* 720 F. Supp. 810 (C.D. Cal. 1989) *aff'd sub nom., Peru v. Wendt*, 933 F.2nd 10013 (9th Cir. 1991). This case, seeking civil restitution of a collection of pre-Columbian artifacts, held the patrimony laws of Peru unenforceable based on the laws' lack of clarity and the absence of evidence of their implementation within Peru.
21. The *United States v. Schultz*, 178 F. Supp 2nd 445 (S.D. N.Y. 2002) *aff'd* 333 F3d 393 (2nd Cir. 2003), *cert. denied* 157 L.Ed. 2nd 891 (U.S., 2004), discussed below in note 31, held that foreign patrimony law of Egypt would be given credence. The appeals court in *Schultz* concluded that "[w]e see no reason that property stolen from a foreign sovereign should be treated any differently from property stolen from a foreign museum or private home" for purposes of federal criminal theft law. 333 F3rd at 47. A change in the AAMD's Code regarding compliance with foreign laws followed later in 2004.
22. The AAMD published a new version of its Professional Practices in Art Museums in 2001. In that document, for the first time, there is a provision directing investigation of provenance as a step in the acquisition process: "The director must ensure that best efforts are made to determine the provenance of a work of art considered for acquisition." (Paragraph 18).
23. J. Paul Getty Museum Acquisition Policy for Classical Antiquities, November 13, 1987, states "[a]ll transactions will be with vendors of substance and established reputations in order that such transactions shall be covered by enforceable warranties." ("Getty Policy 1981").
24. The provision directed Getty staff to contact the International Foundation for Art Research (IFAR) based in New York City to check current lists of stolen art

objects reported as stolen by their owners. This database was later moved in 1991 to London and operates as the Art Loss Register (http://www.artloss.com).

25. J. Paul Getty Museum Acquisition Policy for Classical Antiquities, Revised November 10, 1995. ("Getty Policy 1995").
26. Darraby, Jessica 2006 To Have and To Hold. California Lawyer 26(5): 22–28, citing a 1995 December Art Newspaper interview.
27. Getty Policy, 1995 (rev.).
28. Wilkinson, Tracy and Suzanne Muchnic. 2005 Indictment Targets Getty's Acquisitions. Los Angeles Times 20 May: A1 . A number of these objects are traceable to photographs found in Medici's Swiss warehouse raided by Italian authorities in 1995.
29. Darraby, 2006.
30. Wilkinson, 2005.
31. In 2004, the AAMD published comprehensive new guidelines on acquisition of archaeological materials and ancient art. They were issued after the groundbreaking decision in the *U.S. v. Schultz* case involving a dealer indicted for theft of an object owned by Egypt under its patrimony laws (see note 20 above) and after an announcement of Marion True's indictment in Italy. The 2004 guidelines tighten the requirements for art museums, yet they still do not require compliance with foreign export regulations nor do they prohibit the acquisition of undocumented materials if the acquisition would not provide a direct and material incentive to looting or illegal excavation judged by the length of time the object has been out of the country of origin (suggestion is a minimum of 10 years). For a discussion of the reach of these guidelines, see DeAngelis, Ildikó 2006 How Much Provenance Is Enough: Post Schultz Guidelines for Museum Acquisition of Archeological Materials and Ancient Art, in Art and Cultural Heritage: Law, Policy and Practice, edited by Barbara Hoffman. Cambridge, UK: Cambridge University Press. 398–408. On February 27, 2006, the AAMD also issued guidelines on incoming loans of archaeological materials and ancient art.
32. A moratorium on the acquisition of undocumented antiquities was also declared by the Indianapolis Museum of Art (IMA) on April 16, 2007, which will remain in effect while the IMA "evaluates and reframes" its current policies on the collection of antiquities and ancient art. "We hope it will be a small step towards stemming the tide of illegal excavation or clandestine removal of accidentally discovered objects from countries the world over," said IMA Director and CEO Maxwell Anderson in an internet posting on Apr. 30, 2007.
33. Silver, Vernon 2006 Money and Power at the Met. Bloomberg Markets April: 138–146.

Federal Land Management

• • •

Section Editor: James Van Ness

Introduction

This year there were a number of cases in which the National Historic Preservation Act was lobbed as a tool to contest government action, either by those trying to stop an activity or by those seeking to motivate action by a federal agency. This section will not recount all of those cases but, rather, will focus upon some notable events where use of the law has had, or may have, an impact on federal land management decisions.

Cultural Resources and Mining Claims

In *United States v. Donald E. Eno,*[1] the Interior Board of Lands Appeals (IBLA) considered whether the preservation of cultural resources and values constitutes a competing use of public lands that must be weighed against the economic benefits of mining before operations may begin on a placer claim.

The Hound Dog placer mining claim is a 40-acre claim situated within the Soda Rock Area of the Plumas National Forest in California. The mining claim dates from 1907, when the lands were open to mineral entry. The Soda Rock Area encompasses a unique surface deposit of multicolored travertine, a mineral quarried for building stone. The Hound Dog mining claim is also believed to contain enough gold to make placer mining operations profitable.

The Soda Rock Area is also culturally and spiritually important to the Maidu Indians. Within the area encompassed by the Hound Dog mining claim are located several sites associated with Maidu genesis mythology, including a landslide scar linked to the Ancient Women; the location of one of the sweat lodges where the Ancient Women once lived; and the site of the Earth Maker's heart, the so-called thumping rock. The area was also used in the past by the Maidu for medicinal bathing and for gathering salt grass. In 1982, the Keeper of the National Register of Historic Places determined the Soda Rock Area to be eligible for inclusion in the National Register, and in 2003, the Soda Rock Area was officially listed.

Although this lengthy IBLA opinion spends considerable time sorting through the complicated history of the mining claim, for our purposes the issue boils down to whether the preservation of these Maidu cultural sites is a substantial "other use" (within the meaning of the Mining Claims Rights Restoration Act (MCRRA) of 1955[2]) of the land included within the placer mining claim that must be balanced against the potential economic benefits of mining. The initial Administrative Law Judge (ALJ) concluded that the record failed to establish that the Maidu currently used the Soda Rock Area for cultural purposes, and that, in any case, no such cultural uses could be objectively monetized to establish quantifiable evidence demonstrating the economic value of such a competing use. In addition, the ALJ discounted the significance of the National Register listing as essentially a subjective decision and not determinative. As a consequence, the ALJ declined to consider preservation of the Maidu sites a substantial "other use" of the land encompassed by the mining claim, and issued the claimant, Mr. Eno, a general permission to engage in placer mining operations on the Hound Dog claim.

On appeal by the Forest Service, the IBLA concluded that nothing in MCRRA limits the competing "other uses" that must be considered to only those that are economically quantifiable or measurable. The IBLA also concluded that the National Register listing decision "clearly constituted objective evidence that the land included in the listed area contained substantial cultural resources warranting protection under the [National Historic Preservation Act]."[3] Lastly, while the IBLA did not fault the ALJ for concluding factually that the Maidu do not currently physically use the Soda Rock Area, the opinion does underscore the fact that the Soda Rock Area has been closed to the public since 1963 because of mining, effectively preventing the Maidu from physically using the land.

Having concluded that preservation of these sites and the cultural importance they have for the Maidu people (even if the Maidu's present use of the area is only passive or inchoate) is a substantial "other use" of the land within the meaning of MCRRA, the IBLA opinion next examines the economic value of the land for placer mining and the degree to which suction dredging for gold and quarrying of the travertine would interfere with such cultural uses of the land. The IBLA acknowledges that once general permission to engage in placer mining operations is granted, the Forest Service may not altogether preclude mining on the claim. Nonetheless, the IBLA concludes that the Forest Service does retain the authority to condition its approval of any plan for surface-disturbing operations on the claim by imposing conditions, stipulations, and mitigation measures to protect "other uses" of the land.[4] As a consequence, the IBLA found no error in the ALJ's decision to grant Mr. Eno a general permission to engage in placer mining on the Hound Dog claim.

The Forest Service's appeal may not have prevented Mr. Eno from getting general permission to engage in placer mining on the Hound Dog claim. Nonetheless, and importantly, this IBLA decision does establish that protecting traditional cultural properties—and recognizing the singular importance they have for Indian tribes trying to maintain their cultural identity, even if from a distance—are substantial "other uses" of the public lands that must be weighed before general permission to engage in mining operations that potentially threaten such sites may be granted. And while one may question whether the authority the Forest Service retains to condition actual surface-disturbing mining operations will be adequate to fully protect these sites, this case must still be seen as at least a partial victory for the preservation of cultural resources and other noneconomic uses of the public domain in the face of this country's antiquated mining laws.

Motorized Rafts and the Natural "Soundscape" of the Grand Canyon

Ever since John Wesley Powell first ran the Colorado River in 1869, it has been the dream of many to experience the thrill of floating the river a mile beneath the rim of the towering Grand Canyon. And when *Playboy* magazine in the early 1960s famously published a pictorial of several Playmates shooting some of the largest white-water rapids in the Canyon wearing nothing but life jackets and sneakers, it became evident that the adventure of a lifetime was within the reach of anyone with the wherewithal to book a trip with a commercial river outfitter. Demand surged and remains insatiable—today's intrepid adventurers must book their trips at least two years in advance.

Although not a cultural property law case per se, *River Runners for Wilderness v. Martin*[5] considers an issue with obvious implications for cultural property lawyers—i.e., impairment of the natural soundscape.[6] Early in 2006, the Park Service approved and adopted a new Colorado River Management Plan. The 2006 Plan permits the continued use of motorized rafts, generators for emergencies and inflating rafts, and helicopters to make passenger exchanges. The plaintiffs, a coalition of organizations committed to protecting and restoring the Grand Canyon's wilderness character and unique natural resources, filed suit under the Administrative Procedures Act[7] alleging the Park Service acted arbitrarily and capriciously when it concluded that motorized uses in the Colorado River Corridor do not impair the natural soundscape of the Park within the meaning of the National Park Service Organic Act.[8]

The Park Service based its decision to allow motorized traffic to continue on several considerations. First, because motorized trips take less time to complete, more people can see the Canyon each year from the river if motorized trips continue. Second, motorized trips are frequently chartered for special-needs groups that may be unable to manage a nonmotorized trip. Third, because of their increased mobility, motorized trips can access more locations along the river and help to alleviate overcrowding at popular campsites in the Canyon. And fourth, some individuals simply feel safer when traveling in motorized rafts.

The plaintiffs contended principally that the Park Service failed to consider the cumulative effects of noise from river traffic on the natural soundscape. The district court disagreed. In the court's view, the Park Service both compared river traffic noise to noise-free intervals, and appropriately considered the cumulative effect of river traffic noise when added to other sounds in the Park, such as aircraft overflights. In the court's view, the Park Service correctly concluded that even if all noise from river recreation—motorized and nonmotorized—were eliminated from the Park, there would still be substantial adverse sound effects in the Park from aircraft overflights (which are not within the jurisdiction of the Park Service). Given that the cumulative effects analysis generally demonstrated that motorized river traffic was not the source of serious sound problems in the Park, and that the elimination of such noise would not significantly improve the overall soundscape, the court determined that the plaintiffs had articulated no principled basis upon which the court could conclude that the Park Service should have eliminated motorized noises on the basis of cumulative impacts, but not other human-caused noises such as hiking or nonmotorized raft trips.

As cultural property law and environmental planning practitioners, we generally view cumulative impact analysis as a means to enable us to determine whether the incremental effects of a particular action or undertaking under consideration will, when added to other past, present, and reasonably foreseeable future actions, reach a "tipping point" and precipitate new and irreversible impacts. This case, however, well illustrates that sometimes cumulative impact analysis may make it evident that the incremental effects of a proposed action or undertaking may be, in fact, inconsequential when compared to the effects of other actions over which the action agency has little or no control. In such cases, we may expect courts to take the *River Runners* approach and decline to enjoin an action or undertaking with relatively minor incremental effects if the larger problem would nonetheless continue unabated.

A Deal's a Deal . . .

In an unpublished opinion,[9] the Federal District Court for New Jersey considered the extent to which the National Park Service could rely upon a 1995 Programmatic Agreement (PA) to support a 2004 lease to rehabilitate and adaptively reuse 36 historic structures within the Fort Hancock Historic District.

The Gateway National Recreation Area is located along the waterfronts of New York Harbor in both New York and New Jersey. The Fort Hancock Historic District is part of the Sandy Hook Unit of the Gateway National Recreation Area. The Fort Hancock Historic District was part of the New York Harbor defense system from the 1890s through World War II and contains more than 120 historic structures. In 1995, the National Park Service (NPS) entered into a PA with the Advisory Council on Historic Preservation and the National Conference of State Historic Preservation Officers. The PA specifically listed 13 types of activities in which the NPS could engage without further review by the ACHP or a SHPO, including leasing historic properties where the work under the lease would be limited to preserving, maintaining, repairing, or replacing material and features consistent with the Secretary of the Interior's Standards for Rehabilitation.

In 1999, the NPS issued a Request for Proposals for the lease of a portion of the historic structures within the Fort Hancock Historic District. The vision expressed by the NPS was to return the "elegant buildings at Fort Hancock . . .

to year-round use and . . . to their original function as office and meeting space, transient lodging, and recreation and entertainment facilities." From the 22 proposals that it received, the NPS chose the Wassel Realty Group/ Sandy Hook Partners proposal as the one "most consistent with the preservation of Fort Hancock's historic structures" and evidencing "a commitment to building renovation consistent with the Secretary of the Interior's Standards for Treatment of Historic Properties." In 2004, following the completion of an Environmental Assessment and Finding of No Significant Impact that examined the rehabilitation and reuse of up to100 historic structures in the Fort Hancock Historic District, the NPS entered into a 60-year lease with Sandy Hook Partners covering 36 buildings in the District.

The plaintiffs objected to the lease, alleging that the Sandy Hook Partners' plans for rehabilitating the Fort Hancock buildings would adversely affect the buildings' historic character, and that the lease violated Section 106 of the National Historic Preservation Act because the NPS failed to consult with the SHPO before awarding the lease.

The court disagreed entirely with the plaintiffs' assertions, finding that the NPS had satisfied its obligations under the NHPA before entering into the lease. Specifically, the court noted that the 1995 PA permitted the NPS to lease historic properties within the Fort Hancock Historic District without further review by the ACHP or any SHPO, provided—as was the case with the Sandy Hook Partners lease—the rehabilitation work contemplated would comport with the Secretary of the Interior's Standards for Rehabilitation. Thus, so far as the court was concerned, the 1995 PA authorized the NPS to "perform its own Section 106 review before leasing historical properties under its control without seeking input or further review from the ACHP or SHPO."[10]

This case underscores the fact that there can be a demonstrable savings of time and effort in negotiating a single PA for a program that contemplates multiple similar or repetitive activities, rather than having to engage in repeated individual consultations for each such activity. It is comforting to know that courts recognize this fact and are prepared to rebuff attempts to deny action agencies the benefits of the "deal" they've struck.

Tomb of the Unknowns Monument—Repair or Replace?

The Tomb of the Unknowns Monument in Arlington National Cemetery is the nation's most sacred memorial to American service men and women. Since its opening in 1932, the Tomb of the Unknowns has been visited by countless millions of people who have come to pay their respects to those who have made the ultimate sacrifice for this country. The Tomb of the Unknowns, including the Tomb Monument, is inarguably of transcendent national significance.

While the true significance of the Tomb of the Unknowns lies not in its physical components but rather with the remains of those who rest beneath it, the Tomb Monument has become imbued with its own historic significance. The Tomb Monument, designed by architect Lorimer Rich and sculpted by Thomas Hudson Jones, is eligible for inclusion in the National Register of Historic Places and meets the criteria for consideration as a National Historic Landmark. Unfortunately, the Tomb Monument's 48-ton marble die block (the middle portion of the three-piece Monument containing the sculpted figures, Doric pilasters, and the inscription "Here Rests in Honored Glory An American Soldier Known But To God") has developed two lengthy parallel horizontal cracks, both of which extend partially through the die block.

These cracks were first documented in 1963 and are the result of natural faults or "veining" within the stone. Surface repairs to the cracks were conducted in 1975 and 1989; other than routine cleaning, no other repairs have been made to the Tomb Monument since 1989.

The current controversy centers on whether to repair the Tomb Monument or replace it with a replica monument. The Superintendent of the Arlington National Cemetery has stated that a program of repeated repairs to a deeply flawed die block will not maintain the Monument's condition and appearance in a manner that fully reflects the honor, dignity, and reverence due those it memorializes. Moreover, while suitable marble is currently available from the Yule Quarry near Marble, Colorado (the quarry from whence the original marble was obtained), the amount of suitable marble is limited and there is no certainty it will be available in the future.

The National Trust for Historic Preservation and other preservationist organizations argue that replacing the Tomb Monument with a replica monument is not only inconsistent with the Secretary of the Interior's Standards for the Treatment of Historic Properties but also unnecessary. They characterize the cracks as superficial, visible only at close range, and not apparent to the typical visitor. They argue that with the proper materials, repair expertise, and appropriate monitoring the Tomb Monument can be returned to an acceptable appearance and maintained for many years to come.

Clearly, the decision whether to repair or replace the Tomb Monument is a difficult one, and should be made only in light of the best technical information attainable and only after hearing from veterans organizations, the preservation community, and others with an interest in the outcome. To that end, Senator Daniel Akaka (Hawaii) inserted in the National Defense Authorization Act for Fiscal Year 2008 a provision[11] that requires the Secretary of the Army and the Secretary of Veterans Affairs to jointly submit to Congress a report discussing current plans to replace the Tomb Monument, an assessment of the feasibility of repairing the Monument, and an assessment of the structural identity of the Monument. No action to replace the Tomb Monument may be taken by the Army or the Veterans Adminstration until 180 days after the report is submitted to Congress.

The technology now exists to create almost perfect replicas of many kinds of sculptural and architectural features that may be deteriorating and arguably in need of repair or replacement or protection from the elements. Given this fact, the decision to repair or replace the Tomb of the Unknowns Monument is an important one that warrants our continued attention.

Notes

1. United States v. Donald E. Eno, 171 IBLA 69 (2007).
2. Mining Claims Rights Restoration Act of 1955, as amended, 30 U.S.C. §§ 621 – 625.
3. Eno at 95.
4. 36 C.F.R. Part 228.
5. River Runners for Wilderness v. Martin, No. CV-06-894-PCT-DGC, 2007 WL 4200677 (D. Ariz. 2007).
6. See 36 C.F.R. § 800.5(a)(2)(v).
7. Administrative Procedure Act, 5 U.S.C. §§ 701 – 706.
8. National Park Service Organic Act, 16 U.S.C. §§ 1 and 3.
9. Save Sandy Hook Corporation v. U.S. Department of Interior, Civil Action No. 04-5908 (MLC), Slip Copy, 2007 WL 2704813.
10. Save Sandy Hook, Slip Copy at 19.
11. National Defense Authorization Act for Fiscal Year 2008, H.R. 1585, 110th Cong. § 1048 (2007). P.L. 110-181, Section 2870.

State and Local

• • •

Section Editor: Kelly Yasaitis Fanizzo

Introduction

This State and Local section reviews the historic preservation actions arising in state and local courts, as well as those cases brought in federal court involving state and private entities' compliance with federal law. Because regulation of historic preservation is performed predominantly at the state and local level, it is not surprising that again this year there are a significant number of cases involving zoning actions and permit applications for demolition, alteration, and new construction. Similarly, compliance with state environmental laws, such as New York's State Environmental Quality Review Act, features largely in this section. Other cases involve contractual work on historic properties, the potential use of associated court fees, and an application for tax exempt status. Of note, the Fourth Circuit Court of Appeals heard a case involving criminal contempt for the violation of a preliminary injunction stemming from the terms of a preservation easement. Questions of standing and subject matter jurisdiction also appear in this section.

Free Exercise, Free Speech, and Equal Protection are often the subject of litigation involving the application of historic preservation regulations, as is seen below. In particular, the questions that are raised by the intersection of the First Amendment and historic preservation reveal an interesting debate.

The First Amendment reads

> Congress shall make no law respecting an establishment of religion, or prohibiting the free exercise thereof; or abridging the freedom of speech, or of the press; or the right of the people peaceably to assemble, and to petition the government for a redress of grievances.[1]

When it comes to religious freedom, the balance between unconstitutional burdens and justified protections is delicate. The Supreme Court, in the well-known case *Employment Div., Ore. Dept. of Human Res. v. Smith,*[2] states, "[w]e have never held that an individual's religious beliefs excuse him from compliance with an otherwise valid law prohibiting conduct that the State is free to regulate." Declining to apply the balancing test in *Sherbert v. Verner*,[3] the Court notes,

> The government's ability to enforce generally applicable prohibitions of socially harmful conduct, like its ability to carry out other aspects of public policy, "cannot depend on measuring the effects of a governmental action on a religious objector's spiritual development.". . . To make an individual's obligation to obey such a law contingent upon the law's coincidence with his religious beliefs, except where the State's interest is "compelling"—permitting him, by virtue of his beliefs, "to become a law unto himself," . . . contradicts both constitutional tradition and common sense.[4]

Thus, where the law at issue is a "'valid and neutral law of general applicability'" and lacking religious motivation, there is no need to apply the test for strict scrutiny and compelling government interest.[5] The Court upholds Oregon's criminal prohibition of peyote use.

The Court notes two instances in which a different analysis would have been appropriate. Where other constitutional protections are at stake, "a neutral, generally applicable law" might not meet "constitutional muster."[6] Additionally, the Court asserts that the *Sherbert* test, defined as "governmental actions that substantially burden a religious practice must be justified by a compelling governmental interest," was applied where there was an "individualized governmental assessment of the reasons for the relevant conduct."[7] Unlike the criminal law of general applicability at issue in *Smith*, the State in *Sherbert* was able to consider particular circumstances and had discretion in its determination as to whether an exemption should be allowed for an individual's unemployment benefits. The Court explains that its ruling in *Sherbert* and other similar cases "stand[s] for the proposition that where the State has in place a system of individual exemptions, it may not refuse to extend that system to cases of 'religious hardship' without compelling reason."[8]

Congress responded to the *Smith* decision by enacting the Religious Freedom Restoration Act (RFRA)[9] in 1993. RFRA stated that, at all levels of government, a substantial burden to a person's free exercise of religion must further a compelling government interest and be the least restrictive means possible.[10] In 1997, the Supreme Court again addressed this issue in a landmark case involving a request to modify a Catholic church located in a historic district. The decision in *City of Boerne v. Flores*[11] finds Congress in enacting RFRA to have overstepped its authority pursuant to the Fourteenth Amendment and the separation of powers. The Court stated,

> The substantial costs RFRA exacts, both in practical terms of imposing a heavy litigation burden on the States and in terms of curtailing their traditional general regulatory power, far exceed any pattern or practice of unconstitutional conduct under the Free Exercise Clause as interpreted in *Smith*. Simply put, RFRA is not designed to identify and counteract state laws likely to be unconstitutional because of their treatment of religion.[12]

While the Court did not expressly discuss historic properties in *Smith*, its analysis is often applicable in the preservation arena. In 2000, and in response to *City of Boerne*, Congress enacted the Religious Land Use and Institutionalized Persons Act (RLUIPA).[13] RLUIPA prohibits a land use regulation from substantially burdening a person's free exercise of his religion unless the government shows that regulation to be the least restrictive means possible of furthering a compelling government interest.[14] It is more limited in scope than RFRA as it applies only where the substantial burden comes from a Federally funded activity, where it affects commerce with foreign nations, with Indian tribes or among the States, or where the land use regulation causing the substantial burden allows the government to make "individualized assessments of the proposed uses for the property involved."[15]

This year's section does not directly address RLUIPA; however, a recent example of the conflict that arises in the context of land use regulation and historic religious buildings will be seen in the discussion of *Mount St. Scholastica, Inc. v. City of Atchison*[16] below. An avenue for additional research would be the current discussion surrounding RLUIPA and the development and application of state versions of RFRA.[17]

Compliance with Federal Law

Historic Preservation

In *Friends of Superior, Inc. v. City of Superior*,[18] the plaintiff brought suit to enjoin demolition of the historic Palace Theater, which was built in 1917. On the same day, the defendant demolished the theater, making the suit moot. The plaintiff amended its complaint and alleged that defendants violated Sections 106 and 110(k) of the National Historic Preservation Act (NHPA) and requested an injunction to prevent the City from receiving any federal funds for a project related to the theater's demolition and for the demolition of other historic buildings. The defendant moved for summary judgment.

Section 106 of the NHPA requires a Federal agency to consider the potential effects of a proposed undertaking on historic properties and to afford the Advisory Council on Historic Preservation a reasonable opportunity to comment.[19] Section 110(k) of the NHPA is intended to prevent an "anticipatory demolition."[20]

Prior to this action, the City applied for a Community Development Block Grant Entitlement from the U.S. Department of Housing and Urban Development to demolish two other buildings and for green development at the site. The City later withdrew this application, and no Section 106 review pursuant to the NHPA was done.

The court looked first to whether the Friends had standing to bring this suit. It found that the City's demolition of the theater likely caused an injury to the Friends, whose members enjoyed the aesthetic value of the building. Yet, the court stated that a favorable decision in this case would not remedy that injury, the final necessary requirement for standing. The Friends had asked the court to find (1) the City in noncompliance with the NHPA, (2) the demolition of the theater to be in violation of the NHPA, (3) that the City may not use federal funds for any project related to the demolition, (4) that all federal services, including permits and funding for the related projects, be stopped, (5) that the City may not do anything to threaten other historic properties, and (6) to provide any additional relief available.[21] Because the demolition that caused the injury was complete and not repeatable, the court found the first four requests for relief to be punitive only. The court further found that while the Friends may be injured by the demolition of other historic properties, there was no immediate threat that would allow their fifth request to pass the standing test. The court then dismissed the matter for lack of subject matter jurisdiction.

Free Exercise and Takings

The plaintiff in *Mount St. Scholastica, Inc. v. City of Atchison* is a monastic community whose property must exhibit the "evangelical poverty" of the monastic life. Within its holdings is an administrative building for which the plaintiff argued it had no use. As such, the plaintiff applied for a demolition permit from the City of Atchison. Because of the potential impact to historic properties, the City submitted the permit request to the Kansas State Historic Preservation Officer (SHPO), who suggested as an alternative to demolition that the plaintiff market the property for redevelopment or mothball the building until another use could be found. The plaintiff then submitted its request to the City Commission. Other historic preservation organizations presented guidelines for mothballing the building and a suggestion for potential reuse. The plaintiff rejected both ideas. Since the majority of the City Commission members found that alternatives did exist for the building, the defendant denied plaintiff's request for the demolition permit.

The plaintiff argued that the defendant acted "unreasonably, arbitrarily, capriciously, and in a manner inconsistent" with the Kansas Historic Preservation Act.[22] According to the Historic Preservation Act, the City's governing body may override the SHPO's recommendation where, "based on a consideration of all relevant factors, . . . there is no feasible and prudent alternative to the proposal and . . . the program includes all possible planning to minimize harm to [the] historic property."[23] The defendant claims it considered all relevant factors in making its decision. In determining whether the governing body's decision was arbitrary, the court looks to what could constitute a "relevant factor." Relying on precedent, it noted that such considerations in zoning-change decisions as proximate property uses and neighborhood character as well as those proposed alternatives that are shown to be feasible and prudent could be identified as relevant factors. The court noted further that the plaintiff did not meet its burden of showing that no feasible and prudent alternatives existed for the building. The court held that the defendant took the "required hard look at relevant factors, and made its decision on the evidence."[24]

The plaintiff also alleged that the City's decision deprived it of its rights under the First Amendment, as applied to the states through the Fourteenth Amendment. The court reiterates the Supreme Court's argument in *Smith*, that the Free Exercise Clause does not prevent compliance with a neutral law of general applicability. Thus, "[i]f a law's object is not to infringe or restrict religious practices, the law is neutral. . . . However, if a law that is not neutral or generally applicable burdens a religious practice, it is subject to strict scrutiny."[25] The plaintiff alleged that the Kansas State Historic Preservation Act fell into the latter category and it burdened plaintiff's practice of administering its property in accordance with its principles of evangelical poverty.

The court found the Historic Preservation Act to be neutral (i.e., to protect historic property), but acknowledged the contradictory nature of the relevant tests for determining whether a law is generally applicable, however, in reviewing various Tenth Circuit precedent and state court decisions. It ultimately held that the City's decision-making process under the Historic Preservation Act was one of case-by-case analysis. Thus, following *Sherbert*'s example, the court reviewed the City's decision under the strict scrutiny test: "the burden on religious conduct violates the Free Exercise Clause unless it is narrowly tailored to advance a compelling government interest."[26] In finding historic preservation not to be a compelling government interest, the court concluded that the City's denial of the demolition permit violated the plaintiff's rights under the Free Exercise Clause. The court limited this decision by stating that the Kansas Historic Preservation Act is not unconstitutional as a result, but that the law may not be applied "in a manner that burdens a party's religious beliefs."[27] Thus, the law stands, except when it compromises a religious belief.

The plaintiff also claimed that the City's denial of its permit request constituted a regulatory taking under the Fifth Amendment. The court found this claim to be ripe but without merit. The court determined that because the plaintiff did not allege that the City prevented all economically beneficial use of its property, it was not a "total regulatory taking." The court noted that the plaintiff had not used the administrative building for years and that the plaintiff incorrectly assumed a right to demolish the building. Since the City's actions were limited only to the denial of the demolition permit and the plaintiff had not shown any investment-backed expectations that were affected by that denial, nor had the plaintiff shown an economic impact to its property as a whole, the plaintiff's rights under the Fifth Amendment were not violated.

Free Speech

The plaintiff in *Lusk v. Village of Cold Spring*[28] was a private resident of the Architectural and Historic District of Cold Springs Village, New York. In protesting certain real estate development, he posted a number of signs on his property. The Village issued the plaintiff six violations, to which the plaintiff responded by filing an action in the Southern District of New York, alleging that the Village Code violated his rights under the First Amendment. On appeal, the court reviewed whether a required review by the Architectural and Historic District Review Board for all proposed physical alterations to residential buildings in the historic district is constitutional.

The plaintiff argued a "prior restraint" on his expression and the court noted, "a law requiring prior administrative approval of speech falls within the prior restraint rubric"; and "prior restraints on speech and publication

[are] the most serious and the least tolerable infringement on *First Amendment rights*."[29] The court applied the reasoning of the Supreme Court in *City of Ladue v. Gilleo*[30] to balance the government's interest in regulating speech and the public interest in preserving it.[31] The court agreed with the Village that protecting aesthetic values is a legitimate government interest, but held that the Village's interests do not justify the regulation, and the review period required for the permit process results in timely speech being banned.

In *Riel v. City of Bradford*,[32] the appellants received criminal violation notices for displaying commercial and noncommercial signs without a permit on their private property. In response, they challenged two sign ordinances, the first regulating signs in all of Bradford and the other regulating the historic district, as violating their First Amendment rights. Chapter 125 of the Bradford Code, which is intended to protect the historic features and characteristics of this historic district, prohibits all signs except for those that advertise a public service, business, occupation or profession, which require a permit from the Historical Architecture Review Board. The court found the code to be content neutral and "merely establishes the appropriate relationship between the location and the use of an outdoor sign to convey a particular message."[33] The court held that where the speech concerns some lawful activity and is not misleading, the governmental interests in aesthetics and safety are substantial, the regulation directly advances those governmental interests, and, finally, the burden on commercial signs is not more extensive than is necessary, the code is valid. The court concluded that the City's regulation burdens only off-site commercial signs: the category of speech that receives the least amount of protection under the First Amendment.

Equal Protection

The plaintiff in *Leonard's Linen Serv. v. City of Bloomington*[34] applied for a demolition permit for certain improvements on its commercial property. Although the plaintiff's application was submitted before the implementation of the amended law, the new law was applied to its request and approval of its application was withheld due to the historic significance of the buildings proposed for demolition. The plaintiff alleged that the defendants violated its rights under due process and equal protection, and alleged a conspiracy among governmental officials to deny a permit to prevent development by an individual of the Jewish faith. While the court was critical of due process claims simply to place a matter in federal court, it found facts in dispute on equal protection and denied dismissal of the action.

Compliance with State Law

Environmental Protection

Connecticut The Connecticut Environmental Protection Act (CEPA) creates a cause of action to stop the "'unreasonable destruction of historic structures and landmarks of the state,' which the statute defines as properties 'listed or under consideration for listing' in the National Register" of Historic Places.[35] The plaintiff in *W. Hartford Initiative to Save Historic Property v. Town of W. Hartford* brought a claim under CEPA to preserve the town's Board of Education Building, the West Hartford Town Hall, and the Noah Webster Library, which the plaintiff claimed should be included on the National Register as a historic district. The proposed construction project involved no federal funding or assistance. The buildings were privately owned, and under the NHPA, the owner of a building may object to its listing on the National Register.[36] The Keeper found the district to be eligible.

In reviewing the legislative history of the 1980 amendments to the NHPA, the court stated "the owner consent requirement [to listing the property on the National Register] . . . was adopted to alleviate due process concerns, not because the NHPA or its implementing regulations would place restrictions on owners of properties included in the Register (as we have seen, they do not), but because state and local laws imposing such restrictions could be triggered automatically by Register listing," and state and local zoning authorities are more appropriately utilized to protect historic properties.[37] The court concluded the title transfer was not sufficient to warrant federal jurisdiction over the CEPA claim.

Montana In *Save the Track Found., Inc. v. Tinsley*,[38] the plaintiff asked the court for a preliminary injunction to stop certain capital improvements on and near the oval racetrack included within the Lewis and Clark County Fairgrounds. The racetrack was built in 1870 and had been transferred from the state to the County with the Fairgrounds in 1997. The deed of transfer included the provision that the County would comply with the Montana Antiquities Act (sections 22-3-421, MCA) in its management of the Fairgrounds. In developing a "Footprint" plan for the Fairgrounds, the County's Fair Board held a number of public meetings and solicited public comments. The Board approved the Footprint plan, including proposed construction of an exhibition hall and grandstands in the infield of the racetrack. The court held that the County had been taking the proper steps to comply with the Montana Antiquities Act for the past few years and that none of the work done thus far would require an antiquities permit.

New York In *Ziemba v. City of Troy*,[39] the petitioners requested an injunction to stop the demolition of the Freihofer Bakery Building and the Riverside Club in Troy, New York. They alleged the City of Troy needed to do a State Environmental Quality Review Act (SEQRA) review of the application before issuing the demolition permit. The trial court found the petitioners had standing to bring this claim because they live within two blocks of the proposed demolition and can see the historic buildings from their homes; i.e., they live "within the immediate vicinity of a project that will affect . . . [their] scenic view;" thus, they will suffer a harm not generally shared by the broader public and within the zone of interests, and granted an injunction. The appeals court disagreed by finding the issuance of a demolition permit is a ministerial action and exempted from SEQRA and lifted the injunction.

The court in *Gunthrope-Hardee v. Dormitory Auth. of the State of New York*[40] found that where a project has been completed and the proponent wants only to refinance its existing debt, there is no requirement to complete a SEQRA review. "It must be noted that the logic of exempting completed projects from SEQRA is obvious and consistent with the intent of SEQRA review, namely to determine beforehand the environmental impact of a project and require where appropriate that mitigating steps be taken."[41] The court sympathized that given the facts of this case, it "can understand the moral indignation of the petitioners at what is manifestly an end-run round the SEQRA requirement," but went on to dismiss the claim for failure to state a cause of action.

The court in *Baumgarten v. Town Bd. of the Town of Northampton*[42] considered whether the Town Board gave the required "hard look" under SEQRA for an application to rezone a parcel of land from rural residential to a planned unit development district. Specifically related to historic preservation, an archaeological study was completed and the application was forwarded to the Office of Parks, Recreation and Historic Preservation, which recommended the inclusion of a vegetative buffer to avoid adverse impacts to surrounding historic buildings. The court concluded the town fulfilled the requirements of SEQRA, met the requirements of Town Law § 133, and did not engage in illegal spot zoning.

Easements, Covenants, and Contracts

Hawaii In *Aha Hui Malama O Kaniakapupu v. Land Use Comm'n, State of Haw.*,[43] the appellant challenged the circuit court's dismissal of its claim due to lack of subject matter jurisdiction. The appellants, the Aha Hui Malama O Kaniakapupu (the Hui), are a group that was formed to act as the steward of Kaniakapupu, the historic ruins of Kamehameha III's summer cottage. These ruins are located on state land, which borders a land parcel of roughly 10 acres in Nuuanu, Honolulu, Hawaii. In 1989, the appellees petitioned the Hawaii State Land Use Commission (LUC) to change the land use district boundary from the Conservation Land Use District Boundary to an Urban Land Use District Boundary. The intent of the reclassification was to allow the appellees to subdivide the parcel, construct new and replacement homes, and perform work on the existing units. The LUC approved the reclassification with a covenant that provided right of first refusal to purchase for family members so that the parcel would continue to be used as a private, and not commercial enterprise.

In 2002, Myers listed 2.32 acres of the parcel for sale to the public. The Hui requested the LUC issue an order to show cause why the parcel should not be reclassified as a conservation district due to Myers's failure to comply with the covenant condition regarding right of first refusal for purchase and because such a sale would not be in keeping with the original representations made to the LUC that the property would be used for family enterprise. The Hui also alleged, "selling portions of the Midkiff/Myers Parcel 'will result in the influx of many new people to the Kaniakapupu site and further endanger the preservation efforts carried out to date.'"[44] The Hui requested a hearing on its motion, which the LUC held and subsequently found that the Hui had not presented sufficient evidence that Myers had violated the terms of the covenant. The LUC denied the Hui's motion. The circuit court found that the LUC hearing was not a contested case hearing and, therefore, it lacked subject matter jurisdiction to determine whether a contested case hearing was required.

On appeal, the state supreme court reviewed what constitutes a "contested case" pursuant to state law: "'an agency hearing that 1) is required by law and 2) determines the rights, duties, or privileges of specific parties.'"[45] Noting that the hearing was required by law, the court found that because the matter at issue in the hearing was whether sufficient evidence existed to show Myers's noncompliance with the covenant to issue an order to show cause, "the LUC was not required to—and therefore, did not—determine the Hui's rights and privileges to protect their native Hawaiian culture and traditional practices at Kaniakapupu."[46] In addition, the reclassification of the parcel was not to be determined at the hearing; rather, had the order to show cause been granted, the next step would have been the LUC's determination relating to the rights and duties of the parties. Thus, the court concluded it was not a contested case. The court found again that because it lacked subject matter jurisdiction, it could not review the LUC's decision.

New York The plaintiff in *Bianchi Indus. Serv., LLC v. Vill. of Malone*[47] alleged a breach of contract and fraudulent misrepresentation where the defendant attempted to void the contract between the parties for the demolition and removal of the Flanagan Hotel. The hotel had been condemned due to its deteriorated state and pursuant to the foreclosure proceedings, the defendant sought approval for the demolition from the SHPO and financial grants from HUD. The SHPO approved the demolition of the top three floors of the building but noted the bottom three floors had historic significance. The defendant was confident the issues would be resolved and accepted the plaintiff's bid for the demolition work. After work began, the SHPO notified the defendant of its continuing objections to the demolition. HUD withheld its funds as a result. The defendant replied by telling the plaintiff to stop work and subsequently voided the contract. The motion to dismiss was denied as was a motion for summary judgment, further review into the factual basis of the claim to determine whether the defendant fraudulently misrepresented or withheld the SHPO's objections and the resulting restrictions on the project and HUD funding from the plaintiff.

Virginia The owner of Eastern View Farm, a historic manor house, unsuccessfully appealed his conviction for criminal contempt in *U.S. v. Blackman.*[48] The case arose from a preservation easement held by the NPS. Blackman intended to significantly remodel the house but the NPS denied his renovation plan applications. Blackman elected to remove the porch regardless of the application denial and the NPS responded by seeking a temporary restraining order against any additional renovation work without prior approval. Blackman then requested approval to remove the siding of the house due to its deteriorated condition, which the NPS denied. After the district court issued a preliminary injunction that allowed Blackman to do basic maintenance only on the house without NPS prior approval, Blackman went on to remove the siding from three exterior walls. The district court found Blackman guilty of misdemeanor contempt of court for violating the preliminary injunction. The court of appeals affirmed his conviction.

Compliance with Local Zoning and Permits

Permits: Pennsylvania The court in *Plaxton v. Zoning Bd. of Adjustment*[49] affirmed dismissal of challenges to a construction permit on a historic home. The appellants resided next door to a building where the Philadelphia Historical Commission approved the owner's plans to build additions. Appellants appealed, arguing that the additions would affect the amount of light and air their residence receives, that the permit applicant misstated the size and placement of the additions, and that the work was in violation of zoning regulations. The Philadelphia Board of License and Inspection Review affirmed the decision of the Commission by finding "the approved construction did not affect or destroy historic materials, features or spatial relationships."[50]

Meanwhile, the Philadelphia Court of Common Pleas remanded the case to the Zoning Board for further review by the Department of Licenses and Inspections. The property owners submitted modified plans that included the correct size and placement information, which the Commission and the Department of Licenses and Inspections then approved. The trial court found the cases should be dismissed as moot.

Zoning: Delaware The court in *Friends of Paladin v. New Castle County Bd. of Adjustment & Edgewood Village, LLC*[51] considered whether the decision to allow development of a parcel by the New Castle County Department of Land Use was a zoning or a subdivision issue, thus determining the proper venue for an appeal as either the Board of Adjustment or the Planning Board. The property consisted of a residential complex that the owner wanted to develop into a townhouse community, requiring removal of a potentially historic stone wall. While the Historic Preservation Section stated the wall was not historic due to a lack of integrity, the Historic Review Board disagreed and recommended the application be denied. After some back and forth, the Department of Land Use concluded the wall was historic and could not be removed. The Department instructed the property owner to file any appeal with the Planning Board, but he chose his friendly forum and appealed to the Board of Adjustment, which reversed the Department's decision.

The petitioners asked the court to review the Board of Adjustment's decision and argued that the Board lacked subject matter jurisdiction to hear the appeal because the Department's decision regarding the stone wall as a historic resource was a subdivision decision, not a zoning issue. The court noted the Board of Adjustment's jurisdiction to hear appeals in zoning matters and went on to review the UDC's clear definition of historic resources and related issues as zoning matters. Finding further the Department's decision regarding the historic significance of the wall rested on the criteria listed in that regulation, the court concluded that the Board's jurisdiction to hear the appeal was proper even though the issue arose from the review of a subdivision plan.

Louisiana In *Derbes v. City of New Orleans*,[52] the City of New Orleans appealed the district court's decision to enjoin the City from interfering with Jame Derbes' use of his property for paid events and to dismiss the City's request for a summary judgment regarding the question of whether Derbes' use had achieved nonconforming status under the relevant zoning law. Derbes operates the Benachi House, which is considered to be a local landmark, as a bed and breakfast. Located in a mixed-use neighborhood, the Benachi House has also been hosting paid events consistently since 1993. In 2004, the City Planning Commission and the City Council granted Derbes' request for a conditional use permit to increase the number of guest rooms; however, the Council denied his requests to operate the bed and breakfast while residing in a house that would be built on the Benachi House grounds and to hold "event rentals."[53] Derbes challenged these denials and requested an injunction to stop the City from interfering with the ongoing use of the House for paid events in the district court.

On appeal, the court considered whether the property had achieved a legal nonconforming use, and to do that it next looked to which version of the law applies, the 1993 or 2001. In the 2001 amendments, there was no requirement for written notice of the violation to be given to the City and the time period that must pass from the time of the first violation without the City taking any action is ten years. The earlier versions of the law included written notice requirements and different time periods. The appeals court found that the district court correctly applied the 2001 version of the law to the situation and that Derbes' use of the property had achieved nonconforming status, rendering the injunction unlawful.

Maine The plaintiffs in *McNeil v. Town of Standish*[54] challenged the town of Standish Historic Preservation Commission's grant of a certificate of appropriateness to Robert Higgins for proposed construction of a commercial building and relocation of a historic house and barn within the historic district on an informal request. Acknowledging the letter was not a standard application, the Commission nonetheless approved the proposal with conditions.

The court first addressed the issue of standing, although the case was resolved as a matter of procedural due process. Because Dr. McNeil attended the Commission meeting at which the proposal was presented, he is a party, but the court found he did not suffer a particularized harm as a result of the Commission's decision because he lived almost five miles away from the historic property. Ms. Dudek resided across the street from the property, thus the court found she would suffer a particularized harm distinct from that suffered by the general public, but because only Ms. Dudek's husband attended the Commission meeting, she does not meet the requirement to be a party. To resolve the matter, the court found that the Commission did not make best efforts to notify Ms. Dudek before considering the application as was required. The court stated that notice to one spouse cannot be attributed to the other spouse and the letter requesting approval for the proposal did not constitute an actual or de facto application. Therefore, because of the violation of Standish Historic Preservation Ordinance, the court found Ms. Dudek had standing. Further, since the Commission violated the procedures set forth in the Ordinance to issue a certificate, the Commission's approval of the proposal was not valid.

New Jersey In *Weeden v. City Council of the City of Trenton*,[55] the plaintiffs challenged the Zoning Board of Adjustment's authority to issue a variance to a redevelopment plan. At issue was the proposed development of fast food restaurants with a drive-thru window. The City Council adopted the redevelopment plan "to eliminate those conditions which cause the area to be considered a renewal (blighted) area. . . . The City's intention is to create a mixed-use development, preserving the architectural and historic significance of the Area."[56] The redevelopment plan specified certain goals, including historic preservation, and prohibited drive-in restaurants. The Zoning Board granted the variance, with the approval of the Trenton Landmarks Commission for Historic Preservation, by finding the property to be "uniquely situated" for this particular use. The plaintiffs appealed the decision to the City Council, which affirmed. The plaintiffs then filed a complaint with the superior court, which agreed that the Zoning Board had jurisdiction to approve the variance and that the variance "furthered the purposes of the Redevelopment Plan, and that the project would not cause 'a substantial detriment to the public good or to the intent and purpose of the Redevelopment Plan.'" However, the court found that the Council had not conducted a proper de novo review of the Board's decision. The case was remanded to the City Council for review, and the Council once again approved the variance.

New York In *Greenberg v. City of New York*,[57] New York City appealed the trial court's decision to enjoin its proposed renovations to the fountain basin and fountain plaza in Washington Square Park, a city landmark. Local residents alleged that the city parks department withheld material information relating to the reduction in the size of the plaza and the height of the fountain spray from the Community Board, the Landmarks Preservation Commission, and the Art Commission. The appellate court disagreed with the trial court and found within the record that the city did not withhold material information from the Board or the commissions.

In *In the Matter of Nora Lucas*,[58] the petitioners alleged that the Zoning Board of Appeals (ZBA) arbitrarily and capriciously granted a variance request to a property owner, Benmar Properties, LLC, when the previous property owners' application, alleged to be the same, was denied years before. The variance was to subdivide the parcel in order to construct a second home, when the original application was denied due to the historic nature of the property. A number of residents opposed the Benmar application and noted the location of a number of surrounding, impacted properties that were eligible for listing on the National Register. The court considered whether the ZBA was bound by its earlier decision regarding the variance.

The court found that the ZBA failed to show "a change of circumstances sufficient to justify the contrary result—i.e., that there were substantive differences between the applications or that there has been some other material change in circumstances (such as a change in the character of the neighborhood) to justify the different decision."[59] Thus, the ZBA's granting of the variance was held invalid as arbitrary and capricious for not following precedent. Further, the character of the neighborhood had not changed in the intervening time period.

Pennsylvania In *Royal Bank of America v. Zoning Hearing Board of Schuylkill Township,*[60] the plaintiff appealed an enforcement notice requiring repairs to be undertaken by the Bank on what was alleged to be a historic building. The building was a two-story house originally built in 1873, and used as an office and an apartment. The building was found to be in "cosmetic disrepair."

The Bank challenged the enforcement notice, asserting that the allegation regarding the building's condition was vague, that the building was not a historic structure, and that the Zoning Ordinance's Historic Site Overlay District regulations were invalid and unenforceable because the Pennsylvania Historical and Museum Commission (PHMC) did not certify the historic district. The Township Zoning Hearing Board sustained the claim that the Ordinance lacked clear guidelines for enforcement, but otherwise denied the Bank's requests for relief.

In reviewing the Board's determination that the building was eligible for the Historic Resource's Inventory, the court discussed the inappropriateness of the Township's reliance solely on the building's age as relevant to historic significance. The court highlighted the other requirement of the Ordinance: a determination by a qualified person as to the local historical or architectural significance of the building. The court concluded that although the building is "age-eligible," the Township "failed to show through the testimony of a person possessing the foregoing qualifications that the building had any historic, architectural or archeological value."[61] Thus, the Board abused its discretion in finding the building eligible for the Historic Resource's Inventory and the enforcement notice was dismissed.

Taxes and Use of Fees

Alabama In *Padgett v. Conecuh County Comm'n*,[62] James C. Padgett and the Alabama Preservation Alliance, Inc. (APA) appealed a decision that found the APA to lack standing, denied both plaintiffs relative portions of attorneys' fees and costs, and forfeited the $25,000 deposit that had been given as security for the issuance of a temporary restraining order (TRO). The plaintiffs had alleged the County Commission's intent to use court fees, lodging tax, and revenue warrants to demolish the Conecuh County courthouse, which the plaintiffs argued was historically significant.

On appeal, APA argued it had standing because it is a statewide organization that works to preserve historic buildings, including the courthouse. The court found that because none of APA's members resided in Conecuh County, the county laws on which APA relied to assert its aesthetic and environmental interests did not reach to protect the interests of APA's members, and the APA did not have standing. The court concluded that the TRO was appropriate to enjoin the use of court fees and lodging tax for the proposed demolition and new construction, and inappropriate to enjoin the use of the revenue warrants. Thus the court reversed the forfeiture of the deposit but did not grant attorney fees.

New Jersey In *Univ. Cottage Club of Princeton New Jersey Corp. v. New Jersey Dep't of Envtl. Prot.*,[63] a private, nonprofit eating club affiliated with Princeton University appealed the trial court's decision to affirm the denial of their property tax exemption as a historic site. The exemption was denied because the club did not meet the public accessibility requirements of recently adopted standards to be granted tax-exempt status as a historic site. In response, the club changed its policies and opened the club to the public for no less than twelve days a year. An amendment to the law significantly changed the public access requirements for new applicants and for ongoing certification of already established tax-exempt historic sites.

The court reviewed the timing of the club's application in reference to the new amendments to the law. Finding that the Commissioner's denial of the club's application was arbitrary because it constituted rulemaking that should have been subject to the Administrative Policy Act's notice and comment procedures, the court stated, "in one fell swoop . . . [the Commissioner] upended the prior public access requirement of twelve days, substituted an 'objectively reasonable' standard without defining it, and used that undisclosed standard to deny . . . [the club's] petition outright."[64] The court found the club's application was not subject to the new open access amendment.

Notes

1. U.S. Constitution, Amendment I.
2. 494 U.S. 872, 878–79 (1990).
3. 374 U.S. 398 (1963).
4. *Employment Div., Ore. Dept. of Human Res.*, 494 U.S. at 885 (quoting *Lyng v. Northwest Indian Cemetery Protective Assn.*, 485 U.S. 439, 451 [1988]; *Reynolds v. United States,* 98 U.S. 145, 167 [1879]).
5. *Id.* at 879 (quoting *United States v. Lee*, 455 U.S. 252, 263 [1982]).
6. *Id.* at 881–82.
7. *Id.* at 883–84.
8. *Id.* at 884 (quoting *Bowen v. Roy*, 476 U.S. 693, 708 [1986]).
9. 42 U.S.C. § 2000bb et seq.
10. Greg Groninger, "Religious Freedom Restoration Act Analysis" First Amendment Topics, First Amendment Center (Nov. 16, 2004) at http://www.firstamendment-center.org/analysis.aspx?id=14383 (last visited Nov. 16, 2007).
11. 521 U.S. 507 (1997).
12. *Id.* at 535.
13. 42 U.S.C. § 2000cc et seq.
14. 42 U.S.C. § 2000cc(a)(1).
15. 42 U.S.C. § 2000cc(a)(2).
16. 482 F. Supp. 2d 1281 (D. Kan. 2007).
17. *Id.* See generally "About, State RFRAs," First Amendment Topics, First Amendment Center (Nov. 16, 2004) at http://www.firstamendmentcenter.org/about.aspx?id=14031 (last visited Nov. 16, 2007).
18. No. 06-C-629-S, 2007 U.S. Dist. LEXIS 12826 (W.D. Wisc. Feb. 23. 2007).

19. 16 U.S.C. § 470f.
20. 16 U.S.C. § 470h-2(k).
21. *Friends of Superior, Inc.*, 2007 U.S. Dist. LEXIS 12826 at 5.
22. 482 F. Supp. 2d. at 1283.
23. *Id.* at 1 (quoting Kan. Stat. Ann. § 75-2724(a)).
24. *Id.* at 4.
25. *Id.* at 5.
26. *Id.* at 8 (quoting *Axson-Flynn v. Johnson*, 356 F.3d 1277, 1294 [10th Cir. 2004]).
27. *Id.*
28. 475 F.3d 480 (2nd Cir. 2007).
29. *Id.* at 485 (quoting *Neb. Press Ass'n v. Stuart*, 427 U.S. 539, 559 [1976]).
30. 512 U.S. 43, 48 (1994).
31. 475 F.3d at 490.
32. 485 F.3d 736 (3rd Cir. 2007).
33. *Id.* at 748, 750 (quoting Bradford, Pa., Code § 125-15(E), and Rappa, 18 F.3d at 1067).
34. No.1:06-CV-21-JDT-WTL, 2007 U.S. Dist. LEXIS 21988 (S.D. Ind., Indianapolis Div. Mar. 26, 2007).
35. *W. Hartford Initiative to Save Historic Property v. Town of W. Hartford*, No. 3:06-CV-739 (RNC), 2006 U.S. Dist. LEXIS 58221 (D. Conn. Aug. 18, 2006) (quoting Conn. Gen. Stat. § 22a-19a).
36. See 16 U.S.C. § 470a(a)(6); 36 C.F.R. §§ 60.6(s), 60.3(k).
37. 2006 U.S. Dist. LEXIS 58221 at 20-21.
38. No. CDV-2005-497, 2007 Mont. Dist. LEXIS 101 (Mont. 1st Jud. Dist. Ct., Lewis & Clark County Feb. 15, 2007).
39. 827 N.Y.S.2d 322 (N.Y. App. Div. 3d Dep't 2006).
40. 831 N.Y.S.2d 359 (N.Y., N.Y. County 2006), *aff'd*, 835 N.Y.S.2d 898 (N.Y. App. Div. 1st Dep't 2007).
41. 831 N.Y.S.2d at 3.
42. 826 N.Y.S.2d 811 (N.Y. App. Div. 3d Dep't 2006).
43. 139 P.3d 712 (Haw. Sup. Ct. 2006).
44. *Id.* at 715.
45. *Id.* at 720 (quoting *Pub. Access Shoreline Hawai'i v. Hawai'i County Planning Comm'n*, 903 P.2d 1246, 1252 [Haw. 1995]).
46. *Id.* at 722.
47. 838 N.Y.S.2d 240 (N.Y. App. Div. 3d Dep't 2007).
48. No. 06-4176, 2007 U.S. App. LEXIS 12572 (4th Cir. May 31, 2007).
49. No. 3601, No. 2289, 2006 Phila. Ct. Com. Pl. LEXIS 331 (Pa. Com. Pl., Phila. County, Civil Div. Aug. 14, 2006).
50. *Id.* at 6.

51. No. 591, 2006, 2007 Del. LEXIS 322 (Del. Sup. Ct. July 23, 2007), *aff'g* C.A. No. 05A-08-009-JRS, 2006 Del. Super. LEXIS 423 (Del. Super. Ct., New Castle Dec. 12, 2006).
52. 941 So. 2d 45 (La. Ct. App., 4th Cir. 2006).
53. *Id.* at 4.
54. No. AP-06-07, 2006 Me. Super. LEXIS 256 (Me. Super. Ct., Cumberland County Nov. 2, 2006).
55. 917 A.2d 815 (N.J. Super. Ct. App. Div. 2007).
56. *Id.* at 817.
57. 832 N.Y.S.2d 16 (N.Y. Super. Ct. App. Div. 2007).
58. 836 N.Y.S.2d 486 (N.Y. Super. Ct., Westchester County 2007).
59. *Id.* at 10.
60. No. 06-06492, 2007 Pa. Dist. & Cnty. Dec. LEXIS 57 (Pa. Com. Pl., Chester County Feb. 5, 2007).
61. *Id.* at 11.
62. No. 2041078, 2006 Ala. Civ. App. LEXIS 711 (Ala. Civ. App. Dec. 1, 2006).
63. 921 A.2d 1122 (N.J. Sup. Ct. 2007).
64. *Id.* at 1134.

Tribes, Tribal Lands, and Indian Arts

• • •

Section Editor: Rob Roy Smith

Introduction

Tribal cultural resource protection advocates far too often become mired in fighting for the protections that were to be guaranteed under the patchwork of Federal cultural resource protection statutes, such as the Native American Graves Protection and Repatriation Act and the Archaeological Resources Protection Act, while overlooking a frequent companion of cultural resource issues: tribal religious freedom. Neglect of tribal religious freedom as means to access justice for aggrieved tribes and tribal members might now be a thing of the past. The year 2007 is highlighted by significant sacred site litigation victories in Arizona and Nevada grounded in the guarantees of the First Amendment to the United States Constitution and the Religious Freedom Restoration Act. Might this be the elusive unified approach to cultural resource protection that tribal advocates have been looking for?

This section explores the answer to this timely query by focusing on cultural property issues involving tribes in the courts, the United States Congress, state legislatures, and on a programmatic level; and on Indian Arts and Crafts matters with a particular emphasis on religious freedom.

Tribal Lands, Scared Sites, and Cultural Properties

Religious Freedom Primer

The Free Exercise Clause of the First Amendment to the United States Constitution provides that "Congress shall make no law respecting an establishment of religion, or prohibiting the free exercise thereof . . . ."[1] These simple words mean the right to believe and profess religious doctrine without fear of government regulation or suppression. But the exercise of religion entails more than just belief. The exercise of religion also involves the performance, or in some cases abstention from, certain outward manifestations of those beliefs, whether through acts at ceremonies or simply appearing at special places. Designed to buttress the protections afforded by the Free Exercise Clause, Congress enacted the Religious Freedom and Restoration Act of 1993 ("RFRA"),[2] in part, to "better protect all Americans of all faiths in the exercise of their religion."[3] To do so, Congress used its authority to apply RFRA to the Federal government[4] and broadly decreed that the Federal government "shall not substantially burden a person's exercise of religion" unless the government could demonstrate that "application of the burden to the person (1) is in furtherance of compelling governmental interest; and (2) is the least restrictive means of furthering that compelling interest."[5]

Despite these lofty intentions, RFRA seemed to fall short of protecting tribal religious practices. Until this past year, most Indian religious freedom cases focused on ceremonial peyote use[6] or the use of eagle feathers.[7] Most such cases also resulted in rulings adverse to the Indian advocates seeking to protect what they perceived to be their religious freedoms.[8] Now, however, RFRA has been applied to sacred places and has been used by tribal litigants with success. This success has important ramifications for tribal spiritual practices on federal land.

RFRA and the San Francisco Peaks Litigation

On March 12, 2007, the Navajo Nation, Hopi Tribe, and other southwest tribes scored a major sacred sites victory before the Ninth Circuit Court of Appeals by stopping certain activities of a ski resort in the San Francisco Peaks of Arizona, including the resort's planned use of reclaimed wastewater for snowmaking at the environmentally sensitive and spiritually important site.[9]

The site comprises three 12,000 foot mountains north of Flagstaff. Their peaks are considered sacred by thirteen tribes. The tribes alleged that the wastewater would contaminate the natural resources needed to perform the required ceremonies and would have a devastating impact on their culture and religion. Sacred plants are located in the area. The case involved the important question of whether religious beliefs may block certain land use practices. The answer, at least for these tribes and this site, is yes. This is the first case that has successfully applied RFRA to Indian sacred sites protection.

The Ninth Circuit found that the burden from the project on the religious practices of the tribes falls "roughly into two categories: (1) the inability to perform a particular religious ceremony, because the ceremony requires collecting natural resources from the Peaks that would be too contaminated—physically, spiritually, or both — for sacramental use; and (2) the inability to maintain daily and annual religious practices comprising an entire way of life, because the practices require belief in the mountain's purity or a spiritual connection to the mountain that would be undermined by the contamination."[10] None of the Defendant United States Forest Service's arguments, ranging from multiple use interests to economic interests of the City of Flagstaff or of the resort owners, justified placing such a substantial burden on the tribal members' exercise of religion, according to the court. The court made clear that the Forest Service's approval of the Snowbowl's use of recycled sewage effluent to make artificial snow on the San Francisco Peaks violates RFRA.[11] This is an important decision that sets great precedent for individuals and tribes who seek to protect sites that are both historically sacred and presently culturally and spiritually important to them.

Although this is a sweeping victory for sacred site protection under the RFRA, one must wonder whether the ruling is limited by the particular facts of the case. For instance, the court went to great pains to indicate just how egregious was the Forest Service's decision to permit the reclaimed wastewater in the sacred areas and what an example of government insensitivity to Native religions this case portrayed. The panel stated: "The Forest Service and the Snowbowl now propose to put treated sewage effluent on the Peaks. To get some sense of equivalence, it may be useful to imagine the effect on Christian beliefs and practices — and the imposition that Christians would experience — if the government were to require that baptisms be carried out with 'reclaimed water.'"[12] The court continued: "If Appellants do not have a valid RFRA claim in this case, we are unable to see how any Native American plaintiff can ever have a successful RFRA claim based on beliefs and practices tied to land that they hold sacred."[13]

The San Francisco Peaks litigation may thus be viewed as one extreme on a spectrum of guaranteed religious freedoms that necessitate the protection of sacred sites. The court highlighted the following factors that helped it conclude that the action would impose a burden on the religious exercise of the four tribes: The Peaks are "most sacred" for the Hopi and Navajo; the tribes' religious beliefs have revolved around the Peaks "for centuries"; the religious practices require pure natural resources; the effluent would prevent the creation of "medicine bundles" at the mountain; and, if allowed to go forward, the artificial snow-making process would "fundamentally undermine their entire system of belief" and the associated religious practices.[14] These examples of "substantial burden on [the] free exercise of religion" may now serve as a guidepost to other litigants seeking to use the RFRA to protect sacred sites. Future cases will no doubt challenge these facts, exploring how much less than a "fundamental" altering of a religious system might suffice under RFRA to block destructive land use practices at a sacred site. For instance, what if the practices could take place elsewhere? What if natural resources necessary for the practices could have been obtained elsewhere? Whether something other than the complete destruction of a sacred place that prohibits tribal members from conducting a religious ceremony mandated by their religion would be countenanced under RFRA ultimately remains to be seen. This does not mean, however, that other cases with similar fact patterns cannot be constructed to further the application of RFRA's protections.

This recent case may be referred to in an historical sense as Snowbowl II. In Snowbowl I, the 1980 case of *Wilson v. Block*,[15] the Navajo and Hopi tribes claimed that the construction of the ski area would desecrate their sacred area and sought to bar construction based on the First Amendment "Establishment Clause." In Snowbowl I the court applied the Establishment Clause test of neither promoting nor denying religious practice, and held that to deter the development of the San Francisco Peaks to enable tribal religious practice would be impermissible as unduly promoting religion. The court reasoned that the tribes could practice their religion elsewhere and could collect ritual items from elsewhere on the peaks. Contrast Snowbowl I to Snowbowl II, as in the later case, the court used RFRA rather than the First Amendment, and the court found that snow made from sewage would defile the entire area, making options unavailable on the peak.

An important lesson to be gleaned from the litigation is the substantial testimony in the record created in the lower court, provided by tribal leaders and tribal elders. They spoke of their religious practices and the importance of the Peaks to those practices and beliefs. The court extensively quoted the testimony of tribal elders at the bench trial before the district court describing how the proposed action would have prevented them from performing their ceremonies and, therefore, posed the "substantial burden" required under RFRA analysis.[16] The appellate court was clearly persuaded by testimony that explained the connection between the Peaks and the tribal religions, and the extensive detail provided about tribal religious practices at the Peaks that would be disrupted or blocked altogether. This free expression of normally closely held tribal religious practices stands in sharp contrast to the situation normally confronted by tribal advocates who, in many cases, run into practical difficulties in presenting this critical evidence. Often, and sometimes with much validity, tribal members are reticent to describe religious practices and the religious use of certain places and resources for fear that the resources will be destroyed or that the tribe's unique religious practices will be co-opted by "new-age" leaders. However, the San Francisco Peaks litigation makes clear that for tribes to protect the sites that they hold sacred, they must risk sharing details of those sites with the public. In this case, the reward was clearly worth the risk as the use of reclaimed wastewater was not permitted to go forward.

Before the end of the year, the Ninth Circuit granted rehearing, en banc. Upon rehearing, the court will either cement the application of RFRA and the protections it affords or marginalize the law, diminishing the standard to the one applied in Snowbowl I.

Establishment Clause: Cave Rock

In another religious freedom case focusing on sacred sites, this time addressing a challenge brought by recreational users against a United States Forest Service decision protecting a sacred site, the Ninth Circuit Court of Appeals upheld a decision of the Forest Service to ban "the recreational activity of rock climbing" at Cave Rock.[17] As opposed to the San Francisco Peaks litigation, this case invokes the Establishment Clause and attempts use of the First Amendment to block protections for tribal sacred sites.

Cave Rock is a culturally, historically, and archaeologically significant site to the Washoe people, Native Americans who have lived in the Lake Tahoe area for at least 1500 years. Traditional Washoe view Cave Rock as the site of important mythological events that are central to their cosmology. It is also a symbol of their cultural and religious identity, as under traditional Washoe beliefs, Cave Rock is "the most religious feature within the Washoe religion," and many Washoe compare Cave Rock to a church. Cave Rock is considered so powerful and sacred that the health and integrity of Washoe society may be jeopardized if traditional practices are not observed there. Therefore, the Washoe believe that Cave Rock is to be avoided by all but certain Washoe practitioners.[18]

Unfortunately, Cave Rock is also a popular rockclimbing spot.[19] Climbers have disfigured the rock and added a safety platform. The area is also a historic site, enjoyed for picnics, hiking, and by boaters for its unique vista. The Forest Service decided on a management plan for Cave Rock in 2003 that banned all climbing and removed climbing bolts to "protect Cave Rock's heritage resources."[20] Litigation followed. No Indian tribe or tribal member was a party to the case.

The primary claim by the rockclimbers was that the Forest Service's decision to ban rockclimbing violated the Establishment Clause by elevating religion over multiple use. The court disagreed after an extensive review of the purpose and effect of the Forest Service's decision. The court determined that the Forest Service's decision had a "secular purpose—the preservation of a historic cultural area."[21] To reach this conclusion, the court focused on the fact that the Forest Service's decision to protect Cave Rock was not done with "the predominant purpose of advancing the Washoe religion." Even if Washoe religion did play a role, "the fact that Cave Rock also derives its historical and cultural force in part from its role in Washoe religious belief and practice does not counsel the conclusion that the Forest Service acted with the purpose of advancing religion" because "[h]istorical and cultural considerations motivate the preservation of national monuments that may have religious significance to many or even most visitors."[22] The court concluded that the "fact that Cave Rock is a sacred site to the Washoe does not diminish its importance as a national cultural resource."[23] The court ultimately held that "the Establishment Clause does not bar the government from protecting an historically and culturally important site simply because the site's importance derives at least in part from its sacredness to certain groups."[24]

Cave Rock is an interesting decision, especially when viewed as a companion to the San Francisco Peaks litigation. While both cases secure protections for tribal sacred sites, they present opposite sides of "religious freedom" case strategy. Tribes must remain vigilant to the fact that the First Amendment may be used as both a sword and a shield when it comes to sacred sites. The Cave Rock case also highlights the importance of building a strong record that supports tribal beliefs and practices. The court in Cave Rock made frequent reference to the Washoe Tribe's comments submitted during the Forest Service's comment period on its proposed climbing restrictions.

In addition, tribes might feel that the court reached the "right" result in Cave Rock, but might have done so for the "wrong" reasons. Here, the "sacredness" of Cave Rock to the Washoe people was construed as detrimental to its preservation. Had the tribe's religious beliefs been at the forefront of the Forest Service's decision, rather than the secular justification, the court might have ruled that the Forest Service violated the Establishment Clause. Clearly, this was not the case in the San Francisco Peaks litigation where the tribes' religious practices were fundamental to securing victory under RFRA and, to a lesser extent, the Free Exercise Clause. This distinction must be understood by tribal advocates preparing cases to protect sacred sites using the First Amendment. The lesson is, in the Ninth Circuit, when the First Amendment is invoked to protect a religious site, there must be a prominent secular purpose that may be consistent with religious use.

The Ninth Circuit reasoning is not replicated in other circuits. In the Tenth Circuit, the court reasoned that "the government may accommodate religious practice without violating the Establishment Clause."[25] Like the Ninth Circuit, the Tenth Circuit has come full circle in acknowledgment of protection of tribal sacred sites as components of culture. Unlike the Ninth Circuit, the Tenth Circuit does not require a concurrent secular justification, but rather, views accommodation of religion as distinct from promotion. The Tenth Circuit evolution can be seen in Rainbow Bridge I and II. Rainbow Bridge I is the case of *Badoni v. Higginson*,[26] which arose out of a request of the Navajo Tribe for quiet use of the Rainbow Bridge area, during periods of ceremonial use. The tribe did not request the land but did ask the National Park Service to prevent destructive use of the bridge. The court ruled in 1980 that protection to advantage the tribe would be an unconstitutional promotion of religion. Twenty four years later the court was again asked to review actions of the National Park Service, but this time by climbers who took offense to interpretive signs informing visitors of Native American cultural uses of the park and restricted access which prevented climbing on the bridge. In Rainbow Bridge II the court used the test of reasonable accommodation to uphold NPS.

National Historic Preservation Act

One case brought by an Indian tribe to protect cultural properties under the National Historic Preservation Act (NHPA) is worthy of note in 2007. The Quechan Indian Tribe filed suit against the Bureau of Land Management under the NHPA and the National Environmental Policy Act alleging that the agency failed to properly analyze the potential environmental and cultural resource impacts resulting from a transfer of federal land to the Wellton-Mohawk Irrigation and Drainage District for purposes of building an oil refinery. Before reaching the merits, the Arizona District Court concluded that the Tribe failed to show a strong likelihood of success on the merits of its claims that the agency had failed to take the requisite hard look at the location and needs of the Tribe's cultural resources before approving the land transfer, and denied the Tribe's requested preliminary injunction.[27] The Tribe has filed an appeal of the denial of the injunction.

This case is intriguing as it does not involve tribal lands. The tribe's affected cultural resources are all located on the federal land transferred into private ownership. The issue is the protection of sites as part of the transfer of existing federal obligations with the land.[28] The land is culturally and historically significant to the Quechan. The action appears directed at blocking the eventual construction of an oil refinery in a time of energy crisis, which is in contrast to the cases discussed above, where tribal cultural resources were threatened by recreational use. This litigation will test the strength of historic protection in the face of potentially destructive economic development activities.

Other Sacred Site Protection Efforts

Last year also saw a return to tribal ownership of various sites held sacred to Indian tribes. Tribes also reached new understandings with state and local agencies to protect sacred sites. While these events occurred sans legal action, we mention them here as examples of the law at work in a cooperative environment.

The Cowee Mound in North Carolina and seventy-one surrounding acres were returned to the ownership and stewardship of the Eastern Band of Cherokee Indians in April 2007 after 188 years in private land ownership.[29] This is one of the few undisturbed and unexcavated Indian burial mounds remaining in Western North Carolina. The Tribe has no plans to develop the property. It will be managed under a conservation easement. Cowee was the economic hub of the Tribe, because of its riverside location and proximity to white settlements. Until the late 1770s, approximately eight hundred Cherokee lived in the area.

Similarly, in June 2007, the Ho-Chunk Nation of Wisconsin welcomed the return of the Kingsley Bend Wayside Effigy Mounds from the Wisconsin State Department of Transportation. The site dates to A.D. 600.[30] The mounds are considered some of the finest examples of tribal effigy mounds in the state of Wisconsin. More than one hundred trees have been removed and grass and bushes cut by tribal actors in an effort to return the site to its original environmental condition. The area is believed to have originally held more than twenty mounds, which form various symbols including the natural realms of air, earth, and water.

In August 2007, stories surfaced of enhanced cooperation between Indian tribes in California and state fire protection agencies designed to protect sacred sites from fire and the harm caused by firefighting methods.[31] Tribal members attended fire safety classes to instruct officials as to site locations to help direct bulldozers away from sacred sites. Fire officials and archaeologists say the cooperation has allowed them to protect artifacts during almost every major wildfire in the last few years, and archaeologists and the tribes have successfully worked together to steer both fires and bulldozers away from sacred sites.

Tribes and the Native American Graves Protection and Repatriation Act

This past year also saw litigation, regulatory, and legislative activity concerning the Native American Graves Protection and Repatriation Act (NAGPRA).[32]

Cultural Patrimony, Remains, and Cultural Site Litigation In *Rosales v. United States*,[33] individual tribal members enrolled with the Jamul Indian Village in San Diego County, California, brought suit under NAGPRA against the Department of the Interior and the staff of the National NAGPRA Program, seeking to stop the construction of a hotel and casino project on tribal lands where, according to the plaintiffs, the remains of their decreased relatives and other funerary objects are buried. Employing a litigation strategy that the district court called "baffling," the tribal members did not sue the entities planning to construct the casino, the tribe; rather, they brought suit against the United States claiming that the United States had an affirmative duty under NAGPRA to protect any remains and funerary objects located in the site.[34] The district court denied the tribal members' efforts to obtain a preliminary injunction to block construction at the site, finding that their claims lacked a likelihood of success on the merits and because the plaintiffs could not show irreparable harm. The district court also decided that the proper forum for the case to be heard was not the District of Columbia, where the defendants are located but, instead, the Southern District of California. This is the jurisdiction of the site and the Tribe.[35] On November 28, 2007, the Southern District of California dismissed the complaint with prejudice, for lack of subject matter jurisdiction. The court found that the plaintiffs were individuals seeking to protect alleged tribal interests, and thus overstep the sovereignty of the tribe. The court stated that "Plaintiffs may not make an 'end run' around tribal sovereign immunity by suing the United States."[36] The court found that the parcel in contention was tribal land.[37]

This case, while rather nondescript in the annuls of Indian law, bears mention for two reasons. First, *Rosales* bears some resemblance to a case discussed in last year's *Yearbook*, *Hawk v. Danforth*, where the Chairman of the Oneida Tribe of Indians of Wisconsin alleged violations of NAGPRA caused by the Tribe's covering of burial sites, including those of his ancestors, under a tribally owned parking lot which appeared to be located on tribal lands. The Chairman appeared *pro se* to ask that the court require the Tribe to excavate under the parking lot to find the remains alleged to be buried there. In *Danforth,* the court rejected the claims, finding that to the extent NAGPRA applies where no agency or museum is involved, the statute "applies only to remains or artifacts that are 'excavated or discovered'—not to remains that may still be buried" on federal or Indian land.[38] The court went on to confuse the new discovery on the land and disposition section of NAGPRA, section 3, with the repatriation sections, sections 5–7, but did acknowledge that NAGPRA is a law that deals with disposition of found items, not burials in repose. This is consistent with the Southern District of California decision in *Rosales* that NAGPRA was not triggered, because there were plans to build but no discovery had been made.[39]

Second, the intra-tribal dispute aspect of *Rosales* highlights a growing tension in many tribal communities. Economic development of natural resources is critical for most tribes to achieve self-sufficiency and end the cycle of poverty on Indian reservations. However, development can become controversial when religious and environmental concerns conflict with development goals. Using NAGPRA, a law intended to resolve the property rights of tribes, to litigate within tribes is an unfortunate use of the law.

Regulatory Action

NAGPRA Inventory Reporting Rule

The Department of the Interior published a final rule on March 21, 2007, adding to NAGPRA a new section of the regulations, 43 CFR 10.13. The final rule guides the future applicability of the statute to museums and Federal agencies by providing a uniform set of time parameters to ensure ongoing compliance so that lineal descendents, Indian tribes, and Native Hawai'ian organizations know of the existence and location of cultural items with which they are culturally affiliated and which they may desire to repatriate.[40] The new rules apply only to Native American human remains and cultural items that are already subject to repatriation under NAGPRA and that are "possessed or controlled by Federal agencies and museums." The rule sets forth what is timely continued reporting obligations after NAGPRA's initial reporting period, which was in November 1993 for collection summaries and November 1995 for inventories of human remains and associated funerary objects.[41]

Although the regulations merely codify existing reasonable practices that have been ongoing for more than a decade, the rule fills an important gap and ensures that museums must continue to provide a summary and inventory of tribal cultural properties when new items come into their possession; when a new tribe becomes federally recognized; or for a museum that receives federal funds for the first time. Making an individualized practice uniform provides protection for tribes who require timely information about collections to know whether certain museums hold cultural items that the tribes may claim under NAGPRA. The new rule thus ensures that repatriations of museum collections will be ongoing.

The rule does have some shortcomings. It does not require museums and federal agencies to provide collection information to tribes not federally recognized, although they may do so voluntarily. However, the rule does provide procedures that apply to notifying newly recognized Indian tribes. In addition, the deadlines established for requiring museums and federal agencies to report collection information are relatively long, providing museums and federal agencies with six months to prepare a summary of new holdings or locating a previously unreported holding, and two years to prepare a full inventory upon initial compliance obligations.

Consultation Concerning Future Regulations

On April 11, 2007, the Department of the Interior published a notice of consultation with Indian tribes to discuss the still unpublished regulations for the disposition of unclaimed Native American human remains, funerary objects, sacred objects, or objects of patrimony discovered or excavated from Federal or tribal lands after November 1990.[42] The notice published a list of three consultation meetings and asked tribes to respond to a series of questions asking how the government should distinguish between claimed items and unclaimed items under NAGPRA, and whether the government should treat such items found on Indian reservations differently.[43] Despite the fact that the unclaimed remains provision of NAGPRA has remained unimplemented by

Federal rulemaking for seventeen years, the Federal Register notice did not provide any timeline for the development of the new rules. The issue has been on the Department of the Interior's agenda for some time and it appears likely to remain on the drafting table for more time to come. At present, Federal agencies appear to be addressing disposition issues for new discoveries within the NHPA, Section 106, and NEPA process.

Federal Legislation

The year 2007 again saw efforts to amend NAGPRA. Senators Byron L. Dorgan of (D-ND) and John McCain (R-AZ) introduced the bipartisan "Native American Omnibus Technical Corrections Act of 2007" on September 25, 2007.[44] The bill seeks to amend various Federal laws addressing Indian affairs. The second section of the bill would amend section 2(9) of NAGPRA, 25 U.S.C. § 3001(9), by "(1) by inserting 'or was' after 'is'; and (2) by inserting after 'indigenous to' the following: 'any geographic area that is now located within the boundaries of'" so that the new definition of "Native American" under NAGPRA would read "'Native American' means of, or relating to, a tribe, people, or culture that is or was indigenous to any geographic area that is now located within the boundaries of the United States." The bill would effectively serve as a technical fix to the limitations of the definition of "Native American" highlighted by the Ninth Circuit's *Bonnichsen v. United States* decision in 2004.[45]

It should be noted that NAGPRA does not set a time depth for Native American human remains, relying instead on the factual determination in each case of cultural affiliation of indigenous humans. NAGPRA acknowledges the political nature of federally recognized tribes (tribe) having standing to make a claim, but the claims relate to cultural and not political connectivity. This sequence distinguishes the law from the opinion of the court in *Bonnichsen*. In *Bonnichsen*, the court made a judicial determination that the 9,000-year-old remains were not Native American because the "tribe" could not be determined. Therefore in the Ninth Circuit, only tribal members are Native Americans, the indigenous people of the United States. Thus, when tribes were terminated in the 1950s, the people lost their ethnographic identity as well as their political identity. This new definition of indigenous has not been followed outside of the Ninth Circuit, nor has it been regarded with a straight face by many scientists. In 2007, the USDA Forest Service published a newspaper notice, per NAGPRA, that 10,200-year-old remains, located in a burial cave in southeast Alaska, had a cultural relationship to the present day Tlingit. A disposition was made to the Tlingit.

The current technical corrections bill received favorable treatment and was passed out of the Senate Indian Affairs Committee. This is the third effort. In 2004, Senator Ben Nighthorse Campbell introduced S. 2843 to amend NAGPRA to add the words "or was" to the statutory definition of "Native American" in NAGPRA. The bill did not move out of Committee. In March 2005, Senator McCain introduced S. 536, Native American Omnibus Act of 2005, which contained an amendment to NAGPRA similar to that introduced by Senator Campbell. The amendment to NAGPRA would have added the language proposed by this year's legislative effort. When the change to the law was last proposed, Rep. Doc Hastings (R-WA) introduced counterlegislation that could be filed again in an attempt to provide some scientists with possessory rights to remains in federal possession or control.

State Legislation and Repatriation Measures

The Utah State Legislature passed without opposition the Utah Native American Grave Protection and Repatriation Act— S.B.204 to further repatriation efforts.[46] Under the state law, all "Native American" human remains found on state or nonfederal land will be protected and cared for under the state Native American Graves Protection and Repatriation Act.

The bill amends existing state antiquities laws to provide that the state Antiquities Section assume responsibility for the retrieval, excavation, study, and reporting of human remains found on state or private land, when not found in the context of compliance with other laws, without cost to the landowner. Excavation is to take place within five days. This removes financial burdens from private landowners, ensures timely and proper handling of remains, and ensures that "Native American" human remains are treated in a consistent manner, regardless of land ownership. Second, and more importantly, the bill makes the provisions of the state Native American Grave Protection and Repatriation Act apply to all lands in Utah not covered by the Federal NAGPRA, enabling the potential repatriation of "Native American" remains found on private lands, remains that now fall outside of the coverage of the Federal law. Third, the bill creates a Native American Remains Review Committee to determine cultural affiliation for remains removed from private lands, ensuring tribal participation in the process and providing opportunity for the repatriation of the remains or items with the proper tribe. The legislation's definitions essentially track those of the Federal NAGPRA in a likely effort to ensure consistent application across all lands in the state.

One important difference between the Utah NAGPRA and the Federal NAGPRA is the provision for scientific study. The Utah legislation makes clear that "Native American" remains can only be studied with the approval of the owner of the remains based on a cultural affiliation determination. If no owner is identified, study is to be limited to that necessary to identify ownership. In no event will the remains be kept for study for more than 90 days after ownership is determined.[47]

In Colorado, the Southern Ute Tribe, Mountain Ute Tribe, the Colorado Commission of Indian Affairs, and the Colorado Historical Society developed a NAGPRA protocol approved by the Department of Interior that might prove to be a blueprint for similar plans across the country.[48] The group created the protocol to ensure the repatriation of remains and funerary objects discovered on Colorado State lands or private lands that cannot be culturally affiliated with a specific Indian tribe. The protocol works within the boundaries of state and federal cultural resource laws by shortening the time frame for repatriating inadvertently discovered remains and funerary objects on Colorado State lands and private lands, and addressing an ongoing gap in Federal law by making it possible for the repatriation and reburial of culturally unidentifiable Native American human remains and associated funerary objects that come into the State's possession. As of January 2007, thirty-six tribes had agreed to participate in the voluntary process established by the protocol.

In New Mexico, the state legislature enacted House Bill 73, the "Reburial Grounds Act," directing the state Cultural Affairs Department to designate unmarked reburial grounds on state or federal lands for the reburial of human remains and funerary objects that have not been claimed by a descendent group.[49] The law also requires the Department to define rules for the reinterment of ancestral remains. The Reburial Grounds Act adds a third tier to the existing state process for the reburial of unclaimed remains and funerary objects. First, the State will work to keep unclaimed ancestral remains intact and undisturbed if possible. Second, where preservation is not possible, the unclaimed remains are to be excavated and efforts made to find a culturally identifiable group to claim the remains through consultation. Third, if both prior efforts fail, the Act requires that the unclaimed remains or funerary objects be reburied at a secure and unmarked location on state or federal land. The legislation set aside $150,000 to establish reburial grounds in the state.

While many states have enacted or strengthened their state cultural protection statutes in the wake of NAGPRA, states and tribes now seem to be taking the next step by passing laws that are as or more protective than the Federal NAGPRA, and addressing provisions of the Federal law that remain unimplemented. States and tribes are to be applauded for these efforts. These collaborative processes may yield great success, as the Federal NAGPRA applies only to Federal and tribal lands, leaving remains and funerary objects located on lands within the remainder of the country that might be discovered though construction, excavation, or erosion without sufficient protection and the promise of repatriation to lineal descendents or culturally affiliated tribes.[50]

Indian Arts and Crafts

Indian arts and crafts are a culturally and commercially important part of the lives of many tribal people. This section discusses litigation seeking to use the 1990 amendments to the Indian Arts and Crafts Act (IACA) to file civil actions to collect damages for violations of the IACA and legislative efforts to correct perceived weaknesses in the current patchwork of laws designed to protect Indian artisans and their craft.

Litigation: *Native American Arts*

A case brought under the Indian Arts and Crafts Act and the Indian Arts and Crafts Enforcement Act in 2005[51] by Native American Arts, Inc., representing Ho-Chunk tribal members that accused a St. George, Utah, store owner and internet retailer of misrepresenting goods as being made by Indian artists. The case ended in an agreed settlement protecting Indian artisans and consumers.[52]

The IACA prohibits a person from directly offering or displaying for sale, or selling goods in a manner that falsely suggests that the good is Indian produced or is an Indian product. In *Native American Arts*, an Indian-owned arts and crafts organization sued a non-Indian retailer for selling goods purporting to be Indian made, "Native American," or made by a particular Indian tribe, including artworks, jewelry, dolls, and crafts that were in fact not made by tribe members. Native American Arts argued that it suffered direct competitive loss and advertising injuries as a result of the misrepresentation of Indian products and alleged misappropriation of its business model. The original complaint sought an injunction to stop the sales and damages in excess of eight million dollars.

In the settlement reached in August 2007, Milne Jewelry, Inc., agreed to entry of an injunction that blocks the business from operating in a manner that violates the IACA for a period of five years.[53] Milne Jewelry also agreed to prominently display on its website a disclaimer making clear that "The product is not Indian made or an Indian product . . ." and to post a sign in its retail stores that "None of the products displayed in or offered through the business are Indian products," unless bearing a tag identifying the name of the Indian artisan and his or her tribe.[54] The settlement did not award any damages to Native American Arts. Thus, while the settlement successfully stopped operations by the retail store violating the IACA, this litigation indicates that the IACA is primarily a truth-in-advertising statute that makes it unlawful to sell counterfeit Indian artwork. The IACA is not, however, an effective enforcement or deterrent tool that enables injured Indian arts and crafts dealers to recover for their damages.

Congressional Action

On May 1, 2007, Senator John McCain introduced S. 1255, "The Indian Arts and Crafts Amendments of 2007," designed to protect Indian arts and crafts through the improvement of applicable criminal proceedings to provide for the investigation and punishment of individuals misrepresenting Indian produced goods and products.[55]

This bipartisan legislation is substantially identical to legislation introduced by Senator McCain during the last Congress and would amend the IACA to authorize any federal law enforcement officer (not just the Federal Bureau of Investigation as is currently the case), including an officer under the Indian Law Enforcement Reform Act acting in coordination with a federal law enforcement agency on a violation outside Indian Country, to investigate offenses involving the sale of arts and crafts that are misrepresented as Indian products. The bill would also revise the requirements for initiating civil actions for the misrepresentation of Indian produced goods to make it easier for the enforcement of IACA. The bill was referred to the Senate Indian Affairs Committee where it awaits further action. At the date of this writing, there is no companion legislation in the United States House of Representatives.

Tribal Courts and Tribal Codes

A number of tribes have enacted or are considering enacting tribal code provisions addressing cultural properties. Enforcement of such tribal code provisions would most often occur in tribal court. None of the databases available to the editors of the *Yearbook* revealed any cases or codes on point this year. No known new tribal code sections were enacted or tribal enforcement actions brought concerning cultural properties under tribal law during 2007.

Conclusion

The persistent actions of tribes to proactively protect tribal cultural properties continue to raise awareness of the difficulties tribes face when seeking to protect their culture, beliefs, and sacred places. This awareness seems to be producing results on the state level where tribes are working proactively with states to address the protection and return of tribal cultural properties. The sacred site protection victories of the past year may mark a watershed moment in tribal cultural resource and sacred site protection.

Notes

1. U.S. Const. Amdt. 1.
2. 42 U.S.C. §§ 2000bb–2000bb-4.
3. President W.J. Clinton, Religious Freedom Restoration Act Signing Ceremony, Fed. News Service (Nov. 16, 1993).
4. RFRA was originally universal in its scope, applying to states and local governments as well. However, the U.S. Supreme Court declared that Congress lacked authority to expand the Act beyond the Federal government. *City of Boerne v. Flores*, 521 U.S. 507, 515–16 (1997).
5. 42 U.S.C. §§ 2000bb-1(a) and (b).
6. E.g., *Employment Div., Dep't of Human Resources of Oregon v. Smith*, 494 U.S. 872 (1990) (holding that the prohibition of peyote use under state law is constitutional and, therefore, Oregon may deny unemployment compensation to employees dismissed for use of peyote).
7. E.g., *United States v. Thirty-eight Golden Eagles*, 829 F.2d 41 (9th Cir. 1987) (upholding conviction of Indian religious leader because First Amendment freedoms must yield to compelling government interests in protecting bald eagles).
8. See, e.g., *Badoni v. Higginson*, 638 F.2d 172 (10th Cir. 1980) (holding that agency's decision did not violate the Free Exercise Clause because the Navajo still had access to Rainbow Bridge, despite raised water levels); *Sequoyah v. Tennessee Valley Auth.*, 620 F.2d 1159 (6th Cir. 1980) (holding that the flooding of Cherokee sacred sites was not an abridgement of free exercise where tribe failed to offer sufficient evidence of the centrality or indispensability of site to their religious observance); *Thiry v. Carlson*, 78 F.3d 1491, 1493 (10th Cir. 1996) (denying

RFRA claim where parents sought to stop the construction of a road through the gravesite of their infant).

9. *Navajo Nation, et al. v. U.S. Forest Serv.*, 479 F.2d 1024 (9th Cir. 2007). Rehearing has been granted.
10. *Id.* at 1039.
11. The tribal plaintiffs also made environmental protection claims under the National Environmental Policy Act, one of which, concerning the harm caused by human ingestion of the reclaimed wastewater snow, was upheld by the Court. *Id.* at 1051.
12. *Id.* at 1048.
13. *Id.*
14. *Id.* at 1043.
15. *Wilson v. Block,* 708 F.2d 735 (D.C. Cir. 1983), *cert denied* 464 U.S. 956.
16. *Id.* at 1039–43. The Court noted that the record demonstrated that the harm caused would most greatly be felt by the Navajo and Hopi. *Id.* at 1043.
17. *The Access Fund v. USDA*, No. 05-15585 (9th Cir., Aug. 27, 2007).
18. *Id.*, Slip Op. at 10529.
19. *Id.*, Slip Op. at 10530.
20. *Id.*, Slip Op. at 10533.
21. *Id.*, Slip Op. at 10537.
22. *Id.*, Slip Op. at 10538.
23. *Id.*, Slip Op. at 10539.
24. *Id.*, Slip Op. at 10543 (internal citation omitted).
25. *Natural Arch and Bridge Society v. Alston*, 02-4099, 98 Fed. Appx. 711, 2004 U.S. App. LEXIS 5446 (10th Cir. March 23, 2004).
26. *Badoni v. Higginson*, 638 F.2d 172 (10th Cir. 1980).
27. *Quechan Indian Tribe v. United States Dep't of Interior*, No. 07-0677 (D. Ariz., June 29, 2007).
28. *Muckleshoot Indian Tribe v. United States Forest Service, 177 F.3d 800 (9th Cir. 1999).*
29. http://www.maconnews.com/index.php?option=com_content&task=view&id=618&Itemid=34 (last visited Sept. 27, 2007).
30. http://www.indianz.com/News/2007/003299.asp (last visited Sept. 27, 2007).
31. http://www.latimes.com/news/printedition/california/la-me-tribefires2aug02,1,2564373.story?coll=la-headlines-pe-california (last visited Sept. 27, 2007).
32. Native American Graves Protection and Repatriation Act ("NAGPRA"), 25 U.S.C. § 3001 et seq.
33. *Rosales v. United States*, 477 F. Supp.2d 213 (D. D.C. 2007).
34. *Id.* at 214.
35. *Id.* at 215.

36. *Rosales v. United States*, Case no. 07-CV 0624, Doc. No. 19, p. 9 (Nov. 28, 2007).
37. *Id.* at 10.
38. *Hawk v. Danforth*, 06-C-233, 2006 Lexis 58104 (E.D. Wisc., Aug. 17, 2006).
39. *Rosales*, supra n. 38, at 12-13.
40. 72 Fed. Reg. 13,184 (Mar. 21, 2007).
41. *Id.* at 13,185.
42. 72 Fed. Reg. 18,192 (Apr. 11, 2007).
43. *Id.* at 18,193.
44. S. 2087, 110th Cong. (2007).
45. *Bonnichsen v. United States*, 357 F.3d 962 (9th Cir. 2004), as amended, 367 F.3d 864 (9th Cir. 2004).
46. http://le.utah.gov/~2007/bills/sbillint/sb0204.pdf (last visited Oct. 1, 2007).
47. 25 U.S.C. § 3005(b).
48. Indian Affairs, tribes address burials, Cortez Journal (Feb. 3, 2007), available at http://www.cortezjournal.com/asp-bin/article_generation.asp?article_type=news&article_path=/news/07/news070203_2.htm (last visited Oct. 1, 2007).
49. N.M. H.B. 72 (2007), available at http://legis.state.nm.us/Sessions/07%20Regular/final/HB0073.pdf (last visited Oct. 1, 2007).
50. For example, in Hawai'i, at least fifty sets of bones have been unearthed in an urban Honolulu location where a Whole Foods is being built. Associated Press, Hawaii projects run into graves (May 23, 2007). The Whole Foods dispute follows a dispute on a ten-acre Wal-Mart property a half-mile away where 64 sets of remains were discovered and, after three years, have still not been reburied. *Id.* State law requires construction to cease until remains can be removed, reburied, or otherwise dealt with by the State Historic Preservation Division. *Id.*
51. 25 U.S.C. § 305, et. seq., and 25 U.S.C. § 305e.
52. *Native American Arts, Inc. v. Milne Jewelry Co., Inc.*, No. 05-06203 (D. Utah, Aug. 6, 2007).
53. *Id.* (Agreed Order Between Plaintiff Native American Arts, Inc. and Defendants Milne Jewelry Co, Inc. and Irvin W. Milne at 3 (Aug. 6, 2007)).
54. Agreed Order at 3-4.
55. S. 1255, 110th Cong. (2007).

Marine Environment

• • •

Section Editor: Caroline M. Blanco

Introduction

This section addresses updates on cases, statutes, and particular events related to cultural resources in the marine environment. In 2007, there were three highlights of particular note in the area of submerged cultural resources law. These highlights follow, along with a view by the Section Editor on how some issues in this area might be handled in the future.

Proposed Legislation Amending the R.M.S. Titanic Maritime Memorial Act of 1986

As anticipated in the *Yearbook of Cultural Property Law 2007,* the proposed legislation to implement the International Agreement Concerning the Shipwrecked Vessel RMS Titanic was reintroduced in 2007. The proposed legislation, which was first introduced in 2006, was reintroduced in July of 2007 and is now pending before Congress. As described last year, the proposed legislation seeks to amend the RMS Titanic Maritime Memorial Act of 1986, which designated the RMS *Titanic* as an international maritime memorial, and called for the development of guidelines and an international agreement for the research, preservation, and, if appropriate, salvage of RMS *Titanic* in consultation with the United Kingdom, France, Canada, and other interested nations.

The guidelines and international agreement were finalized, and the proposed legislation, if enacted, would cause the international agreement to enter into force. The proposed legislation, as presented to Congress, reflects a consensus position by all interested federal agencies, and, if passed, would be the most comprehensive legislation in existence addressing the protection and regulation of activities directed at cultural resources in the marine environment.

Litigation

R.M.S. Titanic, Inc. v. R.M.S. Titanic

There has also been a significant development in the litigation before the United States District Court for the Eastern District of Virginia regarding R.M.S. Titanic, Inc.'s exclusive salvor-in-possession status. On October 15, 2007, in the matter, *R.M.S. Titanic, Inc. v. R.M.S. Titanic*,[1] the presiding judge, Chief Judge Rebecca Smith, ordered R.M.S. Titanic, Inc. ("RMST") "to file a motion for a salvage award, with supporting documentation. . . ."[2] RMST filed its motion on November 30, 2007, claiming that it should be construed as an interim salvage award related to artifacts recovered from *R.M.S. Titanic* between 1993 and 2006; RMST claimed that, because it remains salvor-in-possession, it reserves the right to file subsequent motions for salvage awards for artifacts recovered in future expeditions.

In its recently filed Motion for a Salvage Award, RMST argues that the fair market value of the artifacts recovered from the wreck thus far from expeditions occurring between 1993 and 2006 is $110,859,200. RMST then argues that there are no museums that would be willing to spend such an amount to obtain the collection and, thus, RMST should be granted an *in specie* salvage award, subject to appropriate, substantive restrictions regarding the disposition of the collection. In other words, RMST argues that the court should award it ownership rights to the collection in lieu of a monetary award, since no willing buyers are available from which a salvage award could be satisfied. Importantly, however, RMST does acknowledge in its filing the importance of keeping the entire collection intact, in perpetuity, and proposes that the *in specie* award carry with it a covenant to accomplish this result. RMST did not, however, specify particular provisions, but did suggest that the court fashion terms and conditions, such as covenants to run with the collection in perpetuity requiring the artifacts to be kept together as an intact collection that is available for public study, research, and exhibition.[3]

On December 18, 2007, the United States filed a motion seeking an extension of time to consider whether it will seek leave to submit its views as an *amicus curiae* regarding RMST's Motion for a Salvage Award. This filing was made in response to the court's request that the United States, through the United States Attorney for the Eastern District of Virginia, provide oversight to help ensure RMST's compliance with the court's rulings, including the preservation and protection of the artifacts. *See* October 15, 2007 Order. That motion is currently pending.

In sum, of particular significance is the alleged value of the salvage award that RMST is seeking and the manner in which RMST suggests that it be granted—an *in specie* award that has a covenant running with the collection. It will be interesting to see how the court resolves RMST's motion and also how the court reacts to RMST's suggestion that a covenant running with the collection in perpetuity be ordered to ensure the protection and preservation of the artifacts for, in part, the benefit of the public.

The "Black Swan" Case

Another case involving an historic shipwreck, with the code name "The Black Swan," has captured international attention. An American salvage company, Odyssey Marine Exploration, Ltd., claims it has found a sunken wreck located off of the coast of Gibraltar, in international waters, that is valued at over $500 million. Odyssey has already brought up colonial-era silver coins and other artifacts allegedly from the wreck and filed an admiralty lawsuit in the United States District Court in Tampa, Florida, to seek exclusive salvage rights to the wreck. Odyssey claims that it must keep the wreck's location secret to protect it from competing salvagers.

The Kingdom of Spain has taken issue with Odyssey, and filed claims to the wreck and/or its artifacts if either belonged to Spain, or if artifacts were removed from Spain's territorial waters. To press its claim, Spain has urged the court to order Odyssey to disclose the exact location and identity of the wreck. To date, no substantive issues have been resolved in this pending matter. However, according to a case management report filed with the court, both parties have stated that they anticipate being ready for a trial some time after October 1, 2008.

The "Black Swan" case is highlighted in this year's update for the interest and action of the Kingdom of Spain in historic shipwreck matters, which was relatively absent prior to the *Sea Hunt* litigation in the late 1990s. It is also mentioned because it highlights a problem of increasing significance in this area of law: When should a salvor be required to identify a shipwreck and/or its artifacts so that any potential owners may file a claim? This "chicken before the egg" type of dilemma is also faced by agencies charged with managing federal marine protected areas. For example, treasure hunters often argue that they should be allowed to perform test excavations to determine the identity of the wreck; however, potential owners, such as sovereign nations, argue that such intrusive work causes irreparable damage. It is this editor's opinion that perhaps one way to resolve this problem is to first require the salvor to conduct nonintrusive research on the wrecksite, including an extensive document search, so that a reasonable hypothesis regarding the identity of the wreck and/or its artifacts can be made without causing any irreparable damage. Then, for example, if that hypothesis suggests that the wreck and/or its artifacts are reasonably likely to be those of a sovereign nation, the sovereign nation should then be contacted to determine whether it wishes to assert any interest in the wreck and/or its artifacts, or whether it has concerns about how salvage activities are carried out. Although this approach is not without its vulnerabilities (e.g., the nonintrusive research could suggest that the wreck is not that of a sovereign nation but then later test excavations could determine that a sovereign nation does indeed have an interest in the wreck), it does offer more protection to the wreck and provides potential claimants an opportunity to weigh in on whether salvage activities are to be conducted and by what methods.

Editor's Proposal for Protecting Submerged Cultural Resources While Offering Eligible Salvors an Incentive

For decades a dispute has existed between the federal agencies charged with protecting submerged cultural resources and salvors seeking to engage in salvage activities involving historic shipwrecks. Salvors argue that their services are needed to bring the story of historic shipwrecks to the public and that these stories could not be told without their efforts. Federal agencies argue that historic shipwrecks should be left *in situ* (i.e., in place) and should not be disturbed unless scientific reasons justify the destruction of the wrecksite and the investment necessary to conserve and curate the artifacts so that they are preserved in perpetuity. Federal agencies also are concerned that, if artifacts are to be raised from the sea, they be kept together in an intact collection to which the public has access for educational purposes and scientific research.

They thus argue that to ensure that these interests are protected, the artifacts should remain in the public domain and not be dispersed through sale or other means.

To attempt to strike a balance between federal interests and those of qualified salvors, the editor offers the following proposal: Consider a federal regulatory regime in which a qualified salvor could be granted an alienable possessory interest in artifacts, provided the artifacts are kept together in an intact collection and remain available to the public and for scientific research. Under this proposal, the federal government would exercise its sovereign prerogative to claim ownership of abandoned historic shipwrecks lying within waters that are located between state waters (those waters identified in the Submerged Lands Act of 1953, which are located out to three nautical miles from the baseline on the coasts and out to nine nautical miles from the baseline in the Gulf of Mexico) and the United States' 200-mile Exclusive Economic Zone. The National Park Service would be granted regulatory authority over those wrecks lying beyond state waters out to the 12-mile Territorial Sea, and the National Oceanic and Atmospheric Administration ("NOAA") would be granted regulatory authority over those wrecks located between 12 and 200 miles offshore.

Qualified salvors (i.e., those who have demonstrated the ability to carry out the proposed activity in accordance with professional scientific standards, including the conservation and curation of all artifacts in compliance with the regulations found at 36 C.F.R. Part 79) could apply for permits to conduct archaeological research and recovery of those previously abandoned shipwrecks now owned by the federal government. These permit applicants would also have to demonstrate the financial ability necessary to care for the artifacts in accordance with professional scientific standards. The issuance of a permit would also require the applicant to post a bond designed to protect the artifacts in the event that the applicant/permittee becomes insolvent.

If the salvor/applicant can meet these strict requirements and can also establish a scientific reason that would justify the recovery of artifacts, the relevant federal agency could issue the permit. Any such permit, however, would also require that the permittee keep the collection intact and allow for public access for research, education, and/or other public purposes. Under this scenario, the United States retains fee simple ownership of the artifacts but the permittee is granted an alienable possessory interest.

Once a salvor is issued a permit and all artifacts under the permit are recovered, the salvor obtains an alienable possessory interest in the collection, and may sell the artifacts as an intact collection to an eligible buyer, provided that the relevant federal regulatory agency approves the sale and, in particular, agrees that the buyer meets the same eligibility requirements. If the federal regulatory agency approves the sale and finds the buyer to be eligible, the permit granting the alienable possessory interest is then transferred to the buyer. The buyer is then lawfully able to sell the intact collection in the future to another eligible buyer who is willing and able to abide by the permit provisions, and who obtains the approval from the federal government. If at any time the permit is violated, possession of the artifacts would revert to the United States and enforcement action against the permittee could be taken.

This proposed regulatory regime would, of course, require new legislation. While novel and, perhaps, of concern to those who believe that artifacts should not be sold under any circumstances, this approach may be a way to forge public and private partnerships to promote the educational benefits of historic shipwrecks while ensuring their protection and preservation. At all times, the federal government would be in a position to provide the oversight necessary to secure strict adherence to all permit provisions; protection of the artifacts for the public benefit would be the cornerstone of such a regime. With the limited availability of federal funds and the developments in technology allowing for the increased ability to learn more about historic shipwrecks, such a regulatory regime could offer incentives to the private sector while still protecting the nation's underwater cultural heritage.

Notes

1. Civil Action No. 2:93cv902 (E.D. Va.).
2. *R.M.S. Titanic, Inc.*, 2007 WL 3036846 at *2.
3. *See* Memorandum of Law in Support of RMST's Motion for a Salvage Award, at p. 58.

Museum

• • •

Section Editor: Lucille A. Roussin

Introduction

During the year 2007 many of the legal issues in museum acquisitions of stolen antiquities and art looted during World War II continued to be in the forefront of international news. In several momentous settlements, the J. Paul Getty Museum, the Metropolitan Museum of Art, The Boston Museum of Fine Arts, and the Princeton Museum agreed to restitute antiquities to Italy and Greece. As a result of these settlements, charges in courts in Athens and Rome against former Getty Museum curator Marion True have been dropped. It has again been an especially active year for cases and controversies involving the restitution of art looted from Jewish families during the Holocaust.

International

Claims of Italy and Greece to Antiquities in U.S. Institutions

The efforts of Italy and Greece during 2006 to obtain restitution of archaeological artifacts that were stolen over a long period of time have resulted in major settlements. The discovery of a large trove of documentary evidence along with stolen artifacts in warehouses in Geneva and elsewhere more than ten years ago has been the defining element in all the settlements.[1] These restitutions have resulted in a much more amicable and cooperative attitude between the museums and Italy and Greece. An international conference at the University of Milan organized by the committee on cultural heritage law of the International Law Association brought together representatives of the museum community, government and law enforcement officials, and representatives of art dealers.[2]

At another meeting between several American museum directors, current and former members of the Association of Art Museum Directors in North America, and Italian cultural officials, Italian Culture Minister Franco Rutelli stated, "We are ushering in a new era. . . . The phase that was tied to illegal activity through unacceptable channels is closed, and we have arrived at a turning point where we have become partners against illegal traffic."[3] As a result of the cooperation of American museums, Italy has extended loan periods from six months to four years and has offered to widen collaboration on archaeological excavations and other research.[4]

The restitution of significant numbers of classical antiquities to Italy continued in 2007. In 2006, the Metropolitan Museum of Art in New York and the Boston Museum of Fine Arts agreed to return to Italy antiquities that had been illegally removed from Italy over the past three decades. The trend continued this year with the announcement that the Getty and the Princeton University Art Museum will be returning additional ancient art works.

The Getty will return to Italy 40 objects, the largest number of ancient works to be returned at one time.[5] There were negotiations between the Getty and Italian representatives last year during which the Getty agreed to return 26 objects, but the talks broke down over a disagreement about some of the other artifacts claimed by Italy.[6] The 14 objects that were at issue in 2006, all from the controversial Barbara and Lawrence Fleischman Collection, will now be returned.[7] Probably the most prominent of the objects to be returned is the over-life-size statue of a cult goddess, sometimes identified as Aphrodite, and likely to have originated in Sicily. The statue will remain at the Getty Villa on loan until 2010. The Getty and Italy will continue discussions as to the fate of a bronze sculpture, *A Victorious Youth*. As a result of the Getty restitutions, Italy has dropped its civil claim for recovery of the value of these artifacts against former Getty curator Marion True.[8] However, her criminal trial, along with that of dealer Robert Hecht, continues, although the court held sessions only sporadically this year.

The Getty also returned a golden Macedonian funeral wreath and a Kore, or statue of a young woman, both dated to the fourth century B.C., to Greece. Two other antiquities will also be returned to Greece, a grave stele and a small marble relief purchased by J. Paul Getty in 1955. The criminal charges against Ms. True were dropped after her attorney argued that under Greek law the statute of limitations of the jurisdiction where the acquisition took place governed and the three member appeals court dismissed the case.[9]

The Princeton Museum of Art announced that it will return eight artifacts to Italy. According to an agreement concluded on October 30, 2007, Princeton will return four of the objects immediately and will retain four objects on loan for four years, including three ancient vases and an Etruscan head of a winged lion. Princeton's title to seven other objects was recognized. According to the agreement, Princeton students will be given unique research opportunities at Italian excavations and Italy will loan other objects of equal cultural significance.[10]

Two 6th century B.C. marble sculptures have been returned to the Aidone Museum in Aidone, Sicily. The sculptures are acroliths—statues with stone heads and extremities and wooden trunks—and are said to have been looted by tomb robbers from Morgantina, Sicily, in the 1970s. The objects were in the collection of New York businessman Maurice Tempelsman and were on exhibit at the University of Virgina Museums in Charlottesville for the last five years.[11]

For the first time, a private dealer, Jerome Eisenberg of Royal Athena Galleries in New York, has agreed to return artifacts to Italy.[12] The eight Roman and Etruscan artifacts to be returned include a Roman statue, bronze figurines, and several ancient ceramic vases and are worth approximately $500,000. While the statue was probably stolen from a Roman villa, the vases were probably looted from archaeological tomb sites, and one statuette was stolen during an armed robbery in 1975 from a state archaeological office in Ercolano near Pompeii.

Italy has also asked Japan to return antiquities allegedly looted. The Italian government plans to put together a catalogue of some 100 antiquities and will ask the Japanese Cultural Affairs Agency to cooperate in their restitution. About 50 of the objects are in the Miho Museum, a private museum in Shiga, western Japan.[13]

The Italian government has followed up on its request to the Cleveland Museum of Art for information on the acquisition of three South Italian vases by issuing a formal invitation to officials from the museum for discussions in Rome. Timothy Rub, director of the museum, has agreed to the meeting.[14]

Antiquities News

Peru and Yale University have reached an agreement on restitution of the artifacts from Machu Picchu. Hiram Bingham "rediscovered" the Inca site of Machu Picchu in Peru in 1911 and conducted excavations there in 1912 and 1915 with the support of Yale University and the National Geographic Society. Bingham took back to Yale more than 4,000 objects, including human remains, ceramics, and animal bones. In 2001 Alejandro Toledo, Peru's first president of Andean descent, presented a claim for return of the remaining artifacts. Yale claimed that Peru had given the artifacts, whereas Peru claimed that they were on loan. On September 14, 2007, Peru and Yale announced an agreement by which Yale recognized Peru's title to the collection.[15] Yale and Peru's National Institute of Culture will collaborate on an international traveling exhibition. The museum-quality objects, approximately four hundred in number, will be returned to Peru, and a new museum will be built in Cuzco with Yale acting as an advisor. Peru and Yale will share the research rights in the collection. Although the agreement was at first hailed as another creative and collaborative solution to a cultural property solution, the agreement was later criticized because of the small number of objects to be returned to Peru in the next few years and the extended period of time, reportedly another 99 years, in which Yale would retain the remainder of the collection for continued research.[16]

Thirty-eight ancient sculptures, which had been seized by U.S. Immigration and Customs Enforcement and U.S. Customs and Border Protection in September 2005 at the Newark Port of Entry, were returned to Pakistan on January 23, 2007.[17] The artifacts included several Gandharan-type sculptures of the third and fourth centuries A.D., some of the "starving Buddha" type, a relief panel depicting a dance seize, a frieze showing monks meditating, and at least one object dating from the second century B.C. Evidence indicated that they had been looted from archaeological sites in northern Pakistan. The artifacts were contained in two shipments for which the shipper had made a false declaration as to country of origin.

In March a collection of 1,300 artifacts from Afghanistan that were kept in Switzerland for safekeeping since 1999 were handed over to the National Museum in Kabul. The objects were housed in the Afghanistan Museum-in-Exile in Bubendorf, Switzerland, which was set up by a private foundation and is now closed. The return of the works, received from private donors, was financed by Switzerland's National Commission to UNESCO, the Swiss foreign affairs department, and the German defense ministry, which provided the transport.[18]

The Kufa Museum, near the southern religious city of Karbala, Iraq, is seeking restitution of numerous antiquities plundered after the 2003 U.S. invasion. The Kufa Museum held the largest collection of artifacts after the Baghdad Museum. The missing artifacts include engraved bowls with Aramaic transcriptions, pottery, and coins. Officials at the museum believe many of the stolen artifacts have made their way into private collections and auction houses.[19]

Britain's Natural History Museum returned the remains of seventeen Tasmanian aborigines.[20] Australia's Tasmanian community had been fighting for about twenty years to recover the remains, which were taken in the 19th century. While the museum had agreed to the restitution in November 2006 upon recommendation of its Human Remains Advisory Panel, the museum also decided to conduct additional scientific tests before the restitution. The Tasmanian Aboriginal Centre decided to sue to prevent such testing, but a settlement was mediated by which the museum could conduct additional but noninvasive scientific tests, such as measurements, scans, and the making of casts, but DNA and other invasive analyses were not allowed. This and anticipated claims for return of human remains held at Cambridge University, Oxford University, and the National Museums of Scotland are expected to follow the Department of Culture, Media and Sports' Guidance for the Care of Human Remains in Museums,[21] which calls for a balancing of scientific interests against the interests of descendant communities.

Kenya is demanding that the Field Museum in Chicago return the remains of two lions that killed at least 140 Indian workers in the 1890s before being killed by railway engineer Lieutenant-Colonel John Henry Patterson. The lions were the infamous "Maneaters of Tsavo." Patterson sold the remains—the lions' skulls and hides—to the Field Museum in ca. 1916 for $5,000.00. Although Kenya wants them back, Kenyan officials have agreed that they should first be part of an upcoming exhibition on Kenyan history in the United States.[22]

The United Kingdom enacted legislation to provide immunity from seizure for objects that are on temporary loan for exhibition from collections in foreign nations, thus clearing the way for a loan exhibition from Russia's major museums of some 120 French and Russian paintings by artists such as Cezanne, Gaugin, Matisse, Kandinsky, and Malevich.[23] The act provides immunity from seizure in any civil or criminal proceeding and by any law enforcement authorities. A museum that wishes to apply for immunity for objects on loan must first be approved by the Secretary of State; as part of the approval process, the museum must satisfy the Secretary that its due diligence procedures are satisfactory.[24]

Museums must then publish information about each object for which protection is sought before the start of the exhibition and to provide additional information upon request in certain circumstances. Regulations to be issued will specify the information that a museum must provide concerning the objects for which immunity is sought and how far in advance of the loan the information must be provided. These regulations have not yet been promulgated, but draft regulations are available, and public comment was sought by the Department of Culture, Media and Sport before finalizing the regulations.

Two museums have announced new collections of antiquities. The Nasher Museum of Art at Duke University has received a gift of ancient Mediterranean antiquities from an anonymous donor. Kimerly Rorschach, the Nasher's director, says that the museum was provided with documentation that the objects were acquired before 1970. The collection includes about 220 pieces in gold, terra cotta, bronze, ceramic, marble, and amber. Some 45 objects from the gift will be on display in a new exhibit titled "The Past is Present," opening at the Nasher on February 15, 2008.[25]

Fordham University in the Bronx, New York, has established the Fordham Museum of Greek, Etruscan and Roman Art to house a collection given to them by financier and philanthropist William D. Walsh.[26] The collection has some 200 objects, ranging from Mycenaean objects to Roman statues and a child's sarcophagus. It is valued at $5 to $6 million. The acquisition of the collection has been criticized as problematic, since few of the objects have clear provenances.[27]

Litigation Concerning Iranian Antiquities in U.S. Collections

The victims of a bombing carried out by the Palestinian terrorist organization Hamas in Jerusalem in 1997 were awarded damages against Iran as a state sponsor of Hamas. The plaintiffs then sought to attach antiquities that allegedly belong to Iran and are currently in the possession of several U.S. institutions, including the Oriental Institute of the University of Chicago, the Field Museum of Natural History, the Boston Museum of Fine Arts, and Harvard University. Relatively little progress was reported in these suits in 2007.[28]

In the suit against the Oriental Institute, approximately 30,000 ancient cuneiform texts on loan, comprising primarily two collections, the Persepolis Fortification texts and texts from the site of Chogha Mish, are at issue.[29]

The Oriental Institute concedes that these are on loan from Iran and therefore are the property of Iran.[30] It relies on the Foreign Sovereign Immunity Act ("FSIA") as the basis for its defense against attachment of the artifacts. On the other hand, the plaintiffs claim that the artifacts are subject to attachment under the FSIA's exception for "property . . . used for a commercial activity." At the initiation of the attachment proceeding, the magistrate judge held that commercial use is determined by the activities of the foreign sovereign (Iran) and not by the U.S. possessor of the assets at issue.

In the most recent developments in the Chicago case, Iran filed a motion for partial summary judgment and, in response, the plaintiffs filed a motion for additional discovery. The court granted the plaintiffs' request for additional discovery. The plaintiffs argued that they need additional discovery to determine whether the Oriental Institute was acting as Iran's agent so that any commercial activity conducted by the Oriental Institute could be attributed to Iran. In addition, the plaintiffs claimed that the antiquities are "blocked" assets of Iran and can therefore be attached under the Terrorist Risk Insurance Act.[31] In support of that argument, the plaintiffs are seeking to determine whether the Oriental Institute received an attorney opinion concerning the ownership of the artifacts. The plaintiffs are also seeking pleadings from two other cases involving Iranian artifacts. One of these cases is the proceeding before the Iran-United States Claims Tribunal in which the United States may have contested Iran's ownership of the Chogha Mish collection.

Holocaust-Era Looted Art

In *Malewicz, et al. v. City of Amsterdam*, plaintiffs are the surviving heirs of Russian artist Kazimir Malevich, who was recalled to the Soviet Union from Germany in 1928 and left a number of his paintings in Germany with his friend Hugo Haring, who gave them to the Stedelijk (City) Museum of Amsterdam (the Museum) in 1956. In 2005 the heirs brought suit against the Museum for restitution of the paintings in the District of Columbia District Court. The court reserved its ruling because there was insufficient evidence that the expropriation exception of the Foreign Sovereign Immunities Act (28 U.S.C. § 1602, *et. seq.* applied ("FSIA").

In 2007, the City renewed its motion to dismiss on several grounds, including the Act of State doctrine, failure to state a claim under the Federal Rules of Civil Procedure 12(b)(6), the statute of limitations, and lack of jurisdiction under the FSIA. The court rejected the Act of State doctrine, finding that the City's attempt to characterize the acquisition of the Malevich works as an "act of state" stretched the meaning of "official act" too far. Most significantly, the court rejected the City's motion to dismiss under the purview of the FSIA, stating: "the record contains sufficient contacts to establish jurisdiction under the FSIA's expropriation exception."[32]

The vast art collection of Baron Ferenc Hatvany was placed in a private bank vault in Budapest when the pro-Nazi Hungarian government moved to expropriate all Hungarian Jewish property. The family fled the country just before the Nazi takeover of Hungary in March 1944. Among the losses were Courbet's erotic paintings, *L'Origine du Monde* and *Femme Nue Couchée*. The details of the recovery are still unclear, but apparently Hatvany managed to buy back *L'Origine du Monde* in 1946 and then sold it to French philosopher Jacques Lacan; it passed to the French government at his death. The whereabouts of *Femme Nue Couchée* was unknown until 2000, when a Slovakian art and antiques dealer contacted Christie's. The painting was apparently given to a doctor in Bratislava by Russian soldiers in 1945 in gratitude for helping a wounded comrade. The heirs of the doctor have submitted affidavits swearing that this is the true history. Christie's contacted the Commission for Art Recovery, and through attorney Charles Goldstein negotiated for five years, culminating in the restitution of the painting to the Hatvany heirs. The painting was among the works by Courbet on view at the Grand Palais in Paris from October 13, 2007 to January 28, 2008.[33]

Two paintings by the Meister der Heiligen Sippe restituted to Robert and Virginia Stern in 2003 have been donated by them to the Yale Art Gallery. Nothing has been published about the restitution except the donation. The paintings were apparently acquired by the Nazis under duress in 1936. The paintings are now on display as part of "Art for Yale: Collecting for a New Century."[34]

The Israel Museum has put online a catalogue of paintings and objects of Judaica acquired after WWII by the Jewish Restitution Successor Organization. The website, accessible at www.imj.org.il under "World War II Provenance Research On-line," lists over 1,000 objects looted by the Nazis. Most of the works were restituted to the Bezalel National Museum, the predecessor of the Israel Museum, in the early 1950s. Among the most valuable of the 100 or so paintings is Egon Schiele's *The Small City – V* and *Chagall's Praying Jew.*[35]

In March 2007 the four heirs of art dealer Nathan Katz filed a claim with the Dutch government for restitution of 225 paintings and two tapestries held in Dutch museums. The claim became public only in September when the museum directors were informed of the claim by the Dutch Ministry of Culture. The claim includes prized paintings by 17th Century artists Jan Steen, Jacob van Ruisdael, and Gerard Dou. The claim is quite controversial; according to Dutch looted art expert Rudi Ekkart, some of the paintings were sold even before WWII. At least one source has claimed that the paintings were sold voluntarily and at fair market value to Alois Miedl, the dealer for Nazi leader Hermann Goering.[36]

A report released by the Hunt Museum in Limerick, Ireland, has cleared the museum of holding works of art stolen from Jews in Germany during the Holocaust. After such charges were made by the Simon Wiesenthal Center in Paris, the museum started a thorough investigation of its holdings. The report, written by Lynn Nicholas, author of *The Rape of Europa*, concluded that there was no evidence that the Hunts purchased any art from anyone with links to the Holocaust.[37]

A federal judge in California has dismissed a lawsuit against the Norton Simon Museum in Pasadena demanding the return of two paintings by Lucas Cranach the Elder. The suit was brought by Marei von Saher, the heir to art dealer Jacques Goudstikker. In his decision the judge ruled that California's statute of limitations for Holocaust era claims to 2010 is unconstitutional and dismissed the suit based on the state's three year statute of limitations for restitution of personal property. Lawrence M. Kaye of Herrick, Feinstein, the lawyer for Mrs. von Saher, confirmed that she will appeal the decision.[38]

In a legal strategy that is spreading in cases of Holocaust-era art claims, the Museum of Modern Art and the Guggenheim Museum have jointly filed a suit to quiet title to two Picasso paintings in their collections. In March lawyers for Julius H. Schoeps, the grand nephew of German Jewish banker Paul von Mendelssohn-Bartholdy, requested access to the museums' records. Mr. Schoeps claims that the paintings were sold to art dealer Justin K. Thannhauser under duress. The paintings at issue are Picasso's *Boy Leading a Horse* in the Museum of Modern Art and *Le Moulin de la Galette* in the Guggenheim. *Boy Leading a Horse* was donated to the Museum of Modern Art by William S. Paley in 1964 and *Le Moulin de la Galette* to the Guggenheim in 1963 by Thannhauser. Mr. Mendelssohn-Bartholdy sent both paintings to Switzerland in 1933 and thereafter instructed his Paris dealer, Paul Rosenberg, to sell them. They went to Mr. Thannhauser, a well-known Jewish art dealer.[39]

United States

Two cases involving deaccessioning were at the forefront of domestic art issues this year. The Albright Knox Art Gallery sold 20 important Chinese and Indian antiquities on March 15, 2007 at Sotheby's, earning over $18 million. African, Oceanic, pre-Columbian, and American Indian art will be auctioned in May 2008, along with some pre-nineteenth century European art. The rest of the objects to be deaccessioned consist of Chinese export porcelain, mostly plates, tureens, and teacups. The controversy centers on whether it is ethical for the museum to sell these objects in order to boost the museum's endowment. The museum held a meeting forced by the opponents of the measure, but it was approved by a majority of the museum's members. The Albright Knox Gallery is dedicated to modern and contemporary art and the proceeds of the sales will be used for new acquisitions.[40]

The attempt to deaccession four paintings by the Maier Museum of Art at Randolph College (formerly Randolph Macon Women's College) has been stopped by an order of the Virginia Circuit Court of the City of Lynchburg. The paintings at issue are *Men of the Docks*, by George Bellows, *A Peaceable Kingdom*, by Edward Hicks, *Through the Arroyo*, by Ernest Martin Hennings, and *Troubador*, by Rufino Tamayo. The opponents of the sale of the four paintings were granted an extension of six months to raise the $1 million necessary to secure the temporary injunction against the sale of the paintings. They have already raised $500,000, which was delivered to the court on December 3, 2007, and they have until February 15, 2008 to raise the balance, thereby securing the injunction until May 10, 2008. The college wants to deaccession these works to add to its endowment.[41]

In a case between two transportation museums, one in New Jersey and the other in Missouri, each claiming ownership of a historic locomotive that the court called "not a simple souvenir," the matter was resolved, for the time being, by applying the time-honored museum-law concept of loan by default when there is no evidence of express transfer of ownership.[42] A long-term or "permanent" loan was alleged to have been executed in 1953, and the possessor museum argued a "presumption of ownership," due to its long-term "possession and control." The Eighth Circuit remanded the case for final determination with the holding that "When the period of display is indefinite, as it appears to be in the case, we cannot say that, without more, possession and control entitle the museum to a presumption of ownership or continued possession that overcomes a lender's good title."

General Observations for the Year

The strong-arm tactics of the Italians, followed closely by the Greeks, have brought considerable progress in the restitution of stolen antiquities. At the same time, the United States museums involved will benefit by agreements that include long-term loans from Italy and Greece and cooperative agreements for future excavation opportunities.[43] The policy of long-term loans and cooperative excavations has long been advocated by those involved in the issues of cultural heritage preservation and is a welcome change. It should serve as a model for other nations that seek assistance with the preservation of their cultural sites and objects.

The issue of deaccession has become a major issue both in the United States and abroad. The New York State Legislature recently rejected a proposed addition to the New York Cultural Affairs Law that would have broadened a museum's ability to deaccession works that have been in the collection for many years and for which there is no longer a contact. The law would have required extensive public notice. The legislature did not think the proposed amendment provided enough protection to victims of Holocaust-era looting.

In cases of Holocaust-era looted art, there seems to be a reaction on the part of the courts against a liberal interpretation of statutes of limitations and jurisdictional issues. This is in conflict with the Washington Principles enunciated at the 1998 Washington Conference on Holocaust Assets, which called for a more relaxed standard.[44]

Notes

1. The Italian investigations and evidence are discussed in greater detail by Peter Watson & Cecilia Todeschini, THE MEDICI CONSPIRACY: THE ILLICIT JOURNEY OF LOOTED ANTIQUITIES (2006).
2. Elisabetta Povoledo, *Returning Stolen Art: No Easy Answers,* N.Y. TIMES, October 27, 2007 at B13.
3. Elisabetta Povoledo, *Progress Seen in Talks on Antiquities,* N.Y. TIMES, December 1, 2007 at B16.
4. *Id.*
5. Press Release, "Italian Ministry of Culture and J. Paul Getty Trust Reach Agreement," Aug. 1, 2007, available at http://www.getty.edu/news/press/center/italy_getty_joint_statement_080107.html; Elisabetta Povoledo, *Getty Agrees to return 40 antiquities to Italy,* INTERNATIONAL HERALD TRIBUNE, October 1, 2007.
6. Ralph Frammolino and Jason Felch, *Getty Makes New Offer to Italy*, LOS ANGELES TIMES, November 22, 2006, at A1; Peter Popham, *Getty Museum walks out of talks over looted antiquities*, THE INDEPENDENT Nov. 23, 2006, available at http://news.independent.co.uk/world/americas/article2007486ece.
7. David Gill, Looting Matters, http://lootingmatters.blogspot.com/2007/08/getty-will-be-returning.html.
8. Jason Felch and Livia Borghese, *The museum's pledge to return 40 objects is confirmed as civil charges are dropped against former curator,* LOS ANGELES TIMES, September 25, 2007, available at http://msn-list.verweg.com/2007-September/008178.html.

9. Anthee Carassava, *Court Dismisses Case against Ex-Curator,* N.Y. TIMES, November 28, 2007, available at http://topics.nytimes.com/top/reference/timestopics/organizations/g/getty _j _paul _museum/index.html.
10. Elisabetta Povoledo, *Princeton to Return Disputed Art to Italy,* N.Y. TIMES, October 26, 2007 at D1.
11. Elisabetta Povoledo, *Two Marble Sculptures Return to Italy,* N.Y. TIMES, September 1, 2007 available at http://www.nytimes.com/2007/09/01/arts/design/01rest.html?.
12. *Looted Art Returns to Italy from NY*, AP, Nov. 6, 2007; Alessandra Migliaccio and Andrew Davis, *U.S. Art Dealer Eisenberg Returns Eight Antiquities to Italy*, http://www.bloomberg.com/apps/news.
13. *Italy to ask Japan to return antiquities allegedly looted,* INTERNATIONAL HERALD TRIBUNE, January 10, 2007, available at http://msn-list.te.verweg.com/2007-January/006685.html. See also Roussin, Museum, YEARBOOK OF CULTURAL PROPERTY LAW 2007, at 89.
14. Steven Litt, *Italy asks Cleveland museum officials to go to Rome to talk antiquities*, THE PLAIN DEALER, January 30, 2007, available at http://www.cleveland.com/weblogs/print.ssf?/mtlogs/cleve_reviews/archives/print231416.
15. Joint Statement by the Government of Peru and Yale University, Sept. 14, 2007, available at http://www.yale.edu/opa/newsr/07-09-14-01.all.html.
16. Christopher Heaney, *Stealing from the Incas,* Op-Ed, N.Y. TIMES, Oct. 7, 2007.
17. Press Release, Department of Homeland Security returns rare artifacts to the Pakistani government: Stolen statues are from the third and fourth century A.D., available at http://www.ice.gov/pi/news/newsreleases/articles/070123newark.htm; Robert Birsel, *Looted Pakistani artifacts seized in U.S. returned*, REUTERS, March 8, 2007, available at http://in.news.yahoo.com/070308/137/6d13f.html.
18. Afghan artifacts to return home, March 13, 2007, available at http://msn-list.te.verweg.com/2007-March/0070048.html.
19. Iraq. Ransacked provincial museum seeks lost treasures, February 25, 2007, http://www.azzaman.com.
20. Julia Hinde, *Invaluable resource or stolen property?* 1812 TIMES HIGHER ED. SUPP., Sept. 21, 207, at 18.
21. Available at http://www.culture.gov.uk/Reference_library/Publications/archive_2005/guidance_chr.htm; http://www.culture.gov.uk/NR/rdonlyres/0017476B-3B86-46F3-BAB3-11E5A5F7F0A1/0/GuidanceHumanRemains11Oct.pdf.
22. Kenya wants US museum to return maneating lions, Sept. 10, 2007, available at http://msn-list.te.verweg.com/2007-September/008076.html.
23. Tribunals, Courts and Enforcement Act 2007, ch. 15, Part 6, Protection of Cultural Objects on Loan, ss. 134–38. *See also* Department of Culture, Media and Sport Consultation Paper on draft regulations for the publication by museums and galleries of information for the purposes of immunity from seizure, available at http://www.culture.gov.uk/Reference_library/Consultations/2007_current_

consultations/draftregs_immunityfromseizure.htm; John Varoli and Farah Nayeri, Hermitage Won't Send Art to London Without Guarantee from U.K., Oct. 24, 2007, available at http://msn-list.te.verweg.com/2007-October/008417.html.

24. Museums are expected to comply with the due diligence requirements spelled out in the DCMS Guidance, "Combating Illicit Trade: Due diligence guidelines for museums, libraries and archives on collecting and borrowing cultural materials," available at http://www.culture.gov.uk/Reference_library/Publications/archive_2005/illicit_trade.htm. According to this Guidance, museums should borrow items only if they are legally and ethically sound and should be particularly concerned about objects that are not documented before 1970 or that have a provenance gap between 1933 and 1945.
25. Ellen Sung, Nasher Museum acquires ancient treasures, available at http://msn-list.te.verweg.com/2007-February/006845..html.
26. Robin Pogrebin, Fordham Opens Its Gift: An Antiquities Museum, NY Times, December 6, 2007 at E1.
27. *Campuzano et al. v. The Islamic Republic of Iran*, et al., 281 F. Supp. 2d 258 (D.D.C. 2003).
28. For a description of earlier developments, see Patty Gerstenblith and Lucille Roussin, *International Cultural Property,* 41 INT'L LAW. 613 (2007). For a more detailed discussion of this litigation and the impact on cultural objects, *see* Travis Sills, *Judicial Conversion of Culture: Attaching Embodiments of Ancient Culture to Judgments in Civil Proceedings*, in 2007 YEARBOOK OF CULTURAL PROPERTY LAW 237–56 (Sherry Hutt ed. 2007); James A. Wawrzyniak, Rubin v. The Islamic Republic of Iran: *A Struggle for Control of Persian Antiquities in America,* in this issue of the YEARBOOK, pages 223-272.
29. *Rubin v. Islamic Republic of Iran*, 349 F. Supp. 2d 1108, 1110 (N.D. Ill. 2004); 408 F.Supp. 2d (N.D. Ill., 2005); 2007 U.S. Dist. LEXIS 24376 (N.D. Ill, March 19, 2007).
30. Under the Immunity from Seizure Act of 1966, 22 U.S.C. § 2459, art works and cultural objects on temporary loan to U.S. institutions for the purpose of display and exhibition can receive immunity from seizure, attachment or any other legal process. However, such immunity must be conferred before the object enters the U.S. Therefore those artifacts loaned before 1966 were not eligible to receive immunity. Other than the texts at the Oriental Institute, which does not claim ownership, the ownership or loan status of the artifacts at the other U.S. institutions is not clear and may be a significant point of future litigation proceedings.
31. Under the Terrorism Risk Insurance Act ("TRIA"), Pub. L. No. 107-297, 116 Stat. 2322 (Nov. 26, 2002), an amendment to the FSIA enacted in 2002, the artifacts could be attached if they are classified as "blocked" assets. Section 202 of the TRIA is relevant to the case because Iran is not immune under 28 U.S.C. § 1605(a)(7) and because Iran has been designated as a state sponsor of terrorism.

If the assets are "contested," then they are considered to be "blocked." For more discussion of the TRIA aspects, see Gerstenblith & Roussin, *supra* note.

32. *Malewicz v. City of Amsterdam*, 362 F.Supp.2d 298 (D.D.C. 2005); *Malewicz v. City of Amsterdam*, 2007 U.S. Dist. LEXIS 46312 (June 27, 2007).
33. *Adventures of a Masterpiece: a remarkable episode in art history,* THE INDEPENDENT, Sept. 30, 2007, available at http://news.independent.co.uk/europe/article3007147.ece.
34. Evangelia Podaras, *Yale Art Gallery Acquires recovered German Works,* YALE DAILY NEWS, Nov. 28, 2007, available at http://yaledailynews.com/articles/printarticle/22563 .
35. Joseph R. Hoffman, *A Thousand Orphans,* THE JERUSALEM REPORT, Oct. 1, 2007 at 34; Ha'aretz, *Israel Museum launches online catalog of art looted by Nazis,* AP, available at http://ww.haaretz.com/hasen/spages/898354.html.
36. Charmaine Picard, *Dutch museums face largest ever restitution claim*, THE ARTNEWSPAPER, Nov. 22, 2007 at 1; Dinah Spritzer, *Doing 'business' with the Nazis*, THE JERUSALEM POST, Online Edition, http://ww.jpost.com/servlet/Satellite.
37. Shannon Pogatchnik, *Irish Museum Cleared of Nazi Loot Claim*, ASSOCIATED PRESS, September 28, 2007. The full report can be seen at http://www.ria.ie/pdfs/huntreport.pdf.
38. Charmaine Picard, *Norton Simon Museum keeps Cranachs for now*, THE ART NEWSPAPER, October 25, 2007 at 1.
39. Carol Vogel, *Two Museums Go to Court Over the Right to Picassos,* N.Y. TIMES, December 8, 2007 at B7.
40. Bruce Jackson, *The War Against Albright Knox*, N.Y. TIMES, March 21, 2007 at D1. http://artvoice.com/issues/v6n8/war_against_the-_albright_knox; Randy Kennedy, Despite Foes, Buffalo Museum Makes $18 Million in Auction. NY TIMES, March 21, 2007.
41. News Flash: Maier Art Sale Opponents Win Another Court Victory, http://www.artsjournal.com/culturegrrl/2007/12/maier_art_sale_opponents.html; *Jenna Dodge et al., v. Randolph College, f/k/a/The Trustees of Randolph-Macon Woman's College, Inc.* Case no. CL07001917-00, Circuit Court of the City of Lynchburg, Nov. 12, 2007.
42. *Lackawanna Chapter of the Railway & Locomotive Historical Society, Inc. v. St. Louis County, dba. Museum of Transportation,* 2007 U.S. App. LEXIS 19284 (Aug. 14, 2007).
43. This is in accordance with the original Memorandum of Understanding between Italy and the U.S., which was signed in January 2001and renewed in 2005. Federal Register: January 19, 2006 (Volume 71, Number 12).
44. Washington Conference on Holocaust-Era Looted Assets, available at http://www.state.gov/regions/eur/wash_conf_material.html.

PRACTICE AREA 6

Art Market

• • •

Section Editor: Thomas R. Kline[1]

Accelerating the trend seen in 2006, this past year saw art market participants suffering the consequences of past inattention to reasonable due diligence standards in connection with art market purchase and sale transactions and regretfully adjusting their behavior to prevent a repetition of the cycle of careless acquisition and return. During past decades, stolen antiquities and artworks looted from victims of the Nazis circulated freely in the art market, finding their way into prestigious collections, often moving sequentially from collector to collector and ultimately to a museum via donation or purchase. The consequences can be seen in the art market-related developments of the past year, as can the efforts to break the pattern. 2007 also saw more art theft victims, as plaintiffs, faulted and, in several cases, penalized for their past inattention to diligence in pursuing their losses, particularly when lost objects had been exhibited or had traded openly on the art market.

Introduction: 2007 Cautionary Tales

Well-publicized criminal proceedings in Italy and Greece against Dr. Marion True, former curator of the J. Paul Getty Museum in Malibu, who had been actively purchasing antiquities in the market since roughly 1982 when she joined the Getty as a curatorial assistant,[2] have undoubtedly spread fear, if not also loathing, throughout the antiquities-buying community. Dr. True's fortunes have improved somewhat in 2007, although they could hardly have sunk much lower. Basing its decision on the expiration of the California statute of limitations, in late November 2007, a Greek appeals court dismissed criminal charges against Dr. True in connection with the Getty's 1993 purchase of a gold wreath.[3] (Also in 2007, the Getty returned the wreath and three other works to Greece.[4]) Italy dropped its civil case against Dr. True in light of the Getty's agreement to repatriate about forty allegedly looted objects.[5] Other returns remain under discussion between Italy and the Getty, as Italy's criminal prosecution of Dr. True grinds on, with one day of trial each month.[6] New York's Metropolitan Museum of Art and New Jersey's Princeton University also repatriated valuable works to Italy this year (discussed in greater detail below and in the chapter on Museum developments). It remains to be seen whether museum internal investigations or actions by states' attorneys general in California, New York, or New Jersey will take any of these institutions, or their trustees, officers, or curators, to task for the phenomenal waste of acquisition resources—by now in the many tens of millions of dollars nationwide—spent in purchasing looted or at best dubious artwork that has been repatriated over the past two to three years.

Background: Four Decades of Inattention

It is not difficult to see chickens coming home to roost in these various 2007 developments. Museums have long shown the most blatant disregard for diligence standards in major art market transactions. Perhaps most notoriously, in *Making the Mummies Dance: Inside the Metropolitan Museum of Art*, a book that undoubtedly includes considerable puffery, former Met Director Thomas Hoving described the Met's 1960s acquisition of the Lydian Hoard that was later returned to Turkey:

> The material had been purchased by Dietrich von Bothmer [the Met's Curator of Greek and Roman art] over three years starting in 1965. It was called the East Greek treasure for purposes of obfuscation. The hoard had been found by tomb robbers in a village called Elmali near Sardis.
>
> . . . .
>
> "We all believe the stuff was illegally dug up," I told [von Bothmer]. "Drew Oliver [a junior curator in the Greek and Roman Department] has strong evidence. He went to the tomb and says he identified the lower parts of the pair of sphinxes which are now hidden in your storeroom. For Christ's sake, if the Turks come up with the proof from their side, we'll give the East Greek treasure back. And that's policy. We took our chances when we bought the material."[7]

So hot that it stayed in the Met's basement for two decades, the Lydian Hoard was first displayed in the 1980s, when it promptly became the subject of a lawsuit by Turkey. After six years of being on the short side of the litigation, the Met finally returned the Lydian Hoard to Turkey in 1993.[8]

In the early 1970s, not long after acquiring the Lydian Hoard, the Met purchased the far more valuable Euphronios krater (Met director Hoving called it "one of the 10 greatest works created in the Western world"),[9] with a provenance Hoving understood at the time of purchase to be suspicious, if not entirely fabricated.[10] Hoving says he had approached the acquisition of what he soon came to call the "Hot Pot" with the attitude that he "would consciously avoid knowledge of the history of the vase."[11] He later, however, came to believe the purchase may have been legitimate,[12] and the Met fiercely defended its ownership of the krater for more than three decades until, finally in 2006, the Met agreed to return it to Italy.[13]

Art market attitudes had not particularly changed by the late 1980s when the Getty's board of trustees formalized the Trust's ethical policy to facilitate antiquities trading. According to the 2007 statement Dr. True submitted to Italian prosecutor Paolo Ferri, like the Met's high-level officials in the 1960s and '70s, Getty trustees of the 1980s and 90s should have had no illusions about the art market, having been advised "[t]he market in antiquities is perhaps the most corrupt and problematic aspect of the international art trade. Accepting the premise that the majority of antiquities on the market were likely to have been removed from their countries of origin illegally, can we justify collecting these objects at all?"[14]

Demonstrating continuity in museum buying attitudes and market practices rather than irony, in 1993—the same year in which the Met returned the Lydian Hoard to Turkey—the Getty purchased a gold funerary wreath which Dr. True recommended for acquisition despite her reservations about its provenance.[15] That 1993 purchase became the basis for Greece's 2006 criminal indictment of Dr. True, which was recently dismissed,[16] and in 2007 the Getty returned the wreath to Greece along with three less-prominent objects.[17]

Recent Efforts: Greek, Italian, Peruvian, and Cypriot

In 2007, the Cleveland Museum of Art paid a price in credibility when the Louvre withdrew a request to borrow a Greek object the Cleveland Museum acquired on the market from notorious dealers Hicham and Ali Aboutaam. During a visit to Geneva in 2003, Michael Bennett, the Cleveland Museum's curator of Greek and Roman art, purchased a bronze statue called Apollo the Lizard Slayer from Phoenix Ancient Art, a Geneva gallery owned by Hicham and Ali Aboutaam, despite the Aboutaams' reputation and their warning that the provenance was dubious, at best. In December 2003, Hicham Aboutaam had been arrested and charged with smuggling, a felony, and with making false statements related to a silver drinking vessel. In June 2004, he pled guilty to a federal charge of falsifying customs documents related to the same object. Also in 2004, Egypt tried Ali Aboutaam in absentia for antiquities smuggling and sentenced him to 15 years in prison.[18] In 2007, the dubious provenance of the Lizard Slayer bronze caused the Louvre to withdraw its request to borrow the statue after Greece threatened a boycott. According to the *New York Times,* "Greek pressure on the Louvre drew applause from many in the art world, particularly academics who have long criticized antiquities trading as fraught with corruption."[19] This may be the first instance of the international museum community pressuring an American museum on behalf of a source country, and penalizing it for failure to research the provenance of an object diligently.

Italy this year also resolved a dispute with the Princeton University Art Museum over allegedly looted antiquities. Under the deal, Princeton will return eight objects to Italy—four this year and four more in 2011—in exchange for loans of treasures of "equal historical-artistic interest," and Princeton will keep seven other objects that were under discussion between Italy and the museum.[20] Although not deriving from a market purchase, in September 2007 Yale and Peru announced they were taking a similar step by launching a "new conceptual framework for collaboration" on their work on archaeological materials discovered at Machu Picchu. Yale acknowledged Peru's title to all the objects excavated there, and Peru will share with Yale rights in the research collection.[21] In 2006, Peru had threatened to sue Yale over the objects it believed had been excavated at Machu Picchu in the early 1900s by Yale professor Hiram Bingham III.[22] In late 2006, the Boston Museum of Fine Arts also agreed to return thirteen antiquities that Italian officials had claimed were looted.[23] These amicable resolutions may serve as models for other country claimants and American museums that seek to bring amicable closure to the present consequences of past decades of art looting and lack of diligence in art market transactions, and particularly those museums that wish to establish a new paradigm of more judicious collecting and source country–sponsored borrowing.

Additionally in 2007, in a case handled by the author, the Church of Cyprus settled a claim to artworks it located on the art market, announcing in January that it had reached a settlement with the Charles Pankow Foundation for six icons it believed had been stolen and smuggled out of the Turkish-occupied area in northern Cyprus.[24] Looking forward, in 2007, the U.S. State Department renewed its Memorandum of Understanding with the Republic of Cyprus in which it extended existing import restrictions on Cypriot antiquities and Byzantine objects and also granted new protections against the import of ancient coins from Cyprus.[25] This latter step, which will limit the ability of U.S. coin dealers to market unprovenanced Cypriot coins, led coin dealers to complain loudly about unnecessary and burdensome protections.[26] Late in the year, three coin dealer organizations filed suit against the State Department under the Freedom of Information Act requesting documents concerning the review process preceding the U.S.-Cyprus Memorandum of Understanding. The plaintiff-dealers argue that the State Department failed to follow appropriate procedures or to develop a sufficient factual record in recommending renewal of the MOU with provisions covering ancient coins.[27]

These developments presage a shift in the way market participants view their roles—and their risks. Just as Thomas Hoving wrote that he had, in the 1970s, consciously avoided knowledge of the provenance of the Euphronios krater, Dr. True admitted this year to *The New Yorker* that diligence in art market transactions was far from her mind during her antiquities buying in the 1980s and '90s: "There was an etiquette I absorbed. The issue of 'Where did you get this?' was not discussed."[28] Today, market participants must accept that at least some level of diligence is required. Italy's Culture Minister, Francesco Rutelli, made a strong statement in 2007 about the distinct change in the acquiring practices of U.S. museums: "The phase that was tied to illegal activity through unacceptable channels is closed, and we have arrived at a turning point where we have become partners against illegal traffic."[29] Rutelli's reference to "[closing] unacceptable channels" likely meant the Getty Museum's agreement in September 2007 to return to Italy forty antiquities believed to have been looted, and its adoption of a new, very strict set of acquisition guidelines.[30] The Getty's decision to return the artifacts should push other market participants to act diligently *before* entering the market, rather than being forced to unmake so many major transactions after the fact, a messy, embarrassing, and expensive undertaking that can be frowned upon by donors whose funds should have been more carefully spent—and by state regulators.

Were Market Participants Becoming More Diligent in 2007?

It should be unsurprising that the Met and the Getty are the museums pointing the way out of the wilderness they helped to create: the Met with creative settlements that sequence returns and include loans from Italy, and the Getty with its substantial returns to Italy and Greece coupled with the adoption in 2006 of a demanding acquisitions policy.[31] The Getty's October 2006 Policy Statement requires the museum to "undertake due diligence to establish the legal status of an object under consideration for acquisition, making every reasonable effort to investigate, substantiate, or clarify the provenance of the object."[32] For antiquities, the new policy is even more strict, requiring documentation or "substantial evidence" of (1) the object's arrival in the United States prior to 1970, (2) its removal from its probable country of modern discovery before 1970, or (3) its legal export from its probable country of modern discovery after 1970, along with evidence that it has been or will be legally imported into the United States.[33]

On April 16, 2007, the Indianapolis Museum of Art (IMA), following the Getty's model, announced a moratorium on the acquisition of undocumented archaeological objects. For the foreseeable future, IMA will acquire antiquities only if accompanied by documentation that one of the three Getty criteria are met. Arguably stricter than the Getty policy, IMA's guidelines cannot be satisfied with substantial nondocumentary evidence. Both the Getty and IMA policies turn on 1970 because that was the year of adoption of the UNESCO Convention on the Means of Prohibiting and Preventing the Illicit Import, Export and Transfer of Ownership of Cultural Property.[34] The 1970 UNESCO Convention was intended to aid countries in the protection of antiquities at risk of plunder by controlling trade in those objects.[35] This step puts the IMA on track with the Getty at the forefront of American antiquities-acquiring institutions and more in tune with the antiquities policy of the International Council of Museums (ICOM) than other U.S. museums.[36]

The ICOM Code of Ethics states that an acquiring museum's due diligence "should establish the full history of the item since discovery or production."[37] Even the Getty's and IMA's codes are not this strict, but they still surpass the recent policy established by the Association of Art Museum Directors (AAMD), which allows museums to acquire poorly documented antiquities that have been out of the ground for more than ten years, if there is a substantial collections-related reason to do so; for example, if the "art is in danger of destruction or deterioration" or "the acquisition would make the work of art publicly accessible, providing a singular and material contribution to knowledge, as well as facilitating the reconstruction of its provenance thereby allowing possible claimants to come forward."[38]

One decision in 2007 demonstrates that courts may not have fully realized that art market participants can no longer be allowed to validate their own negligent practices. In its July 2007 decision in *Lindholm v. Brant*, the Supreme Court of Connecticut ruled against the plaintiff who sought return of Andy Warhol's *Red Elvis*, a painting she claimed her art dealer had sold without her permission. The court reasoned that the defendant-purchaser had followed standard industry practice in the transaction and should, therefore, be treated as a buyer in the ordinary course of business, even though he had failed to conduct diligence concerning the dealer's authority to sell. The court accepted the defendant's expert testimony that "the vast majority of art transactions . . . are 'completed on a handshake and an exchange of an invoice.'"[39] The issue in *Lindholm* was authority to sell under the Uniform Commercial Code (not provenance or provenience), so the case should not be cited as a general endorsement of lack of diligence in art market transactions; nonetheless, it is a troubling throwback to the wild-and-crazy days when Met Director Hoving was excited to make the mummies dance.

Perhaps more typical of the reception that careless art market participants can expect to face in court is the grilling received by the attorney for Julius Schoeps recently in a case seeking restitution of a Picasso painting:

> Now, I know that no one in the art world is just interested in money or in buying and selling paintings for profit. That of course is utterly ridiculous. They're all guided by their belief in truth and beauty.[40]

At least partly for this reason—courts' reluctance to enforce consistent standards of diligence upon buyers—the impact of market problems such as those of the Getty and the Cleveland Museum on the antiquities market is difficult to gauge, except in one way. The market spoke loudly this past year when Sotheby's held two very successful antiquities auctions of objects that were well known and documented to have been out of their countries of origin for a long time. On June 7, 2007, Sotheby's sold the bronze figure *Artemis and the Stag* for $28.6 million, at the time the most expensive sculpture ever sold at auction;[41] the sculpture had been in the collection of the Albright-Knox Art Gallery since 1953 and heavily published.[42] That record was surpassed on December 5, 2007, when Sotheby's auctioned the even better-known Guennol Lioness, reportedly obtained from a site outside Baghdad in the early 1900s, for $57.2 million, far more than the projected $14–18 million.[43] The Lioness had been displayed at the Brooklyn Museum of Art for more than 50 years.[44] Thus, the market itself is starting to put value on a relatively clean provenance. Sotheby's and Christie's have, in recent years, provided considerable advice and support to their consignors, particularly in the area of artworks that may have changed hands in Europe during the National Socialist Era and, thus, the question at the end of 2007 is how much other market participants are receiving the message that old habits must now fade away.

What Are Market Participants Doing to Be Diligent?

Among judges, lawyers, museums, dealers, collectors, law professors, and commentators there is no shortage of discussion about the proper standards for diligence in art market transactions. There is, however, a severe shortage of *agreement* about appropriate standards, and how and when to apply them. The Art Dealers Association of America's (ADAA) 2006 Nazi Era Guidelines; the American Association of Museums' (AAM) 1999 Nazi Era Guidelines; and the AAMD's 1998 Nazi Era Guidelines, 2004 Report on Acquisition of Archeological Materials and Ancient Art, and 2006 Report on Incoming Loans of Archaeological Material and Ancient Art[45] all present market participants with a menu of advice and instructions that may assist art or antiquities buyers in determining what steps to take and what minimal standards may apply to put a buyer in good faith. In May 2007 the AAMD issued a position paper entitled "Art Museums and the Identification and Restitution of Works Stolen by the Nazis."[46] The paper lists several questions museum directors are advised to ask in order to, among other things, "ensure continued transparency in the acquisition and presentation of their collections," such as:

> Has the museum identified . . . all objects in its collection that underwent a change of ownership between 1933 and 1945, and that were in continental Europe between those dates?
>
> Has the museum made public the results of its provenance research, and is it continuing to do so?
>
> . . . [I]s the museum balancing a swift and compassionate response to claimants with its responsibility as an institution to act with care and prudence in protecting the works it holds in the public trust?
>
> Before purchasing a work or accepting a gift or loan with an incomplete ownership history, has the museum undertaken additional research to determine its Nazi-era provenance?

Case law provides some additional assistance to market participants in art and antiquities transactions. In 1989, the U.S. District Court in Indianapolis decided *Autocephalous Greek-Orthodox Church of Cyprus v. Goldberg,* a marketplace due diligence case in which, ironically, Dr. Marion True testified in support of claims by the Church of Cyprus to recover mosaics stolen from the Turkish-occupied area of Cyprus. The Court found that an Indiana dealer had failed to act in good faith by purchasing mosaics in Europe without conducting a sufficient inquiry into the background facts of the transaction: "A purchaser establishes his good faith by showing that he took steps to inquire into the seller's capacity to convey property rights and that such steps reasonably resolved such doubt."[47]

The ADAA has made some steps to provide advice to clients on the importance of due diligence in art transactions, claiming partial credit for the increasing interest in diligence and transparency in the art market: "Today, partly owing to the efforts of the ADAA, sellers of art are much more concerned with establishing clear title in advance of a transaction."[48] However, only in 2006 did the ADAA introduce its Guidelines Regarding Art Looted During the Nazi Era which urged "greatly increased scrutiny . . . being given to provenance" as a result of the Nazis' art looting.[49] In introducing the policy, however, the ADAA excused the *lack* of information in some chains of title:

> [The ADAA] recogniz[es] that many art works do not have complete chains of provenance and never will. Sellers of works of art through the years have often, for perfectly legitimate reasons, chosen to remain anonymous. And provenance has not routinely been recorded for works of relatively low value, including many contemporary works, watercolors and drawings and most prints. As the value of these works has risen, provenance has become a matter of increased interest and concern. However, the inability to conclusively establish the ownership of a work during the Nazi period does not necessarily mean that the work in question was looted.[50]

These sentiments echo the testimony given by Gil Edelson, ADAA's Vice President and Counsel, before Congress in July 2006, complaining that "provenance has not routinely been recorded for works of modest value . . . and works on paper" and that "many collectors prefer to remain anonymous." Edelson also defended his constituents by pointing out that while dealers' invoices customarily list the provenance of the work, such documents are often lost or contain erroneous information.[51] Most notably, the ADAA's Guidelines maintain the sanctity of the dealer-client relationship:

> If evidence of looting is discovered and there is no evidence of restitution, the dealer should not proceed to acquire or sell the object, and should notify the seller. Depending on the circumstances of the particular case, additional steps may be prudent or necessary, such as notifying appropriate government authorities or other interested parties of the dealer's findings. However, dealers are not law-enforcement agents, and dealers may also have a duty to protect the confidentiality of their clients.[52]

Since issuing its Guidelines, the ADAA has not taken the next obvious step of asking its member art dealers to begin to apply similar procedures when there is no taint of the Holocaust, so that due diligence can assume the same role in art in purchases and sales transactions that it does generally in American business.

Other dealer associations have also made efforts to self-police. Under the American Numismatic Association's Code of Ethics, a member agrees "[t]o neither buy nor sell numismatic items of which the ownership is questionable."[53] Similarly, the Ancient Coin Collectors Guild (ACCG) adopted a Code of Ethics in 1995, stating in part that "Coin Collectors and Sellers will not knowingly purchase coins illegally removed from scheduled archaeological sites or stolen from museum or personal collections, and will comply with all cultural property laws of their own country."[54] These codes are open to many criticisms, such as the limitation against dealing in coins from "scheduled archaeological sites." Since dealers in ancient art generally disclaim knowledge of the provenience or find spot of an antiquity, this turn of phrase provides almost no restriction on individual dealers.[55] Also, these codes using terms like avoiding "questionable" objects and not "knowingly" dealing in looted art put the dealer's knowledge at issue, meaning that a dealer may—like Thomas Hoving in the 1970s—avoid evidence of theft. In other words, a coin dealer who deliberately remains ignorant may continue to deal within the confines of the industry's code of conduct, if not the law, which does not sanction conscious avoidance of the truth. Nor do these codes address the sensitive issue that an object may have been illegally exported from the country even if there is no evidence of theft. While illegal export may not alone be the basis for a legal claim against an antiquity in the United States, it can be a red flag of more serious problems and could, by itself, preclude later museum interest in the object under policies like ICOM's, the Getty's, and IMA's.

Developments Concerning Victim Diligence

Victim diligence can be considered directly related to buyer diligence, since art market participants seeking to act in good faith benefit from the information made available by and on behalf of theft victims. As early as 1980, courts were beginning to address the need for diligence by art theft victims, and the relationship between that diligence and art market transactions. In *O'Keeffe v. Snyder*, the Supreme Court of New Jersey addressed Georgia O'Keeffe's effort to recover three allegedly stolen paintings from the defendant Snyder's gallery. The Court reversed the trial judge's grant of summary judgment to O'Keeffe and, in remanding the case, the New Jersey Supreme Court instructed the lower court to determine whether O'Keeffe had been adequately diligent in trying to recover her paintings at the time of the theft, whether there was a method for alerting the art world about the theft other than talking to colleagues, and whether registering the paintings with the Art Dealers Association of America would put a reasonably prudent person on notice of the theft.[56]

The 1991 case *Solomon R. Guggenheim Foundation v. Lubell* also addresses victim diligence issues. Defendants in that case purchased a Marc Chagall gouache from an art dealer in 1967 and in 1986, the Guggenheim asked Mrs. Lubell to return it to the museum, telling her it had been stolen years before. The appellate court declined to impose *any* standards of diligence on the victim museum in the context of the defendants' statute of limitations defense, but held that in New York the theft victim's alleged lack of diligence would be addressed in the context of the defendants' laches defense, which entails a weighing of the claimant's delay and the acquirer's prejudice.[57] As a result, since *Lubell*, several good faith possessors in New York have succeeded on a laches defense where the claimant could show no history of diligence. For example, in *Greek Orthodox Patriarchate of Jerusalem v. Christie's*, the court granted defendants' motion for summary judgment, finding that plaintiff Patriarchate had not been sufficiently diligent in waiting almost seventy years to begin pursuing the Archimedes Palimpsest, a tenth-century manuscript.[58]

When it comes to assessing victim diligence, courts in 2007 were generally unforgiving, holding claimants strictly responsible for past failures to actively seek out claims and pursue them. In the much-publicized case by the heirs of Jewish art collector Margarete Mauthner against Elizabeth Taylor, *Orkin v. Taylor*, the Ninth Circuit affirmed the Central District of California's dismissal of a complaint seeking recovery of Van Gogh's *Vue de l'Aisle et de la Chapelle de la Saint-Rémy*. Mauthner fled Nazi Germany in 1939, leaving her belongings behind and, eventually, Elizabeth Taylor purchased *Vue de l'Aisle* at auction in April 1963.

The Ninth Circuit agreed with the district court that the plaintiffs' state law claims were time-barred, holding that plaintiffs could reasonably have discovered the whereabouts of their property much earlier.[59] The Court reasoned that Taylor's acquisition of the painting in 1963 was well-publicized, that her ownership of it was published in a 1970 *catalogue raisonné*, and that she had offered it for sale in 1990.[60]

In December 2007, the Museum of Modern Art and the Solomon R. Guggenheim Foundation jointly filed for declaratory judgment in the Southern District of New York in Manhattan, asking the Court to rule that Picasso's *Boy Leading a Horse* and *Le Moulin de la Galette* were not forcibly sold and belong to the museums. The claimant is Julius H. Schoeps, great-nephew of the paintings' original owner, the German Jewish banker Paul von Mendelssohn-Bartholdy. Schoeps demanded that MoMA and the Guggenheim turn over the paintings in November 2007, asserting that his great-uncle sold them under duress in Nazi Germany. Although MoMA and Guggenheim did not recently acquire these paintings through the market, their response is instructive to gauge the thinking of American museums in 2007 as they approach Holocaust claims, many of which do concern objects that were the subject of market transactions over the decades since the end of World War II. According to MoMA's director Glenn Lowry, the museums did "an enormous amount of research, which confirmed what we already knew: There is absolutely no evidence that these paintings were sold under duress."[61] Of course, MoMA and the Guggenheim's rationale for their aggressive stance is undoubtedly based at least in part on Schoeps' shaky background in making similar claims for another Picasso; in November 2006, he forced the withdrawal of *Portrait de Ángel Fernández de Soto* from a Christie's auction at the eleventh hour, only to have federal court dismiss his case; Schoeps refiled his case in state court, but a New York state judge dismissed the suit this year, saying that Schoeps did not legally represent his great-uncle's estate.[62]

This new approach to restitution claims, where museums use declaratory judgment suits to beat claimants to the courthouse is gaining traction and may represent a hardening of attitudes towards Holocaust claimants. It was followed successfully in recent years by the Detroit Institute of Art and the Toledo Museum of Art, which in January 2006 filed declaratory judgment actions against the heirs of Martha Nathan regarding the heirs' claims to van Gogh's *The Diggers* and Gauguin's *Street Scene in Tahiti*.[63] (Courts in Michigan and Ohio granted both plaintiff-museums' motions to dismiss the heirs' counterclaims, finding that the heirs' claims were barred by the states' statutes of limitations, at least in part for the theft victim's failure to diligently search for the object.[64]) Then again, at least with respect to Schoeps' claim, MoMA and the Guggenheim reportedly made their restitution files available to him prior to filing their declaratory judgment action. Only when Schoeps continued to press his claim *after* seeing that research did the museums pursue declaratory judgment actions.

Virtually at the close of 2007, December 27 to be exact, the U.S. District Court in Rhode Island addressed the question of victim diligence, holding that a claimant's diligence had been sufficient to support summary judgment against the defendant possessor on her laches defense. In *Vineberg v. Bissonette*, in which the author represented the plaintiff trustees of the Dr. and Mrs. Max Stern Foundation, the court held that Dr. Stern, a Jewish art dealer in prewar Germany who had been ordered by Nazi officials to sell his inventory, did not lose title to the artwork he had been required to auction. Defendant Maria-Louise Bissonnette had inherited the painting from her mother and argued that the Stern Foundation had delayed unreasonably in finding her and suing for recovery of the painting at issue. Since Dr. Stern had pursued his losses after the war and the Foundation had continued those efforts, the court held that the diligence was reasonable. In reaching this decision, the court was mindful of the "chaotic events of World War II in Europe and the perverse actions of the Nazi regime as directed against the Jewish population of Germany and other European countries."[65] In granting the plaintiff's motion for summary judgment on replevin, and ordering the defendant to turn over the painting, the court observed that records had been lost, complicating the search, and ruled that the claimant must only show that recovery efforts were reasonable under the circumstances presented, not whether they were perfect.[66] The court also noted that defendant Bissonnette and her family had held the painting continuously since the war, for the most part keeping it in their apartment, and so could not demonstrate significant prejudice by reason of any delay on the part of Dr. Stern or the Foundation that succeeded to his rights.

Conclusion

Concepts of openness, enhanced transparency, and due diligence have been seeping into the art marketplace over the past few years, gradually replacing the prior decades of buyers, particularly museums, consciously ignoring the origins of antiquities and other artworks they acquired. These concepts are most strongly presented in the AAMD's 2006 policy on incoming museum antiquities loans[67] and in the ICOM Code of Ethics. The Getty acquisition guidelines, accepted this past year by IMA, and the many 2007 returns of antiquities claimed by source countries presage U.S. museums paying greater attention to avoiding or minimizing the risks inherent in market transactions. These developments can be expected to be event-forcing, with more and more buyers asking questions and with dealers, rather than making excuses, providing their clients with assistance in developing the information they need to make informed purchasing decisions. Likewise, with art buyers becoming increasingly diligent, theft victims who do not provide their information to the art market can expect to see their conduct judged harshly by museum acquirers and by courts.

Notes

1. The author thanks L. Eden Burgess for her assistance in the preparation of this chapter.
2. Perhaps because the tide seems to be changing, Dr. True gave a lengthy interview in December about her trial and the charges against her that appears in the December 17, 2007 issue of The New Yorker. Hugh Eakin, *Treasure Hunt,* NEW YORKER, Dec. 17, 2007.
3. Anthee Carassava, *Greek Court Dismisses Case Against Ex-Curator,* N.Y. TIMES, Nov. 27, 2007.
4. Jason Felch, *Charges are Dropped in Getty Case*, L.A. TIMES, Nov. 27, 2007.
5. Elisabetta Povoledo, Progress Seen in Talks on Antiquities, N.Y. TIMES, Dec. 1, 2007; Elisabetta Povoledo, Italy and Getty Sign Pact on Artifacts, N.Y. TIMES, Sept. 26, 2007.
6. Ildikó DeAngelis, Interview With Italian Prosecutor Paolo Ferri in Rome, Italy, March 2007. See pp. 11–31 of this edition of the YEARBOOK.
7. Thomas Hoving, MAKING THE MUMMIES DANCE: INSIDE THE METROPOLITAN MUSEUM OF ART 217 (2003).
8. Michel Bessières, *We have to change the buyer's attitude* (interview of Turkish journalist Özgen Acar), UNESCO COURIER (April 2001), at http://www.unesco.org/courier/2001_04/uk/doss27.htm.
9. Russell Berman, *Met Chief To Discuss 'Hot Pot' in Rome,* N.Y. SUN, Nov. 11, 2005.
10. Hoving, MAKING THE MUMMIES DANCE at 310–20.
11. *Id.* at 310.
12. *Id.* at 338–40.
13. Randy Kennedy and Hugh Eakin, *The Met, Ending 30-Year Stance, Is Set to Yield Prized Vase to Italy,* N.Y. TIMES, Feb. 3, 2006.
14. Eakin, *Treasure Hunt* at 65.

15. Jason Felch, *Charges are dropped in Getty case*, L.A. Times, Nov. 27, 2007.
16. *Id.*
17. Ancient wreath returns to Greece, BBC News, March 30, 2007, at http://news.bbc.co.uk/2/hi/europe/6505971.stm.
18. Barry Meier, *Art Dealer Pleads Guilty In Import Case*, N.Y. Times, June 24, 2004.
19. Ron Stodghill, *Do You Know Where That Art Has Been?*, N.Y. Times, March 18, 2007.
20. Ariel David, *Princeton, Italy strike deal to repatriate 8 antiquities*, Associated Press, Oct. 31, 2007, at http://www.philly.com/inquirer/magazine/ 20071031_Princeton_Italy_strike_deal_to_repatriate_8_antiquities.html.
21. Joint Statement by the Government of Peru and Yale University, Sept. 14, 2007, at http://www.yale.edu/opa/newsr/07-09-14-01.all.html.
22. Diane Orson, NPR's All Things Considered, Peru Seeks Return of Machu Picchu Artifacts, March 30, 2006, at http://www.npr.org/templates/story/ story.php?storyId=5298164.
23. Elisabetta Povoledo, *Boston Museum Returns 13 Ancient Works to Italy,* N.Y. Times, Sept., 29, 2006; www.mfa.org/collections/index.asp?key=2656.
24. Cyprus Embassy Press Release, Smuggled icons returned to lawful owner—the Cyprus Church, Jan. 11, 2007, at http://www.cyprusembassy.net/home/ index.php?module=article&id=3915.
25. In October 2007, Dr. Pavlos Flourentzos, Director of the Department of Antiquities of Cyprus, gave a brief but informative interview to SAFE (Saving Antiquities For Everyone), explaining the importance of coins to Cyprus' cultural heritage. The interview is available at http://www.savingantiquities.org/feature_cyprusinterview.php.
26. See, e.g., Letter from Federation of European Numismatic Trade Associations (FENAP) to U.S. Secretary of State regarding Cypriot import restrictions, July 25, 2007, at http://www.accg.us/issues/news/fenap-expresses-concern-to-us-state-department/.
27. *ACCG, et al., v. U.S. Dept. of State,* Civ. Act. No. 07-02074 (D.D.C. Nov. 15, 2007). The ACCG's Complaint is available at http://accg.us/issues/news/complaint.pdf.
28. Eakin, *Treasure Hunt*, at 64.
29. Povoledo, *Progress Seen*.
30. Povoledo, *Italy and Getty Sign Pact*.
31. Policy Statement, Acquisitions by the J. Paul Getty Museum, Oct. 23, 2006, at http://www.getty.edu/about/governance/ pdfs/acquisitions_policy.pdf.
32. *Id.*
33. *Id.*
34. Convention on the Means of Prohibiting and Preventing the Illicit Import, Export and Transfer of Ownership of Cultural Property, http://exchanges.state.gov/culprop/ unesco01.html.

35. Indianapolis Museum of Art Declares Moratorium on Acquisition of Archeological Objects Lacking Adequate Provenance, April 16, 2007, available at http://www.imamuseum.org/sites/default/files/ IMA%20Moratorium.pdf.
36. ICOM Code of Ethics for Museums, 2006, http://palimpsest.stanford.edu/icom/ethics.html.
37. *Id.*
38. AAMD, Report on Acquisition of Archeological Materials and Ancient Art, June 4, 2004, at http://www.aamd.org/papers/documents/TaskForceReportwithCoverPage_Final.pdf.
39. *Lindholm v. Brant*, 925 A.2d 1048 (Conn. 2007).
40. Transcript, *Schoeps v. The Andrew Lloyd Webber Art Foundation*, 06CV12934 (S.D.N.Y.), Nov. 7, 2006, before Judge Rakoff, at 37.
41. Sotheby's press release, Sotheby's Sets a New World Record for Sculpture at Auction, June 7, 2007.
42. Sotheby's press release, The Albright-Knox Art Gallery in Buffalo, New York Renowned for Modern and Contemporary Art, to Auction Antiquities and Other Historic Works, November 10, 2006.
43. Carol Vogel, *Tiny Lioness Commands Many Millions*, N.Y. TIMES, Dec. 6, 2007; Rita Delfiner, *Roarrr! Ancient Lion Gets Record $57M*, N.Y. POST, Dec. 6, 2007; Sotheby's press release, Sotheby's Sets a New World Record for Sculpture at Auction, Dec. 5, 2007.
44. Sotheby's press release, The Guennol Lioness; Sotheby's to Sell One of the Last Known Masterworks of Ancient Near-Eastern Art Now in Private Hands, September 14, 2007.
45. ADAA, Guidelines Regarding Art Looted During the Nazi Era, at http://www.artdealers.org/publications/loot.html; AAM, Guidelines Concerning the Unlawful Appropriation of Objects During the Nazi Era, at http://www.aam-us.org/museumresources/ethics/nazi_guidelines.cfm; AAMD, Report of the AAMD Task Force on the Spoliation of Art during the Nazi/World War II Era (1933-1945), June 4, 1998, at http://www.aamd.org/papers/guideln.php; AAMD, Report on Acquisition of Archeological Materials and Ancient Art, June 4, 2004, at http://www.aamd.org/papers/documents/TaskForceReportwithCoverPage_Final.pdf; AAMD, Report of the AAMD Subcommittee on Incoming Loans of Archaeological Material and Ancient Art, Feb. 27, 2006, at http://www.aamd.org/papers/documents/Loans_and_PressRelease.pdf.
46. Available at http://www.aamd.org/papers/documents/Nazi-lootedart_clean_06_2007.pdf.
47. *Autocephalous Greek-Orthodox Church of Cyprus v. Goldberg*, 717 F. Supp. 1374 (S.D. Ind. 1989), *aff'd* on other grounds, 917 F.2d 278 (7th Cir. 1990).

48. Jane Kallir, A Brief History of the ADAA, at http://www.artdealers.org/who.history.html.
49. Art Dealers Association of America, Guidelines Regarding Art Looted During the Nazi Era, at http://www.artdealers.org/publications/loot.html.
50. *Id.*
51. Testimony of Gilbert S. Edelson at 3, Administrative Vice President and Counsel, Art Dealers Association of America before the Subcommittee on Domestic and International Monetary Policy, Trade and Technology of the House Committee on Financial Services, July 27, 2006: www.financialservices.house.gov/media/pdf/072706gse.pdf.
52. ADAA Guidelines ¶ A.4 (emphasis added).
53. American Numismatic Association, Federal Charter, Bylaws and Codes of Ethics, at http://www.money.org/Content/NavigationMenu/AboutANA/FederalCharterBylawsCodeofEthics/0605_bylaws.pdf.
54. ACCG Code of Ethics, at http://www.accg.us/issues/news/code.
55. See Nathan T. Elkins, Codes of Ethics vs. the Financial Interest, SAFECORNER, Sept. 20, 2007, at http://safecorner.savingantiquities.org/2007/09/codes-of-ethics-vs-financial-interest_20.html.
56. *O'Keeffe v. Snyder*, 416 A.2d 862 (N.J. 1980).
57. *Solomon R. Guggenheim Foundation v. Lubell,* 569 N.E.2d 426 (N.Y. Ct. App. 1991).
58. *Greek Orthodox Patriarchate of Jerusalem v. Christie's*, 1999 U.S. Dist. LEXIS 13257 (S.D.N.Y. Aug. 30, 1999).
59. The Ninth Circuit also held that the Holocaust Victims Redress Act did not create a private right of action against private art owners.
60. *Orkin v. Taylor*, 487 F.3d 734 (9th Cir.), *cert. denied*, 128 S. Ct. 491 (2007).
61. *Schoeps v. The Andrew Lloyd Webber Art Foundation*, 06CV12934 (S.D.N.Y.); Carol Vogel, *Two Museums Go to Court Over the Right to Picassos*, N.Y. TIMES, Dec. 8, 2007.
62. Vogel, Two Museums.
63. In May 2007, the heirs withdrew their appeal of the lower courts' findings that the statutes of limitations barred their claims and challenged the museums to submit the claims to binding arbitration. Rowland & Associates and Schink & Studzinski, Press Release, Nathan Heirs Withdraw Appeals Of Statute Of Limitations Ruling And Challenge Museums To Submit Claims To Arbitration On The Merits, May 10, 2007, at http://www.mmdnewswire.com/nathan-heirs-withdraw-appeals-of-statute-of-limitations-ruling-and-challenge-museums-to-submit-1617-2.html.
64. *Detroit Inst. of Arts v. Ullin*, 2007 U.S. Dist. LEXIS 28364 (E.D. Mich. March 31, 2007); *Toledo Museum of Art v. Ullin*, 477 F. Supp. 2d 802 (N.D. Ohio 2006).
65. *Vineberg v. Bissonnette*, 06-cv-211 (D.R.I. Dec. 27, 2007) (ML) slip op. at 14.

66. *Vineberg v. Bissonnette*, 06-cv-211 (D.R.I. Dec. 27, 2007) (ML); Ray Henry, *Court: Painting sold under Nazi pressure belongs to Jewish dealer,* ASSOCIATED PRESS, Dec. 28, 2007, at http://www.boston.com/news/local/rhode_island/articles/2007/12/28/court_painting_auctioned_by_nazis_belongs_to_jewish_mans_estate/.
67. AAMD, Report of the AAMD Subcommittee on Incoming Loans of Archaeological Material and Ancient Art, Feb. 27, 2006, at http://www.aamd.org/papers/documents/Loans_and_PressRelease.pdf.

International Cultural Property

• • •

Section Editor: Patty Gerstenblith

Introduction

The year 2007 saw advances in international law, particularly an increasing number of countries entering the international treaty regime, with an increasing number of ratifications and implementing legislation for both the 1970 UNESCO Convention and the 1954 Hague Convention. Museums in the United States continued the trend from 2006 of restitutions to foreign countries, particularly Italy and Peru, and new agreements of cooperation. Greater activity in European countries, including litigation and new legislation, has been another characteristic of this past year.

International Conventions and Agreements

The 1954 Hague Convention

The 1954 Hague Convention on the Protection of Cultural Property in the Event of Armed Conflict was adopted in the wake of the large-scale cultural looting and destruction perpetrated by the German Nazi regime during World War II. It currently has 119 States Parties with Japan being the most recent country to join. However, the two largest military powers, the United States and the United Kingdom, are not parties, although they both signed the treaty in 1954.

In the aftermath of the 2003 Gulf War, the United Kingdom announced in May 2004 that it would move toward ratification of the main Convention and both the First and Second Protocols. Although President Clinton transmitted the main Convention and First Protocol to the Senate in 1999, no further action was taken until February 2007 when the State Department placed both instruments on its list of law of war treaties that the administration wants to see the Senate take up during the current Congress. The Senate Foreign Relations Committee has not as yet, however, scheduled hearings. Furthermore, the State Department recommended that the Senate ratify only the second part of the First Protocol, which is concerned with the status of cultural objects illegally removed from occupied territory. This recommendation has been controversial with the cultural heritage preservation community, and the Senate may not consider the First Protocol at all.

Germany, which ratified the First Protocol in 1967, is the first nation to enact specific implementing legislation for it. This legislation prohibits the import of cultural goods removed in violation of the protocol from occupied territory of another States Party any time after November 11, 1967.[1] This legislation will enter into force with Germany's accession to the 1970 UNESCO Convention on the Means of Prohibiting and Preventing the Illicit Import, Export and Transfer of Ownership of Cultural Property (1970 UNESCO Convention).[2]

The 1970 UNESCO Convention and Its Implementation

The 1970 UNESCO Convention is the primary instrument that addresses the international movement of cultural materials.[3] Four nations joined the 1970 UNESCO Convention this year—New Zealand, Norway, Montenegro, and the Republic of Moldova—while Greece joined the 1995 Unidroit Convention on Stolen or Illegally Exported Cultural Objects. New Zealand, which joined the Unidroit Convention in late 2006, enacted new comprehensive legislation that incorporates implementation of both conventions into its domestic law.[4] In addition to regulating the export of protected cultural objects from New Zealand, the legislation prohibits the import into New Zealand of unlawfully exported protected foreign objects[5] and allows reciprocating states to bring actions to recover stolen or illegally exported protected objects.[6]

Germany also enacted implementing legislation for the 1970 UNESCO Convention this year, although it will not formally join the convention until January 2008. Under this legislation, Germany will not allow the import of any illegally exported cultural objects that have been individually classified in an accessible inventory by the country of origin one year prior to removal. In addition, the country of origin must place archaeological objects in the inventory within one year of the time when the country of origin gains knowledge of the excavation.[7]

On December 29, 2006, Switzerland and Peru signed an agreement pursuant to the Swiss implementation of the 1970 UNESCO Convention, the Federal Act on the International Transfer of Cultural Property.[8] The Swiss-Peru agreement provides for the return of stolen cultural goods, particularly archaeological objects, from Switzerland to Peru.[9] In November, Switzerland and Peru announced the publication of a "red list" of Peruvian artifacts that are most at risk for looting and theft. At the same time, Swiss authorities returned a Chancay ceramic bowl, dating to about A.D. 1200, that had been intercepted by Swiss customs.[10]

In the United States, nations must enter into additional bilateral agreements under the Convention on Cultural Property Implementation Act ("CPIA").[11] During 2007, the United States extended its agreements for an additional five years with four countries: Peru, Cyprus, Mali, and Guatemala.[12] No new requests for agreements were presented and no new agreements were finalized. The State Department has still taken no action on China's request for an agreement with the United States, which was considered by the Cultural Property Advisory Committee in early 2005.

Probably the most controversial development was the inclusion of ancient coins on the list of designated archaeological materials in the renewal of the U.S.-Cyprus agreement.[13] The extended agreement also restricts the import of Byzantine ecclesiastical materials, which had previously been covered under an emergency action. The import restriction applies to coins of Cypriot types made of gold, silver, and bronze, including but not limited to issues of the ancient kingdoms of Amathus, Kition, Kourion, Idalion, Lapethos, Marion, Paphos, Soli, and Salamis dating from the end of the sixth century B.C. to 332 B.C.; issues of the Hellenistic period (332 B.C.–30 B.C.), and provincial and local issues of the Roman period from about 30 B.C. to A.D. 235. This is the first time that coins have been included in a memorandum of understanding with any country, and the inclusion has precipitated a significant backlash from the coin dealer and collector community.

In February 2007, the State Department announced that it had completed the delegation of authority relating to emergency import restrictions on Iraqi cultural materials.[14] The Emergency Protection of Iraqi Cultural Antiquities

Act, enacted in 2005, allows the president to impose import restrictions on Iraqi cultural materials that left Iraq illegally after 1990.[15] This authority has now been delegated to the Assistant Secretary of State for Educational and Cultural Affairs, but no import restrictions have yet been imposed pursuant to this legislation.

Recoveries, Restitutions, and Claims

Recoveries and Restitutions

Manuscripts The FBI Art Crime Team assisted in the recovery of 15th century Spanish maps stolen from Madrid. At the request of the Spanish National Police and Civil Guard, the FBI assisted in the recovery of the two maps from an edition of Ptolemy's Geographia that were stolen from the Spanish National Library in Madrid earlier in the year. United Kingdom, Australian, and Argentinean authorities have recovered nine other maps. Spain has charged a citizen of Uruguay, Cesar Gomez Rivero, with the theft. Rivero is considered a fugitive and is believed to be in South America.[16]

Return of Sculpture to Cambodia The United States recovered and returned to Cambodia the head of an Angkor-era sculpture that had been stolen and smuggled out of Cambodia. The artifact, a sandstone head of a celestial dancer, or apsara, from the twelfth century, was returned in accordance with the U.S.-Cambodia memorandum of agreement of 2003.[17]

Return of Artifacts to Peru In June 2007, the United States returned to Peru a cache of 412 pre-Columbian artifacts that had been seized in 2005.[18] The recovered artifacts included clay burial vessels of pre-Inca cultures, gold and silver jewelry, and quipus (knotted strings believed to have been used as counting devices) from the Inca culture. The individual who was attempting to sell the artifacts was arrested in an undercover operation and ultimately pled guilty to the sale and receipt of stolen goods.

Statues Returned to Pakistan Thirty-eight ancient sculptures, which had been seized by U.S. Immigration and Customs Enforcement and U.S. Customs and Border Protection in September 2005 at the Newark Port of Entry, were returned to Pakistan on January 23, 2007.[19] The artifacts included several

Gandharan-type sculptures of the third and fourth centuries A.D., some of the "starving Buddha" type, a relief panel depicting a dance seize, a frieze showing monks meditating, and at least one object dating from the second century B.C.[20] Evidence indicated that they had been looted from archaeological sites in northern Pakistan. The artifacts were contained in two shipments for which the shipper had made a false declaration as to country of origin.

Human Remains Returned to Tasmania Britain's Natural History Museum returned the remains of seventeen Tasmanian aborigines.[21] Australia's Tasmanian community had been fighting for about twenty years to recover the remains, which were taken in the nineteenth century. While the museum had agreed to the restitution in November 2006 upon recommendation of its Human Remains Advisory Panel, the museum also decided to conduct additional scientific tests before the restitution. The Tasmanian Aboriginal Centre decided to sue to prevent such testing, but a settlement was mediated by which the museum could conduct additional but noninvasive scientific tests, such as measurements, scans, and the making of casts, but DNA and other invasive analyses were not allowed. This and anticipated claims for return of human remains held at Cambridge University, Oxford University, and the National Museums Scotland are expected to follow the Department of Culture, Media and Sports' Guidance for the Care of Human Remains in Museums,[22] which calls for a balancing of scientific interests against the interests of descendant communities.

Peru/Yale Agreement on Restitution

Hiram Bingham "rediscovered" the Inca site of Machu Picchu in Peru in 1911 and conducted excavations there in 1912 and 1915 with the support of Yale University and the National Geographic Society. Bingham took back to Yale more than 4,000 objects, including human remains, ceramics, and animal bones. In 2001 Alejandro Toledo, Peru's first president of Andean descent, presented a claim for return of the remaining artifacts. Yale claimed that Peru had given the artifacts, whereas Peru claimed that they were on loan. On September 14, 2007, Peru and Yale announced an agreement by which Yale recognized Peru's title to the collection.[23] Yale and Peru's National Institute of Culture will collaborate on international traveling exhibitions. The museum-quality objects, approximately four hundred in number, will be returned to Peru, and a new museum will be built in Cuzco with Yale acting as an advisor. Peru and Yale will share the research rights in the collection. Although the agreement was at first hailed as another creative and collaborative solution to a cultural property problem, the agreement was later criticized because of the small number of objects to be returned to Peru in the next few years and the extended period of time, reportedly another ninety-nine years, in which Yale would retain the remainder of the collection for continued research.[24]

United Kingdom Immunity from Seizure Legislation

The United Kingdom enacted legislation to provide immunity from seizure for objects that are on temporary loan for exhibition from collections in foreign nations.[25] The act provides immunity from seizure in any civil or criminal proceeding and by any law enforcement authorities. A museum that wishes to apply for immunity for objects on loan must first be approved by the Secretary for Culture, Media and Sport; as part of the approval process, the museum must satisfy the Secretary that its due diligence procedures are satisfactory.[26]

Museums must then publish information about each object for which protection is sought before the start of the exhibition and in certain circumstances provide additional information upon request. Regulations to be issued will specify the information that a museum must provide concerning the objects for which immunity is sought and how much in advance of the loan the information must be provided. These regulations have not yet been promulgated, but draft regulations are available,[27] and public comment was sought by the Department of Culture, Media and Sport before finalizing the regulations.

Claims

Sch'yen Collection A large group of incantation bowls on loan from a private Norwegian collection to the University College London (UCL) is at the center of a dispute concerning their origin and proper disposition.[28] The collection was created by a wealthy retired Norwegian businessman, Martin Sch'yen, and includes primarily different types of ancient writings.[29] The Sch'yen collection loaned most of its incantation bowls (654) to UCL in 1995 for them to be stored, studied, and catalogued. Incantation bowls, dating to the fifth to eighth centuries A.D., contain inscriptions in Aramaic, an ancient Hebrew language, mostly from the Bible, and were placed under buildings as magical protections. The vast majority of them, if not all, come from within modern Iraq.

After a documentary aired in 2003 questioned the origins of much of the Sch'yen collection, UCL initiated an investigation as to whether UCL was holding the bowls in violation of UK law that prohibits the handling of antiquities that were or might have been removed illegally from Iraq after 1990.[30] UCL then set up a committee of inquiry in 2005, which produced a report on the status of the bowls in July 2006. It is said that the report, which has not been made public, concluded that the Jordanian documents that accompanied the bowls were not "convincing" and that the bowls, even if they left Iraq before 1990, would be considered stolen property under Iraq's national ownership law of 1936.[31] Despite this, Sch'yen might have acquired good title if he possessed the bowls for more than six years in good faith. In March 2007, the Sch'yen Collection announced it would sue UCL to return the bowls. This litigation was settled in June with a press release stating that "no claims adverse to the Sch'yen Collection's right and title have been made or intimated. . . ."[32] The press release also stated that the bowls had been returned to the Collection (presumably in London where the Collection is also based) and that UCL agreed to make a payment to the Collection. UCL has also refused to release the report of its inquiry committee. Iraq is now reportedly investigating whether to bring a claim before the bowls leave London and is asking for assistance from the British government.[33]

Odyssey Marine Exploration Odyssey Marine Exploration, Inc., a company engaged in deepwater exploration of historic wrecks and recovery of artifacts for commercial sale, announced the recovery of over 500,000 silver and gold coins and other artifacts from a colonial-era shipwreck code-named "Black Swan."[34] Odyssey claims that the wreck is not yet identified and refuses to disclose its exact location; the wreck is described as located one mile west of the Straits of Gibraltar in international waters, beyond the territorial waters or contiguous zone of any nation, and at a depth of 1,100 meters. The discovery was announced after Odyssey had imported the artifacts into the United States; the artifacts are being cleaned and conserved and will then be offered for sale.

Odyssey has filed three admiralty claims (or arrests) for wrecks located in the Atlantic Ocean and in the western Mediterranean in federal court in the Middle District of Florida.[35] Spain has entered all three as a claimant, asserting ownership of any Spanish property that might be located at these sites. In addition, Spain is seeking to dismiss Odyssey's filings because Odyssey had not described the defendant *res* (the shipwrecks) with sufficient detail.

British Litigation Concerning Iranian Artifacts

Two cases involving Iran as the plaintiff in British courts were of interest to cultural property lawyers in 2007.

Iran v. Berend

The first case involved questions of acquisition of movable property and choice of law. A French collector, Denyse Berend, placed for auction at Christie's in London a fragment of an Achaemenid limestone relief, taken from the eastern staircase of the Apadana structure (or audience hall) of Persepolis, dating to the first half of the fifth century B.C.[36] Berend purchased the relief at a public auction in New York in 1974 and took possession of it in Paris, also in 1974. When Berend transferred the relief to London, Iran sued and received a temporary injunction restraining the sale. While both parties agreed that Iran had good title to the relief before 1974, the court held that the question of title should be decided according to the *lex situs* where the title that is now in dispute (Paris) was purported to have been acquired.

Iran first tried to argue that under French conflict of laws principles, a French court would apply the doctrine of *renvoi*, thereby utilizing the law of Iran (the country of origin) to resolve the title dispute. The British court held, however, that there was no compelling or overarching doctrinal basis for applying *renvoi* to movable property under the facts of this case. The court then turned to the resolution of the dispute under French domestic law. According to French law, a possessor may acquire title either by possession for three years in good faith under article 2279 of the Civil Code (acquisition of title by possession) or by possession that is continuous, uninterrupted, peaceful, public, and unequivocal (Art. 2229) for thirty years under article 2263 of the Civil Code (acquisition of title by thirty-year prescription). In this case, both parties conceded that the possessor had acted in good faith. The current possessor was therefore allowed to maintain her title to the relief. It sold at auction in October 2007 for £580,500.

Iran v. Barakat

The second case involved the application of Iran's national ownership law of antiquities to determine the disposition of a cache of antiquities imported into England by a dealer, Barakat.[37] The antiquities at issue include jars, bowls, and cups made of chlorite that allegedly were excavated illegally in the Jiroft region of southern Iran and date to the third millennium B.C. The sites in the Jiroft region were excavated only in recent years but had been subjected to looting for several years before. Iran based its claim of title to the antiquities on its laws pertaining to antiquities.

The trial court first examined various laws of Iran that pertain to its archaeological heritage, in particular the laws of 1930 and 1979. In examining these laws, the court concluded that none made a clear statement of ownership, vesting title to undiscovered antiquities in the nation. Although Iran had failed to prove its ownership interest in the antiquities, the court turned to consider, in *obiter dictum*, the question of whether, even if Iran's law were clearly a vesting law, its ownership claim could be vindicated. The court cast this issue in terms of the justiciability of Iran's claim. Because acquisition by means of a national ownership law is a method available only to sovereigns, the court characterized such laws as public in nature and held that Iran's claim was not justiciable.

Iran's appeal of the trial court decision was decided on December 21, 2007, with the appellate court reversing on the two main points. The appellate court held that, under conflict of laws principles, ownership of the antiquities should be determined by the law of the *lex situs* (Iran) and that Iran's 1979 Legal Bill denies the attributes of ownership of antiquities to the finder and, instead, confers both ownership and an immediate right to possession on the nation. In considering the second issue, the appellate court concluded that Iran's national ownership law was not the type of public law that precluded recognition of the ownership rights that Iran's law created in British courts, thus distinguishing between the question of recognition and that of enforcement. In reaching this conclusion, the court relied in part on the U.S. precedent established in *U.S. v. Schultz,* which recognized Egypt's national ownership law as vesting an ownership interest in undiscovered antiquities in the nation.[38] Finally, the court further held that even if Iran's ownership law were a public law, there was no reason to view it as nonjusticiable on the grounds that Iran's claim is an attempt to enforce the public law of another nation in UK courts. Citing to international conventions to which the United Kingdom is a party, including the 1970 UNESCO Convention and the European Union's Council Directive 93/7 on the Return of Cultural Objects Unlawfully Removed from the Territory of a Member State, the court concluded that it is consistent with British public policy to recognize the ownership claim of a foreign nation to antiquities that are part of its cultural heritage. The decision in this case is highly significant for the legal regime that aims to protect the world's archaeological heritage and harmonizes the U.S. and UK judicial approaches to the status of national ownership of looted antiquities.

Practice Area Discussion

This section will consider different methods of implementation of the 1970 UNESCO Convention, particularly that of the United States where this has become a controversial issue. Most nations that have ratified the convention grant across-the-board recognition of other States Parties' export controls on cultural materials. This means that nations require an export license from the country of origin before permitting the importation of those cultural materials that are subject to export control.[39] In contrast, the United States and Switzerland require other States Parties to enter into an additional agreement that restricts the import of archaeological and ethnological materials.[40] The United Kingdom, at the time of its ratification, stated that its current system of import and export regulation was sufficient for implementing the Convention, but it later, at the end of 2003, enacted a statute that created a new criminal offense.[41]

The most complex method of implementation for the 1970 UNESCO Convention is that adopted by the United States under the Convention on Cultural Property Implementation Act (CPIA).[42] The CPIA establishes a mechanism by which other nations that are party to the 1970 UNESCO Convention may request that the United States impose import restrictions on designated categories of archaeological and ethnological materials that are subject to pillage pursuant to either a bilateral agreement or an emergency action. The statute mandates four requirements: that the nation's cultural patrimony is in jeopardy from pillage of archaeological or ethnological materials; that the nation has taken internal measures consistent with the UNESCO Convention to protect its cultural heritage; that other nations with a significant import trade in the same cultural materials are taking similar actions to control the trade; and that import restrictions are in the interest of encouraging international exchange of cultural materials for scientific, cultural, and educational purposes.[43] The criteria for an emergency action focus on whether a crisis exists with respect to a particular category of cultural remains.[44]

The Cultural Property Advisory Committee (CPAC) reviews a nation's request. CPAC has eleven members: Three represent the general public, three are experts in anthropology or archaeology, three are experts in the international sale of antiquities and ethnographic materials, and two represent the interests of museums. CPAC evaluates the request and makes recommendations as to whether the statutory criteria are satisfied. The recommendations are sent to a State Department official to whom is delegated the authority to make a decision as to whether the statutory criteria are satisfied for a bilateral agreement and/or an emergency action.

If the statutorily mandated determinations are found, then the United States may enter into a bilateral agreement (or Memorandum of Understanding) with the requesting nation that will restrict the import of the designated materials into the United States. Such agreements last for a maximum of five years but may be renewed an indefinite number of times. Emergency actions last for a maximum of five years and can be renewed only once for an additional three years. The import restrictions apply to designated categories of archaeological and/or ethnological materials. Such materials can still enter the United States if they left the country of origin before the effective date of the import restriction or if they are accompanied by an export license.

As previously discussed, the decision this past summer to include coins in the extension of the agreement with Cyprus has proven to be particularly controversial. The lobby of coin dealers and collectors has objected vociferously to this action because coins have never before been covered by an agreement under the CPIA. On November 15, 2007, the Ancient Coin Collectors Guild filed a Freedom of Information Act suit against the State Department, seeking the release of documents pertaining to its consideration of requests for agreements from Italy, China and Cyprus and of the inclusion of Cypriot coins.[45]

Market participants have frequently criticized the fact that CPAC holds closed meetings and that the transcripts and other documents, including CPAC's report to the decision maker, are kept confidential. However, these objections fail to note that the public sessions with opportunity for public comment both in writing and in person are not mandated by the statute and were added to the committee's procedures to accommodate a wider expression of public viewpoints. They also seem to exaggerate the role of CPAC, whose function is purely advisory, while the CPIA confers the actual decision-making function on the U.S. president, who has delegated it to a State Department official. While the outcome of the FOIA suit is still in the future, the question is whether the coin lobby is seeking only this information or whether it wishes ultimately to challenge the inclusion of coins in the U.S.-Cyprus agreement on substantive grounds. A clearer understanding of both the CPIA and CPAC's function is crucial for a proper evaluation of this action with respect to Cypriot coins and the other import restrictions[46] that the United States has imposed under the UNESCO Convention.

Notes

1. Transformation Act of 25 April 2007; Implementation Act of 18 April 2007. Matthias Weller, "Portable Antiquities: The German Legal System," paper presented at conference, "Portable Antiquities in the Modern European Context: Law, Ethics, Policy and Practice" University of Pecs, Pecs, Hungary, July12–13, 2007 (presentation on file with author).
2. See *infra* note 7 & accompanying text.
3. 823 U.N.T.S. 231, 10 I.L.M. 289 (1971).
4. Protected Objects Act 1975, as revised 2007, available at http://www.legislation.govt.nz/browse_vw.asp?content-set=pal_statutes. Full analysis of this legislation falls outside the scope of this article.
5. The definition of foreign protected object tracks the definition of cultural property used in the 1970 UNESCO and Unidroit Conventions. Part 1, section 2(1).
6. Part 1, section 10.
7. Implementation Act of 18 April 2007, *supra* note 1, section 6(2), sentences 1–3. This same legislation also replaces Germany's legislation implementing EC Directive 93/7/EEC. The Report of the EC Commission of 21 Dec. 2005 indicates that Germany has been involved in five returns of cultural objects through diplomatic channels; two cases are pending; there have been 12 applications for searches for cultural objects, and three court proceedings for return (two to Greece and one to France).
8. Available at http://www.kultur-schweiz.admin.ch/arkgt/files/kgtg2_e.pdf.
9. Swiss and Peruvian experts have presented a "red list" of Peru's cultural heritage that is particularly at risk from looting and illegal art traffickers, Nov. 14, 2007, available at: http://www.museum-security.org/wordpress/?p=68; Liste rouge des antiquités péruviennes en peril, available at http://www.news-service.admin.ch/NSBSubscriber/message/fr/15822.
10. *Id.*
11. 19 U.S.C. §§ 2601–2613.
12. For amendments to and extensions of the agreements, see, respectively: http://exchanges.state.gov/culprop/PeruMOU2007EXT.pdf; http://exchanges.state.gov/culprop/CyprusAmendExt2007FRN.pdf; http://exchanges.state.gov/culprop/Mali2007MoU.pdf; http://exchanges.state.gov/culprop/Gt07ExtFRN.pdf.
13. See Section IIID of the list of designated materials subject to import restriction.
14. Delegation of Authority, No. 296, Fed. Reg. Feb. 22, 2007, Vol. 72, No. 35, p. 8054.
15. Pub. L. 108-429, Title III, § 3002.
16. FBI Press Release, Nov. 8, 2007, FBI Recovers 15th Century Spanish Maps Stolen from Madrid, available at http://www.fbi.gov/pressrel/pressrel07/stolenmaps110807.htm.

17. Press Release, U.S. Returns Ancient Artifact Stolen from Cambodia, July 30, 2007, available at http://www.southeastasianarchaeology.com/2007/07/31/stolen-apsara-head-returned-to-cambodia/.
18. Alfonso Chardy, *Peru given recovered artifacts: The United States formally turned over to Peru 412 pre-Columbian archaeological artifacts recovered from a smuggler,* THE MIAMI HERALD, June 14, 2007.
19. Press Release, Department of Homeland Security returns rare artifacts to the Pakistani government: Stolen statues are from the third and fourth century A.D., available at http://www.ice.gov/pi/news/newsreleases/articles/070123newark.htm.
20. Robert Birsel, *Looted Pakistani artifacts seized in U.S. returned*, REUTERS, Mar. 8, 2007, available at http://in.news.yahoo.com/070308/137/6d13f.html.
21. Julia Hinde, *Invaluable resource or stolen property?* 1812 TIMES HIGHER ED. SUPP., Sept. 21, 207, at 18.
22. Available at http://www.culture.gov.uk/Reference_library/Publications/archive_2005/guidance_chr.htm; http://www.culture.gov.uk/NR/rdonlyres/0017476B-3B86-46F3-BAB3-11E5A5F7F0A1/0/GuidanceHumanRemains11Oct.pdf.
23. Joint Statement by the Government of Peru and Yale University, Sept. 14, 2007, available at http://www.yale.edu/opa/newsr/07-09-14-01.all.html.
24. Christopher Heaney, *Stealing from the Incas*, Op-Ed, N.Y. TIMES, Oct. 7, 2007.
25. Tribunals, Courts and Enforcement Act 2007, ch. 15, Part 6, Protection of Cultural Objects on Loan, ss. 134–38. *See also* Department of Culture, Media and Sport Consultation Paper on draft regulations for the publication by museums and galleries of information for the purposes of immunity from seizure, available at http://www.culture.gov.uk/Reference_library/Consultations/2007_current_consultations/draftregs_immunityfromseizure.htm.
26. Museums are expected to comply with the due diligence requirements spelled out in the DCMS Guidance, "Combating Illicit Trade: Due diligence guidelines for museums, libraries and archives on collecting and borrowing cultural materials," available at http://www.culture.gov.uk/Reference_library/Publications/archive_2005/illicit_trade.htm. According to this Guidance, museums should borrow items only if they are legally and ethically sound and should be particularly concerned about objects that are not documented before 1970 or that have a provenance gap between 1933 and 1945.
27. *Supra* note 25.
28. Michael Balter, *University Suppresses Report on Provenance of Iraqi Antiquities*, 318 SCIENCE 554–55 (Oct. 26, 2007).
29. The collection includes over 720 manuscripts and other types of ancient written documents. See http://www.schoyencollection.com.

30. Statutory Instrument 2003 No. 1519 was enacted in response to UNSCR 1483 and is available at http://www.hmso.gov.uk/si/si2003/20031519.htm. Section 8 prohibits the import or export of illegally removed Iraqi cultural property and created a criminal offense for "[a]ny person who holds or controls any item of illegally removed Iraqi cultural property . . . unless he proves that he did not know and had no reason to suppose that the item in question was illegally removed Iraqi cultural property."
31. Antiquities Law No. 59 of 1936, and the Two Amendments, No. 120 of 1974 and No. 164 of 1975. Article 3 states: "All antiquities in Iraq whether movable or immovable that are now on or under the surface of the soil shall be considered to be the common property of the State. No individuals or groups are allowed to dispose of such property or claim the ownership thereof except under the provisions of this Law."
32. Quoted in Balter, *supra* note 28, at 555.
33. Iraq asks Britain to return hundreds of missing artifacts, Azzaman, Nov. 8, 2007, available at http://www.azzaman.com/english/index.asp?fname=news%5C2007-11-8%5Ckurd.htm.
34. Press Release, Odyssey Marine Exploration Announces Third Quarter 2007 Results, Nov. 7, 2007, available at http://biz.yahoo.com/bw/071107/20071107006637.html?.v=1.
35. The claim involving the historic wreck Black Swan is *Odyssey Marine Exploration, Inc. v. The Unidentified Shipwrecked Vessel,* Case No. 8:2207cv00614 (M.D. Fla. 2007).
36. *Islamic Republic of Iran v. Berend*, [2007] EWHC 132 (QB), [2007] 2 All ER (Comm) 132.
37. *Republic of Iran v. Barakat Galleries Ltd.*, [2007] EWHC 705 (QB), TLQ/06/0601; *rev'd*, [2007] EWCA Civ. 1374.
38. *United States v. Schultz*, 333 F. 3d 393 (2d Cir. 2003).
39. In addition to the new legislation of New Zealand that follows this paradigm, see *supra* notes 4–6 & accompanying text; Canada and Australia are other examples of nations that have adopted this system.
40. See *supra* note 8 & accompanying text.
41. Dealing in Cultural Objects (Offences) Act 2203, ch. 27, available at http://www.opsi.gov.uk/acts/acts2003/20030027.htm. This statute creates a criminal offense for dealing in cultural objects that are "tainted"—that is, those that were removed from structures or sites in violation of local law.
42. 19 U.S.C. §§ 2601–13.
43. 19 U.S.C. § 2602(a)(1)(A)–(D). An exception to the third requirement allows the United States to enter into a bilateral agreement, even if another nation with a significant import trade is not engaging in similar actions, so long as the U.S. restrictions will be of substantial benefit in deterring the situation of pillage. 19 U.S.C. § 2602(c)(2).

44. 19 U.S.C. § 2603.
45. *Ancient Coin Collectors Guild et al. v. U.S. Dep't of State* (D.D.C. 2007); complaint available at http://www.accg.us/issues/news/complaint.pdf.
46. A chart of emergency actions and bilateral agreements is available at http://exchanges.state.gov/culprop/chart.html.

Enforcement Actions

Section Editor: David Tarler[1]

Introduction

This year's review of federal enforcement actions includes three second-time violators of the Archaeological Resources Protection Act (*Brady; Harelson;* and *Burroughs*). One case (*Brady*) marks the first time that an earlier criminal conviction for "violation" of ARPA has been used as the basis for doubling the amount of an ARPA civil penalty for a second "violation" of the Act.

In the district of Hawaii, the first defendants convicted of violating 18 U.S.C. § 1170 (b), one of the criminal provisions of the Native American Graves Protection and Repatriation Act, were sentenced in 2007 (*Carta and Taylor*). This case appears to mark the first time that anyone has been convicted of *obtaining* protected cultural items *in violation of NAGPRA* from nonfederal or nontribal land.

Two more sentences in the district of Oregon linked to "Operation Bring 'em Back" are reported this year (*Maxwell; Harelson*). Begun in 2000 to target the illegal excavation and trafficking in Native American human remains and cultural items, and archaeological resources, "Operation Bring 'em Back" has been a joint investigation involving law enforcement personnel and archaeologists from the Bureau of Land Management; U.S. Forest Service; Internal Revenue Service; Bureau of Alcohol, Tobacco, and Firearms; Oregon State Police Wildlife Division; and Central Oregon Drug Enforcement Team. The Operation has yielded the seizure of over 100,000 items; the recovery of two skulls of Native American children; the discovery of illegal excavation at over 100 cultural sites on public lands in Oregon managed by the Bureau of Land Management, Forest Service, and Fish and Wildlife Service; a determination of damages in excess of $1 million; and the execution of numerous search warrants. Several of the "Operation Bring 'em Back" defendants have been methamphetamine addicts and traffickers (search warrants yielded four meth labs). Six of them were convicted of drug trafficking in federal or state court.

The last two volumes of the *Yearbook* have, together, reported four federal prosecutions involving the theft of documents from libraries. In three of those cases, the statute of conviction was the Theft of Major Artwork statute (18 U.S.C. § 668), and in one case, the statute of conviction was the Archaeological Resources Protection Act (16 U.S.C. § 470ee (c)). One of those four cases involved thefts from the National Archives and Records Administration, in Washington, D.C. This year, another library theft case is reported (*McTague*). Again, the National Archives was the victim and the target was its Philadelphia branch. Altogether, since 2002, there have been four convictions for theft of documents from the National Archives. In three of the four cases, the defendants were caught only after they offered stolen Archives materials for sale on eBay and the items' provenance was recognized by members of the public. That the National Archives and Records Administration appeared not to have obtained commercial values for the stolen items for use at sentencing is vexing. This value, or loss, could possibly be *the* single most important specific offense characteristic used to determine the defendant's offense level and, thus, his or her sentence. If the court does not have an accurate commercial value—assuming that such a value is ascertainable—the resulting sentence cannot reflect the seriousness of the offense, and can neither adequately serve its deterrent and retributive purposes nor further the protection of cultural heritage.

A prosecution for the offense of misrepresentation of Indian-produced goods and products, in violation of the Indian Arts and Crafts Act (*Morris*), has had repercussions beyond the conviction and sentencing of the individual defendant. The cooperative, three-state investigation of the crime by the Federal Bureau of Investigation and the National Park Service resulted in the execution of a Memorandum of Understanding (MOU) between the FBI and the Department of the Interior regarding DOI assistance in the investigation of crimes involving the Indian Arts and Crafts Act. The MOU, which became effective on August 13, 2007, gives the Bureau of Indian Affairs, Bureau of

Land Management, Bureau of Reclamation, Fish and Wildlife Service, and National Park Service nationwide jurisdiction to investigate possible violations of the Act on a case-by-case basis, and complements the agencies' independent law enforcement jurisdiction on DOI-managed lands. In addition, the FBI and DOI bureaus will cooperate on these investigations by, among other things, sharing intelligence and investigative reports. Whether this MOU should serve as a template for future agreements regarding the investigation of other crimes against cultural heritage is a matter that the FBI and DOI might wish to address.

Finally, the nonimposition of a Guideline sentence, nonuse of all the Guideline-specific offense characteristics, or decision to charge a crime carrying a considerably lower maximum sentence all have resulted in some sentences that appear to be lower than otherwise would be indicated by strict use of U.S. Sentencing Guideline § 2B1.5 (*Kirk and Whitling; Morris; Marcillo-Aviles; Tulino*).2 A hard look at this phenomenon might be warranted.

The Archaeological Resources Protection Act

The Archaeological Resources Protection Act (ARPA; 16 U.S.C. §§ 470aa-mm) prescribes criminal punishment (at 16 U.S.C. § 470ee) for persons who:

(a) excavate, remove, damage, or otherwise alter or deface any archaeological resource located on public lands or Indian lands, or attempt to do so, without a permit (16 U.S.C. § 470ee (a));

(b) sell, purchase, exchange, transport, or receive, or offer to sell, purchase, or exchange any archaeological resource removed from public lands or Indian lands in violation of (a), or any provision, rule, regulation, ordinance, or permit in effect under any other provision of federal law (16 U.S.C. § 470ee (b));

(c) sell, purchase, exchange, transport, receive, or offer to sell, purchase, or exchange, in interstate or foreign commerce, any archaeological resource excavated, removed, sold, purchased, exchanged, transported, or received in violation of any provision, rule, regulation, ordinance, or permit in effect under state or local law (16 U.S.C. § 470ee (c)); or

(d) counsel, procure, solicit, or employ another to violate (a), (b), or (c) (16 U.S.C. § 470ee (d)).

An ARPA offense is a general intent crime. The government must prove that the defendant knowingly committed the offense conduct.[3]

ARPA also provides for the assessment of civil penalties for violations on public lands and Indian lands (16 U.S.C. § 470ff). In the case of a second or subsequent violation of ARPA, the amount of a civil penalty may be double the amount that would have been assessed if such violation were the first violation (16 U.S.C. § 470ff (a); 43 C.F.R. § 7.16 (a)(2); 36 C.F.R. § 296.16 (a)(2); 32 C.F.R. § 229.16 (a)(2); and 18 C.F.R. § 1312.16 (a)(2)). Intent is not an element of a civil violation of ARPA.[4]

United States v. Mark Anthony Brady[5]

Mark Anthony Brady was ordered by the U.S. district court to pay an ARPA civil penalty assessed by the Bureau of Indian Affairs in the amount of $24,204, which was double the amount that could have been assessed if his ARPA violation were a first violation. The U.S. Attorney filed a civil action to enforce and collect the penalty (pursuant to 31 U.S.C. § 3711) after Brady forfeited his right to contest the assessment administratively and judicially.[6]

Brady and Stephen Owens were apprehended in the act of excavating archaeological resources belonging to a precontact period village site known as the CK Canyon Site, which is located on the San Carlos Apache Indian Reservation. A damage assessment determined that the cost of restoration and repair of the archaeological resources involved in the violation conduct was $12,102, but the BIA assessed Brady an ARPA civil penalty for double that amount, based on the agency's determination that the prohibited act he committed on the San Carlos Apache Indian Reservation was his second violation of ARPA. (An action against Stephen Owens for destruction of tribal property was brought by the San Carlos Apache Indian Tribe in tribal court, and the BIA is considering whether to assess him an ARPA civil penalty.)

Brady was one of the first defendants convicted under ARPA. On November 3, 1979, three days after ARPA became law, he and three others were apprehended at an archaeological site in the Clifton Ranger District of Apache-Sitgreaves National Forest, in Arizona. Damages caused by the four defendants to the archaeological resources were determined to be $38,479. Brady pled guilty to one felony count of excavating, removing, and injuring archaeological resources in violation of ARPA (16 U.S.C. § 470ee (a)) and one felony count of injuring government property in violation of 18 U.S.C. § 1361. He was sentenced, in 1980, to six months' imprisonment, but the sentence was suspended and, instead, he received 36 months of probation. In 1981, the United States attempted to collect from the four defendants, jointly and severally, the $38,479 in damages pursuant to the Debt Collection Improvement Act of 1966 (31 U.S.C. § 3711), but in 1982, the debt was declared uncollectible by the Department of Justice.

In assessing Brady an ARPA civil penalty double the amount that could have been assessed if his ARPA violation were a first violation, the BIA determined that a prior *criminal conviction* under the ARPA statute constitutes a "violation" for purposes of doubling the amount of a *civil penalty* if the person in question subsequently commits an act prohibited by the ARPA regulations. As the validity and amount of the penalty are not subject to review in a civil action to collect an ARPA civil penalty (16 U.S.C. § 470ff (b)(2)), the U.S. district court did not directly address the BIA's calculation of Brady's civil penalty. Nevertheless, the fact that a prior ARPA criminal conviction has subjected a subsequent ARPA violator to double the otherwise maximum civil penalty amount begs the question of whether or not a prior ARPA *civil* "violation" subjects a subsequent ARPA offender to the enhanced *criminal penalties* provided by the law for a second or subsequent "violation" (16 U.S.C. § 470ee (d)).[7]

United States v. Vincent E. Williams, Fenton E. Terembes, Jr. & Jeremy L. Burroughs[8]

Vincent Williams pled guilty to one misdemeanor count of violation of ARPA (16 U.S.C. § 470ee (a)) and Fenton Terembes, Jr. and Jeremy L. Burroughs each pled guilty to one felony count of violation of ARPA (16 U.S.C. § 470ee (a)). Williams was sentenced to 12 months of probation and ordered to pay restitution to Fredericksburg & Spotsylvania National Military Park in the amount of $1,471. Terembes was sentenced to 24 months' imprisonment followed by 12 months of supervised release. Burroughs was sentenced to 18 months' imprisonment followed by 36 months of supervised release. Terembes and Burroughs also were ordered, jointly and severally, to pay restitution to Fredericksburg & Spotsylvania National Military Park in the amount of $57,265. In addition, the three defendants forfeited their equipment and the approximately 200 artifacts they removed from the park, including a Confederate belt buckle that Terembes had removed from Spotsylvania Battlefield and sold for $3,300, and which the Park subsequently recovered.

Using metal detectors, the three defendants excavated more than 460 holes atop or around the Civil War earthworks on the Spotsylvania Battlefield at Fredericksburg & Spotsylvania National Military Park, in Virginia. The 8,000-acre park commemorates the Civil War Battle of Fredericksburg, the Chancellorsville Campaign (encompassing the battles of Chancellorsville, Second Fredericksburg, and Salem Church), the Battle of the Wilderness, and the Battle of Spotsylvania Court House.

Burroughs now has two felony convictions for violation of ARPA. His first conviction was in 1998. Along with another person, he was apprehended, again on Spotsylvania Battlefield, while in possession of metal detectors, digging equipment, and archaeological artifacts; an investigation tied the two suspects to 34 holes. Burroughs and the other defendant each pled guilty to one felony count of violation of ARPA (16 U.S.C. § 470ee (a)). Each was sentenced to 24 months of supervised probation and ordered to pay restitution to Fredericksburg & Spotsylvania National Military Park in the amount of $1,374.

United States v. Felix Sidney Maxwell and Randy Dean Wools[9]

Felix Sidney Maxwell and Randy Dean Wools each pled guilty to one felony count of conspiracy to violate the Archaeological Resources Protection Act (18 U.S.C. § 371; 16 U.S.C. § 470ee(a)) and one misdemeanor count of theft of government property (18 U.S.C. § 641). Wools was sentenced to six months of imprisonment followed by 36 months of supervised release, and ordered to pay restitution to the Bureau of Land Management in the amount of $20,000. During his term of supervised probation, Wools was banned from entering federal lands. Maxwell was sentenced to 60 months of probation, including eight months of electronically monitored home detention, and ordered to pay restitution to the Bureau of Land Management, in Oregon, in the amount of $25,961. In addition, during the period of his probation, Maxwell has been banned from entering any property managed by the Bureau of Land Management, U.S. Forest Service, National Park Service, Bureau of Indian Affairs, or U.S. Fish and Wildlife Service.

Maxwell and Wools excavated, injured, and removed archaeological resources from public lands managed by the Bureau of Land Management, U.S. Forest Service, National Park Service, Bureau of Indian Affairs, and U.S. Fish and Wildlife Service. Their 18 U.S.C. § 641 convictions stem from the theft of a historic canoe from the Paisley Ranger Station, in Fremont National Forest, in January 2005.

Maxwell and Wools are two of the defendants convicted as part of "Operation Bring 'em Back," an investigation begun in 2000 to target the illegal excavation and trafficking in Native American human remains and cultural items and archaeological resources.

United States v. James E. Burton[10]

James E. Burton pled guilty to one felony count of violation of ARPA (16 U.S.C. § 470ee (a)) and one felony count of injuring government property in violation of 18 U.S.C. § 1361. He was sentenced to 24 months of supervised release, including 180 days of home confinement, and ordered to pay a fine in the amount of $2,000 and restitution to Ashley National Forest in the amount of $12,382. Burton also was ordered to forfeit his interest in the 2004 Honda ATV he used to commit the offenses. Burton excavated, removed, and injured precontact era archaeological resources at Red Hand Rock Shelter and East Fork Rock Shelter in the Flaming Gorge District of the Ashley National Forest, in Utah.

United States v. Bryan Keith Gary, Kristi L. Hendricks, and Tina Todd[11]

Bryan Keith Gary and Kristi L. Hendricks each pled guilty to one felony count of violation of ARPA (16 U.S.C. § 4700ee (a)). Gary was sentenced to 24 months' imprisonment and Hendricks was sentenced to 12 months and one day of imprisonment. In addition, Gary and Hendricks each were ordered to pay restitution to the Francis Marion and Sumter National Forests in the amount of $800. Tina Todd was approved for entry into the pretrial diversion program. As a result, her trial has been continued until the July 2008 term of the court.

Gary, Hendricks, and Todd excavated, disturbed, and removed archaeological resources from a site located in the Long Cane Ranger District of the Sumter National Forest, in South Carolina, which had been occupied during the Early Archaic, Middle Archaic, Late Archaic, Early Woodland, and Mississippian cultural periods. A site damage assessment found that approximately 93 square yards of the site were disturbed to a depth of up to 12 inches. The cost of restoration and repair of the site was determined to be $19,985 and the archaeological value of the archaeological resources involved in the offense conduct was calculated to be $49,632.

United States v. Jonathan Keith Carroll and Christopher William Pelchat[12]

Jonathan Keith Carroll and Christopher William Pelchat each pled guilty to one misdemeanor violation of ARPA (16 U.S.C. § 470ee (a)). Each defendant was sentenced to 12 months of supervised probation and 25 hours of community service at Chesapeake & Ohio Canal National Historical Park, in Maryland, and ordered to pay restitution to the Park in the amount of $2,569, forfeit their metal detectors and digging tools, and write a letter of apology to the National Park Service. In addition, the defendants were banned from entering any National Park for two years (except to perform their community service) and were banned from possessing tools of excavation on National Park Service property for life.

Pelchat and Carroll excavated the grave of Mary Blackwell Ohr, whose husband, Dr. Charles H. Ohr, was a mayor of Cumberland, Maryland and a Maryland state senator. Mary Ohr died in 1875 and is buried in the Brent/Blackwell/Widmeyer family cemetery, in Hancock and within the present-day park. Her grave is marked with a large, elaborate headstone and is surrounded by a three-foot tall wrought iron fence. The defendants dug a hole five feet deep, and through Ohr's casket and remains, in search of jewelry that they believed might be buried with her. In addition, using metal detectors, Pelchat and Jonathan Carroll, together with Carroll's father, James A. Carroll, dug approximately 25 to 30 holes in the area of the adjacent historic homestead of the Brent/Blackwell/Widmeyer families, which dates back to 1779.[13] A citizen who provided information that led to the arrest and prosecution of the three men subsequently received a $1,000 reward from the National Park Service.

U.S. v. Joseph M. Mercurio, Tonya C. Mercurio, Daniel M. Fisher, and Thomas J. Luecke[14]

Joseph M. Mercurio, Daniel M. Fisher, and Thomas J. Luecke each pled guilty to one felony count of violation of ARPA (16 U.S.C. § 470ee (a)), and Tonya C. Mercurio pled guilty to one misdemeanor count of violation of ARPA (16 U.S.C. § 470ee (a)). All four defendants were sentenced to 24 months of probation. Joseph Mercurio's sentence included four months of home detention and Fisher and Luecke's sentences included six months of home detention.

In December 2005, under cover of darkness and with the aid of a tent and a heater, the defendants traveled from Ohio to Kentucky and, using digging equipment and rakes, excavated, injured, and removed archaeological resources belonging to a documented Early Woodland cultural period site located on an old flood plain of Barren River Lake, which is today an island managed by the U.S. Army Corps of Engineers. Following a tip by a Lake neighbor, the defendants were observed digging at the site and apprehended. In their possession were found archaeological artifacts and the bone of a child aged 11 or younger. The cost of restoration and repair of the site was determined to be $30,102 and the archaeological value of the archaeological resources involved in the defendants' offense conduct was calculated to be $42,915.

United States v. Richard C. Kirk and David A. Whitling[15]

Richard C. Kirk pled guilty to one felony count of violation of ARPA (16 U.S.C. § 470ee (a)) and David A. Whitling pled guilty to one misdemeanor count of violation of ARPA (16 U.S.C. § 470ee (a)). Kirk was sentenced to 24 months of supervised probation, including six months of home detention. Whitling was sentenced to 24 months of supervised probation. Both defendants also were ordered to participate in a program for treatment of narcotic addiction or drug or alcohol dependency.

In February 2006, Kirk and Whitling traveled from Ohio to Kentucky and, under cover of darkness, used digging equipment and a rake to excavate, injure, and remove archaeological resources belonging to the same Early Woodland cultural period site at Barren River Lake that had been looted, in December 2005, by Joseph M. Mercurio, Tonya C. Mercurio, Daniel M. Fisher, and Thomas J. Luecke (see above).[16] Following a tip by a Lake neighbor, the two were apprehended as they were leaving the site by boat. In their possession were found archaeological artifacts.

The cost of restoration and repair of the site was determined to be $11,580 and the archaeological value of the archaeological resources involved in the defendants' offense conduct was calculated to be $58,721. Despite the defendants' admissions that they had looted the same site on previous occasions, the sentencing judge rejected the Government's argument that Kirk and Whitling's offense levels should be increased by two levels for their engaging in a pattern of misconduct involving cultural heritage resources.[17]

United States v. Jack Lee Harelson[18]

Following a stipulated facts trial, Jack Lee Harelson was found guilty of one felony count of counseling, procuring, soliciting, and employing another person to offer for sale, via the Internet and by other means, archaeological resources that had been, and were to be, excavated and removed from public lands, in violation of ARPA (16 U.S.C. §§ 470ee (d), (a) & (b)). Harelson was sentenced to 18 months' imprisonment, to be served in the custody of the Oregon Department of Corrections concurrent with Harelson's term of imprisonment for his conviction in Jackson County (Oregon) case No. 041053FE, followed by 12 months of supervised release.

Jack Lee Harelson recruited Brian Doland to excavate and remove archaeological resources from public lands in Oregon and from Elephant Mountain Cave, a rock shelter located in Nevada's Black Rock Desert and managed by the Bureau of Land Management. Harelson had been excavating Elephant Mountain Cave, perhaps one of the most important archaeological cave sites in the Great Basin, since 1980. Harelson also recruited Doland to offer for sale, via the Internet and by other means, those archaeological resources that were to be removed from public lands under this scheme, as well as additional archaeological resources that Harelson already had removed from public lands, including Elephant Mountain Cave. Unbeknown to Harelson, Brian Doland was acting as a paid government informant.

In 1996, Harelson was convicted by a jury in the Josephine County Circuit Court, under Oregon law, for first degree theft and tampering with physical evidence in connection with his looting of Elephant Mountain Cave. He was sentenced to 30 days in jail and ordered to pay a fine in the amount of $20,000. Harelson and his then-wife had removed numerous artifacts from Elephant Mountain Cave—they included a pair of 10,000-year-old sandals—as well as two baskets from the Archaic cultural period, each containing the 2,000-year-old mummified body of a child (a boy and a girl). After removing the bodies and assorted artifacts—such as woven nets for catching rabbits, obsidian blades, and deer-hoof rattles—from the baskets, Harelson placed the bodies in plastic garbage bags and buried them in his back yard, while keeping the baskets, the artifacts, and the children's skulls.[19] On these facts, the Bureau of Land Management assessed Harelson an ARPA civil penalty in the amount of $2,525,316, in 2002.[20]

Harelson always claimed he had buried the children's skulls together with their bodies, and did not know the whereabouts of the skulls—they were missing when the bodies were exhumed—when, in fact, he himself transferred the skulls to Doland (the paid government informant) in 2002. The Pyramid Lake Paiute Tribe asserts that the tribe is culturally affiliated with the disinterred human remains from Elephant Mountain Cave.

In 2005, a Jackson County (Oregon) jury found Harelson guilty of trying to hire a hit man to kill Harelson's former partner in an opal mining venture because the partner assisted the State in Harelson's archaeological looting conviction.[21] According to tape recordings, an informant told Harelson he knew a hit man, and Harelson offered to pay the hit man to do the job. After being shown a photograph of the corpse of his ex-partner, Harelson paid for the murder in opals worth $10,000. In fact, the informant was Brian Doland, the hit man was an undercover law enforcement agent, and the photograph of the murder victim had been staged. Harelson was sentenced to ten years' imprisonment, and it is with this term of imprisonment that Harelson was ordered to concurrently serve his sentence for violation of ARPA.

As Harelson was sentenced to 18 months' imprisonment, the judge did not address the issue of whether or not Harelson's prior ARPA *civil* "violation" subjected him to the enhanced *criminal penalties* provided by the law for his second "violation" (16 U.S.C. § 470ee (d)). The U.S. Attorney for the District of Oregon did not do so, either.

Harelson is one of the defendants convicted as part of "Operation Bring 'em Back," an investigation begun in 2000 to target the illegal excavation and trafficking in Native American human remains and cultural items, and archaeological resources.

United States v. Douglas L. Turner[22]

Douglas L. Turner pled guilty to one misdemeanor count of violation of ARPA (16 U.S.C. § 470ee (a)). He was sentenced to twelve months of probation and 80 hours of community service at the Yakima Training Center and ordered to pay a fine in the amount of $1,000. Also, during his twelve-month period of probation, Turner was banned from entering the Yakima Training Center (except to perform his community service).

Turner excavated and removed archaeological resources from the Yakima Training Center, in Washington, after he and three other persons entered the Center pursuant to an Outdoor Recreation Orientation Permit. The Yakima Training Center is public land managed by the Department of Defense (Army). The permit stipulated that under no circumstances were archaeological or Native American cultural sites to be disturbed, and warned that such disturbances, along with the removal of artifacts, were punishable under federal law. After the four had entered the Center, the Grant County Public Utility District Cultural Resources Specialist and another PUD employee observed them walking around the shoreline of the Columbia River, near Hanson Creek, in disregard of a sign reading "U.S. Army Military Reservation No Trespassing." Turner appeared to be picking up items from the ground and putting them in his pocket. After speaking with Turner, the PUD employees called the Yakima Training Center Police who, in turn, contacted the Washington Department of Fish and Wildlife. On being questioned, all four members of the group denied picking up artifacts, but subsequently, Turner admitted that he had been searching for, and had removed, artifacts and that he knew his actions were unlawful. A search of his vehicle yielded 35 stone artifacts.

The Antiquities Act of 1906

In the late nineteenth century, with the cessation of wars between the United States and Indian tribes and the opening of vast territories through the expansion of the railroads, pristine archaeological sites in the West became accessible, and vulnerable, to anyone with a curiosity for the past. Sensing that the cultural heritage was becoming endangered, Congress passed the Antiquities Act in 1906 (16 U.S.C. §§ 431-433). The Antiquities Act required the Executive Branch to institute a permitting scheme "for the examination of ruins, the excavation of archaeological sites, and the gathering of objects of antiquity" on lands under federal jurisdiction (16 U.S.C. § 432). The Act also gave the President of the United States the discretionary authority "to declare by public proclamation historic landmarks, historic and prehistoric structures, and other objects of historic or scientific interest that are situated upon the lands owned or controlled by the Government of the United States to be national monuments" (16 U.S.C. § 431). Lastly, the Antiquities Act prescribed criminal punishment for persons who "appropriate, excavate, injure or destroy any historic or prehistoric ruin or monument, or any object of antiquity, situated on lands owned or controlled by the Government of the United States, without the permission of the Secretary of the Department of the Government having jurisdiction over the lands on which said antiquities are situated" (16 U.S.C. § 433).[23]

A criminal violation of the Antiquities Act is a Class B misdemeanor. Thus, the U.S. Sentencing Guidelines do not apply to any count of conviction under the Act, and a court may impose any sentence authorized by the Act (United States Sentencing Commission, *Guidelines Manual*, § 1B1.9). The maximum sentence authorized by the Antiquities Act is incarceration of up to 90 days and a fine of $5,000 for an individual or $10,000 for an organization (per the Criminal Fine Improvements Act of 1987, 18 U.S.C. § 3571 (b)(6) (individuals) & § 3571 (c)(6) (organizations); 18 U.S.C. § 3559 (a)(7)).

A split of authority exists among the circuits on whether or not the criminal enforcement section of the Antiquities Act is unconstitutionally vague in violation of the due process clause of the Constitution. In *U.S. v. Diaz,*[24] the trial judge admitted the testimony of a witness qualified as an expert, who offered an opinion on the meaning of "object of antiquity," a legal term that was left undefined in the Act. The witness testified that the term has reference not only to the age of an object but also to the use for which the object was made and to which it was put, and that, consequently, three- or four-year-old face masks removed from a medicine man's cave on the San Carlos

Indian Reservation were objects of antiquity. As a consequence of the opinion testimony, Diaz was convicted of violation of the Antiquities Act. On appeal of the conviction,[25] rather than hold that the trial court judge had committed reversible error in admitting opinion testimony on the meaning of a legal term, which is a matter of law for the judge to decide, the United States Court of Appeals for the Ninth Circuit held that the criminal enforcement provision of the Antiquities Act, by use of undefined terms of uncommon usage, was fatally vague in violation of the due process clause of the Constitution. By contrast, in *U.S. v. Smyer*,[26] the United States Court of Appeals for the Tenth Circuit upheld the convictions of the defendants under the Antiquities Act for looting 800–900-year-old archaeological resources belonging to the Mimbres culture from the Gila National Forest. Disagreeing with the Ninth Circuit's holding that the term "object of antiquity" was unconstitutionally vague, the Tenth Circuit judges relied on Webster's International Dictionary to determine that the legal term meant "times long since past" and to hold that, when measured by common understanding and practice, the challenged language conveys a sufficiently definite warning as to the proscribed conduct.

United States v. Anthony Joseph Tulino[27]

Anthony Joseph Tulino pled guilty to one count of violation of the Antiquities Act (16 U.S.C. § 433). He was sentenced to 24 months of probation and 50 hours of community service and ordered to a pay a fine in the amount of $500. In 1990, Tulino removed from a display case at the Old Orchard Museum at Sagamore Hill National Historic Site the .38 Model 1892 Colt double-action, six-shot revolver believed to have been carried by Lieutenant Colonel (and later, President) Theodore Roosevelt at the charge up San Juan Hill, during the Spanish-American War. In 2006, following a tip from a friend of Tulino, the FBI recovered the revolver.

An inscription on the revolver reads "July 1st, 1898, San Juan, Carried and Used by Colonel Theodore Roosevelt, From the Sunken Battle Ship Maine." The gun was contained in the armory of the battleship *U.S.S. Maine* when the ship sank in Havana Harbor on February 15, 1898. During the salvage of the ship, it was recovered by a relative of Theodore Roosevelt, who gave it to him. Its value has been estimated to be between $250,000 and $500,000.

Sagamore Hill National Historic Site, in Oyster Bay, New York, was the home of Theodore Roosevelt from 1885 until his death in 1919. It is owned by the United States and managed by the National Park Service. The revolver also is owned by the National Park Service.

As the statute of conviction is a Class B misdemeanor, the sentencing judge did not apply the U.S. Sentencing Guidelines. Had the defendant been charged under the theft and embezzlement of Government property statute (18 U.S.C. 641), he *would* have been sentenced under U.S. Sentencing Guideline § 2B1.5. Assuming Tulino had a Category I criminal history, his offense level would have been at least 19, which carries a sentence of 30–37 months' imprisonment.[28]

Misrepresentation of Indian Produced Goods and Products

The offense of Misrepresentation of Indian Produced Goods and Products (18 U.S.C. § 1159, also known as the Indian Arts and Crafts Act) is the act of offering or displaying for sale, or selling, any good in a manner that falsely suggests it is Indian-produced, an Indian product, or the product of a particular Indian or Indian tribe or Indian arts and crafts organization that is resident within the United States. The term "Indian tribe" includes both federally and state-recognized Indian groups. Misrepresentation of Indian Produced Goods and Products is a general intent crime. A first violation is a Class E felony and a second or subsequent violation is a Class C felony.

United States v. Rose Morris[29]

Rose Morris pled guilty to two counts of violation of misrepresentation of Indian produced goods and products. The first count, representing a first violation, was a Class E felony and the second count, representing a second violation, was a Class C felony. The defendant was sentenced to 60 months of probation, during which she is prohibited from incurring new credit charges, opening additional lines of credit, or negotiating or consummating any financial contracts without prior approval from the probation officer. Also, she must give the probation officer access to any requested financial information and personal income tax returns, authorize the release of credit information, and provide other business financial information in which Morris has a control or interest. In addition, Morris was ordered to pay restitution totaling $49,590 to the individual victims of her offense. The U.S. Attorney argued to the judge that he should follow the U.S. Sentencing Guidelines and sentence Morris to 24 months' imprisonment, but the judge demurred.

Morris admitted to selling as many as 500 rugs to buyers in the Four Corners area of New Mexico, Arizona, and Colorado which she claimed were

Navajo-made when, in fact, they were not. The rugs were discovered to be non-Navajo—mostly fakes from Mexico and India—when some buyers sought appraisals of their rugs for insurance purposes. The victims contacted the FBI, which, together with National Park Service investigators, launched an investigation that included several controlled "buys" from Morris. Those purchases were determined to be fakes by an expert at the Museum of Indian Arts and Culture, in Santa Fe.

In 2006, the New Mexico legislature appropriated $70,000 for the State to study and propose rules to establish a certification stamp for arts and crafts made by Indians in New Mexico. That appropriation was vetoed by Governor Richardson.

Illegal Trafficking in Native American Human Remains and Cultural Items

The Native American Graves Protection and Repatriation Act (NAGPRA) includes a criminal enforcement section (Pub. L. No. 101-601, § 4, 80 Stat. 3048, 3052 (1990)). Codified at 18 U.S.C. §1170, the law contains two subsections. One subsection (18 U.S.C. § 1170 (a)) criminalizes the knowing sale, purchase, use for profit, or transportation for sale or profit of the human remains of a "Native American" (per the definition at 25 U.S.C. § 3001 (9)) without the "right of possession" (per 25 U.S.C. § 3001 (13)). The other subsection (18 U.S.C. § 1170 (b)) criminalizes the knowing sale, purchase, use for profit, or transportation for sale or profit of other NAGPRA-defined "cultural items" (per 25 U.S.C. §§ 3001 (3) (A), (B) & (C)) obtained in violation of NAGPRA. Regardless of value or loss, a first violation is a misdemeanor and a second or subsequent violation is a felony. Illegal trafficking in Native American human remains and cultural items is a general intent crime.

United States v. John Andrew Carta and Daniel Warren Taylor[30]

John Andrew Carta and Daniel Warren Taylor each pled guilty to one misdemeanor count of conspiracy to sell, use for profit, and transport for sale and profit Native American cultural items obtained in violation of the criminal provisions of NAGPRA (18 U.S.C. § 371; 18 U.S.C. § 1170 (b)). Carta was sentenced to 12 months' imprisonment followed by 12 months of supervised release, but died on February 27, 2007, prior to the date on which he was to report to prison (April 2, 2007). Taylor was sentenced to 11 months' imprisonment.

Carta and Taylor removed 158 moepu, or Native Hawaiian funerary objects (as defined by NAGPRA, 25 U.S.C. § 3001 (3)), from Kanupa Cave, a burial cave for lesser Hawaiian chiefs and part of a network of lava-tube caves in South Kohala, on the island of Hawaii. Some of the objects had originally been interred in Kanupa Cave, but were removed by collector Joseph S. Emerson, in 1858, and later sold to the Bernice Pauahi Bishop Museum, in Honolulu, and the Peabody Essex Museum, in Salem, Massachusetts. Pursuant to NAGPRA, the museums repatriated the ex-Emerson Collection items and additional funerary objects to several Native Hawaiian organizations, and the items were reburied in Kanupa Cave, in 2003. Some of the Native Hawaiian cultural items removed by Carta and Taylor still bore labels indicating that they belonged to the Emerson Collection.

Taylor sold two of the items from Kanupa Cave, a piece of kapa (bark cloth) for $150 and a fisherman's bowl and cover for $2,083. He also offered items for sale by advertising them on the Internet and approaching private collectors. These items included a lei niho palaoa (a whale-tooth pendant hanging from a human-hair necklace) for $40,000, and a kupee (a bracelet) for $5,600. At least one collector who recognized the provenance of the items contacted federal authorities, triggering an investigation by the Office of the Inspector General of the U.S. Department of the Interior, who was assisted, at the outset, by the Hawaii Attorney General's Office and the Hawaii Department of Land and Natural Resources.

When first approached, Taylor only admitted to having possession of the items he was asked about, not all of them. Subsequently, though, he allegedly helped investigators locate Carta, and wore a wiretapping device to help gain evidence against his co-defendant. All of the items removed from Kanupa Cave were recovered except for the piece of kapa.

This case represents the first prosecution in the district of Hawaii for violation of the criminal provisions of NAGPRA. As the defendants pled guilty and did not reserve any issues for appeal, no judicial opinion was issued. Nevertheless, the legal premise for the violation of 18 U.S.C. § 1170 (b) might be interesting to contemplate. Prior to this case, every violation of 18 U.S.C. § 1170 (b) had clearly occurred on "Federal lands" (as defined by 25 U.S.C. § 3001 (5)) or "tribal land" (as defined by 25 U.S.C. § 3001 (15)). In those cases, the legal premise was that the defendants did not belong to the class of possible owners of Native American cultural items excavated or discovered on federal or tribal land after November 16, 1990, as provided by Section 3 of NAGPRA (25 U.S.C. § 3002 (a)) and, thus, they had *obtained* the cultural items in question *in violation of NAGPRA*. By contrast, Kanupa Cave is on land owned by the State of Hawaii, and *unless* the cave, in fact, is administered for the benefit of Native Hawaiians pursuant to the requirements of NAGPRA (25 U.S.C. § 3001 (15)(C)), then the offense did not occur on "tribal land." In that event, some legal reasoning other than violation of the ownership provisions in Section 3 of NAGPRA would be required in order to prove that, when the defendants took Native Hawaiian cultural items from *state land*, they obtained them in violation of NAGPRA.

Smuggling Goods into the United States

There are four ways in which the crime of smuggling might be committed, in violation of 18 U.S.C. § 545. The first way is by clandestinely introducing, or attempting to introduce, into the United States merchandise that should have been invoiced, with the intent to defraud the United States. The second way is by passing, or attempting to pass, a false, forged, or fraudulent invoice through Customs, with the intent to defraud the United States. The third way is by importing into the United States merchandise, knowing that the importation is contrary to law. The fourth way is by receiving, concealing, buying, selling, or facilitating the transportation, concealment, or sale of merchandise, knowing that the merchandise was imported contrary to law. Proof of a defendant's possession of such merchandise creates a rebuttable presumption of the defendant's guilt.

A violation of the smuggling statute is a Class E felony (18 U.S.C. § 3559), and carries a maximum term of imprisonment of five years. Upon conviction, an individual may be fined up to $250,000 and an organization may be fined up to $500,000 (18 U.S.C § 3571).

United States v. Cecilia Marcillo-Aviles[31]

Cecilia Marcillo-Aviles, also known as Ana Cecilia Marcillo Muirragui, pled guilty to one count of knowingly importing and bringing into the United States nine pre-Columbian artifacts contrary to law, in violation of 18 U.S.C. § 545. She was sentenced to time served, and ordered to pay a fine in the amount of $500. Also, she was ordered to forfeit the nine pre-Columbian artifacts seized from her and listed in the criminal information, and 156 additional artifacts seized from her.

The defendant, together with her daughter, Susan Aviles, and Edgar Nakache, solicited buyers for approximately 600 pre-Columbian artifacts from Ecuador by, among other things, contacting the International Council of Museums, in Paris. ICOM, in turn, contacted France's National Central Bureau of Interpol, which contacted the Ecuadoran National Police, which contacted the FBI's Legat office in Santiago, Chile (whose jurisdiction includes Ecuador), which contacted the FBI's Miami Division, which, through the FBI Art Crime Team, conducted an undercover investigation of the matter.

An undercover agent contacted Nakache, who represented that he was a broker for the artifacts, that the owner was an Ecuadoran woman, that some of the collection was located in Miami, and that he was offering the collection for sale for $2.5 million. Through information contained on a website provided by Nakache, law enforcement agents identified Cecilia Marcillo-Aviles as the possible proprietor of the artifacts. Subsequently, the agents met with the defendant, Nakache, and Susan Aviles at Aviles's Miami home, where they viewed several artifacts. The defendant stated that her husband had collected the artifacts being offered for sale over a 40-year period, that the rest of the artifacts were at her house in Ecuador, and that, through connections at the airport in Ecuador, she could bring the rest of the collection into the United States without a problem. Also, both the defendant and Nakache admitted they knew that selling the artifacts was illegal.[32] At a subsequent meeting, also at the Aviles residence, an academic expert joined the law enforcement agents and, together, they examined 13 artifacts, which the expert deemed to be authentic. During this meeting, Aviles, too, admitted she knew that selling the artifacts was illegal. During yet a later meeting, at two Miami storage units, the undercover agent viewed additional artifacts.

During the undercover operation, Nakache raised the asking price for the entire collection to $5 million. At some point, the undercover agent and Nakache agreed that, initially, the agent would purchase 150 artifacts for $2 million. The agent would receive the artifacts at the Aviles residence and, in return, would transfer the money to the defendant's bank account. On the day of the buy, the undercover agent joined the defendant, Aviles, and Nakache as they loaded the artifacts from the storage units and transported them to the Aviles residence. Upon receiving the undercover agent's signal that the artifacts were in the residence, law enforcement agents entered the residence, where they found 165 pre-Columbian artifacts.

After being read his Miranda rights, Nakache confessed to knowing that selling the artifacts was illegal, and further stated that Aviles told him that removing the artifacts from Ecuador and selling them was against the law. He also stated that the defendant had smuggled the majority of the artifacts into the U.S. both on a private jet and a commercial airliner.

Initially, the U.S. Attorney charged all three suspects. Later, the charges against Nakache and Aviles were dismissed.[33]

Marcillo-Aviles's sentence of "time served" amounted to six months. The disparity between this sentence and her sentence under U.S. Sentencing Guideline 2B1.5 is vexing. Assuming Marcillo-Aviles had a Category I criminal history, her offense level would have been at least 23, which carries a sentence of 46–57 months imprisonment.[34]

Theft and Embezzlement of Government Property

The first paragraph of 18 U.S.C. § 641 creates the crime of theft of Government property, which is the unlawful taking of "a thing of value of the United States." The second paragraph of the statute concerns the unlawful possession of that property after it has been stolen.

In order to prove theft of Government property, the Government must prove that, at the time of the alleged unlawful act, the United States owned, or had possession of and control over, the property in question; that the defendant stole that property; and that the defendant intended to deprive the Government of the use and benefit of that property.[35] The law provides for both a felony and a misdemeanor offense, depending on the value of the property stolen, with the dividing line between a misdemeanor and a felony offense being $1,000. Thus, in order to prove felony theft of Government property, the Government also must prove that the value of the property in question was greater than $1,000. "Value" is defined in the statute. It means "face, par, or market value, or cost price, either wholesale or retail, whichever is greater" (18 U.S.C. § 641).

United States v. Michael J. Barstad[36]

Michael J. Barstad pled guilty to one misdemeanor count of theft of Government property. He was sentenced to six months' imprisonment and ordered to pay a fine in the amount of $1,000 and restitution to Apostle Islands National Lakeshore in the amount of $101.

Barstad ripped down a plexiglass display case in the visitor center at Apostle Islands National Lakeshore, in Wisconsin, and stole a pair of brass binoculars used in the Civil War. The barrels of the binoculars are inscribed with the names of a dozen battles. The binoculars once belonged to famed lighthouse keeper Ed Lane, whose family gave them to the National Park Service. The commercial value of the binoculars is believed to be between $3,500 and $10,000.

Barstad was apprehended after he offered the binoculars for sale on eBay. A person who had seen the eBay offer coincidentally saw a flyer publicizing the theft and alerted the National Park Service.

United States v. Denning McTague[37]

Denning McTague pled guilty to one felony count of theft of Government property. He was sentenced to 15 months' imprisonment followed by 24 months of supervised release, during which he may not engage in physical contact with archival material without the prior consent of the Court. Also, McTague was ordered to pay a fine in the amount of $3,000 and restitution to the National Archives and Records Administration in the amount of $175.

McTague is the owner and operator of Denning House, a business that he took over from his mother, in 1993, and which has described itself as a purveyor of rare and unusual books, maps, manuscripts, interesting paper, and Americana. He also has worked as a local history specialist at the Nyack Library, in New York. During the summer of 2006, McTague stole 164 items from the Archival Operations of the National Archives—Mid Atlantic Program, in Philadelphia, and later sold some of them on eBay. He committed the thefts while serving an unpaid internship that had been arranged by the State University of New York so that McTague could satisfy one of the requirements for a Master of Arts degree in Library Science. Most of the stolen items were archival materials relating to the American Civil War that McTague was supposed to be arranging and organizing for the upcoming sesquicentennial of the War, which begins in 2011. Among them were a letter from Confederate cavalry commander J.E.B. Stuart and an order from the War Department to the armies of the Republic announcing the death of President Lincoln. Of the 164 items stolen, 161 were recovered, either through search warrants or through contact with the eBay buyers.

The National Archives did not discover the theft. It was discovered after a member of the public saw a stolen document being offered for sale on eBay, recognized its provenance from having done research at the National Archives, and alerted the Archives. When a special Agent of the Inspector General's Office of the National Archives, with the assistance of the FBI, executed a search warrant at McTague's home, he admitted his crimes. He said that he had no difficulty in removing the items from the Archives, claiming that security was virtually nonexistent. He merely took the documents, placed them inside a pad of yellow paper, and then placed the pad in the backpack inside his locker. To assure himself that his theft had gone undetected, McTague waited about one month after his internship ended before offering the documents for sale on eBay.

To determine value or loss for purposes of calculating McTague's offense level and hence his sentence, the United States valued the J.E.B. Stuart letter at $5,000, while, altogether, the other 163 documents were valued at more than $5,000 and less than $25,000. As the National Archives and Records Administration did not obtain and offer a commercial value for the items, presumably the U.S. Attorney added together the actual sales amount realized by McTague for the items, which was $9,000, and his asking prices for the unsold items and offered the sum of those amounts as the value of the cultural heritage resources involved in the offense conduct.

With the conviction of McTague, there now have been four convictions for theft of documents from the National Archives and Records Administration in recent years. In 2002, Shawn P. Aubitz, an archivist and curator, and 18-year employee at the same Philadelphia branch of the Archives where McTague interned (as well as a part-time history instructor at Bucks County Community College), was convicted of a felony under 18 U.S.C. § 654 (Employee of the United States Converting the Property of Another). He was sentenced to 21 months' imprisonment and ordered to pay a fine in the amount of $73,792. Aubitz stole "hundreds" of documents, at least 59 of which were recovered. In 2005, Howard W. Harner, Jr., a member of the public, was convicted of a felony under 18 U.S.C. § 668 (Theft of Major Artwork). He was sentenced to 24 months' imprisonment followed by 24 months of supervised release, and ordered to pay a fine in the amount of $10,000. Harner is known to have stolen 109 documents, 43 of which had been recovered by the time he was sentenced. Also in 2005, Samuel Richard "Sandy" Berger, a former National Security Advisor to President William Clinton, was convicted of a misdemeanor under 18 U.S.C. § 1924 (Unauthorized Removal or Retention of Classified Documents). He was sentenced to 24 months of probation and ordered to pay a fine in the amount of $50,000 and the administrative costs of his probation in the amount of $6,905, and to perform 100 hours of community service. Berger is known to have stolen five documents, two of which were returned to the Archives and three of which he admitted destroying.

Aubitz, Harner, and McTague were caught only after they offered stolen Archives materials for sale on eBay and members of the public recognized the items' provenance and alerted NARA. Berger was observed by NARA personnel in the process of stealing items and apprehended.

Notes

1. The section editor wishes to thank Elise Foster for her technical assistance.
2. For a complete and reader-friendly history, presentation, and explanation of U.S. Sentencing Guideline § 2B1.5, see Paula J. Desio, *Crimes and Punishment: Developing Sentencing Guidelines for Cultural Heritage Resources Crimes*, in LEGAL PERSPECTIVES ON CULTURAL RESOURCES 61–84 (Jennifer R. Richman & Marion P. Forsyth eds., 2004).
3. For a discussion of the intent, or *mens rea*, required to be proved in an ARPA criminal prosecution, see Marion P. Forsyth & David Tarler, *Model Jury Instructions in ARPA Prosecutions: Removing the "Lynch-Pins,"* in PRESENTING ARCHAEOLOGY IN COURT 127–142 (Sherry Hutt, Marion P. Forsyth & David Tarler eds., 2006).
4. For a detailed treatment of ARPA civil penalties, see Elise Foster, U.S. Dep't of Agric., USING ARPA CIVIL PENALTIES TO PROTECT ARCHEOLOGICAL RESOURCES ON PUBLIC AND INDIAN LANDS (Sherry Hutt & David Tarler, Nat'l Park Serv., eds., 2007).
5. *United States v. Mark Anthony Brady*, No. CV 07-00401 PHX-NVW (D. Ariz. judgment on the pleadings Aug. 17, 2007).
6. Where the person served with a notice of assessment has not filed a timely request for a hearing, the notice of assessment constitutes the final administrative decision (43 C.F.R. § 7.15 (h)(2); 36 C.F.R. § 296.15 (h)(2); 32 C.F.R. § 229.15 (h)(2); and 18 C.F.R. § 1312.15 (h)(2)). Judicial review of a final, administrative order assessing a civil penalty is available if a petition for review is filed within 30 days from the date the order was issued (16 U.S.C. § 470ff (b)(1)), but if, as in this case, a petition for judicial review is not filed, the Federal land manager may then request the U.S. Attorney to institute a civil action in the U.S. district court to collect the penalty. In that action, the validity and amount of the civil penalty are not subject to review (16 U.S.C. § 470ff (b)(2)).
7. In the case of a first felony violation of ARPA, the statutory maximum term of imprisonment is two years. In the case of a second or subsequent "violation," the statutory maximum term of imprisonment is five years. 16 U.S.C. § 470ee (d).

8. *United States v. Vincent E. Williams, Fenton E. Terembes, Jr. & Jeremy L. Burroughs*, No. 3:07 CR 181 (E.D. Va. sentence June 13, 2007 (Williams), Sept. 24, 2007 (Terembes, Jr.) and Nov. 5, 2007 (Burroughs)).
9. *United States v. Felix Sidney Maxwell and Randy Dean Wools*, No. CR-06-60038-AA (D. Or. sentence Sept. 18, 2006 (Wools) and Apr. 4, 2007 (Maxwell)).
10. *United States v. James E. Burton*, No. 2:07 CR 0065 (D. Utah sentence Oct. 4, 2007).
11. *United States v. Byran Keith Gary, Kristi L. Hendricks, and Tina Todd*, No. 8:07-CR-19-HFF (D.S.C. sentence June 20, 2007 (Gary and Hendricks), and continuance order June 27, 2007 (Todd)).
12. *United States v. Jonathan Keith Carroll and Christopher William Pelchat*, No. 06-M-592-TMD (D. Md. sentence Jan. 16, 2007).
13. On February 20, 2007, James A. Carroll pled guilty to one count of excavating cultural or archaeological resources in violation of 36 C.F.R. § 2.1 (a)(6), and was ordered to pay restitution to the Park in the amount of $1,016.
14. *United States v. Joseph M. Mercurio, Tonya C. Mercurio, Daniel M. Fisher, and Thomas J. Luecke*, No. 1:06 CR-36-01-TBR (W.D. Ky. sentence Apr. 2, 2007).
15. *United States v. Richard C. Kirk and David A. Whitling*, No. 1:06 CR 41-R (W.D. Ky. sentence Apr. 2, 2007).
16. In fact, some of the defendants in the two cases were acquainted.
17. United States Sentencing Commission, *Guidelines Manual*, § 2B1.5 (b)(5) and comment. (n.6).
18. *United States v. Jack Lee Harelson*, No. CR 05-60102-1-AA (D. Or. sentence Dec. 19, 2006).
19. Harelson's ex-wife was granted immunity and assisted the Government in its prosecution of Harelson. The appellate court affirmed those convictions but reversed Harelson's convictions for abuse of a corpse on statute of limitations grounds. *Oregon v. Harelson*, 938 P.2d 763 (Or. Ct. App. 1997).
20. *Jack Lee Harelson v. Bureau of Land Management*, No. ARPA 97-1 (Dep't of Interior, Off. of Hearings & Appeals Dec. 6, 2002), *adopted*, No. D 2003-28 (Dep't of Interior, Ad Hoc Bd. of Appeals Apr. 5, 2004). The civil penalty amount included damages to the archaeological value in the amount of $1,758,767 and restoration and repair costs in the amount of $766,549. At his hearing before an administrative law judge, Harelson argued that the ARPA civil penalty was time-barred by the statute of limitations for judicial actions commenced by the United States. The ALJ found against Harelson, and reiterated a general rule that statutory limits for the commencement of *judicial actions* for damages on behalf of the United States do not limit *administrative proceedings* within the Department of the Interior conducted to determine liability and fix the amount the Government claims to be due (*Harelson*, at 10, citing *Marathon Oil Co.*, 149 IBLA 287, 290 (1999)). For further discussion of limitations periods with respect to ARPA civil penalties, *see* Roberto Iraola, *The Archaeological Resources Protection Act – Twenty Five Years Later*, in 42 DUQ. L. REV. 221, 255-56 (2004).

21. A jury acquitted Harelson of soliciting the murders of two other people involved in his archaeological looting convictions, an Oregon State Police officer and the judge who presided over Harelson's 1996 trial.
22. *United States v. Douglas L. Turner*, No. 2:07CR02081-JPD (E.D. Wash. sentence Aug, 24, 2007).
23. For a more extensive treatment of the Antiquities Act, see THE ANTIQUITIES ACT: A CENTURY OF AMERICAN ARCHAEOLOGY, HISTORIC PRESERVATION, AND NATURE CONSERVATION (David Harmon, Francis P. McManamon & Dwight Pitcaithley eds, 2006) and Richard Waldbauer & Sherry Hutt, *"Cultural Property" Begins: The Centennial of the Antiquities Act*, in YEARBOOK OF CULTURAL PROPERTY LAW 2006, 147–174 (Sherry Hutt ed., 2006).
24. *U.S. v. Diaz*, 368 F. Supp. 856 (D. Ariz. 1973).
25. *U.S. v. Diaz*, 499 F.2d 113 (9th Cir. 1974).
26. *U.S. v. Smyer*, 596 F.2d 939 (10th Cir. 1979).
27. *United States v. Anthony Joseph Tulino*, No. 06 CR 746 (E.D.N.Y. sentence Mar. 2, 2007).
28. The revolver is a "cultural heritage resource" for purposes of applying sentencing guideline § 2B1.5 (United States Sentencing Commission, *Guidelines Manual* § 2B1.5, comment. (n.1 (C) & (F)). It was manufactured in 1892, so it is an "archaeological resource," as defined by the Archaeological Resources Protection Act (16 U.S.C. § 470bb (1), and *see also* 43 C.F.R. § 7.3 (a)), and it also is an object in the care, custody, or control of a "museum" *and* worth at least $100,000, so it is an "object of cultural heritage," as defined by the Theft of Major Artwork statute (16 U.S.C. § 668 (a)(1) & (2)). A total offense level of 19 is calculated by starting with a base level of 8, adding 12 levels because the value of the revolver exceeds $200,000, adding another 2 levels because the revolver was on, in, or in the custody of the national park system, and subtracting 3 levels for the defendant's acceptance of responsibility.
29. *United States v. Rose Morris*, No. 1:05 CR 1378-001 JC (D.N.M. sentence Dec. 5, 2007).
30. *United States v. John Andrew Carta and Daniel Warren Taylor*, No. 1:06 CR 00157 (D. Haw. sentence Jan. 31, 2007 (Carta) and June 24, 2007 (Taylor), and order for dismissal Oct. 15, 2007 (Carta)).
31. *United States v. Cecilia Marcillo-Aviles*, No. 07-20040-CR-JORDAN (S.D. Fla. sentence Feb. 2, 2007).
32. Ecuadoran law prohibits the sale or export of the artifacts in question. Ecuador also asserts ownership of this class of artifacts.
33. Criminal Complaint, *United States v. Edgar Nakache, Susan Aviles, and Cecilia Marcillo-Aviles*, No. 1:06-mi-02767-WCT (S.D. Fla. July 21, 2006). Initially, all three suspects were charged with smuggling, as well as the sale and receipt of stolen goods (18 U.S.C. § 2315, also known as the National Stolen Property Act).

34. The pre-Columbian artifacts are a "cultural heritage resource" for purposes of applying sentencing guideline § 2B1.5 (United States Sentencing Commission, *Guidelines Manual* § 2B1.5, comment (n.1 (C)). They are more than 100 years old—some of them are 3,000–4,000 years old—so they are an "archaeological resource" as defined by the Archaeological Resources Protection Act (16 U.S.C. § 470bb (1), and *see also* 43 C.F.R. § 7.3 (a)). A total offense level of 23 is calculated by starting with a base level of 8, adding 16 levels because the value of the 165 artifacts exceeds $1,000,000, adding another 2 levels because the offense was committed for pecuniary gain or otherwise involved a commercial purpose, and subtracting 3 levels for the defendant's acceptance of responsibility.
35. Leonard Sand, John S. Siffert, Walter P. Loughton, Steven A. Reiss & Nancy Batterman, MODERN FEDERAL JURY INSTRUCTIONS—CRIMINAL VOLUMES § P 23A.01 (Theft of Government Property) (2005).
36. *United States v. Michael J. Barstad*, No. 07-CR-0020-X-01 (W.D. Wis. sentence Aug. 22, 2007).
37. *United States v. Denning McTague*, No. 2:07-cr-00141-SD (E.D. Pa. sentence July 12, 2007).

ARTICLE

Ownership Issues and Archaeological Reports

Kelly Yasaitis Fanizzo[1]

Introduction

Each summer the archaeology departments of numerous universities launch field schools to record archaeological data from new sites; various entities provide grants for independent studies; and Federal agencies, states, tribes and private contractors employ archaeologists to excavate and record sites in the course of infrastructure development. The reports that result expand the body of knowledge and fulfill certain statutory obligations for the recipients of Federal contributions. It is foreseeable that the contents of archaeological reports will inform future studies, development decisions, and published materials. Reports compiled after archaeological excavation on public lands are to be undertaken in the public interest and must begin with a permit issued by a Federal agency. Thus, the legal questions for archaeologists and those who represent them are:

- Who owns an archaeological report?
- What rights does the archaeologist have in the work he or she prepares after completing the research?
- Do individuals who may have contributed to both the research and the archaeologist's understanding of the material past have any rights in the final report?
- Are there limits to the subsequent use of the reports?

Archaeology is the study of the material past. Physical remains provide the means for archaeologists to reconstruct human histories and cultural stories.[2] Archaeology as a discipline necessarily involves physical property through the artifacts recovered, yet it also involves intellectual property in the expressed interpretation of the information gathered. Intellectual property rights protect the products of the human intellect. Just as a novelist might have certain rights in a work of fiction that he or she has created, archaeologists may have certain intellectual property rights in the developed products of their research. The aim of this article is to provide practical information on the ownership issues that can arise in the context of archaeological reports. Although the topic lends itself to a number of situations, this article will address the nongovernmental, that is, the private academic archaeologist who, pursuant to his or her own research and discretion, requests a permit through the Archaeological Resources Protection Act (ARPA)[3] to excavate an archaeological site on public land and subsequently prepares a report for future use based on that research.

To answer the questions listed above this article will take a hypothetical archaeologist through the provisions of ARPA, explaining the intent and purpose of this law, and through the complexities of the copyright laws, putting archaeology and archaeological reports into the context of intellectual property law. This article will also touch on other possible aspects of intellectual property law that may be relevant in the context of such a report. I'd like to introduce Dr. Raines, a consultant who received his graduate degree in archaeology from the University of Pennsylvania. He is currently working to build upon his dissertation work researching Pristine Site 001 in Red Earth National Park, New Mexico. He hopes to incorporate the results of this research in the seminar he plans to teach next year. Dr. Raines has recently identified a new site in the park he thinks may provide additional information and insight to his ongoing research, and thus, has applied through the National Park Service (NPS) for an ARPA permit. Assuming Dr. Raines obtains a permit, what rights does he, or anyone else, have in a subsequent archaeological report?

Why These Questions Are Relevant Today

The question of ownership in archaeological reports has been an emergent issue for the last few decades. With the ongoing use and ease of technology, there exists increased pressure to put additional knowledge into the global commons. Disseminating information learned from archaeology is necessary because in most cases, the archaeologist destroys the resource by conducting the research.[4] Further, archaeological resources are generally understood to be held in the public interest, and archaeologists, as stewards, need to be conscious of their responsibility to maintain the integrity of the archaeological record, protect the resource, and share the information as it belongs to humankind. ARPA, the law that specifies the authority for scientific extractive use of public lands, recognizes that archaeological resources are public assets under the stewardship responsibility of Federal land management agencies.

For the archaeologist, publishing archaeological reports is often helpful, if not necessary, to advance in one's career, or simply to make a profit. Thus, knowledge of the intellectual property rights that exist in the report created is imperative for appropriate attribution, control, and economic gain.

At the heart of the discussion of intellectual property rights in archaeological reports is the debate over ownership of heritage. Archaeology tells human histories. For scientists, the knowledge to be gained from an archaeological site is universal and its story should be shared with the world. For descendants of subject cultures, certain knowledge is private or sacred and related only to a single few or group, and should remain contained or confidential. Codes of ethics for archaeologists address this conflict by stating that an archaeologist should publish his or her work, usually within a reasonable amount of time from the discovery, and tempering this provision by noting the need for sensitivity to protect the resource and the people about whom it reports.[5] When the sites from which the data are obtained are on public lands, the need to resolve ownership issues becomes critical, since an ARPA permit conveys superior and singular access to a site.

Indigenous societies, including Native American tribes, have traditional knowledge that has been sought by others since the time of first contact. Often, this knowledge helps inform archaeological research. The term "traditional knowledge" has been used as an umbrella phrase to include a number of other, more specific categories of folklore, art, designs, information, and practices.[6] For purposes of this article, the term "traditional knowledge" will refer to oral histories, stories, narratives, and other tradition-based information that may provide the archaeologist insight to the culture with which the site is affiliated, provide depth to the meaning and significance of the artifacts uncovered, or establish a context in which the archaeologist may then place his or her finds that would otherwise be unknown.

In addition to the rights the archaeologist may claim in his work, use of traditional knowledge in the development of an archaeological report adds additional layers of ownership. What rights do the indigenous tribes have in the information they might provide or that may otherwise come into the possession of the archaeologist? How does the archaeologist account for the potentially multiple layers of intellectual property or use rights in the final report?

Intellectual property rights in the context of traditional knowledge have risen to the forefront in many professional and academic discussions on archaeology. Archaeologists lodge the self-criticism that "[a]rchaeology will not move beyond being a colonist enterprise unless it actively seeks to understand the underlying issues of ownership and control of material and intellectual property as related to cultural knowledge and heritage."[7] While this article will not fully explore this conflict, it will highlight where the debate is ongoing today and how addressing questions about intellectual property rights in archaeological reports may help to define the attributes of ownership.

The goal of this article is to provide model language that may be either incorporated in the permit terms or developed as a separate agreement that Dr. Raines, and the reader, can rely upon in his future research and writing. Realizing that this model will not be universally applicable, hopefully it, as well as the discussion throughout this article, will allow the archaeologist to ask pertinent questions and to hold an intellectual property rights conversation in the context of relevant law.

What Are Archaeological Reports and How Are They Created?

ARPA: Intent and Purpose

In response to a 9th Circuit court decision[8] that weakened the enforceability of the Antiquities Act of 1906, and thus arguably left archaeological sites more vulnerable to looting and vandalism, Congress enacted ARPA.[9] The purpose of this law was to strengthen the government's ability to protect archaeological resources and to help illicit trade in artifacts from public and Indian lands.[10] ARPA's expressly stated purpose is

> to secure, for the present and future benefit of the American people, the protection of the archaeological resources and sites which are on public lands and Indian lands, and to foster increased cooperation and exchange of information between governmental authorities, the professional archaeological community, and private individuals having collections of archaeological resources and data.[11]

Some legal scholars further interpret this purpose in the context of the Kennewick Man case to state that ARPA, by not expressly limiting scientific research on archaeological resources, protects archaeological sites specifically for such study.[12]

In addition to its criminal provisions, ARPA strengthens the permitting requirements of the Antiquities Act[13] to specifically require

(1) the applicant is qualified, to carry out the permitted activity,

(2) the activity is undertaken for the purpose of furthering archaeological knowledge in the public interest,

(3) the archaeological resources which are excavated or removed from public lands will remain the property of the United States, and such resources and copies of associated archaeological records and data will be preserved by a suitable university, museum, or other scientific or educational institution, and

(4) the activity pursuant to such permit is not inconsistent with any management plan applicable to the public lands concerned.[14]

The law also adds a criminal sanction for the excavation, removal, damage, alteration, or the attempt thereto, to any archaeological resource on public or Indian lands without a permit.[15]

Dr. Raines knows that prior to conducting any archaeological investigation that involves excavation, shovel-testing, coring, pedestrian surveys, underwater archaeology, photogrammetry, or rock art documentation, he must seek a permit from the NPS as the Federal land manager.[16] He submits an application to the NPS Regional Office, and based upon his qualifications, his proposed research which would relate directly to the park's ongoing interpretation and management of its resources, and the arrangement he has with the University of Pennsylvania's Museum to maintain and safeguard all subsequent archaeological resources and records, he receives a permit.

Tribal Considerations

The site where Dr. Raines proposes to excavate is located near the ancestral home of the Pueblo tribe. In the time he has been researching in this area, Dr. Raines has developed a very good working relationship with the tribe. The tribal council has trusted him with certain insights and information. He hopes, with this new research proposal, he will be able to work with the tribe again to learn more about their traditional uses for the area.

ARPA expressly recognizes tribal sovereignty and property rights on tribal lands.[17] Defining the term "Indian lands," the law goes on to state that no permit for excavation on Indian lands may be issued without "obtaining the consent of the Indian or Indian tribe owning or having jurisdiction over such lands. The permit shall include such terms and conditions as may be requested by such Indian or Indian tribe."[18] Further, if the work is to be done on public lands, the regulations require that the Federal land manager notify any Indian tribe of a permit application where the proposed work may result in harm to a site of religious or cultural significance to that tribe.[19]

ARPA instructs Federal land managers to solicit information relating to the location of sites of religious or cultural significance from Indian tribes identified to have aboriginal or historic ties to their jurisdictional lands to supplement the information available for land management purposes.[20] The law encourages Federal land managers to develop through consultation with Indian tribes or other Native American groups conditions for which the tribes may be provided with special notifications after a permit has been issued.[21] For instance, a tribe may request the Federal land manager to notify and consult with its official representative or other members should any human remains be discovered during the course of the permitted work. These conditions should be included within the terms of the permit so that a process for this notification is established.

Other Considerations

While ARPA jurisdiction applies to Federal and Indian lands, which does not include lands within the exterior boundaries of an Indian reservation, other laws such as the National Historic Preservation Act[22] (NHPA) and the Native American Graves Protection and Repatriation Act[23] (NAGPRA) include these areas within statutory boundaries. ARPA permits may be required for excavation done pursuant to the NHPA and NAGPRA on private lands that are within tribal boundary areas. Such permits are administered by the Bureau of Indian Affairs. It should be noted that in regard to the NHPA, ARPA expressly provides in its regulations that "[i]ssuance of a permit in accordance with the Act and this part does not constitute an undertaking requiring compliance with [S]ection 106 of the Act of October 15, 1966 (16 U.S.C. 470f). However, the mere issuance of such a permit does not excuse the Federal land manager from compliance with [S]ection 106 where otherwise required."[24]

As briefly noted above, at least 30 days prior to issuing a permit on nontribal lands, the Federal land manager must notify any Indian tribe that attaches cultural or religious importance to a site that may be harmed during the course of the work.[25] If so requested during that period, the Federal land manager may consult with tribal representatives to find ways to avoid or mitigate any such harm that would then be incorporated into the terms of the permit.[26]

The National Environmental Policy Act (NEPA)[27] requires the responsible Federal official to assess the effects on the environment from the issuance of an ARPA permit and determine appropriate action. In coming to this determination, consultation with tribes and other culturally associated groups is a must.

Permit Terms

ARPA specifies certain terms and conditions that the Federal land manager must include in all permits:

(1) The nature and extent of work allowed and required under the permit, including the time, duration, scope, location, and purpose of the work;

(2) The name of the individual(s) responsible for conducting the work, and if different, the name of the individual(s) responsible for carrying out the terms and conditions of the permit;

(3) The name of any university, museum, or other scientific or educational institutions in which any collected materials and data shall be deposited; and

(4) Reporting requirements.[28]

ARPA also recognizes the sensitivity required in dealing with locational information for archaeological sites due to the potential harm that might come to the resources.[29] The regulations prohibit the disclosure of "information relating to the nature and location of any archaeological resource," unless the Federal land manager determines the disclosure of that information furthers the purposes of ARPA and does not risk harm to the resource, or a State Governor provides a written request for such information within a state, giving assurances to protect the area from harm.[30]

The Federal land manager may also include additional terms in the permit necessary to protect public safety, the work area and other legitimate land uses, and other resources.[31] Where the work is to be done on Indian lands, the Federal land manager must include the conditions the landowner and the tribe request. Where the work is to be done on public lands, the Federal land manager must include any conditions that may have been developed in consultation with Indian tribes that attach religious or cultural importance to sites potentially harmed by the work, or any conditions specifying circumstances for special notification to an Indian tribe.[32]

Where the work done pursuant to the permit will last longer than one year, the permit shall provide for a review by the Federal land manager at least annually.[33] Generally the permit will stipulate the number of reports or products to be submitted as a result of the research, timelines for those draft and final submissions, and certain requirements to restore the land to the "satisfaction" of the Federal land manager upon completion of the work.[34] The permit may also require a plan to provide for the inadvertent discovery of human remains.[35] By initiating the work subject to the permit, the permittee accepts the terms and conditions of the permit.[36]

Archaeological Reports

It has been said that "[a]rchaeologists have a duty, both to colleagues and to the general public, to explain what they are doing and why."[37] The archaeological report is where the archaeologist unveils the information he or she has gathered in the public and scientific interest from the archaeological excavation, how it was gathered, and the archaeologist's subsequent analysis of that information. For example, components of an archaeological report may include a description of the proposed work and its location, a list of qualified personnel, a project history, information on the site's setting (environmental and cultural), any previous research that was done, the methods employed, the results, an analysis, an evaluation of those methods, and possibly identified areas for future research.

The Secretary of Interior's Standards for Archeological Documentation provide a series of general objectives and standards, which are then followed by more detailed Guidelines for archaeologists conducting and writing up their research. Under "Reporting Results," the Guidelines state that the archaeological report, at a minimum, should include

1. Description of the study area;
2. Relevant historical documentation/background research;
3. The research design;
4. The field studies as actually implemented, including any deviation from the research design and the reason for the changes;
5. All field observations;
6. Analyses and results, illustrated as appropriate with tables, charts and graphs;
7. Evaluation of the investigation in terms of the goals and objectives of the investigation, including discussion of how well the needs dictated by the planning process were served;
8. Recommendations for updating the relevant historic contexts and planning goals and priorities, and generation of new or revised information needs;

9. Reference to related on-going or proposed treatment activities, such as structural documentation, stabilization, etc.;
10. Information on the location of original data in the form of field notes, photographs, and other materials.[38]

The Guidelines go on to discuss the need in certain cases for sensitivity and the confidentiality of locational information due to potential threats to the sites and to protect the privacy of traditional practitioners.

Dr. Raines notes that according to the NPS, "[t]he final report is a public document and cannot be copyrighted. Information compiled in the final report may be used by the NPS for cultural resource management purposes. Information collected during the research project, however, may be used by permittees in other publications that can be copyrighted."[39] We will now discuss future publication of archaeological reports and the extent of intellectual property rights.

Putting Intellectual Property Law in the Context of Archaeology

Intellectual Property Rights

To understand intellectual property, we start by defining a few key terms. What is property? It can be something you own, possess, or have some sort of legal title to. Inherent in the term "property" is the idea of "right." An individual or entity has a right to something; while what that right conveys may vary, it generally includes an ability to exclude use or access by others or to control use. The type of property established will lay a foundation for the bundle of rights that may be associated with it. Ownership is the "bundle of rights allowing one to use, manage, and enjoy property, including the right to convey it to another. Ownership implies the right to possess a thing, regardless of any actual or constructive control."[40] It is important to note the legal concept of "constructive possession," which provides that one may control or hold title to a property without physically possessing it.[41]

From this broad understanding of property and ownership stem categories of property with more specific characteristics. One type of property is personal property. Personal property is "any moveable or tangible thing that is subject to ownership."[42] This can be any number of things, such as a chair, shovel, or camera; anything that is not associated with land. From our very early days, we understand on some level the concept of personal property and the ownership thereof as we label objects as "mine" or ask for "my toy."

When the category of personal property is intangible property it is "property that lacks a physical existence."[43] A physical existence describes that which you can hold or touch. For instance, a piece of paper may be personal property, but the value of the stock option or the amount of the gift certificate that is described on that paper is intangible property. As one scholar has summarized, "'intangible property' (i) has value; (ii) derives its value from what it represents (rather than its physical manifestation); (iii) can be owned and transferred; and (iv) confers on its owner a legally enforceable right to a benefit which allows the owner to exclude others from exploiting the property."[44]

Intellectual property is a type of intangible property. Intellectual property is a "commercially valuable product of the human intellect, in the concrete or abstract form." It is intangible property that is produced by the human intellect. Much of the value of intellectual property is based on its potential for commercial exploitation or profit. It follows then that intellectual property rights are those "intangible rights protecting [the] commercially valuable products of the human intellect."[45] This category of property rights includes copyright, trademark, and patent protection in the marketplace. In each, "their value depends significantly on the information they embody and on the commercial value of exploiting that information."[46] Further, it is important to recognize that, just as is the case with tangible property, Dr. Raines cannot assert ownership beyond the interest he has received. Permission for access and use does not convey blanket ownership rights to all data in his notes. Understanding where ownership begins and ends is critical to understanding rights in archaeological reports.

Copyright

In the United States, the principles of copyright were first seen in the Articles of Confederation and later in the U.S. Constitution (art. 1, §8, cl. 8).[47] By 1976, Congress had gone through a number of iterations of the law to produce the existing Copyright Act.[48] The purpose of the Copyright Act is to provide authors with some measure of protection so that they will be encouraged to put their ideas out into the commons. The stated goal of copyright law is thus "to promote the Progress of Science and useful Arts."[49] To achieve this goal, the law gives authors a monopoly to allow them to benefit commercially from work; that monopoly is limited, though, as will be discussed later. As expressed by some scholars, "[n]othing would be more abhorrent to the underlying policy of copyright, and of all intellectual property law, than to restrict access to material that is, and should be, in the public domain."[50] The primary intent of copyright law is to encourage societal and intellectual development; following this is the individual author's protection and benefit.

There exists copyright protection in "original works of authorship fixed in any tangible medium of expression, now known or later developed, from which they can be perceived, reproduced, or otherwise communicated, either directly or with the aid of a machine or device."[51] The Copyright Act goes on to list possible categories of "works of authorship," and includes "literary works; musical works . . . ; dramatic works . . . ; pantomimes and choreographic works; pictorial, graphic, and sculptural works; motion pictures and other audiovisual works; sound recordings; and architectural works."[52] As stated, this protection does not extend to the underlying facts, idea, concept, or principle.[53] Raw data or ideas, where there is no creative input in the expression, are not protected.[54] A distinction is thus made between creation and discovery: a person who discovers a fact has not created it.[55] Facts exist independent of the author's creation. This principle relates directly to the purpose of copyright: "[t]he underlying facts may be used by a subsequent author as part of his own expression, or for any other purpose. In this way, the product of the original author's intellect is protected while the public store of information is increased."[56]

Another concept to define is that of the public domain. The public domain is the field of creative works, expressions, inventions, and the like that either receives no intellectual property protection or the applicable protection for which has lapsed.[57] This material is freely available at no cost; it belongs to and exists for the benefit of the public. However, material in the public domain cannot be copyrighted by another individual "as is." Authors may build upon a work that exists in the public domain, and after inserting their own originality, develop a different copyrightable work.

Historical facts are considered raw data and are not copyrightable. As the court in *Hoehling v. Universal Studios, Inc.*[58] stated, "the protection afforded the copyright holder has never extended to history, be it documented fact or explanatory hypothesis. The rationale for this doctrine is that the cause of knowledge is best served when history is the common property of all, and each generation remains free to draw upon the discoveries and insights of the past." The court goes further to find "[w]here...historical facts, themes, and research have been deliberately exempted from the scope of copyright protection to vindicate the overriding goal of encouraging contributions to recorded knowledge," what is copyrightable in a historical account is only the author's original expression.[59]

The primary requirement for a work to qualify for copyright protection is originality. "Originality" is not defined in the Act, so its definition must come from the courts' interpretation of the term in copyright cases. The Supreme Court has said this is a very low threshold, that "only a slight amount will suffice"; "originality requires independent creation plus a modicum of creativity."[60] In other words, the author must exercise some subjective control or influence in the final product. An interesting point raised by the *Feist* Court is that originality does not equate to novelty; where two independent persons develop similar expressions, if ignorant of each other, each work is copyrightable.[61]

Generally, copyright vests in the author or coauthors of the work.[62] Where there is a collective work with multiple authors, the copyright is assumed to vest only for that portion each author contributes to the larger work. Without the express transfer of copyright to another author, no one author owns the copyright for the entire work.[63] To take this in a slightly different direction, copyright protection exists only for those portions of "a work that are original to the author."[64] When an author has copyright protection, he or she has the exclusive rights to do, or authorize reproductions or copies of, the work, derivative works, the distribution of copies to the public by sale or lease, and the public performance or display of the work.[65] Additionally, the author of a work of visual art has the rights of attribution and integrity.[66] The author may transfer or convey his or her copyright or any of the exclusive rights therein in whole or in part in an instrument of conveyance that is in writing and signed by the author.[67]

In contrast to the type of work being proposed by Dr. Raines, a "work for hire" is defined as "a work prepared by an employee within the scope of his or her employment; or a work specially ordered or commissioned for use as a contribution to a collective work . . . if the parties expressly agree in a written instrument signed by them that the work shall be considered a work made for hire."[68] With a work made for hire, the employer or other person for whom the work was prepared owns the copyright in the work, unless the parties expressly agreed and signed a written instruction to alter this understanding.[69] Therefore, it is presumed not to be a work for hire unless expressly stated. But if it is a work for hire, it is presumed that the employer owns the content unless otherwise expressly stated.

"The right to make *limited* use of a work that is otherwise subject to restrictions is the hallmark of *copyrighted* works: after all, every copyright is only a set of rights subject to the right of the public to make at least *some* use of the work."[70] To infringe a copyright is to violate any of the exclusive rights of the copyright owner.[71] Two elements are required to prove infringement: "(1) ownership of a valid copyright, and (2) copying of the constituent elements of the work that are original."[72] Therefore, to prove infringement the copyright owner must show "the existence of those facts of originality, of intellectual production, of thought, and conception."[73] Some scholars note that proving infringement is often problematic and assert that "[c]opyright [generally] is . . . very difficult to monitor or enforce."[74] Despite this concern, there are certain remedies for infringement, such as injunctions against the infringing use, the impounding or disposition of the infringing work, and certain damages, as well as costs and attorney's fees.[75] There are also criminal penalties where the purpose of the willful infringement is for "commercial advantage or private financial gain," or where the reproduction or distribution of the infringing works in a set time period exceeds a retail value of $1,000.[76]

Copyright protection has certain limitations. Time, for one, limits its reach in that a copyright in any work created on or after January 1, 1978, exists from the time of the work's creation for the duration of the life of the author plus seventy years after his death.[77] Where there is more than one author for any one copyrighted work, the copyright extends for the life of the last surviving author plus seventy years.[78] Where the work is created anonymously, the copyright term is ninety-five years from the time of first publication, or 120 years from the time of its creation, whichever expires first.[79] The time limits of copyright law are one of the aspects that make it a difficult fit for the protection of indigenous traditional knowledge, assuming that the knowledge was intended for dissemination in the marketplace and is neither private nor public domain.

A second, well known limitation on copyright protection is the doctrine of fair use. The fair use limitation states that certain reproduction or copies of a copyrighted work "for purposes such as criticism, comment, new reporting, teaching . . . , scholarship, or research" do not constitute an infringement of the copyright.[80] In order to determine, on a case by case basis, whether a subsequent use is a fair use, the Act sets out factors to consider:

(1) the purpose and character of the use, including whether such use is of a commercial nature or is for nonprofit educational purposes;

(2) the nature of the copyrighted work;

(3) the amount and substantiality of the portion used in relation to the copyrighted work as a whole; and
(4) the effect of the use upon the potential market for or value of the copyrighted work.[81]

The fair use limitation clearly provides for deference to nonprofit educational or scholarly uses. If the use is for individual commercial profit, regardless of whether it may also be educational, it typically is argued not to constitute a fair use. In addition, where the subsequent work copies the entirety of the original work, the courts often do not find it to be a fair use. "A powerful argument against fair use is that it may be a detriment to the economic success of a copyrighted work."[82] However, when the subsequent use is factual, and not a creative, fictional work, courts look very closely at the potential public benefit in considering the possible damage to the copyright holder.[83] The reasoning behind the fair use concept is the priority order given to the goals of copyright. As one scholar notes, "[i]f the author's creative contribution is very small, so should be his protection."[84]

Another limitation on the exclusive rights contained in the Copyright Act worth pointing out is for reproductions by libraries and archives. Certain conditions are attached to this limitation; for example, the reproduction must not be for any direct or indirect commercial advantage, the collections of the library or archive must be either open to the public or available to all persons doing research in a particular field, and the reproduction must contain a notice of the copyright or a legend stating that the work may be protected by copyright.[85]

Patent, Trademark, Trade Secret, Privacy

While copyright law is the focus of this article, it is helpful to point out other potential intellectual property rights that may have some relevance for archaeology. This section is intended only to provide enough information so that the reader, and our Dr. Raines, might be able to identify a potential issue and raise the question.

Patent An individual who "invents or discovers any new and useful process, machine, manufacture, or composition of matter, or any new and useful improvement thereof" may be able to obtain a patent.[86] This allows the patent holder to exclude others from using or selling that machine or process. To receive a patent, the inventor must meet the criteria of novelty (that is, newness), nonobviousness, and usefulness.[87] A patent grants the following rights to the patent holder and his or her heirs or assigns "the right to exclude others from making, using, offering for sale, or selling the invention throughout the United States or importing the invention into the United States, and, if the invention is a process, . . . the right to exclude others from using, offering for sale, or selling throughout the United States, or importing into the United States, products made by that process, referring to the specification for the particulars thereof."[88] A very important point to note is the distinction between patents and copyright. A patent can protect the underlying ideas or concepts that made the machine or process useful, whereas a copyright cannot.[89]

Patents are typically available for such things as machinery; industrial processes; electronic products, including computer software; chemicals; and ornamental designs.[90] There are three common types of patents: utility patents (e.g., machines, manufactures, compositions), design patents (i.e., that protect only the aesthetic design and visual uniqueness), and plant patents (i.e., that protect the distinct variety or type of human-made plant).[91] A patent is used often in the context of ethnobotany, for example, to protect "inventions with commercial potential based on traditional plant knowledge."[92]

Trademark A trademark is a "word, phrase, logo, or other graphic symbol used by a manufacturer or seller to distinguish its product or products from those of others. The main purpose of a trademark is to designate the source of goods or services. In effect, the trademark is the commercial substitute for one's signature."[93] To be eligible for protection, the trademark must be distinctive; in fact, the level of protection provided relates directly to the level of distinctiveness of the trademark.[94] There exists what is termed a "spectrum of distinctiveness" that puts in order the increasing levels of distinctiveness for certain trademarks and ranges from the most distinctive, the "fanciful" trademark, which receives the highest level of protection, to the least distinctive, "generic" terms, which receive no protection.[95] The relative strength of a trademark's distinctiveness is based on its uniqueness, its universally understood connotation (i.e., its intended use), and its lack of inherent linguistic meaning.[96]

Trademarks can be viewed as similar to design patents because they protect unique visual features. In the realm of archaeology, trademarks are often involved with reproduced images and designs, sometimes in the form of replicated artifacts for sale as souvenirs, or t-shirts with certain images on them.

Trade Secret A trade secret is

> a formula, process, device, or other business information that is kept confidential to maintain an advantage over competitors; information—including a formula, pattern, compilation, program, device, method, technique, or process—that (1) derives independent economic value, actual or potential, from not being generally known or readily ascertainable by others who can obtain economic value from its disclosure or use, and (2) is the subject of reasonable efforts, under the circumstances, to maintain its secrecy.[97]

Trade secrets may include technical information, such as certain designs, formulas, or techniques; or it may include business information, such as cost or pricing estimates, pre-decisional negotiating information, information on business opportunities, or personnel information.[98] Its economic value is recognized in certain legal protections that attempt to prevent the theft of trade secrets.[99] Typically, protection for trade secrets stems from state law.

Trade secret protection may coexist with copyright, for instance, in a writing or picture; however, it is important to note that the publication and/or distribution of the copyrighted work may destroy the trade secret rights.[100] A trade secret need not meet the "novelty" test of a patent, and there is no set duration to its protection provided its secrecy is maintained.[101] In the context of archaeological reports, confidentiality agreements may work to maintain the status of a trade secret; yet it is important to remember that determining whether protection for a trade secret exists at all depends on the analysis of a number of criteria, including the extent to which the information is "widely known" and "the value of the information to the claimant or its competitors, the cost of developing the information, and the extent to which the claimant has taken efforts to maintain the secrecy of the information."[102]

Privacy Privacy law appears to be a multifaceted and somewhat malleable concept;[103] however, certain legal principles are relevant to a discussion of archaeological reports. Under tort law, privacy law provides protection against "unreasonable intrusion upon the seclusion of another . . . ; or (b) appropriation of the other's name or likeness . . . ; or (c) unreasonable publicity given to the other's private life . . . ; or (d) publicity that unreasonably places the other in a false light before the public."[104] It is worthwhile to expand upon the concept "intrusion upon seclusion," which provides that "[o]ne who intentionally intrudes, physically or otherwise, upon the solitude or seclusion of another or his private affairs or concerns, is subject to liability to the other for invasion of his privacy, if the intrusion would be highly offensive to a reasonable person."[105] While legal scholars note that this aspect of privacy law has not yet been applied to the protection of traditional knowledge or expression, it might be a useful tool for tribal members to employ against the misappropriation of such knowledge.[106]

Generally, the protection offered under privacy law as the "right to be left alone" applies to the single individual. Thus, in the context of traditional knowledge, the question can be raised whether the protection could apply to a collective, tribal group where the "quintessential concept of selfhood is shifted from one person to one people" and the protection is for something owned by the group.[107] The United States Supreme Court has determined that privacy vests in the individual,[108] but the case did not also remove the concept of group ownership of private property. Thus, groups can hold property that is private and not for disclosure without appropriate permission.

Applying Intellectual Property Protections to Archaeological Reports

What is copyrightable in an archaeological report? The ownership of a copyright is distinct from ownership of the material object in which the work may be embodied and the artifact from which the information might stem.[109] For instance, purchasing the final bound archaeological report conveys ownership of the report but not ownership of the intellectual property contained within the report.

As was discussed earlier, raw data, historical facts, and ideas without creativity in their expression are not copyrightable. Field observations, methods of data collection, discoveries, measurements, survey results, and inventory lists would not be subject to copyright protection. However, recall that the originality threshold is very low; thus the narrative analysis and theoretical discussions and interpretations that are included in the final report should be copyrightable. The archaeological report may be a compilation. Compilation is defined by the Copyright Act as "a work formed by the collection and assembling of preexisting material or of data that are selected, coordinated, or arranged in such a way that the resulting work as a whole constitutes an original work of authorship."[110] The copyright protection for a compilation or derivative work does not include the preexisting material.[111] Theoretically, the ability of the author to exclude others from the unauthorized reproduction of his or her work is maintained while allowing some level of subsequent use.

Traditional Knowledge in the Context of Intellectual Property Law

What about the traditional knowledge that might come from interviews with tribal elders or ethnographic studies? Is this information copyrightable, what aspects of it, and if so, by whom—an individual member of the tribe, or the tribe as a whole? Applying intellectual property protections to traditional knowledge is difficult for a number of reasons. Whether the current legal system can accommodate the unique factors and non-Western concepts inherent in traditional knowledge is a topic of much discussion today.[112] Certain scholars argue that there is no clear answer, for instance, as to how traditional knowledge may be protected under copyright's limited definition of an "author."[113] Others argue that "[t]he United States government has yet to come out with a broad legislative solution that strikes an adequate balance between the claims of the indigenous people and the traditional goals of intellectual property law."[114] Even other scholars argue that while "no single solution is likely to meet all the needs of indigenous and traditional communities and to protect [traditional cultural expressions][115] in a comprehensive manner," looking to a "menu of [legal and moral] options" may provide sufficient protection.[116] Perhaps some of the questions of legal theorists could be answered, and clear guidance given to archaeologists, by examining the basic legal tenets outlined in the first part of this article. Facts cannot be owned and traditional knowledge holders may not be "authors" when they have not willfully placed knowledge or ideas into commerce. Also, access to ideas for use does not convey ownership. Keeping straight the layers of "rights" may help to resolve questions of privacy, access, use, and full ownership.

While certain generalizations may be made in this discussion, one reason intellectual property law as a whole is often at odds with traditional knowledge is the variability that exists among the many cultures. This is why certain scholars again point to a "body of law," encompassing various aspects of national and international intellectual property law, rather than a single piece of legislation, as the most appropriate remedy.[117]

As was discussed previously, copyright law requires originality and fixation in "any tangible medium of expression," and has a limited duration. The concept of originality may not translate into traditional or sacred knowledge because the stories, songs, or other traditional cultural expressions "do not spring from an individual author but are purposefully based on or *copied exactly from* creative works that have come before."[118] The question of fixation also becomes problematic for many traditional expressions that are fixed by the indigenous group in multiple mediums. In addition, traditional knowledge is often that which is passed from elder to youth and has been shaped over the generations. Its significance does not diminish with time. As such, the issue of temporal limitations on the protection allowed is typically at odds with the development and provision of this knowledge.[119] Thus, it is likely that a great deal of traditional knowledge does not necessarily fit into the rubric of copyright.

Making a derivative work from traditional knowledge may extend some protection.[120] For instance, a photograph of a traditional image might receive copyright protection provided the required level of originality existed. But, what is the basis upon which to gauge the required level of originality?[121] "Taking a photo does not imply any exclusive right in the preexisting material."[122]

There is an alternative means of protection, for those works that might otherwise fall into the public domain, in the concept of character or moral rights. The Visual Rights Act of 1990[123] (VARA) is the United States' version of moral rights. It provides for the rights of attribution and integrity for works of visual art.[124] VARA defines a visual art as "a painting, drawing, print, or sculpture . . . [or] a still photographic image produced for exhibition purposes only," and adds certain additional caveats to each of those categories.[125] It specifically excludes from the definition commercial or functional items. As much of the traditional knowledge relevant to an archaeological report consists of oral stories and traditions, VARA may have little relevance currently to Dr. Raines' archaeological report. Other countries are currently contemplating expansion of such protection to "indigenous communal moral rights."[126]

Who Owns Archaeological Reports as a Matter of Law and Ethics

In theory, Dr. Raines, in describing his interpretations and learned opinions in the final archaeological report, will hold copyright to his original expressions. But what constitute those original expressions? A question to ask might be whether there exists any creativity in the scope and design of the research. For instance, it has been noted that, "[a]s with all research, to some extent the answers the archaeological research gives depend on the questions that were asked and the assumptions that were made."[127] It appears decided, however, that the methods of uncovering the underlying facts and the source data, such as the location of site, are not original and thus, are not copyrightable. "Copyright does not preclude others from using the ideas or information revealed by the author's work. It pertains to the literary [work] . . . in which the author expressed intellectual concepts."[128] Dr. Raines may copyright his discussion, analysis, and conclusions. Others will have access to his data and may copyright their expressions.

As to the data set, earlier courts attempted to develop another kind of copyright protection for factual compilations based upon the amount of work the compiler put into the product. Often termed the "sweat of the brow" concept, this copyright protection was to reward the hard efforts of the compiler. As pointed out by the *Feist* Court,[129] however, the sweat of the brow theory incorrectly extended copyright protection to the facts of the compilation, rather than just their selection and arrangement. Congress has since clarified this point, on the recommendation of the U.S. Copyright Office, by revising the Copyright Act to make the originality requirement clear.[130] In regard to the work done pursuant to an ARPA permit, it is imperative to recognize that public assets are put at the disposal of the researcher; thus, there exists a public expectation for a quality data set in exchange for the exclusive access and primary use.

Access and Use of Report: Professional Best Practices

Virtually all scientists will argue that access to raw data, without another's subjective interpretation placed upon it, allows for different perspectives to be developed and different angles of the story to be told. They would further argue that the subsequent "conjunction of differing opinions. . . . is more likely to result in a synthesis that is accurate."[131] The Society for American Archaeology states in its Principles of Archaeological Ethics that intellectual property is part of the archaeological record and should be treated with the same stewardship as that which is afforded to the physical artifacts. It goes on to note, in Principle 5, that, "[i]f there is a compelling reason, and no legal restrictions or strong countervailing interests, a researcher may have primary access to original materials and documents for a limited and reasonable time, after which these materials and documents must be made available to others."[132] Thus, the SAA recognizes the obligation not to hoard data or delay sharing the information.

The Register of Professional Archaeologists' Code of Conduct provides a specific ten-year time limit to the archaeologist's "right of primacy with respect to analysis and publication of the data."[133] After that ten-year period, or earlier if the archaeologist chooses not to publish his research, the RPA states that the information "should be made fully accessible to other archaeologists for analysis and publication."[134] Further, the RPA's Code of Conduct urges an archaeologist not to enter into a contract that would prohibit including his or her own interpretations and conclusions in the report, or that would prevent using the data gathered for a report in the future.

It is generally accepted that the type of access allowed is based on the type of information contained and/or the type of use proposed. For instance, access may be limited by the need for sensitivity or confidentiality, as was discussed earlier in the Secretary of Interior's Standards and as is expressed in ARPA. Beyond this established limitation, though, can there be other limitations on the use of the information contained in the final archaeological report?

There are strict standards for the protection of human subjects for research and testing, specifically for the issue of informed consent.[135] Informed consent is understood to be a process, an ongoing voluntary permission given by the research subject to participate in the research.[136] Some scholars have noted that in the context of ethnographic research, the researcher must discuss with his or her subjects the fact that he or she is specifically studying cultural practices.[137] "Cultivating an ethical climate for ethnographic research requires trust among all involved in the process of implementing a research project."[138] Further, informed consent requires the ethnographer to fully explain the intent of the research, how the research will be conducted, how the information provided will be used and held, and all potential benefits and risks that may stem from the research.

The issue of control of access to information is not new. As many have argued, "[h]istorically, controlling access to information has been a way to control people, socially and politically."[139] Academic freedom has often been termed the stalwart defender of free thought and access to information. Yet, even with the scholarly research Dr. Raines proposes, there still exists a concern with the "appropriation, misrepresentation, or misuse of knowledge, loss of control of knowledge, and loss of access to the products of research or their benefits" that may be held by the tribal groups he is working with.[140] In the context of intellectual property ownership and access, it is important to realize the economic drivers behind copyright and other intellectual property protections as potentially conflicting with the cultural concerns and moral sense of collective ownership that permeates the belief systems of many indigenous groups.[141]

Encouraging greater collaboration with indigenous parties—specifically here, with the tribes from whom Dr. Raines hopes to gain additional insight and knowledge, the development of agreements, even beyond the requirements already existing in the ARPA regulations—is highly advantageous for both the archaeologist and the tribes. This would allow for the conditional provision of information and control of the information dissemination. Through such agreements, issues such as access may be decided in a sensitive manner. Examples of suggested terms and conditions to address access to information are discussed in the next section.

Suggested Model Language

Generally, standard ARPA permit conditions include a provision such as

> Permittee shall submit a clean, edited draft final report to the agency official for review to insure conformance with standards, guidelines, regulations, and all stipulations of the permit. The schedule for submitting the draft shall be determined by the agency official.[142]

The final report referred to here is the one that Dr. Raines must turn in to the NPS Regional Office, which cannot be copyrighted and which furthers the knowledge sharing purposes of ARPA. Additionally, because raw data cannot be copyrighted, Dr. Raines cannot claim a copyright in the permit terms or elsewhere to protect the facts he has uncovered in his research. That information would belong in the public domain. Beyond this, however, Dr. Raines would be able to use the information gathered to develop another report including his own analyses and interpretations that would be copyrightable.

As is seen in many standard permit conditions, though, certain limitations may apply to that use. For instance, the confidentiality provision regarding site locational information is extended to any subsequent uses of that information via the following standard permit term:

> Permittee shall not disclose archeological site locational information, collected under the authority of this permit, to any other entity, public or private, at any time, except with the specific approval of the Federal permitting agency. The permittee shall not publish, in printed format, on the internet, on film, or through other methods, without the approving official's prior permission, any locational or other identifying archeological site information that could compromise the Government's protection and management of archeological sites.[143]

> Further, the permit may require the permittee to "submit a copy of any published journal article and any published or unpublished report, paper, and manuscript resulting from the permitted work (apart from those [otherwise] required . . .), to the approving official and the appropriate official of the approved curatorial facility."[144] The permit may also require the permittee to specify in any subsequent publication where the work was performed in relation to the Federal property (e.g., which National Forest).[145]

Another important point to consider here is that should Dr. Raines have applied for a permit to conduct research on Indian lands, as required by ARPA, the permit would include as special permit conditions any specific terms the landowner and tribe might request. In all likelihood, these conditions would include limitations on the use of the information gathered, as well as any traditional knowledge provided. If Dr. Raines were conducting his research on public lands, but involving work that might harm properties of religious or cultural significance to the Pueblo tribe, the special permit conditions might include certain limitations or protocols developed in consultation with the tribe. These terms would include methods to minimize or mitigate potential harm to the properties, and in theory, might include certain restrictions on the use of the information provided as a manner of mitigation. For instance, special permit conditions could prohibit specific uses that would be offensive to the tribe.

There is no requirement under ARPA to include special permit conditions that discuss the control of traditional knowledge, outside the confidentiality provisions for locational information already discussed, since ARPA is specific to archaeological sites and not nonarchaeological ethnographic knowledge. Yet given the potential privacy issues of present-day people involved, the permit should account for the use of study data. The Secretary of the Interior's Guidelines for Archeological Documentation allow for confidentiality provisions to protect traditional religious practices as well as the physical location of the site. Additionally, the National Historic Preservation Act, in Section 304, allows for information relating to the "location, character, or ownership of a historic resource" to be withheld from public disclosure if such a disclosure might "cause a significant invasion of privacy," or "impede the use of a traditional religious site by practitioners."[146] Building upon these examples, one way in which Dr. Raines and the NPS Regional Office, as the Federal land manager, might acknowledge the sensitivity and intellectual property rights that exist in the traditional knowledge of the Pueblo tribe is by voluntarily working with the tribe to negotiate an additional special permit condition that states

> The agency official shall not make available to the public any information relating to the traditional, cultural, religious or sacred practices or beliefs of an Indian tribe that are provided to the agency official or the permittee as a result of the research being conducted pursuant to this permit without the prior approval of the Indian tribe. The permittee shall not include any such information in any subsequent published or unpublished report, paper, or manuscript resulting from the permitted work without the prior approval of the Indian tribe.

Through this term, a tribe might be able to provide sensitive information to help inform the research and the agency's land managing policies, but still receive a similar level of protection as that given to site locational information. If the tribe chooses in a certain instance not to provide prior approval for the release of such information, it could be argued that there exists a risk of harm to the tribe's traditional practices or beliefs. It should be noted, however, that a written request from a State Governor might require this information to be released per the process outlined in the regulations.[147] Additionally, subsequent research into the applicability of the Freedom of Information Act might be required to determine the feasibility of this suggested permit term.

An additional caveat is due here: the researcher may receive information from an individual within a tribe, but that does not convey rights that a tribe would have or would confer. It cannot be assumed that individually given information is individually owned and that the speaker has the authority to disclose this information for any further use.

Copyright Protection

Dr. Raines' copyright protection in a subsequent archaeological report would vest automatically as this protection is generally self-executing once the work is fixed in a tangible medium.[148] He may, however, consider registering his copyright in the report with the U.S. Copyright Office. Registering a copyright within three months of its original publication extends protection retroactively to the date of original publication.[149] This is important because it sets the date of copyright ownership unquestionably.

Depending on how involved the Pueblo tribe is in the development of the report, Dr. Raines and a designated tribal representative may be considered coauthors with separate identifiable rights for their respective contributions. It is important to remember, though, the discussion above regarding the complications of applying copyright protection to traditional knowledge. A joint authorship agreement would allow for the parties to share rights in the work. [150] Neither coauthor would have the ability to exclude the other from use of the intellectual property. Similarly, neither coauthor would be able to use the property in such a way as to diminish or deplete the other's potential use (i.e., any sale of rights that would foreclose the other's ability to use the property). [151] Because of this, each coauthor would need to account to the other for any benefits of his use if that use excludes the other or causes damage or a diminishment in value to the property.

A joint authorship agreement may be developed to stipulate the specific rights and arrangement for uses between the parties. Without such an agreement, though, copyright protection would most likely still apply with certain presumptions such as

1. Each co-author will own an equal ownership share in the work. This will occur even if one of the co-authors has contributed a greater quantity of the work than the other co-authors.
2. Each co-author will own an "undivided" interest in the entire work. This means that if the publishing project consists of illustrations and text that the artist and the writer will each own fifty percent of the entire work, i.e., the art and the text.
3. Any co-author, without the permission of [his/her] fellow co-authors, may grant non-exclusive rights to the work to third parties. However, a co-author may only grant exclusive rights to the work to third parties if the co-author obtains the prior consent of the other co-authors.
4. Each co-author has a duty to account to the other co-authors for any profits obtained from the exploitation of the work.
5. A co-author has the right to assign his/her ownership share in the work to a third party or to bequeath his/her ownership share to his/her heirs.
6. Each co-author will be entitled to equal authorship credit for the work upon its publication. [152]

Licensing It has been argued that archaeologists exert control over information by deciding what research to pursue and what results and analysis to publish. [153] Noting the dichotomy between the exclusive rights provided in copyright protection and the lack of protection provided to information in the public domain, a suggestion offered by a number of scholars is the development of a "cultural-heritage-license." [154]

A license is a contract, a legal agreement among the signatory parties. [155] The Pueblo tribe in this instance would be the licensor, who would be allowing the licensee, Dr. Raines, certain uses of their traditional knowledge. This type of agreement does assume the tribe's ownership of the traditional knowledge. As to who within the tribe, a designated representative or the collective, may have this ownership right would need to be ascertained. Further discussion might also be needed as to whether any fees or consideration might be appropriate for this license.

Dr. Raines and the Pueblo tribe could negotiate this license after he has completed the requirements of his ARPA permit and submitted his final report to the NPS; thus, through a license he could meet the special permit condition of seeking the prior approval of the Indian tribe to use the knowledge provided to him in a certain subsequent publication.

The terms of this license could include any number of the following, and would require significant consultation between Dr. Raines and the Pueblo tribe. These terms are intended only to offer suggestions for consideration, and are not intended to be incorporated as stated in any agreement.

> Licensee agrees to maintain the integrity of the information as much as possible in its original context and provided in such a way as is consistent with the stated beliefs and values of the licensor.
>
> Licensee agrees to identify/keep anonymous the origin and affiliation of the information provided.
>
> Licensee agrees to provide the licensor with a preliminary draft of his work prior to any public dissemination or publication of said work for the licensor's review and comment. Should there be any dispute between the licensee and the licensor, or should the licensor object to the licensee's interpretation, expression, description, or analysis of the information provided by the licensor, the licensor may prohibit the licensee from using the information in the work.
>
> This license applies only to the ABC work of the licensee. Any subsequent use by the licensee of the information provided is prohibited without the prior approval of the licensor.
>
> "Licensee agrees to report back to the licensor at least once every year regarding any new public use of the information covered by this license of which the licensee is aware. Report will include, at a minimum, location of use, a brief description of the use, and contact information for at least one person responsible for said use."[156]
>
> Licensee agrees to provide the licensor with # copies of the final work.

It would be necessary to define the terms used in this license, such as "information provided" and "ABC work." Again, who from the tribe would be the appropriate party or official representative to sign this license would need to be clarified. Additionally, greater detail might be helpful to outline the specific use agreed to by the parties. As a final term, Dr. Raines might consider including language to the effect that "Nothing in this agreement affects or alters the rights under copyright law" for the remaining content of this work.[157] That way, the terms of the license are restricted to the input provided by the tribe.

Conclusion

The terms and language suggested above should be the subject of ongoing research. For, while intending to put archaeological reports in the context of intellectual property law and highlight discussion areas that affect the subsequent ownership issues, this article admittedly leaves a number of questions unanswered. For instance, where is the line between scientific fact and traditional belief? In the discussion of intellectual property law, it is interesting to consider that in copyright and tribal belief, neither can be owned. What if the two contradict each other? How, if at all, can copyright terms or intellectual property law more broadly be translated and made applicable to traditional knowledge?

At the time this article is being written, a number of initiatives are in motion to consider those and many other related questions of scientific integrity and law. Those discussions will have far reaching effects. Thus, through an attempt to provide practical information on the property rights that arise in the context of archaeological reports, it becomes clear that the issue of who owns archaeological reports has multiple, varied, and often, complex layers.

Notes

1. The author would like to thank Sherry Hutt and David Tarler for their valuable insight and guidance, and Tom McCulloch for his thoughtful review. The opinions expressed in this article belong solely to the author.
2. George P. Nicholas & Kelly P. Bannister, *Intellectual Property Rights and Indigenous Cultural Heritage in Archaeology*, in INDIGENOUS INTELLECTUAL PROPERTY RIGHTS, LEGAL OBSTACLES AND INNOVATIVE SOLUTIONS 312 (Mary Riley ed., 2004).
3. 16 U.S.C. § 470aa et seq. (1979).
4. Ryan M. Seidmann, Authorship and Control: Ethical Issues of Student Research in Archaeology, 14 ALB. L.J. SCI. & TECH. 451, 455–56 (2004).
5. Register of Professional Archaeologists, Code of Conduct and Standards of Research Performance, 1.1c, 6.3, at http://rpanet.org/conduct.htm (last visited Mar. 14, 2007).

6. See, e.g., Intellectual Property Needs and Expectations of Traditional Knowledge Holders, WIPO Report on Fact-Finding Missions on Intellectual Property and Traditional Knowledge (1998–1999) (Apr. 2001) 25, available at http://www.wipo.int/tk/en/tk/ffm/report/index.html (last visited Nov. 26, 2007) (defining "traditional knowledge" as "tradition-based literary, artistic or scientific works; performances; inventions; scientific discoveries; designs; marks, names and symbols; undisclosed information; and all other tradition-based innovations and creations resulting from intellectual activity in the industrial, scientific, literary or artistic fields").
7. George P. Nicholas & Kelly P. Bannister, *Copyrighting the Past? Emerging Intellectual Property Rights Issues in Archaeology*, 45 CURRENT ANTHROPOLOGY 327, 329 (2004).
8. *U.S. v. Diaz*, 499 F.2d 113 (9th Cir. 1974).
9. National Park Service, Department of the Interior, Archeology, NADB Permits, Legislative History, (2007) http://www.cr.nps.gov/archeology/TOOLS/permits/legislative.htm.
10. Sherry Hutt, Caroline Meredith Blanco, Walter E. Stern, & Stan N. Harris, CULTURAL PROPERTY LAW, A PRACTITIONER'S GUIDE TO THE MANAGEMENT, PROTECTION, AND PRESERVATION OF HERITAGE RESOURCES 53 (2004).
11. Archaeological Resources Protection Act of 1979, 16 U.S.C. §§ 470aa–470mm (1979), 16 U.S.C. § 470aa(b).
12. Ryan M. Seidemann, The Reason Behind the Rules: The Archaeological Resources Protection Act of 1979 and Scientific Study, ExpressO Preprint Series, Paper 1874, 3, 8 (2006), available at http://law.bepress.com/expresso/eps/1874 (last visited Feb. 20, 2007) (reacting to Magistrate Judge John Jelderks's quote that the "remains must be made available for study to 'qualified professionals,' 'subject to the type of reasonable terms and conditions that normally apply to studies of archaeological resources under ARPA.'" *Bonnichsen v. U.S.*, 217 F. Supp. 2d 1116, 1166, 1167 [D.Or. 2002]). The author acknowledges in a footnote to this text that ARPA has other purposes as well, including the "reassertion of federal ownership of resources on federal land and the protection of archaeological resources for educational display and for public access to ruins." *Id.* at 8, FN 31.
13. 16 U.S.C. § 432. The Antiquities Act left each agency to determine its own standards for issuing a permit.
14. *Supra* note 11, at 50; 16 U.S.C. § 470cc(b)(1)-(4).
15. 16 U.S.C. § 470ee(a).
16. National Park Service, Department of the Interior, Archeology Program, Permits for Archeological Investigations: Managers, (2007), at http://www.cr.nps.gov/archeology/npsGuide/permits/managers.htm.
17. *Supra* note 11, at 97.
18. 16 U.S.C. §§ 470bb(5), 470cc(g)(2).
19. 43 C.F.R. § 7.7(a).

20. 43 C.F.R. § 7.7(b)(1).
21. 43 C.F.R. § 7.7(b)(4).
22. 16 U.S.C. § 470 et seq. (1966).
23. 25 U.S.C. 3001 et seq. (1990).
24. 43 C.F.R. § 7.12.
25. 43 C.F.R. § 7.7(a).
26. 43 C.F.R. § 7.7(a)(3).
27. 42 U.S.C. 4321, 4331-4335 (1969).
28. 43 C.F.R. § 7.9(a).
29. 16 U.S.C. § 470hh.
30. 43 C.F.R. § 7.18.
31. 43 C.F.R. § 7.9(b). In National Parks, a special use permit will detail additional terms.
32. 43 C.F.R. § 7.9(c).
33. 43 C.F.R § 7.9(g).
34. *Supra* note 17.
35. *Supra* note 17. Note: in NAGPRA such planning is termed an "Intentional Excavation."
36. 43 C.F.R. § 7.9(d).
37. Colin Renfrew & Paul Bahn, ARCHAEOLOGY, THEORIES, METHODS, AND PRACTICE 573 (4th ed. 2004).
38. National Park Service, Department of the Interior, Archeology and Historic Preservation: Secretary of the Interior's Standards and Guidelines, as amended and annotated, at http://www.cr.nps.gov/local-law/arch_stnds_7.htm (last visited Feb. 20, 2007).
39. *Supra* note 17.
40. BLACK'S LAW DICTIONARY 1138 (8th ed. 2004).
41. *Id.* at 1201.
42. *Id.* at 1254.
43. *Id.* at 1253.
44. Danni Dunn & Donald F. Brosnan, TRANSFERRING INTELLECTUAL PROPERTY, 724 PLI/Tax 317, 324 (2006).
45. *Supra* note 41, at 824.
46. *Supra* note 45, at 325.
47. Lisa Michelle Weinstein, Ancient Works, *Modern Dilemmas: The Dead Sea Scrolls Copyright Case*, 43 AM. U.L. REV. 1637, 1651 (1994).
48. 17 USC 101 et seq.
49. Cindy Alberts Carson, *Raiders of the Lost Scrolls: The Right of Scholarly Access to the Content of Historic Documents*, 16 MICH. J. INT'L L. 299, 335 (1995) (quoting the United States Constitution).

50. *Id.* at 336. A caveat is required here to note that this would apply to access to information in final archaeology reports.
51. 17 U.S.C. § 102.
52. 17 U.S.C. § 102(a).
53. 17 U.S.C. § 102(b).
54. *Feist Publications, Inc. v. Rural Telephone Service Co.*, 499 U.S. 340, 345 (1991).
55. *Id.* at 347.
56. Cindy Alberts Carson, *Laser Bones: Copyright Issues Raised by the Use of Information Technology in Archaeology*, 10 HARV. J. L. & TECH. 281, 295–96 (1997).
57. *Supra* note 41, at 1265.
58. 618 F.2d 972, 974 (2d Cir. 1980).
59. *Id.* at 980.
60. Feist, 499 U.S. at 345–46.
61. *Id.* at 346.
62. 17 U.S.C. § 201(a).
63. 17 U.S.C. § 201(c).
64. Feist, 499 U.S. at 348.
65. 17 U.S.C. § 106.
66. 17 U.S.C. § 106A.
67. 17 U.S.C. §§ 201(d), 204(a).
68. 17 U.S.C. § 101.
69. 17 U.S.C. § 201(b).
70. Edward Samuels, The Public Domain in Copyright Law, 41 journal of the copyright soc'y 137, 166 (1993), available at http://www.edwardsamuels.com/copyright/beyond/articles/public.html#fn91 (last visited Nov. 26, 2007). (emphasis supplied).
71. 17 U.S.C. § 501(a).
72. Feist, 499 U.S. at 361.
73. *Id.* at 346–47 (quoting *Burrow-Giles Lithographic Co. v. Sarony*, 111 U.S. 53, 59-60 (1884)).
74. *Supra* note 8, at 342 (discussing copyright in the context of ethnobotany).
75. 17 U.S.C. §§ 502, 503, 504, 505.
76. 17 U.S.C. § 506(a); punishment for this infringement per 18 U.S.C. § 2319.
77. 17 U.S.C. § 302(a).
78. 17 U.S.C. § 302(b).
79. 17 U.S.C. § 302(c).
80. 17 U.S.C. § 107.
81. 17 U.S.C. § 107.
82. *Supra* note 49, at 1669.
83. *Supra* note 49, at 1669.
84. *Supra* note 58, at 313.

85. 17 U.S.C. § 108(a).
86. 35 U.S.C. § 101.
87. *Supra* note 45, at 327.
88. 35 U.S.C. § 154(a).
89. Craig J. Madson, *Patents*, in AMERICAN BAR ASSOCIATION, THE INTELLECTUAL PROPERTY HANDBOOK, A PRACTICAL GUIDE FOR FRANCHISE, BUSINESS AND IP COUNSEL 231 (William A. Finkelstein & James R. Sims III eds., 2005).
90. *Id.* at 232.
91. *Id.* at 234.
92. *Supra* note 8, at 342.
93. *Supra* note 41, at 1530.
94. Christopher P. Bussert, *Trademarks—U.S.*, in AMERICAN BAR ASSOCIATION, THE INTELLECTUAL PROPERTY HANDBOOK, A PRACTICAL GUIDE FOR FRANCHISE, BUSINESS AND IP COUNSEL 4 (William A. Finkelstein & James R. Sims III eds., 2005).
95. *Id.* at 5.
96. *Id.* at 8.
97. *Supra* note 41, at 1533.
98. Henry C. Su, *Trade Secrets*, in AMERICAN BAR ASSOCIATION, THE INTELLECTUAL PROPERTY HANDBOOK, A PRACTICAL GUIDE FOR FRANCHISE, BUSINESS AND IP COUNSEL 276-78 (William A. Finkelstein & James R. Sims III eds., 2005).
99. See 18 U.S.C. § 1832.
100. *Supra* note 99, at 284.
101. *Supra* note 45, at 334.
102. *Supra* note 45, at 335.
103. Molly Torsen, *"Anonymous, Untitled, Mixed Media": Mixing Intellectual Property Law with Other Legal Philosophies to Protect Traditional Cultural Expressions,* 54 AM. J. COMP. L. 173, 193 (2006) (referencing Ken Gormley, One Hundred Years of Privacy, 1992 WIS. L. REV. 1335 (1992)).
104. Restatement (Second) of Torts § 652A(2) (1997).
105. *Id.* at § 652B.
106. *Supra* note 103, at 195 (noting specifically that the "reasonable person" concept may be troublesome for "Western cultures judging non-Western cultures").
107. *Supra* note 103, at 193-94.
108. See generally *Lawrence v. Texas*, 539 U.S. 558 (2003).
109. 17 U.S.C. § 202.
110. 17 U.S.C. § 101.
111. 17 U.S.C. § 103(b).
112. *Supra* note 111, at 174.
113. Susan Scafidi, WHO OWNS CULTURE? APPROPRIATION AND AUTHENTICITY IN AMERICAN LAW 148 (2005).

114. Paul Kuruk, *Protection Folklore under Modern Intellectual Property Regimes: A Reappraisal of the Tensions between Individual and Communal Rights in Africa and the United States*, 48 AMERICAN U. L. REV. 769, 824 (1999) (referencing Michael F. Brown, *Can Culture be Copyrighted?*, 39 CURRENT ANTHROPOLOGY 193, 195 [1998]).
115. *Supra* note 103, at 177 (using the term "traditional cultural expression" as defined by the World Intellectual Property Organization; meaning "music, art, designs, names, signs and symbols, performances, architectural forms, handicrafts and narratives"; Traditional Cultural Expressions [Folklore], World Intellectual Property Organization, Program Activities, at http://www.wipo.int/tk/en/folklore/ [last visited Nov. 26, 2007]).
116. *Supra* note 103, at 174 (quoting WIPO, Traditional Cultural Expressions/Expressions of Folklore, Legal and Policy Options, Intergovernmental Committee on Intellectual Property and Genetic Resources, Traditional Knowledge and Folklore, Sixth Session, para. 2, WIPO Doc. WIPO/GRTKF/IC/6/3 [Dec. 1, 2003]).
117. *Supra* note 103, at 178.
118. Synopsis to Accompany Intellectual Property and Traditional Cultural Expressions, a presentation by Molly Torsen at Santa Clara Law School's Conference on Intellectual Property Protection for Traditional Knowledge and Cultural Expressions, November 9, 2007, available at http://www.wipo.int/tk/en/folklore/culturalheritage/pdf/torsen_santaclara_synopsis.pdf (last visited Nov. 28, 2007) (speaking in the context of "traditional cultural expressions").
119. *Supra* note 116, at 149.
120. *Supra* note 103, at 188.
121. See generally *Burrow-Giles Lithographic Company v. Sarony*, 111 U.S. 53 (1884).
122. 17 U.S.C. § 103(b).
123. 17 U.S.C. § 106A (1990).
124. 17 U.S.C. §§ 101(1),(2).
125. 17 U.S.C. §§ 101(2)(A)-(C).
126. *Supra* note 103, at 188 (referring to legislation in Australia; Australian Copyright Council, Article for Australian Intellectual Property Rights Bulletin, Indigenous Communal Moral Rights, July 16, 2003).
127. *Supra* note 58, at 316.
128. *Supra* note 51, at 331–31 (quoting House Comm. on Judiciary, Copyright Law Revision, H.R. Rep. No. 1476, 94th Cong., 2d Sess. 56 [1976], reprinted in 1976 U.S.C.C.A.N. 5659, 5670).
129. 499 U.S. at 353.
130. Feist, 499 U.S. at 354.
131. *Supra* note 58, at 316.
132. Society of American Archaeology, Principles of Archaeological Ethics, Principle No. 5: Intellectual Property, at http://www.saa.org/ABOUTSAA/COMMITTEES/ethics/principles.html (last visited Mar. 14, 2007).

133. *Supra* note 6, at VI, 6.3.
134. *Supra* note 6, at VI, 6.3.
135. United States Department of Health and Human Services, Office of Human Research Protections, Policy Guidance (2007), at http://www.hhs.gov/ohrp/policy/index.html#research; 45 C.F.R. § 46.116.
136. United States Department of Health and Human Services, Office of Human Research Protections, Tips on Informed Consent (2007), at http://www.hhs.gov/ohrp/humansubjects/guidance/ictips.htm.
137. Jonathan T. Church, For the Record, Should all Disciplines be Subject to the Common Rule? Human Subjects of Social Science Research, ACADEME (Jan. 2002), at http://www.aaup.org/publications/Academe/2002/02mj/02mjftr.htm.
138. American Anthropological Association, Statement on Ethnography and Institutional Review Boards, adopted by AAA Executive Board June 4, 2004, at http://www.aaanet.org/stmts/irb.htm (last visited July 5, 2007) (putting ethnographic research into the context of the "Federal Policy for the Protection of Human Subjects").
139. *Supra* note 51, at 317.
140. *Supra* note 8, at 331.
141. Rebecca Tsosie, *Cultural Challenges to Biotechnology: Native American Genetic Resources and the Concept of Cultural Harm*, 35 THE JOURNAL OF LAW, MEDICINE & ETHICS 396, 398–99 (2007).
142. United States Department of the Interior, Permit for Archaeological Investigations (2007), at http://www.blm.gov/az/cultural/CRUP_Permit_AZ.doc.
143. *Id.*
144. *Id.*
145. U.S. Department of Agriculture, Forest Service, Permit for Archaeological Investigations (2006), at http://www.fs.fed.us/r4/ashley/heritage/contractors/FS_2700_32_Cultural_Resource_PERMIT.doc.
146. 16 U.S.C. 470w-3(a). It should be noted that Section 304 of the NHPA is limited to information relating to a "historic resource," which is a term defined in the statute as "any prehistoric or historic district, site, building, structure, or object included in, or eligible for inclusion in the National Register, including artifacts, records, and material remains related to such a property or resource" (16 U.S.C. 470w(5)).
147. 43 C.F.R. § 7.18(a)(2).
148. Arthur R. Miller & Michael H. Davis, INTELLECTUAL PROPERTY, PATENTS, TRADEMARKS, AND COPYRIGHT 392 (1990).
149. Susan Upton Douglass, *Copyrights*, in AMERICAN BAR ASSOCIATION, THE INTELLECTUAL PROPERTY HANDBOOK, A PRACTICAL GUIDE FOR FRANCHISE, BUSINESS AND IP COUNSEL 199 (William A. Finkelstein & James R. Sims III eds., 2005).
150. Lloyd L. Rich, *Copyright Ownership: The Joint Authorship Doctrine*, THE PUBLISHING LAW CENTER (1995), at http://www.publaw.com/joint/htm.
151. *Supra* note 148, at 377.

152. *Supra* note 150.
153. *Supra* note 2, at 325.
154. Eric C. Kansa, Jason Schultz & Ahrash N. Bissell, *Protecting Traditional Knowledge and Expanding Access to Scientific Data: Juxtaposing Intellectual Property Agendas via a "Some Rights Reserved" Model,* 12 INT'L J. OF CULTURAL PROP. 285, 286 (2005).
155. Arlene Bielefield & Lawrence Cheeseman, INTERPRETING AND NEGOTIATING LICENSING AGREEMENTS, A GUIDEBOOK FOR LIBRARY, RESEARCH, AND TEACHING PROFESSIONS 3(1999).
156. *Supra* note 154, at 301.
157. *Supra* note 155, at 94.

ARTICLE

A Proposed Model Tribal Cultural Resources Protection Code

• • •

Trinidad Contreras

Introduction

For the past few centuries Federal Indian Policy embodied a concerted effort to erase tribal histories and traditions under the assumption that a prosperous future for Native Americans required the destruction of their past. However, in 1990, when the Native American Graves Protection and Repatriation Act (NAGPRA) was passed by Congress, the United States government conceded that Native Americans and Native Hawaiians rely on this enduring cultural heritage as vital to their survival.

Dr. Tom Holm, in his article entitled "Peoplehood: A model for the extension of sovereignty in American Indian Studies,"[1] argues that the "Peoplehood Matrix" is a core assumption for American Indian Studies and a theoretical construct based solely on indigenous knowledge. Deriving from the work of Cherokee anthropologist Dr. Robert K. Thomas, Holm expands on Thomas's notions regarding the Peoplehood. Both Thomas and Holm perceived four aspects of a Peoplehood existed and that these features were interwoven and interdependent; language, sacred history, ceremony/ceremonial cycle, and land are the entities that interact with one another. The attributes of a Peoplehood are universal to indigenous cultures and this conceptual framework was developed to be a primary theoretical assumption for the academic field of Indigenous Studies.

Understanding how these four aspects interact is critical. Not only do they support one another, they cannot exist independently. These facets of the Peoplehood account for the specific social, cultural, political, economic, and ecological behavior embedded in indigenous worldviews and lifeways. By carefully explaining the significance of each aspect, this article presents an argument in favor of the assertion of tribal sovereignty. From this tribal foundation, I will build an argument that, due to independent tribal status prior to the arrival of Europeans in North America, treaties and other sovereign contracts made with Europeans are valid. These treaties, both ratified and unratified, hold the United States government responsible for breaching these agreements, and it is the responsibility of the signatory tribes to hold the U.S. government to its fiduciary responsibility in land claim and cultural property disputes.[2]

Having a distinct language not only makes a group unique, it also creates an exclusive worldview. With language as the source and vehicle in which sacred histories are transmitted, the function and meaning of oral tradition becomes multilayered. Origin, creation, migration, and other stories transmitted among community members and the messages and lessons embedded in these core narratives take on different meaning depending on the person's role and age within the community. Language becomes the tool to describe the natural surroundings, and it is this environment which controls the lexicon and capacity of the language. Place-name is a good example of the relationship between language and ties to the land. Place-names usually denote places that have a cultural significance; they describe the area in the context of their people's history and serve as constant visceral reminder of its importance. Language can also be controlled from within the group; for example, religious leaders and clans are privy to a language separated from the general lexicon because of its ceremonial significance and the power of spoken word. These sacred words can only be articulated by those who have been trained for healing and religious leadership.

Language affects tribal society and helps illustrate the complex social organization tribal communities possess. Sacred history becomes the instrument to address groups' origination and instills core values. Detailing ties of kinship, the significance of ceremony, life lessons, and the meanings behind place-names are just a few of the topics covered in a group's sacred history. As members obtain more knowledge and grow within the community, social customs and political structures arise, thus leading to a social order.

Culturally significant markers in the environment, which are present in sacred histories, become places with great power, because they are usually places that groups identify as the origins of life. Burial sites are also chosen for the spiritual energies. These places are central to the worldview of a culture group. Tribes long removed from their ancestral homelands still experience a connection when they return to those places. Hence there is great attachment and meaning associated with these landscapes.

The ceremonial aspect of Peoplehood demonstrates the difference between indigenous lifeways and that which Western culture calls "religion." To most Americans religion takes place when it is most convenient, or for about two hours once a week. Indigenous cultures have a belief system that is lived every day and is central to daily activities. Ceremony encompasses a sacred language, a particular landscape, and specific stories. Sacred histories explain when, where, and how ceremonies are to be conducted. Ceremonies often coincide with significant natural events such as lunar cycles, solstices, blooming of plants, and changes of the seasons and can include other celestial cycles, bodies, or events.

NAGPRA and Development of Tribal Code

The Native American Graves Protection and Repatriation Act (NAGPRA) is an important piece of legislation, because it represents recognition that sacred objects and cultural patrimony of Native peoples are other than museum specimens. Rather, such items must be respected, protected, and treated as living spiritual entities. NAGPRA also centers on Native communities as sources for resolving legal questions. Through their own laws and codes, tribal court systems, and leadership, tribes are able to interpret and respond to issues regarding sacred objects and cultural patrimony as they intersect the NAGPRA process. Consequently, tribal law must include legislation that protects and enforces tribal interest in its Native art, religion, and culture. Contrary to the history of federal policies directed toward Native Americans that discouraged the continuation of tribal religions and culture, NAGPRA has made traditional lifeways and attitudes of Native Americans the focal point. It becomes essential that tribes be understood. NAGPRA relies upon tribal history and cultural traditions. Thus, NAGPRA will be applied by a tribe under its own cultural and legal standards. For example, NAGPRA requires that requests for repatriation come from the tribal community, causing its provisions to rely upon initiative. The concept of property and the right to transfer title to property is a crucial concept that tribes must clearly define in law and code. NAGPRA requires the definition of an object to come from its tribal owner and not from anthropologists, commercial art dealers/consumers, or museum authorities. NAGPRA seeks to resolve the pending questions of ownership of Native American human remains, funerary and sacred objects, and items of cultural patrimony that are not in control of the tribe.

NAGPRA also obligates federal land managers to consult with federally recognized tribes in the event any NAGPRA protected items materialize on federal lands.[3] The law creates a scenario that disrupts projects if agencies fail to have a permit or a memorandum of agreement as to how to proceed prior to a discovery.[4] In the same manner, excavations on tribal lands, either intentional or inadvertent, must incorporate official tribal action. On tribal lands, tribal consent and permit authorization must be obtained prior to moving forward with any scientific study or development.

NAGPRA provides tribes a vehicle through which they can locate and retrieve tribal property and human remains held in museum and federal agency custody for over a century. Once these items are acknowledged to be tribal property and placed under tribal control, the tribe must decide the direction to be taken. Human remains can be reburied according to tribal custom, or a museum may continue in its role as caretaker, at the behest of the tribe. Cultural items may be reincorporated into ceremonial usage or may be housed in a museum of the tribe's preference, whether it is tribal, private, or public. It should be noted that if a tribe is inclined to sell an item previously identified as an item of cultural patrimony, the action runs counter to NAGPRA's intention, thus risking invalidation of repatriation.

The Archaeological Resources Protection Act and Tribal Code

The Archaeological Resources Protection Act (ARPA) recognizes tribal sovereignty and property rights over cultural property on tribal land and tribal interests on federal land. It preserves the government-to-government relationship between the federal government and tribes. Tribes may identify religious and cultural sites so they may find protection from harm or destruction, while simultaneously keeping these specific locales confidential from public record.[5]

ARPA's criminal and civil enforcement provisions permit tribes to receive restitution. Restitution may include the cost of repairing sites, cultural items, and purification of religious items or reburial of ancestors. ARPA forfeiture provisions make the tribes the owners of forfeited items, including vehicles and tools used in the offense in addition to the seized contraband.

According to 16 U.S.C. §470cc, ARPA allows tribes to issue permits to grant studies to take place on tribal lands. In the event a tribe does not have a code readily established, the federal code is adopted and exercised by the Bureau of Indian Affairs on behalf of the tribe. Tribes must give consent for permits that will be issued for activities on tribal lands. As a result, tribal code is the authority for tribal member activities; these codes control or restrict tribal members from conducting excavations on tribal lands. For any activities taking place on federal lands, where there is potential impact on cultural or religious sites, the federal land manager of the responsible agency must notify affected tribes of all activities prior to issuing a permit for scientific data collection.[6]

Due to the sensitivity and cultural significance of religious or cultural sites, tribes have reason to resist disclosure of this information. ARPA exempts information about the specific location of Indian sites from federal disclosure requirements, and makes it unlawful to disclose this information.[7]

Methods of Examining Existing Tribal Codes

Tribes have exercised management and control of cultural resources for a long time, even before the passage of NAGPRA and similar pieces of legislation.[8] When the federal government amended the National Historic Preservation Act (NHPA) in 1992, federal agencies were given a process for communicating with tribal agents, in the person of a tribal historical preservation officer (THPO). The future of tribal cultural management brightens as more and more tribes develop tribal museums and cultural centers and more Indians return home with academic credentials to become the professionals to staff these institutions.[9]

Prior to suggesting a model for tribes yet to establish a cultural protection code, it is instructive to review those in existence. For this purpose tribal codes were obtained from several databases listed on the Tribal Court Clearinghouse website.[10] More than125 tribal codes are available for examination online. However, the codes are not presented in their entirety, or may not specifically address the preservation of historical and cultural resources. All of the tribal codes on the Clearinghouse website were surveyed; only about ten percent of the available codes had notable provisions for this survey. Yet the data collected have provided an exceptional baseline for comparison of existing tribal codes designed to protect historical and cultural tribal resources.

A table of the tribal codes was then prepared to identify the following: (1) the name of tribe, (2) the applicable chapter or section of tribal code, (3) the year it was enacted and/or amended, (4) a brief description of the code, section by section, emphasizing several characteristics such as variety of terms and definitions used, civil and criminal penalties, and the permit process, including terms and conditions of permit approval. Table 1 indicates, by tribe, terms defined in tribal ordinance. Table 2 provides a comparison of existing tribal codes.

Comparative Analysis of Preexisting Tribal Codes

Table 1 illustrates the variety of terms used by tribes in ordinances. This characteristic is a good place to point out the variety one might encounter when examining approaches to protection of cultural resources and objects of cultural patrimony. Another trait of these ordinances, seen in Table 2, illustrates a tribe's effectiveness to assume the responsibility of protecting cultural resources and regulating archaeological activities, is the length of the ordinance and the complexity of its scope. Such views will inform the model. The next step in a code is the establishment of a department, committee, or council that will possess the authority and responsibility to carry out tribal policies with regards to issuance of archaeological permits.

Cultural Resource Entities

Ho-Chunk, Warm Springs, Tohono O'odham and Red Cliff Chippewa ordinances do not have provisions in their Natural or Cultural Resource codes for the establishment of a cultural resource protection agency. On the other end of the scale, Mille Lac Chippewa, Colville, Eastern Band Cherokee, and Siletz all have detailed codes that establish a department, committee, or council. In the Chickasaw code, authority and responsibility lie with the governor to "recover all remains," utilizing all legal and just means inherent in the sovereign powers of the Chickasaw Nation. The Fort McDowell Yavapai tribe has an archaeological officer rather than a department.

TABLE 1

Tribe	*Terms defined in Ordinance*
Chickasaw	Artifact, Chickasaw Nation, Chickasaw Tribal Government, Remains
Colville	Council, Board, Department, Archaeological resource, Effect, Historic property, Colville register of historic and archaeological properties or Colville register, National register, Reservation, Undertaking, ARPA, NHPA
Eastern Band of Cherokee	Agriculture or Silviculture activities, Burial site, Cemetery, Cultural patrimony, Duly authorized law enforcement official, Disturb, Grave goods, Human remains, Person, Tribal historic preservation officer (THPO)
Fort McDowell Yavapai	No terms
Ho-Chunk	Custodian, Owner, Nation, Property or National property, Nation lands
Mille Lac Band of Chippewa	Archaeological resources, ARPA, Band's register of historic and archaeological properties, Board, Department, Effect, Historic Property, National Register, NHPA, Undertaking
Red Cliff Band of Chippewa	Cemetery, Burial ground, Artifact, Monument, Ruin, Historic, Prehistoric, Federal Antiquities Act
Siletz	Agricultural use, Archaeological activities, Burial item or funerary object, Ground disturbing activity, Human remains, Land use action, Object of cultural patrimony, Person, Protected object, Protected site, Sacred object
Tohono O'odham	Archaeological resources, ARPA, Band's register of historic and archaeological properties, Board, Department, Effect, Historic Property, National Register, NHPA, Undertaking
Warm Springs	Archaeological material, Archaeological site, Ceded area, Cultural material, Cultural site, Historic site, Indian, Protected lands, Protected objects, Reservation, Tribal council, Tribe

TABLE 2

Breakdown of Code

Sec. 1 Defines: cemetery, burial ground, artifact, monument, ruin, historic, prehistoric, antiquity and Indian

Sec. 2 States Red Cliff's Authority to assign permits within their jurisdiction

Sec. 3 Asserts penalties for any unauthorized access, destruction or injury to protected items. Penalties range from $10-$5000

Sec. 4-4-1 Colville Cultural Resources Protection Chapter

Sec. 4-4-2 Legislative Findings - Federal Laws- Preemption: (a) Federal Archeological Resources Protection Act of 1979, (b) no federal permit for excavation or removal... can be issued without consent of Tribes, (c) no exchange or disposition ... without consent of the Tribes, (d) The National Historic Preservation Act declares national policy to work in partnership with Tribes

Sec. 4-4-7 Damaging or Adverse Effects- Prohibited Acts

Sec. 4-4-8 Permits

Sec. 4-4-11 Colville Register of Archaeological and Historic Properties

Sec. 4-4-15 Enforcement: Criminal Offense (b)(1) A fine of not less than $10 or no more than $500; (2) A jail term of not less than one day nor more than six months; (3) Forfeiture of any articles seized

Sec. 19-2 Violations; Penalites: Fine not exceeding five hundred dollars ($500) or by imprisonment not to exceed six (6) months, or both , and in addition forfeit...

Sec. 19-5 Permit; Conditions: No permit shall be issued for a period of more than one year, but permits may be renewed.

Sec. 19-8 Fees; Bonds: (a) $25 per week, (b) the permittee shall, prior to the issuance of the permit, post a bond payable to the Tribe

Sec. 490.001: Tribal Policy and Legislative Intent: Tribe affirms its commitment to preserving, protecting and promoting tribal culture and heritage. Including management of ancient and contemporary cultural use sites and materials which are a fundamental in the recognition of traditional lifeways, values and histories of the Tribe. It is also recognized that these are an invaluable, irreplaceable and endangered tribal resource. 490.001(2): Inclusive list of acts... 16 USC § 461, Historic Sites, Buildings, and Antiquites; 16 USC § 469, Reservoir Salvage Act of 1960; 16 USC § 469(a)(1), Archaeological and Historic Preservation; 16 USC § 4709, National Historic Preservation; 376 C.F.R. 800, Protection of Historic and Cultural Property; 42 USC § 4321, National Environmental Policy; 43 USC § 1996, American Indian Religous Freedom Act...

Table 2, continued

Sec. 490.105 Criminal Penalties: fined not more than $500 or imprisoned not more than six months, or both.

Sec. 490.110 Civil Penalties: punishable by a maximum of $500 (infraction).

Sec. 490.120 Forfeiture of Contraband

Sec. 490.125 Seizure of Security

Sec. 490.130 Removal from Reservation

Sec. 490.200 Tribal Council Permission Required

Sec. 490.600: subsection (2) be initiated only after prior written notification to the State Historic Preservation Office and with the prior written consent of the appropriate Indian tribe…(3) determination of appropriate tribe … shall consult with the Commission on Indian Services which shall designate the appropriate tribe.

Sec. 490.700 Purchase of Artifacts by the Middle Oregon Indian Historical Society: to assist in the protection and preservation of the Tribes' culture. The Middle Oregon Indian Historical Society … purchase or receive donations of artifacts and other materials...

Sec. 3 Definitions: (A) "Archaeological resources" means any material remains of past human life… (B) "Material remains of past human life or activities" means physical human habitation, occupancy … (C) "Chairman" means the Chairman … (D) "Federal Act" means 1) Antiquites Act of 1906; 2) Archaeological and Historic Preservation Act of 1974; 3) National Historic Preservation Act of 1966; 4) American Indian Religous Freedom Act of 1973, 5)... 6) National Environmental Policy Act of 1969.

Sec. 4 Prohibited Acts: (A) resource located on the Papago (TO) Reservation, unless such activity is pursuant to a permit issued under Section 7 or is exempted by section 5(B).

5 Permit, Exemptions: (A) Permits are required… to conduct excavations and/or removal of archaeological resources from the Papago Reservation … (B) Exceptions: first shall receive the written consent to conduct such surveys or studies from District Council ...

Sec. 5 Interference Prohibited - (b) A violation of this Section shall be punishable to the furthest extent of Wisconsin Criminal Law and Ho-Chunk Nation law.

Sec. 9.003 Definitions: (cc) Burial item or funerary object, (d)…(e) Human remains …

Sec. 9.005 Cultural Specialist: Council shall appoint Cultural Specialist … coordinate the Cultural Resources Protection Program.

Table 2, continued

Sec. 9.010 Application for Permit

Sec. 9.019 Required Permit Conditions

Sec. 9.027 Criminal Penalties: Not more then five thousand dollars ($5,000), or imprisoned for not more than one (1) year, or both, per infraction

Sec. 9.028 Civil Penalties: fine of five thousand dollars ($5,000) and/or exclusion from tribal lands.

Sec. 9.030 Forfeiture: deemed contraband and forfeited to the Tribe

Sec. 15-301 Title: Tribal Legislature of the Chickasaw Nation

Sec. 15-305 Powers Granted to Governor: Governor of the Chickasaw Nation to recover all remains

Sec. 70-1 Excavation of skeletal remains: (b) any reburial shall be in a manner ... first approved by the Tribal Council of the Eastern Band of Cherokee Indians.

Sec. 70-2 Sanctity of ancestors who are buried throughout the aboriginal Cherokee lands: (d) if anyone outside the Cherokee nations is in possession of artifacts... should be returned to the proper tribes for reburial.

Sec. 70-604 Penalties: (1) failure to report disturbance of burial site ... shall forfeit not less than $100 nor more than $1,000, (2) disturbs ... shall forfeit not less than $500 nor more than $2,000, (3) intentionally causes or permits ... disturbance to burial site... shall forfeit not less than $1,000 nor more than $5,000, (4) disturbs a burial site for commercial gain not related to the use of the land... may be fined not to exceed two times the gross value gained or two times the gross loss caused by the disturbance, whichever is greater, plus court costs and the costs of investigation and prosecution, reasonably incurred.

The Eastern Band Cherokee code reveals the attention to detail of tribes with extensive codes. The Cherokee code establishes the Tribal Historical Protection Officer (THPO), who maintains records of the past for future generations. The THPO must develop a file that identifies historic properties within reservation boundaries; conduct a history of these areas; manage the collection and catalogue of locations; and issue permits for excavation projects. The THPO is also responsible for developing and maintaining a tribal registry, for any tribal member to view, that includes burial sites, so that these sites are not disturbed. Finally, the Cherokee code creates a tribal repository for any items of cultural patrimony discovered on tribal lands that the tribe has decided not to reintroduce into cultural practices and lifeways. Access and usage of these items for education or research is controlled by the Board of Directors, subject to the approval of the tribal government.

In a similar fashion, the Siletz code creates the Cultural Heritage Committee (CHC) to advise the tribal council in providing oversight over all cultural resource management activities. The council appoints or delegates authority to a general manager to appoint a cultural specialist. The specialist must make presentations to the tribal council with regard to ongoing projects. The position is also responsible for developing regulations for monitoring, identifying, and inventorying protected sites and objects. The CHC makes recommendations for tribal, state, and federal historical registries. Unique among all other codes, the Siletz code has a provision to develop procedures and standards for a limited release of confidential information. The code also requires the CHC to cooperate with the State Historic Preservation Office and the National Historic Preservation Office in the best interests of the tribe, to protect cultural resources.

Sections 4-4-5 and 4-4-6 of the Colville Code and Subchapter 11 of the Mille Lac Chippewa ordinances are also excellent examples of detailed and polished codes.

Permit Guidelines, Terms, and Conditions

All of the tribes with the exception of Ho-Chunk and Chickasaw have permit provisions in their ordinances. The tribal provisions are:

Red Cliff Chippewa: For archaeological sites under Red Cliff jurisdiction, examination of ruins, burial grounds, cemeteries, and excavation activity must be granted by the tribal council. Permission is given to qualified institutions and persons who agree to be subject to the rules and regulations prescribed by the tribal council.

Mille Lac Chippewa: The application process for a permit requires information on the proposed work and the individuals involved. It must include a sketch plan and legal description of the proposed area or site. The applicant must then sign the application and take an oath to abide by the provisions set forth in the laws of the Mille Lac Band. Once the application is complete and ready for review, it gets filed with either the Board or the Director of the Cultural

Department. To be granted approval the application must meet the following requirements: (1) personnel are demonstrably qualified to carry out the project or study, (2) resources found are to remain tribal property, and (3) the work does not conflict with preexisting management plans.

The Board has six months from the submission date to make a decision on permit applications and if necessary the Board may exercise, with written notification to the applicant, an unlimited amount of three month extensions to complete a review. Decisions are made in writing via certified mail to the applicant. Once the permit is granted it is nontransferable, a bond may be required, and the permit term is for three years with possible renewal. However, if work is not initiated within six weeks, or failure to "diligently" prosecute such work after it has begun occurs, a void permit results, without Board orders or proceedings. The permittee is required to report monthly and quarterly to the Board, with summaries of the work performed (monthly) and catalogs of collections and/or photographs (quarterly). If there are items which are to leave reservation boundaries, a temporary removal license is required to accompany all artifacts at all times while off reservation.

Suspension and revocation of permits occur when a violation of permit provisions or other applicable laws has occurred, circumstances have changed so that the criteria of permit requirement are no longer met, or misrepresentation occurred on the permit application.

Colville: Language and provisions are verbatim of the Mille Lac Chippewa.

Ft. McDowell Yavapai: Permits are issued by the archaeological officer of the community to qualified persons, organizations, and museums. Permits are issued on the condition that sites are returned to their original conditions and that all property or objects remain under tribal control. Permits are issued for one-year terms but can be renewed. A bond of $25 per week in advance must be posted prior to issuance of permit, to assure the site is restored.

Tohono O'odham: There are exceptions for activities *not* requiring permits: (1) projects involving archaeological surveys or studies not involving collections or disturbance of resources. Nonmembers if the tribe must receive written consent of the respective district council; (2) collection or recovery done by employees or agents of the Tohono O'odham; (3) official tribal archaeological management; (4) federal agents carrying out duties under archaeological management; and (5) work done under federal permits prior to the enactment of this ordinance.

Issued by the Chairman at his "absolute discretion," permits are issued to qualified persons. An outline of the proposed work must be submitted, including an outlet for public written dissemination of results. In addition, the outline must include the names and contact information of those involved with the permit, identify the location where temporarily removed items will be housed and under what conditions, and supply certification of the hosting authority.

The Chairman, after consultation with the affected district(s), decides if the work will benefit the tribe, and if the applicant is qualified the Chairman will make a decision on the permit application. If the study/survey is to be conducted on allotted land, consent of the Indian landowner is required. Also, the applicant is required to employ qualified members of the Tohono O'odham community to conduct the proposed work, if their services are available.

Terms and conditions stipulate that if possible the work must be open to the public in cooperation with schools and other educational programs. Initiation of work constitutes acceptance of terms. Failure to correct a situation that led to a permit suspension and permit termination by the Tohono O'odham are causes for a permit to be lost. Appeals can be petitioned in writing to the Council and a final decision is made within 90 days.

Warm Springs: Requires Tribal Council permission through the Land Use Committee. Procedural rules are developed by the Land Use Committee.

Siletz: Any person, including tribal departments, must obtain a permit prior to commencement of ground-disturbing activity. The application must describe the proposed activity, location (including maps), and any identified protected sites or objects in the vicinity. The Cultural Resources Program then makes recommendations to the Cultural Heritage Committee and Tribal Council to approve or deny the application. All information must be shared with the Cultural Resources Program. All activities must be respectful of tribal culture and religion. No burial items are to be removed without express written permission. Finally, reports shall be issued throughout the activity period.

Eastern Cherokee: All tribal members, tribal employees, lessees, individuals, organizations contracted with tribes, and government agents shall have a permit issued by the Tribal Historical Preservation Office (THPO). All applications are reviewed by the THPO and applicants are notified within 30 days of a decision. An archaeological review is required to accompany the permit application in the event the area or site has not previously been examined. The archaeological review consists of a file search within the tribal registry and an archaeological field study. Appeals of a denied permit application can be made in writing within 14 days of notification of denial. The tribal council decision is final.

There are lands that are excluded from field or archaeological surveys (see Sec. 70-404). Archaeological studies and surveys must be conducted by a qualified archaeologist, and tribal members doing work are to be paid. All nontribal members must also possess an ARPA permit. Finally, any surveys conducted on fee land within reservation boundaries must contact the Office of the State Archaeologist of North Carolina to determine the process to obtain a permit and provide notice to the THPO.

Penalties: Civil and Criminal

Red Cliff Chippewa: Any person who shall appropriate, excavate, injure, or destroy any Indian cemetery, Indian burial mound, or burial ground including items as well as skeletal remains, historic or prehistoric ruins or monuments, or any object of antiquity situated on lakes within the boundaries of the Red Cliff Reservation or within the territory of the Lake Superior Chippewa without the written permission of the Red Cliff Tribal Council having jurisdiction over said lands shall be subject to civil forfeiture of not less than $10 nor more than $5,000.

Colville: Criminal- In the event a defendant is found guilty, the court may impose: (I) A fine of not less $10 or more than $500; (II) A jail term of not less than one (1) day nor more than six (6) months; (III) Forfeiture of any articles seized.

Civil- The Colville Confederated tribes may bring a civil action against any person who is alleged to have engaged in any activity which violates the law, including non-tribal members. The tribes may also bring an action for forfeiture of any articles possessed in violation of the law.

Chickasaw: No provisions in Chapter 3 Preservation of Land and Natural Resources

Tohono O'odham: No provisions in Chapter 1 Archaeological Resources Protection

Fort McDowell Yavapai: No provisions in Chapter 19 Antiquities and Archaeological Sites

Warm Springs: Criminal- Any Indian who knowingly violates, or counsels, procures, solicits, or employs any other person to violate, any prohibition contained in WSTC 490.100 shall, upon conviction, be fined not more than $500, or imprisoned not more than six months, or both. Such person may be also subject to the civil penalties provided for in WSTC 490-110.
Civil- Any person violating the provisions of this Chapter commits a civil infraction punishable by fine or exclusion from the reservation pursuant to WSTC Chapter 300. The infraction shall be punishable by a maximum fine of $500. The trial of any such infraction shall be by the Court without a jury and the prosecution shall have the burden of proving the alleged infraction by a preponderance of the evidence. There shall be no appeal from a judgment involving such an infraction.

Ho-Chunk- There is no criminal or civil provision.

Siletz: Criminal- Any person who knowingly violates, or counsels, procures, solicits or employs any other person to violate, any prohibition contained in the ordinance shall, upon conviction, be fined not more than five thousand dollars ($5000), or imprisoned for not more than one (1) year, or both, per infraction. There may also be an assessment of civil penalties and damages.
Civil- Any person violating the provisions of this Ordinance commits a civil infraction punishable by a fine of five thousand dollars ($5,000) and/or exclusion from tribal lands.

Eastern Cherokee Band: Penalties- (1) Any person who fails to report the disturbance of a burial site or the cataloged land contiguous to a cataloged burial site as required, shall forfeit not less than $100.00, nor more than $1,000.00. (2) Any person who intentionally disturbs a burial site which is not cataloged, without the authorization of the Tribe, shall forfeit not less than $500.00, nor more than $2,000.00. (3) Any owner who intentionally causes or permits any activity which disturbs a burial site after receiving notice from the tribe without the authorization shall forfeit not less than $1,000.00, nor more than $5,000.00. (4) Any person who disturbs a burial site for commercial gain, not related to the use of the land, where a burial site is located, or who disturbs a cataloged burial site for commercial gain related to use of the land where a burial site is located, may be fined not to exceed two times the gross value gained or two times the gross loss caused by the disturbances, whichever is greater, plus court costs and the cost of investigation and prosecution, reasonably incurred.

Overview of Model Code

The following Cultural Resource Preservation Code is intentionally broad to primarily address the criteria set forth in NAGPRA. NAGPRA informs the code as it is the only federal statute focused solely upon property rights and protection of Native American cultural property. The code also allows a tribe to request items beyond NAGPRA from public and private museums, individuals, and the Smithsonian Institution under the National Museum of the American Indian Act (NMAIA) and other laws, such as ARPA. As a vehicle to establish and maintain cultural programs and archives, the model code also permits tribes to seek grants and enter into contracts with curators and museum entities to ensure the preservation of cultural or religious items through the creation of a cultural division within the tribal administration infrastructure. The model also establishes a permit system for excavation or scientific studies conducted on tribal lands, while simultaneously creating civil and criminal penalties for violating terms of a permit, or excavating without a permit. Tribes should implement provisions that are culturally specific or relevant to reinforce their own unique traditional common law, ideals, societal roles, and cultural needs.

Section 1: This is the context section, with a citation, findings, purpose, and definitions. The definitions are drawn from two sources: an indigenous lens or point of view and NAGPRA. Tribes should be careful when defining terms like "cultural item," because of the variety of definitions currently used in various pieces of legislation. Code definitions should be broad enough to encompass not only items protected within NAGPRA but also those found in NMAIA and ARPA. For example, under NAGPRA, cultural items include not only human remains but also funerary or sacred objects and items of cultural patrimony. A term that needs to be addressed by specific code is "cultural affiliation." It has been established under NAGPRA that museums and federal agencies have the initial burden to determine cultural affiliation for human remains and their associated funerary items, in an inventory, which culturally affiliated tribes may request. Tribes initiate claims for other cultural items, generally referred to in the summary of the collection. When making a claim, the initial burden of proof lies with the tribe, which is where tribes can utilize the traditional knowledge of elders in combination with other tribal experts who have relevant academic credentials. "Right of Possession" definitions should include the legal standard for the property right. This includes cultural items found on tribal lands as well as items found on private or federal lands.

Section 2: Establishes the functions and authority of the Cultural Resources Preservation Department/Commission/Council. It must be able to continue to function regardless of political changes within the tribe, in order to facilitate the return of cultural items. The selection process will differ among tribes based on respective tribal and traditional practices. The tribal governing body must consider the most appropriate means of selecting religious leaders since in some tribes traditional members may not want to participate in secular political activities of a tribe.

This section also establishes a Cultural Rights and Resources Checklist, which outlines the administrative assessment for preservation projects affecting cultural resources. Section 2 delineates the method in which sites can be nominated for the Tribal Cultural Resource Register and puts forth the eligibility requirements for the National Register of Historic Places.

Section 3: The Cultural Resource Permits section provides a process for archaeological excavations and scientific studies to be conducted on tribal lands. NAGPRA, NEPA, and NHPA assume an ARPA-like tribal permit will issue for actions on the tribal lands. Failure to obtain a permit prior to excavation of any kind will result in penalties. The tribe should establish a timeline for review of permits when they seek to monitor appropriate activity.

Section 4: The civil and criminal enforcement section provides for penalties for violations under tribal law. Fines and imprisonment have been established, but can be altered by tribes to impose greater penalties and reflect individual concerns of the tribe.

Title _____
_____Tribe Code of Laws

CULTURAL RESOURCES PRESERVATION CODE

CHAPTER _____.01 TITLE, FINDINGS, PURPOSE AND DEFINITIONS

_____.01.010 Title

The title of this code shall known as "Title_____
Cultural Resources Preservation Code."

_____.01.020 Findings

Beyond the memory of man, the _______Nation/Tribe/Band/People used traditional lands, sites and communities within the established boundaries of the Reservation/Rancheria/Reserve freely, continuous and uninterrupted for maintaining a traditional lifeway, a lifestyle inherited from ancestors through the tribe's language, sacred history, ceremonial cycle and ties to the aforementioned land base. From these intertwining entities from which Indigenous knowledge is created, maintained and passed down to the next generation, members discover the tribe's language, resources, traditions, culture and spiritual values. It is this unique heritage that still exists today and is evident in the lives of tribal members' belief systems and practices. The______(Nation/Tribe/Band/People) hereby find and declare that the integrity of the _______traditions, cultural heritage and values are not to be dominated by the United States government. In addition, the _________ (Nation/Tribe/Band/People) also recognize the existence of unregulated activities affecting cultural resources interferes with tribal sovereignty and leads to the destruction of sacred lands, sites and other religious or cultural items of the _________Nation/Tribe/Band/People.

The ______tribal council finds that the spirit and purpose of the code should guide and inform the Cultural Resources Preservation Commission in carrying out its duties, roles and responsibilities under this code. The Commission shall seek to ensure: All existing and any new federal legislation must be administered on tribal land in a manner that maintains and enhances the jurisdictional integrity, authority and perpetuity of the (______Nation/Tribe/Band/People) as an independent and self-governing sovereign nation.

The ability of the (______) people and the (______Nation/Tribe/Band/People) to sustain customs, practices and traditions of its culture shall not be adversely affected by federal or state law or policies.

The (_______Nation/Tribe/Band/People) may receive federal funding for the maintenance, operation and control of any and all federal programs intended to benefit the ______people directly from the federal government.

Appropriations by Congress for the benefit of the ________people and the (_______Nation/Tribe/Band) should also include sufficient funds to cover the costs of negotiations or litigation wherever necessary to resolve jurisdictional issues or conflicts of interest between federal, tribal and state authorities.

Congress acknowledges the inherent sovereignty of the (_________ Nation/Tribe/Band/People) by insuring no legislation, regulation or policy is enacted without the participation and full consent of the (Nation/Tribe/Band/People).

The National Historic Preservation Act (NHPA), 16 USC § 470, declares it a national policy to develop working partnerships with Tribal governments for the protection of cultural resources, providing a mechanism by which Tribal governments may carry out the provisions of the Act, including the power to nominate sites to the National Register of Historic Places. The (__________ Nation/Tribe/Band/People) find that effective tribal procedures must be established to carry out these activities, and to assert priorities under NEPA, approach tribal claims in the NAGPRA process, and replace ARPA provisions with tribal permitting requirements.

_____.01.030 Purpose

As a sovereign entity, the (__________Nation/Tribe/Band/People) desires to manage the (Nation/Tribe/Band/People's) cultural resources in a spirit of stewardship. The purpose of this code is to provide a framework to ensure the (________Nation/Tribe/Band/People's) cultural resources are preserved and protected through well-informed decisions that involve sound decision making principles.

It shall be the policy of the (________ Nation/Tribe/Band/People) to:

- Preserve and manage cultural resources in ways that contribute to meeting social, environmental, spiritual, economic and other needs of present and future generations.
- Provide leadership and technical assistance in the preservation, protection and conservation of cultural resources by developing a culturally appropriate cultural resources management program, and by sponsoring educational programs for the general public and training programs for tribal members and employees and by consulting or cooperating with other government agencies.
- Administer cultural resources in the jurisdiction or control of the (Nation/Tribe/Band/People) on land within the traditional territory of the (Nation/Tribe/Band/People) in a spirit of stewardship and for the inspiration of present and future generations.

___.01.040 Definitions

Our Culture: Our beliefs, spirituality, language, epistemology, what we eat, how we live, everyday activities, attitudes and values passed down in oral or sacred histories.

Cultural Practice: An intangible aspect of our way of life which is especially valued by the Nation/Tribe/Band/People. Although intangible by nature, cultural practices may be associated with or dependent on cultural resources, such as language, oral traditions, ideology, family life, subsistence techniques, graphic arts, handicrafts, music, dance and many other aspects of traditional life.

Cultural Resource Management: The range of activities aimed at understanding, preserving and providing for enjoyment of cultural properties. This means the (___ Nation/Tribe/Band/People) is the administrator, caretaker and protector of these properties and resources. Activities include research, planning for actions affecting cultural resources and the stewardship of those resources.

Traditional Cultural Property: A people's cultural practices, customs, beliefs rooted in a collective history and important in maintenance of a unique traditional cultural identity. These are inherent properties passed down from time immemorial by ancestors, to be passed on to future generations.

Adverse Effect: A reasonable likelihood of more than moderate adverse consequences for cultural resources in any given site or area. (1) This determination is based on the context of a proposed action or development. (2) The intensity of a proposed action, including the magnitude and duration of an impact and the likelihood of its occurrence. (3) The relationship between a proposed action and other similar actions which are individually insignificant but may have a cumulative impact.

Ancestral or Human Remains: The physical remains, articulated and unarticulated bones, bone fragments, associated artifacts, where decomposition has occurred of any deceased human being(s) that is reasonably believed to be Native American or has been identifiable through available evidence.

Archaeological Resource: Any material remains of human life or activities which are at least one hundred years old and of archaeological value.

Burial Site: Any natural or prepared physical location, whether originally below, on or above the surface of the earth, into which, as part of a death rite or ceremony, an individual(s) human remains are deposited. All burial sites are sacred sites and defined as protected sites or funerary objects and are also protected as part of the original cultural integrity of the burial.

Commission/Council/Department: The Cultural Resources Preservation Commission/Council/Department as established by the tribe is _____.

Consultation: A formal, direct contact with the Tribal leader, or his/her designee, by any governmental agency or private entity. Such consultation shall be for the specific purpose of seeking tribal participation concerning decisions related to affected cultural resources, as required by federal and state statutes.

Cultural Resources: In the traditional view, but not limited to, four major categories: language, including traditional place names found in oral or sacred histories; traditional cultural properties; historic sites; and archaeological resources. It also means any material remains of the past, present or future human life or activities which are of cultural significance, as determined by the council. Such materials include but are not limited to: pottery, basketry, weapons, weapon projectiles, tools, structures, rock paintings and carvings.

Cultural Resources Management System: The comprehensive system for the identification, protection, and preservation of cultural resources developed and approved by the Commission/Council/Department. The Cultural Resources Management System shall be based on the principles of baseline information or history and include at a minimum: this code, the cultural resources preservation plan, cultural resources register, regulations and policies approved and adopted by the Commission/Council/Department.

Cultural Site: A geographic locality containing tribal cultural resource properties and archaeological resources.

Indian: Any person of Indian blood and who is a member of a federally recognized Indian tribe or any other person on a Reservation/Reserve/Rancheria who is recognized by the community as an Indian, including Canadian First Nations or an Alaskan Native.

Museum collections are: Any private, local, state or federal agency including institutions of higher education, which has possession or control of tribal cultural resources.

NAGPRA is: The Native American Graves Protection and Repatriation Act of 1990, PL 101-601, 25 U.S.C. 3001-3013.

NHPA: The National Historic Preservation Act of 1966, 16 U.S.C. § 470.

National Register: The National Register of Historic Places, administered under the guidelines of the Secretary of the Interior and the Keeper.

Natural Resources: A material source of wealth occurring in a natural state, such as floral, faunal, mineral or elemental resources.

Protected Site: The act or process of applied measures designed to defend or guard a property or site from deterioration, loss or attack. In the case of building or structures, such treatment is of a temporary nature and anticipates future historic preservation treatment. Cultural resources or archaeological sites may have temporary or permanent protective measures.

CHAPTER ______.02
Cultural Resources Preservation Department/Commission/Council

___.02.010 Establishment and Authority of the Cultural Resources Preservation Department/Commission/Council

.011 The Cultural Resources Preservation Department/Commission/Council is hereby created and shall be the agency responsible for the protection, preservation, and conservation of cultural resources. It will also undertake cultural resources management planning; perform the functions of a Tribal Historic Preservation Office for the (____________ Nation/Tribe/Band/People).

.012 The Cultural Resources Preservation Department/Commission/Council shall prepare a comprehensive Cultural Resources Preservation Plan which shall consist of a report or a series of reports on all manner of cultural resources and the historic preservation program. These reports shall describe the preservation program. The program shall be given a philosophy or rationale behind the choices made for the current and future projections of the preservation program by the (Department/Commission/Council) and approved by the tribe . The plan shall also be reviewed and approved by the governing body of the (________ Nation/Tribe/Band/People).

.013 The Cultural Resources Preservation Department/Commission/Council shall prepare an annual budget for the program which shall be reviewed and approved by the governing body of the (__________ Nation/Tribe/Band/People).

.014 The Cultural Resources Preservation Department/Commission/Council shall ensure clear roles and responsibilities for staff are developed to monitor any activities that might affect cultural resources as economic fluctuations occur within Reservation/Reserve/Rancheria boundaries.

.015 The Cultural Resources Preservation Department/Commission/Council shall designate a director for the Tribal Historic Preservation Department/Commission/Council, who will be authorized to inform other tribal, federal, state and local governments and private organizations on matters pertaining to cultural resource preservation to achieve the goals set forth by the Cultural Resources Preservation Plan.

.016 The Cultural Resources Preservation Department/Commission/Council shall prepare and submit to the Secretary of Interior a plan describing the functions of the Cultural Resources Preservation Department/Commission/Council and of the Tribal Historic Preservation Officer.

___.02.020 Cultural Rights and Resources Checklist Policy

The Cultural Rights and Resources Checklist Policy addresses projects that require permits, consultations, review, comments or recommendations regarding activities that may affect cultural resources on tribal land and their preservation. Tribal reviews shall be based on the following checklist which shall include the following information:

1. Project name.
2. Area, site, or location identified.
3. Funding sources to determine regulatory requirements or compliance procedures.
4. Whether the area, site, location, of a project is listed or eligible to be listed on the Cultural Resource Register and/or the National Register of Historic Places.
5. Listing of tribal, federal, state, or local permits or licenses and applications.

6. A report that indicates the potential adverse effects on cultural resources or properties.
7. Whether the project is to take place on or off the reservation, but affecting sites on the reservation.
8. Acknowledgment of the consultation process with the ___________ Nation/Tribe/Band/People.
9. Agreement to comply with the Cultural Resources Preservation Department/Commission/Council's Code of regulations, policies and procedures.

___.02.030 Nominations to the Cultural Resource Register

.031 The Cultural Resources Preservation Department/Commission/Council is authorized to nominate all sites, buildings and objects within the Reservation/Reserve/Rancheria that qualify for listing on the Cultural Resource Register.

.032 The Cultural Resources Preservation Department/Commission/Council shall:

1. Conduct a comprehensive survey of all historical and cultural resource properties on the Reservation/Reserve/Rancheria.
2. Compile an inventory, including basic information about the location and history of each property.

.033 Based on the evaluation of information described in the inventory of all historical and cultural resource properties, each item will be assigned into a category of significance, subject to the approval of the governing body of the (___________Nation/Tribe/Band/People). Recommendations to modify or limit actions affecting a cultural and/or historic property can be made by appropriate religious leaders or respected members of the community who are regarded by the community as cultural experts.

___.02.040 Nominations to the National Register of Historic Places

The Cultural Resources Preservation Department/Commission/Council shall prepare nomination forms for those properties that appear to be eligible for placement on the National Register of Historic Places.

___.02.050 Tribally Owned Properties

The Cultural Resources Preservation Department/Commission/Council shall initiate measures and procedures to provide for the maintenance, preservation, rehabilitation or restoration of tribally owned and registered sites at the standard prescribed by the director of the Cultural Resources Preservation Department/Commission/Council.

___.02.060 Promotion of Preservation Efforts

The Cultural Resources Preservation Department/Commission/Council is authorized to take the following actions for the purpose of promoting cultural resources and historic preservation efforts in the following way:

1. Develop and make available to tribal agencies information and advice concerning professional methods and techniques for identifying, preserving, stabilizing, improving and restoring and maintaining cultural resource sites and historic properties.
2. Advise tribal agencies in the evaluation, identification, preservation, improvement and maintenance of historical and cultural resources.
3. Encourage public interest and participation in cultural resource management and historical preservation.
4. Encourage training and education in the field of tribal cultural resource management, archaeological and historical preservation.
5. Prepare and maintain a current list of tribally produced and non-Indian archaeologists, anthropologists, historians and other relevant professionals approved to perform services related to cultural resources and historic preservation efforts and activities for the _______ Nation/Tribe/Band/People.
6. Employ professional and support staff as employees or independent contractors within the confines of the approved budget to fulfill the purposes of this code.

___.02.070 Annual Report

The Cultural Resources Preservation Department/Commission/Council shall submit annually a comprehensive report of its activities and report the results of its studies to the governing body of the ________ Nation/Tribe/Band/People. Reports shall include a summary of actions undertaken by the Department/Commission/Council such as permits issued, review of nominations to the tribal and federal registry and other aforementioned responsibilities.

CHAPTER ________.03 CULTURAL RESOURCES REGISTER

___.03.010 Nomination and Acceptance

The Cultural Resources Register is established for the purpose of which shall be to serve as the register for the _________ Nation/Tribe/Band/People. This register shall include tribal cultural resources and properties, historic sites, buildings, structures and objects of significant cultural value. The Cultural Resources Preservation Department/Commission/Council shall prepare a comprehensive review of the nomination for presentation to the governing body of the (___________ Nation/Tribe/Band/People).

___.03.020 Undertakings Upon Listed Properties or Properties Eligible to be Listed

Any person or entity applying for a permit to conduct an undertaking within tribal Reservation/Reserve/Rancheria boundaries shall inform the Cultural Resources Preservation Department/Commission/Council whether the proposed activity may affect any property listed on or eligible to the Cultural Resources Register.

___.03.030 Cultural Resource Permits

.031 Application: Any person proposing to visit or inspect cultural resources, undertake cultural resource inventories, alter, collect, excavate, disturb or remove cultural resources or otherwise cause an adverse effect to cultural resources shall apply for a Cultural Resources Preservation Permit from the Cultural Resources Preservation Department/Commission/Council.

.032 Each application must be accompanied by a written outline of the proposed work. The application must supply, but is not limited to the following: detailed account of all individuals involved in the undertaking, contact information, proposed start and end date, project time frame, the primary investigator, acknowledgment that all material(s) removed shall remain in tribal custody, and methods of preservation of cultural items.

.033 The application must be accompanied by a detailed map and description of the particular site in question and the effects associated with such an undertaking.

.034 Each application shall be accompanied by a completed checklist which is administered and approved by the Cultural Resources Preservation Department/Commission/Council.

.035 Once the permit has been approved by the Cultural Resources Preservation Department/Commission/Council and the governing body of the (__________Nation/Tribe/Band/People), the application is filed and a courtesy copy will be provided to the applicant.

___.03.040 Time Frame for Processing Permit Applications

The Cultural Resources Preservation Department/Commission/Council Director shall make a decision to issue or deny a permit within forty-five calendar days after the date of the completed application. The Director may extend this date for an additional fifteen days, however; the applicant must be notified with a written explanation of the factors requiring additional time. Once the Director has made a decision to issue or deny a permit, the applicant shall be notified via registered mail in writing of this decision.

___.03.050 Terms and Conditions of Cultural Resources Preservation Permit

All permits issued by the Cultural Resources Preservation Department/Commission/Council shall include the following terms and conditions:

.051 Each permit shall identify the individual(s) who shall be responsible for carrying out the terms and conditions of the permit.

.052 The permit shall contain provisions requiring restoration of the site to its former condition.

.053 Every permit shall not be transferable unless the Director of the Cultural Resources Preservation Department/Commission/Council gives written permission.

.054 The duration of the permit shall not exceed twelve months under its original or modified terms and conditions.

___.03.060 Suspension and Revocation of Permit

The Cultural Resources Preservation Department/Commission/Council may suspend or revoke a permit based on any of the circumstances listed below.

.061 A permit may be suspended or revoked upon determination by the Director of Cultural Resources Preservation Department/Commission/Council that the continuation of activities would not be in the best interests of the Nation/Tribe/Band or its people.

.062 A permit may be suspended or revoked if terms and/or conditions of the permit have been violated or are superseded by other applicable laws, regulations or policies.

.063 A permit may be suspended or revoked upon determination by the Director of Cultural Resources Preservation Department/Commission/Council that the materials in the application of the permit were misrepresented or did not follow standard procedures delineated by the Cultural Resources Preservation Department/Commission/Council.

___.03.070 Damaging or Adverse Effects Prohibited

a. No person shall excavate, remove, damage or otherwise alter, deface, destroy any cultural resource or historic property on land within Reservation/Reserve/Rancheria boundaries. This shall not apply to employees engaged on official business on behalf of the Cultural Resources Preservation Department/Commission/Council.

b. No person shall sell, offer to sell, purchase, exchange, transfer, transport, or receive any cultural or historical resource if it is removed or excavated within Reservation/Reserve/Rancheria boundaries. This shall not apply to employees engaged on official business on behalf of the Cultural Resources Preservation Department/Commission/Council.

c. No person shall engage in ethnographic research within Reservation/Reserve/Rancheria boundaries without written authorization.

CHAPTER__________.04 ENFORCEMENT

___.04.010 Violations

It shall be unlawful for any person to perform any act which is prohibited under this Code, or to fail to do any act that is required under this Code.

___.04.020 Criminal Penalties

The tribal Court may impose one or all of the following penalties for violating the provisions found within this Code:

1. A fine of not more than $5,000.
2. A jail term not to exceed one year.
3. Forfeiture of any article seized by reason of illegal activities prohibited by this Code.

___.04.030 Civil Assessments

.031 Individuals violating the prohibitions of this Code shall be subject to civil assessment imposed by the Cultural Resources Preservation Department/Commission/Council.

.032 Violations of the provisions shall be grounds for withdrawal of the privilege of doing business with the___________ Nation/Tribe/Band/People. The final determination is made by the governing body of the ________ _Nation/Tribe/Band/People.

.033 Any person not a member of the __________ Nation/Tribe/Band/People who visits or inspects cultural properties within the exterior boundaries of the Reservation/Reserve/Rancheria without a valid permit shall be committing trespass. Such individuals determined to be in trespass after a hearing before the Cultural Resources Preservation Department/Commission/Council shall be assessed a civil forfeiture of not to exceed $500 for the first offense and not to exceed $1000 for any subsequent offenses.

.034 Any individual within the exterior boundaries of the Reservation/Reserve/Rancheria who alters, collects, damages, defaces, destroys, excavates, removes or sells cultural properties or who collects ethnographic data without explicit permission or valid permit shall be liable, after a hearing before the Cultural Resources Preservation Department/Commission/Council, for civil damages to be determined in the following manner:

1. Full costs of restoration of cultural resources.
2. Enforcement and administration costs associated with the civil action.
3. Cost of disposition of cultural properties, including costs of curation.
4. Costs associated with documentation, approved testing, and evaluation of the cultural property in order to assess a plan for its restoration.

Notes

1. Wicazo Sa Review (Spring 2003).
2. *Johnson v. M'Intosh*, 21 U.S. (8 Wheat) 543 (1823); *Worcester v. Georgia*, 31 U.S. 515 (1832).
3. 43 C.F.R. section 10.5, 25 U.S.C. 3005.
4. Inadvertent discovery regulations, 43 C.F.R. section 10.3.
5. 16 U.S.C. section 470cc(c).
6. 16 U.S.C. 470cc(c).
7. Federal Freedom of Information Act (FOIA), 5 U.S.C. section 552, ARPA exemption of sites from FOIA disclosure, 16 U.S.C. section 470hh.
8. Chickasaw Nation (Sec. 15-307); Confederated Tribes of the Colville Reservation (Title 4 Ch. 4); Confederated Tribes of Siletz (Sec. 9); Warm Springs Reservation (Ch. 490); Little Traverse Bay Bands of Odawa Indians (Sec. 4 Ch.8); Tohono O'odham (Title 8 Ch. 1); Eastern Band of Cherokee (Ch. 70); Elk Valley Rancheria ((Part 2 Sec. 48); Ft. McDowell Yavapai Community (Ch. 19); Ho-Chunk Nation (Title 7 Sec. 2); Lummi Nation (Title 40); Mille Lac Band (Title 10); Nisqually Nation (Sec. 14-05).
9. Note also that the 1992 amendments to the National Historic Preservation Act (NHPA) established Tribal Historic Preservation Offices to replace state offices and their functions for those tribes that desire to do so,16 U.S.C. 470a(d)(2), and that Traditional Cultural Places (TCPs) may be nominated to the National Register of Historic Places to afford protection. 16 U.S.C. 470a(d)(6). As of December 2007, there were 76 THPOs.
10. http://www.tribal-institute.org/lists/codes.htm . The Tribal Court Clearinghouse website maintained by the Tribal Law and Policy Institute, which is a Native American–owned and operated nonprofit corporation organized to design and deliver education, research, training, and technical assistance programs that promote the enhancement of justice in Indian country.

Rubin v. The Islamic Republic of Iran
A Struggle for Control of Persian Antiquities in America

James A. Wawrzyniak, Jr.

Winner of the 2007 LCCHP Law School Writing Competition

Part I. Background

In 2003, a group of American plaintiffs won a $90 million default judgment against the Islamic Republic of Iran. This is the story of how they tried to execute that judgment.

The Underlying Claim

The incident that prompted the litigation was a suicide bombing on the afternoon of September 4, 1997, at a crowded pedestrian mall on Ben Yehuda Street, Jerusalem, Israel.[1] Five members of the plaintiff group were present that day, and suffered life-altering injures. As the court later found, the bombers packed their bombs with "nails, screws, pieces of glass, and chemical poisons to cause maximum pain, suffering, and death."[2] This vicious cocktail resulted in one plaintiff suffering multiple shrapnel wounds to his lower body, a shard of glass in his left eye, and a permanent hematoma to his left leg.[3] Another had a burned cornea and partially severed ear.[4] A third had, among other injuries, burns covering 40 percent of his body and more than one hundred shrapnel-induced entry wounds.[5] The other plaintiffs present that day were injured in similarly painful ways. In addition, four of the victims' family members (not present that day) sought recovery for the emotional injuries caused by watching their loved ones suffer and for the time and effort required to provide full-time care to them in the attack's immediate aftermath. Altogether, then, nine individuals (sometimes called the "Rubin plaintiffs" after the lead plaintiff in the group) sustained injuries as a direct result of the terrorist attack.

Hamas claimed responsibility for the bombing.[6] Israeli police wasted no time arresting two Hamas operatives and bringing them to trial.[7] Both were subsequently convicted by an Israeli criminal court on multiple counts of murder, attempted murder, and membership in a terrorist organization.

Soon thereafter, the Rubin plaintiffs brought civil actions for damages against Hamas[8] (for actually carrying out the bombing) and the Islamic Republic of Iran[9] (for providing material support and finance for the bombing). The action against Iran was brought in United States District Court for the District of Columbia on July 31, 2001.[10] The plaintiffs named Iran, the Iranian Ministry of Information and Security (MOIS), Ayatollah Ali Hoseini Khamenei, Ali Akbar Hashemi-Rafsanjani, and Ali Fallahian-Khuzestani as defendants.[11] The individual defendants were high-ranking members of the Iranian government at the time of the bombing.

The district court noted jurisdiction based upon the Foreign Sovereign Immunities Act (FSIA), 28 United StatesC. § 1602 et seq. None of the defendants made an appearance. The case was consolidated with another civil action in which the plaintiffs alleged injuries stemming from the same terrorist bombing, and a hearing was held to obtain relevant evidence upon which a default judgment award could be entered.[12] Experts testified that Iran provided terrorist training and economic assistance to Hamas worth $20 million to $50 million annually during the 1990s.[13] Much of the money was funneled through MOIS, a powerful Iranian instrumentality with more than 30,000 employees and a budget of several hundred million dollars.[14] Experts also testified that Iranian governmental support for terrorism was an "official state policy," supported by the highest-ranking members of the government.[15] A certain Mahmoud Abu Hanoud was determined to be the mastermind behind the 1997 bombing and the critical link between Iran and Hamas.[16]

Foreign states have generally been thought immune from the jurisdictional reach of United States courts.[17] This long-standing rule of immunity flows from principles of international law concerning "grace and comity" among sovereigns.[18] Due to its control of foreign relations, the executive branch was traditionally accorded deference to decide when it was acceptable for a court to override the presumption of immunity and subject a sovereign to suit.[19] In 1976, however, Congress decided that a comprehensive statutory scheme should supplant the ad hoc decision making of the executive.[20] This was thought fairer for both foreign sovereigns and American parties with grievances against those sovereigns.

The new statutory scheme was codified as the Foreign Sovereign Immunities Act (FSIA).[21] The FSIA retained the presumption that a foreign sovereign was generally immune from suit in United States courts for its sovereign actions.[22] However, it also decreed, in accordance with an influential State Department letter known as the Tate Memorandum[23], that the commercial activities and property of a foreign sovereign would generally not be immune.[24] More relevant to this case, a further exception to sovereign immunity was carved out in 1996 to cover terrorist actions by foreign states. Thus, a sovereign is stripped of immunity from suit in every case where (1) "money damages are sought against a foreign state for personal injury or death that was caused by an act of torture, extrajudicial killing, aircraft sabotage, hostage taking, or the provision of material support or resources . . . for such an act"; (2) the defendant nation is designated a "state sponsor of terrorism"; and (3) the claimant is a "national of the United States."[25]

The Rubin plaintiffs alleged that Iran's sovereign immunity was revoked by this so-called terrorism exception. The court agreed. First, it is well-settled that a deadly terrorist attack is considered an act of "extrajudicial killing," even if the plaintiffs bringing suit were not killed.[26] Second, the U.S. Department of State has designated Iran a state sponsor of terrorism continuously since 1984.[27] Finally, based on the plaintiffs' uncontroverted expert testimony, the district court found the Iranian defendants had materially supported Hamas. Therefore, the court concluded that 28 U.S.C. § 1605(a)(7)'s terrorism exception to foreign sovereign immunity applied, giving it jurisdiction to hold Iran liable for injuries sustained by the plaintiffs as a result of the 1997 bombing.[28]

The court awarded the plaintiffs both compensatory and punitive damages. Compensatory damages for those physically injured were based on pain and suffering, loss of prospective income, and medical expenses; their caretakers recovered for their emotional suffering and grief ("solatium"). The sum of the nine plaintiffs' awards totaled approximately $71.5 million.[29] In addition, the court thought it appropriate to award punitive damages, because "punitive damages are intended to punish the defendants for the terrorist act."[30] The district court followed earlier precedents in awarding $300 million in punitive damages.[31] Courts that had addressed similar fact patterns had often awarded $300 million in punitive damages per terrorist act, reaching that figure by tripling Iran's estimated annual budget for supporting terrorist groups. The final judgment was rendered on September 10, 2003.

Preliminary Execution Suits

Obtaining the initial judgment against Iran was the easy part. Since representatives of the Islamic republic decided not to contest the suit, the Rubin plaintiffs provided uncontroverted evidence linking Iran and its top government officials to the Hamas-led suicide bombing. Without an adversarial party blocking their way, the litigation progressed smoothly. Attempting to recover on their judgment, however, would prove entirely more difficult.

On June 1, 2004, the Rubin plaintiffs sought to execute upon two Bank of America accounts containing funds belonging to the Consulate General of Iran.[32] The funds were associated with the former Iranian embassy in Washington, D.C. and had been safeguarded by the U.S. State Department since 1979. When the plaintiffs filed a motion for writ of execution, the State Department quickly moved to quash it.[33] The plaintiffs claimed the money was subject to execution under the Terrorism Risk Insurance Act of 2002 (TRIA), § 201(a), while the United States argued Iran was immune under the Vienna Convention on Diplomatic Relations. The latter protects diplomatic assets located abroad, including Iran's former embassy. The district court sided with the plaintiffs. It found that the money in the accounts was not "being used" for diplomatic purposes as required under the Vienna Convention, and therefore was subject to attachment and execution under TRIA § 201.[34] Unfortunately, the plaintiffs did not receive any funds, because an earlier judgment creditor had a prior lien upon them.[35]

The plaintiffs' next attempt was in New York. They sought to attach and execute against three Iranian-controlled bank accounts held by the Bank of New York.[36] The plaintiffs again claimed the assets held by the bank were subject to execution under TRIA § 201, this time under a provision that allowed for recovery against certain "blocked assets" of foreign nations. Following a similar case decided two years earlier, however, the U.S. district court determined the Iranian banks should retain ownership of the accounts; the plaintiffs could not execute against them.[37]

Finally, the plaintiffs sought to attach, sell, and recover upon an Iranian residence located in Lubbock, Texas.[38] The home was located near Lubbock's Reese Air Force Base, where the former Iranian crown prince had received fighter jet training.[39] The U.S. district court sitting in Amarillo agreed that the building could be attached by the plaintiffs and issued an order directing the sale of the property. On January 4, 2005, U.S. Marshals sold it for approximately $390,000.[40] Thus, several years and hard-fought execution battles later, the Rubin plaintiffs had managed to recover only a pittance of their multimillion dollar judgment.

Illinois and Massachusetts Execution Suits

Within the year, the Rubin plaintiffs had decided upon a new approach: executing upon Persian antiquities in museum collections across the country. It mattered little whether the museums claimed full and complete ownership or only a temporary possessory interest; the plaintiffs propounded legal theories that would allow attachment either way. After registering their judgment in federal district courts in Illinois, Massachusetts, and Michigan, the plaintiffs began serving summonses and subpoenas.[41] "Upon information and belief," they asserted that the museums held antiquities that could be attached by the plaintiffs as judgment creditors of Iran. Once attached, the invaluable collections would be sold to the highest bidder at auction to raise money to pay the plaintiffs' judgment award.

Needless to say, the museums were not happy. They began to fight the summons, subpoenas, and discovery requests. Although still in its relative infancy, the litigation may continue a long time more.[42]

Soon after the initial flurry of activity, the plaintiffs retrenched and consolidated their efforts to focus on two jurisdictions: the Northern District of Illinois (Eastern Division) and the District of Massachusetts. The unfortunate defendants were (1) in Illinois, the University of Chicago's Oriental Institute and the Field Museum of Natural History and (2) in Massachusetts, Harvard University, several Harvard University art museums, and the Museum of Fine Arts in Boston.

The Oriental Institute at the University of Chicago is one of the leading centers for the study of archaeological records in the Near East.[43] Its research goal is to integrate "archaeological, textual, and art historical data to understand the development and functioning of the ancient civilizations of the Near East from the earliest Holocene through the Medieval period."[44] It regularly sponsors archaeological expeditions in the Near East, including Iran, Egypt, Sudan, Syria, and Turkey.[45] As a corollary to its research activities, the Institute also operates a museum.

From the Oriental Institute, the Rubin plaintiffs sought to attach the "Persepolis Fortification archive" and the "Chogha Mish collection." The Persepolis archive was principally discovered during several field seasons of work at the site of Tall-i-Bakun in the plain of Persepolis starting in 1928 and continuing into the 1930s.[46] It consists of tens of thousands of whole and fragmented clay tablets stamped with seal impressions and dated to the period of the Achaemenid Persian Empire (ca. 550–330 B.C.).[47] The seals and impressions, written in the Elamite cuneiform alphabet, served an important textual role in the Persian imperial system.[48] Since the tablets were found in a citadel at the site of the ancient city, they were called the Persepolis Fortification tablets. Due to their vast number and dating, the archive is important to a wide range of scholars, from linguists and sociologists to historians and classicists. Around 1935, the Oriental Institute and the National Museum of Iran entered into an agreement to allow researchers at the Institute to catalogue and study the Persepolis collection in the United States.[49] The tablets are periodically returned to Iran as the Institute completes study of them.[50] Gil Stein, director of the Institute, estimates that more than two-thirds of the collection has been returned to Iran, leaving only 8,000 tablets and 11,000 fragments remaining in the U.S.[51]

The Chogha Mish collection is the product of excavations at Chogha Mish, Iran, between 1961 and 1978.[52] The excavations yielded evidence of cultures in the area much earlier than had previously been known. The evidence also extended backward the known length of human occupation on the plain by more than a millennium (to ca. 6000 B.C.). The results added knowledge of the Archaic period to the already well-known Susiana prehistoric.[53] Before transportation to the United States, the Institute and the Iranian government entered into a similar study-and-return understanding as had been more formally written up with regard to the Persepolis Fortification collection.[54] In 2005, study of the Chogha Mish collection was completed and the Institute prepared all remaining materials for shipment back to Iran. The U.S. State Department halted the shipment, however, because a claim related to the collection is currently pending in the Iran-U.S. Claims Tribunal in The Hague.[55] Although the Institute is not a party to that proceeding, it must await the outcome before transporting the collection.

The Field Museum of Natural History was founded to highlight various exhibits during the World's Columbian Exposition in Chicago in 1893. It has grown beyond its original mission of housing biological and anthropological collections to researching and exhibiting more than twenty million wide-ranging objects.[56] Since the museum's focus is on natural history—as opposed to human history—most of the Persian antiquities in its collection are never seen by the general public. Instead, they are used for study by researchers.

From the Field Museum the plaintiffs claimed a right to execute upon the so-called Herzfeld collection. The Herzfeld collection consists of a group of objects Professor Ernst Herzfeld of Princeton University collected during his many years of archaeological excavations of Persian sites in Iran and neighboring countries during the 1920s and 1930s. The collection contains about 500 pieces of prehistoric pottery, about 500 pieces of objects in metal (mostly bronze) such as weapons and horse trappings, about 200 ornaments such as seals and figurines, and various lists, photographs, and related documentation.[57] Herzfeld sold the collection to the Field Museum in 1945 for $7,300.[58]

Harvard University and its constituent art museums were parties in the Massachusetts litigation.[59] Founded in 1636, Harvard is the oldest institution of higher education in the United States. It currently enrolls approximately 18,000 degree-earning candidates in ten principal academic units.[60] There are three main art museums on its campus. According to its website, these Harvard museums "house more than 160,000 objects of art that range in date from ancient times to the present, and come from Europe, North America, North Africa, the Middle East, South Asia, East Asia, and Southeast Asia."[61]

The Museum of Fine Arts (MFA) is one of the oldest art museums in the United States. Founded in Boston in 1870, it has the second biggest collection in the Western Hemisphere—surpassed only by the Metropolitan Museum of Art in New York. Its mission statement begins, "The Museum of Fine Arts houses and preserves preeminent collections and aspires to serve a wide variety of people through direct encounters with works of art."[62] Its collection from the ancient Near East includes more than 7,000 years of art from Nubia, Egypt, Iraq, Iran, Turkey, Cyprus, Greece, and Italy. Objects include architectural elements, sculpture, painting, and coinage.[63]

Unlike the detailed items sought to be attached for execution in the Illinois litigation, the Rubin plaintiffs cast a wider net over the collections at the MFA and Harvard. They alleged generally that the parties possessed collections of antiquities owned by Iran. The only specific claim was that "at least six antiquities on display at the Sackler Museum[64] at Harvard University that relate to the ancient civilization at Persepolis" "may be the property of Iran."[65] The university has contended those reliefs were donated to the museum by Grenville L. Winthrop on his death in 1937.[66]

Asserting that they did not hold any antiquities owned by Iran, Harvard and the MFA (together referred to as "trustee process defendants") moved to quash the summonses and to dissolve any attachments. They wrote, "the Harvard parties possess no Iranian antiquities that belong to the government of Iran or any of the other judgment debtors."[67] They further claimed that even if they did hold Iranian property, it would be immune from attachment under the FSIA. In response, the plaintiffs filed a motion for partial summary judgment, arguing that the trustee process defendants did not have standing to assert the sovereign immunity of Iran's property from attachment and even if they did, the property would not be immune under the FSIA. First, they said that since the antiquities were on display in a museum open to the public, the antiquities fell within the commercial use exception to the FSIA. Second, notwithstanding any available immunity under the FSIA, the property was subject to attachment and execution under TRIA § 201 as a "blocked asset" of Iran. Harvard and the MFA opposed the plaintiffs' motion for partial summary judgment, contending that the immunity of the property from attachment was an issue that could be raised properly by them or even by the court *sua sponte*.

In Illinois, the legal arguments put forth by both sides were similar to those in Massachusetts. The main difference stemmed from the Oriental Institute's concession that Iran owned the property in question. It acknowledged the Persepolis Fortification archive and the Chogha Mish materials were only on loan to the United States for cataloguing and studying; ownership remained with the National Museum of Iran. This factual stipulation differed from that asserted by the Field Museum, which pursued the same approach as the MFA and Harvard in arguing that it—not Iran—owned the collection the plaintiffs sought to attach. Thus, while the MFA and Harvard could put forth a joint defense, based upon shared factual assertions, the Oriental Institute and Field Museum found themselves arguing different positions.

As in Massachusetts, the earliest motions in the Illinois litigation revolved around the question of whether the Oriental Institute and Field Museum (referred to as "citation respondents") had standing to assert that the materials were immune from attachment under the FSIA. The plaintiffs argued that foreign sovereign immunity is an affirmative defense available to the sovereign alone. As such, only Iran had standing to assert its property was immune from attachment under the FSIA. The Oriental Institute and the Field Museum disagreed, characterizing the issue of sovereign immunity in jurisdictional terms and arguing that any party to the litigation could raise it. The Field Museum sought to quash the attachment on the additional ground that it alone owned the antiquities at issue.

Part II. The Legal Issues: FSIA and TRIA

The first step for the Rubin plaintiffs trying to recover the money owed them was to register their judgment against Iran in federal district courts in Northern Illinois and Massachusetts.[68] Under 28 U.S.C. § 1963 and Fed. R. Civ. P. 69(a), those courts acquired supplemental jurisdiction over the matter, even with regard to third parties in possession of property owned by Iran.[69] Rule 69(a) sets forth the general mechanism by which a judgment creditor can seek property in satisfaction of a judgment. In relevant part, it provides that proceedings in aid of executing a judgment follow the practices of the state in which the judgment has been registered, "except that any statute of the United States governs to the extent that it is applicable."[70] The Foreign Sovereign Immunities Act (FSIA) and the Terrorism Risk Insurance Act (TRIA) are two such federal statutes. Each is addressed in turn.

A. Standing under the Foreign Sovereign Immunities Act

In accordance with long-standing international practice, the FSIA sets forth a default rule that the noncommercial property of a foreign sovereign is immune from attachment and execution.[71] Section 1609(a) reads, "the property in the United States of a foreign state shall be immune from attachment arrest and execution except as provided in sections 1610 and 1611 of this chapter."[72]Although sections 1610 and 1611 describe several exceptions to the default rule of immunity, they fail to explain which parties to an attachment proceeding have standing to raise the immunity issue.

Positions of the Litigants The Rubin plaintiffs argued that Section 1609(a), and the FSIA more generally, provided that sovereign immunity was an affirmative right exercisable only by the foreign state itself. On their reading, Congress intended to codify international practice, which focused on upholding notions of "grace and comity" among sovereigns in foreign courts. Since the sovereign's personal dignity was at stake in any foreign lawsuit, it should not be forced to contest a case it disliked. Under this reading, only Iran could raise the issue of whether the property in question was immune from attachment under the FSIA; the third-party respondents did not have standing.

Turning to the legislative history behind the FSIA, the plaintiffs pointed out that the House report on the matter stated that Congress intended to make the FSIA "an affirmative defense which must be specially pleaded."[73] This authority was strengthened when cited approvingly by the Supreme Court in an important sovereign immunity decision.[74]

In response, the third-party respondents in both Illinois and Massachusetts argued they had standing to assert that the antiquities at issue were nonexecutable assets under the FSIA. For purposes of determining the standing question alone, they assumed the property belonged to Iran. They argued that sovereign immunity was a question of subject matter jurisdiction. Since the scope of every federal court's powers is limited by Article III of the U.S. Constitution, every federal judge must affirmatively verify that the court possesses subject matter jurisdiction over a case *before* considering the merits of the claims. Since sovereign immunity is a threshold jurisdictional issue, any party—even the court itself—can and must raise it before proceeding to the merits of the claims. On this theory, the third parties in possession of the antiquities could raise the question of whether the property was immune under the FSIA just as surely as Iran could.

The third-party respondents also contested the plaintiffs' resort to legislative history. They argued it was unnecessary where, as here, the meaning of the statute was clear on its face. The language of section 1609, referring to "the property in the United States of a foreign sovereign," clearly showed that the immunity ran with the property—not the sovereign.[75] Thus, whoever was in possession of the property had standing to raise the FSIA issue. Finally, even if resort to legislative history were appropriate, the plaintiffs' citation of a single sentence from a House report was not sufficient to prove anything. Although the Supreme Court had also cited it, the Court did so in a footnote, not the main text of the opinion.[76]

Decision of the Illinois Court The district court in Illinois was first to address the FSIA standing issue. District Judge Blanche M. Manning adopted Magistrate Judge Martin C. Ashman's report and recommendation.[77] She agreed that the sovereign immunity conferred by the FSIA was personal to the sovereign and no one else had standing to raise it. Judge Manning thought *Verlinden B.V. v. Central Bank of Nigeria*, cited by both sides, was inapposite for two reasons. First, she thought its command that a district court evaluate sovereign immunity *sua sponte* was created by 28 U.S.C. § 1330(a), not the FSIA.[78] Since § 1330(a) was relevant in *Verlinden* but not here, no guidance could be drawn from that part of the opinion. Second, she noted the sovereign immunity afforded under § 1330(a) dealt with immunity from suit, not from the attachment of property.[79] As the FSIA treated immunity from suit differently than immunity from attachment, it was unwise to look at precedents concerning the former to figure out how to treat the latter. Finally, she concluded that since one party generally cannot assert the rights of another,[80] only Iran could assert its affirmative right to sovereign immunity from attachment.

In elaborating further on the last point, the judge noted there were only a limited set of instances where one party could assert another (absent) party's rights. A two-part test must be met: first, the party to the litigation must itself have suffered an injury-in-fact; second, prudential considerations must favor permitting the litigating party to assert the absent party's rights.[81] The Oriental Institute and the Field Museum had presented only weak arguments on the injury-in-fact they were likely to suffer. Perhaps they thought the mere possibility of losing the antiquities in their collections would be such a profound injury as to not warrant elaboration. Yet their failure to show a real injury led Judge Manning to accept the magistrate judge's conclusion that they had not met the first prong of the test.[82] She therefore concluded, "the citation respondents give this court no reason to decline to adopt the magistrate judge's conclusions."[83]

Despite the third parties' having failed the first prong of the test, the court nevertheless considered the second prong as well. In considering the prudential considerations of the case, Judge Manning focused on the closeness of the relationship between the museums and Iran, as well as Iran's ability to assert its rights for itself. Even assuming the Oriental Institute were holding property for Iran as a bailee, that possessory interest alone was insufficient to find the requisite alignment of parties' interests.[84] Since asserting another's rights is so rarely allowed for fear of prejudicing the absentee party or granting relief to a party not entitled to it, the museums had to show their interests regarding the property were almost exactly aligned with Iran's. The argument that neither the museums nor Iran desired the plaintiffs to attach the property was insufficient.

The court also found no reason why Iran could not assert its own right to sovereign immunity in the Illinois court. It cited several recent instances where Iran had made appearances in United States district courts to assert various claims.[85] Moreover, the suggestion that the courts of the United States were hostile to Iran was dismissed as unfounded. Since it was not overly expensive or difficult for Iran to make an appearance in the present litigation to assert its right to sovereign immunity, it was obligated to do so.

Decision of the Massachusetts Court When the standing issue came before the district court in Massachusetts three months later, District Judge George A. O'Toole, Jr. reached the opposite conclusion. He held that third parties in possession of sovereign property did have standing to assert the property was immune from attachment under the FSIA on behalf of the absent foreign state.[86]

Judge O'Toole began his discussion by focusing on the statute under which the plaintiffs had registered their original judgment: 28 U.S.C. § 1963. He found that section 1963 automatically conferred jurisdiction upon the Massachusetts court to adjudicate claims relating to the execution of the previous validly issued judgment.[87] For that reason, he dismissed the trustee process defendants' argument that the FSIA presented a threshold question of subject matter jurisdiction as "largely irrelevant here."[88] He was perfectly capable of adjudicating the issue of sovereign immunity under section 1609 itself.

Thus, Judge O'Toole turned to the main issue: did the third-party trustee respondents have standing to assert that the sovereign property at issue was immune from attachment? Without hesitation, he answered in the affirmative.[89] First, on a plain reading of 28 U.S.C. § 1609, there was no indication that raising the immunity question was reserved solely to the foreign sovereign itself. The language states, "the property in the United States of a foreign state" "shall be immune from attachment arrest and execution except as provided in sections 1610 and 1611 of this chapter."[90] If Congress had wanted to limit standing to the foreign sovereign alone, it could have clearly said so. Second, the judge thought the Supreme Court's opinion in *Verlinden* offered little guidance, since the discussion of subject matter jurisdiction there was centered on the FSIA's provisions regarding immunity from suit; neither 28 U.S.C. § 1609 nor execution immunity more generally was addressed.[91] Thus, any statement indicating that immunity was a personal right of the sovereign was inapplicable. Finally, Judge O'Toole reasoned that since subject matter jurisdiction in any particular case turned on the existence of an exception to the general rule of immunity, a district court should determine whether or not immunity was available in every case—whether or not raised by the sovereign.[92]

As required under Rule 69(a), the judge then examined the state law on the issue. He found nothing in Massachusetts statutes or cases barring third parties from explaining to a court why property in their possession was immune or exempt from attachment.[93] Therefore, neither state attachment laws nor federal statutes barred a third party from raising the rights of an absentee foreign sovereign. The MFA and Harvard could assert that the property held in their possession—if found to be owned by Iran—was nevertheless immune from attachment and execution under the FSIA.

Conclusions Both courts erred in their sovereign immunity analyses. Since the federal appellate courts will review the standing issue de novo,[94] they may reach different conclusions than their district court counterparts.

Judge Manning in Illinois was wrong to describe the FSIA's grant of immunity as an affirmative right, exercisable only by the sovereign. The FSIA should be treated like all other jurisdictional provisions of the federal courts: raisable by any party to the suit, as well as the court itself. Federal courts are courts of limited jurisdiction. Their authority to reach the merits of a case extends only as far as generally contemplated by Article III of the U.S. Constitution and specifically allocated by congressional statute.[95] Maintaining the delicate balance of power between the national and state governments in our federal system requires every federal court to critically assess whether it properly has subject matter jurisdiction over every case presented to it. It is not a task to be taken lightly. Without the constraining force of this jurisdictional requirement, federal courts could hear every case brought before them, even though the parallel state court system may have more expertise in the particular area of law, more stake in the outcome, or more judicial resources to devote to it.[96] Thus, on numerous occasions, the U.S. Supreme Court has held that subject matter jurisdiction must be determined in the affirmative before any proceedings on the merits may begin.[97] Thus, for example, in *Duke Power Co.*, the Court stated, "As a threshold matter, we must address the question of whether the District Court had subject-matter jurisdiction over appellees' claims, despite the fact that none of the parties raised this issue and the District Court did not consider it."[98]

Beyond the overarching policy considerations at stake, the best interpretation of 28 U.S.C. § 1609 also counsels in favor of granting third parties standing to raise the sovereign immunity issue. First, the provision is in Title 28 of the U.S. Code, which deals with subject matter jurisdiction. As just discussed, an issue of subject matter jurisdiction may be raised by any party to the litigation, including the court.[99] Second, the U.S. Supreme Court, although not totally clear on the point, seems to regard the provision as one that can be raised by any party. In the important *Verlinden* footnote cited by the Rubin plaintiffs, for example, the Court said a district court must decide whether the FSIA applies, "even if the foreign state does not enter an appearance to assert an immunity defense."[100] Third, the FSIA requires a court to send notice to a defaulting foreign state before applying other provisions of the Act. This shows Congress contemplated a situation where sovereign immunity could attach to certain property under the FSIA, even though the issue was never raised by the foreign sovereign.[101] Although Judge Manning tried to envision a very narrow range of situations in which that provision could apply under her reading of the statute,[102] nothing in the text or legislative history reveals why it should be so constrictively construed.

In Massachusetts, District Judge O'Toole erred when he casually assumed that the court acquired jurisdiction over the attachment proceedings as a result of the Registration of Judgments provision in 28 U.S.C. § 1963.[103] Due to special considerations present with judgments arising out of the FSIA, the act of registering a judgment in another district court should not automatically give rise to subject matter jurisdiction in the registering district. While ancillary enforcement jurisdiction under section 1963 would be appropriate in many situations, cases and controversies arising under the FSIA are different.[104] Congress has created a bifurcated jurisdictional scheme with regard to foreign sovereigns that must be respected. For suits against a sovereign, federal court jurisdiction is governed by a presumption in favor of immunity, 28 U.S.C. § 1604, and exceptions to the presumption, *Id.* § 1605. For attachment and execution proceedings against a sovereign, jurisdiction is governed by an analogous presumption, 28 U.S.C. § 1609, and exceptions-to-presumption regime, *Id.* §§ 1610 and 1611. Unlike other types of actions that proceed through federal courts, therefore, suits against a foreign sovereign must be affirmatively checked for subject matter jurisdiction *twice*—once before suit and again before execution. This is a statutory command and courts are not free to dispense with it.[105] Judge O'Toole erred in failing to question whether jurisdiction over the matter was appropriate under the execution provisions of the FSIA.

The judge suggested that registration of a judgment in his court automatically maintained jurisdiction.[106] The First Circuit case he relied upon correctly noted that since enforcement proceedings were "a continuation of the original action, the federal court retains residual jurisdiction flowing from its original authority to render a judgment in the case."[107] Overlooked in that opinion, however, was an important qualifier: "The question of whether such [enforcement] jurisdiction should be exercised may well vary with the nature of the underlying basis for federal jurisdiction and the nature of the postjudgment claims made."[108] In typical enforcement proceedings not involving a foreign sovereign, it is perfectly appropriate and efficient for the enforcement court to maintain jurisdiction on the same basis for which it had been granted for the original claims. For sovereign immunity claims, however, the grant of authority for the court to begin the suit is insufficient for it to reach the sovereign's property. A new and independent inquiry into the attachment provisions of the FSIA must be conducted. In failing to recognize that, Judge O'Toole's suggestion that the court acquired jurisdiction as soon as the plaintiffs registered their judgment was mistaken.

Even though Judge O'Toole's reasoning was flawed, his conclusion was correct. The federal courts must have jurisdiction to hear the plaintiffs' case. The only other alternatives are an attachment proceeding in state court or no proceeding at all, both of which are untenable outcomes. Due to the international nature of the plaintiffs' claims, the federal government must be involved. Allowing 50 different state courts to adjudicate claims against foreign sovereigns like Iran—and thereby conduct a form of foreign policy—would be an intrusion into the federal government's authority to conduct relations with foreign nations. If both the federal and state courts were closed to them, however, plaintiffs would have no remedy at all. Without the opportunity to attach and execute upon Iranian assets, their $90 million judgment would be meaningless. To ensure the plaintiffs are not denied a remedy for their right and to ensure a cohesive foreign policy, the federal district courts must take jurisdiction over this case.

B. Commercial Use Exception in the Foreign Sovereign Immunity Act

Although the FSIA provides a default rule of attachment immunity for a foreign sovereign's property, the "commercial use" exception can overcome the presumption. Section 1610(a)(7) of Title 28 provides:

> The property in the United States of a foreign state, as defined in section 1603(a) of this chapter, used for a commercial activity in the United States, shall not be immune from attachment in aid of execution, or from execution, upon a judgment entered by a court of the United States or of a State after the effective date of this Act, if . . . the judgment relates to a claim for which the foreign state is not immune under section 1605(a)(7), regardless of whether the property is or was involved with the act upon which the claim is based.

This commercial use exception stems from the notion that a sovereign should be protected against suit when acting in an official governmental capacity, but not when it enters the commercial arena as a market participant.[109] The question presented in the Rubin litigation was whether using the Persian antiquities for research and display in museums, as well as for publication in books sold for profit, constituted "commercial use."

Positions of the Litigants The plaintiffs' first main argument sought to establish that the commercial use exception encompassed use of the property by any party, not just the foreign sovereign. Hence, if the Oriental Institute or Harvard University were using the objects commercially, they would fall into the exception to immunity.[110] This argument was textual. Comparing the FSIA's language describing the exception from immunity *from attachment* with the exception from immunity *from suit* revealed that while the latter specifically referenced activity "by the foreign state," the former did not.[111] From this, the plaintiffs reasoned Congress had made a deliberate choice to allow all commercially used property owned by the foreign sovereign—regardless of who used it—to be attached and executed upon.[112] The plaintiffs also cited dicta in a district court case in Massachusetts that suggested the commercial use exception would indeed apply to property used commercially by a third party.[113]

The second part of the argument sought to establish that by showcasing the antiquities in question in museums, and publishing and selling books related thereto, the third-party respondents had engaged in a commercial activity. It is undisputed that the Illinois respondents have studied and translated the Persepolis and Chogha Mish collections and have published their findings in books.[114] The FSIA provision on this point commands a court to examine the "nature" of the activity, as opposed to its "purpose" to determine if it constitutes commercial use.[115] If the nature of the use is one that a private (nonsovereign) individual could engage in, it is described as commercial. Using this framework, numerous courts have held that publishing and selling academic treatises constitutes commercial activity.[116] Indeed, even a museum displaying art items in the United States has been described as commercial in at least one recent opinion.[117] Thus, the plaintiffs tried to convince the courts that the commercial use exception could be triggered by third-party use, and that the museums' use of the Persian antiquities at issue was commercial.

Sometime later in the litigation, the plaintiffs advanced a second main argument: The third-party respondents in control of Iranian property were agents of Iran. They argued that nations, by their very nature, must act through human agents.[118] Hence, only agents of a foreign sovereign could engage in any "commercial use" of the sovereign's property. The plaintiffs cited eight specific statements they claimed showed the University of Chicago and its Oriental Institute were agents of Iran.[119] For example, the director of the Institute wrote to the Iranian ambassador, "Looking forward to the opportunity of giving You [sic] a full account of our activities in behalf of Your Government . . . ."[120] Similarly, a member of the Institute wrote to Iran's

Minister of Education, "I hoped that our work of the past years had proved our conscientiousness and our eagerness to cooperate loyally with the High Imperial Government."[121] The plaintiffs reasoned that if a court agreed that the third-party respondents were acting as agents of Iran, they would no longer have to prove the more difficult argument that a third party's commercial use of property placed the property in the FSIA's commercial use exception.

Third-party respondents—Harvard, MFA, Oriental Institute, and Field Museum—asserted that the FSIA's "commercial use" exception covered the commercial use of property only by the sovereign itself.[122] They denied that the slightly different phraseology used in the FSIA provisions covering immunity from suit and immunity from attachment was intended to result in different outcomes; rather, it was simply a stylistic drafting decision. Moreover, the Supreme Court's analysis of the statute providing immunity from suit, 28 U.S.C. § 1605, should be considered binding in the attachment context, *Id.* § 1610.[123] The provisions are so intimately related that persuasive analogies can be made between them. Since the Court had previously held that property must be used by the sovereign in order to subject the sovereign to suit, the same should be true for subjecting a sovereign's property to attachment proceedings. Property should fall into the commercial use exception if and only if the sovereign used the property in that manner. In this case, Iran had not used the property at any point since it came to the United States. It had received no money from the display of the antiquities in the museums or the publication and sale of any books. Therefore, the commercial use exception of the FSIA was not applicable.

The respondents further asserted that as not-for-profit institutions, engaged in scholarly and academic pursuits, their actions in relation to the antiquities should not be considered "commercial."[124] The antiquities collections were put to a scholarly use—not a "business, trade or traffic" use.[125]

As to the plaintiffs' agency argument, the third-party respondents denied such a relationship existed. The Oriental Institute characterized the agreement wherein it had accepted delivery and safekeeping of the Persepolis and Chogha Mish antiquities as one of bailment.[126] Bailment occurs "upon the delivery of personal property by one person (the bailor) to another (the bailee) who holds the property for a certain purpose under an express or implied-in-fact contract."[127] Thus, the Institute characterized its relationship as a normal contractual one wherein one party takes possession of another's property—in this case, for scholarly study. The Harvard parties, on the other hand, flatly denied any relationship between the Persian antiquities in its collection and the Iranian government.[128] They said, "Harvard has never taken direction from the government of Iran or any of its instrumentalities or officials about the uses to which any of the Iranian antiquities in its collection may be put."[129]

Shortly after the Illinois court held only Iran had standing to assert its sovereign immunity,[130] Iran entered the proceedings to do so.[131] Iran reiterated the third-party respondents' position that only property put to commercial use by the sovereign itself could qualify for the exception to immunity in the FSIA.[132] It corroborated the point that neither the National Museum of Iran nor any other instrumentality of Iran had used the antiquities for a commercial purpose in the United States; the objects were in the complete possessory control of the Oriental Institute.[133] Finally, Iran noted that the burden of proving the commercial use exception to immunity was on the plaintiffs, not Iran or the third-party respondents.[134]

Decision of the Illinois Court The court in Illinois sided with the third-party respondents. First Magistrate Judge Ashman, then District Judge Manning held that foreign property was immune from execution unless used for a commercial purpose *by the foreign sovereign.* [135, 136] Examining the text of section 1610(a)(7), they found nothing to support the sweeping construction advocated by the plaintiffs. Allowing property used by anyone—not just a foreign sovereign—to fall within the commercial use exception was not the most reasonable interpretation of the text. Moreover, other courts had already come to the conclusion that only property used commercially by the foreign state should be stripped of its immunity.[137]

They agreed it was sensible, from a policy perspective, for Congress to limit the exception from immunity to property used by the foreign sovereign. If a foreign sovereign did not live up to its business bargain, commercial parties could legitimately expect to attach and execute upon those business assets alone. Moreover, the long-standing international norm existing before the enactment of the FSIA made it more difficult to attach sovereign property than to bring suit against a sovereign.[138] The plaintiffs' interpretation would have reversed that norm, while respondents' position remained faithful to it.[139]

As of this writing, the Illinois court had not ruled on the plaintiffs' agency argument.

Decision of the Massachusetts Court In Massachusetts, Judge O'Toole reached the same conclusions as the judges in Illinois. He thought that upon reading the "plain language" of the FSIA, it was clear Congress intended to allow execution upon sovereign property only when the sovereign itself was engaged in its commercial use.[140] He quoted the purpose section of the FSIA, 28 U.S.C. § 1602, to infer that foreign sovereigns "risk losing their sovereign immunity where they themselves engage in commercial activities beyond their borders."[141] He thought the slightly different language used in section 1605 (suit immunity) and section 1610 (attachment immunity) amounted to "a distinction without a difference."[142] He burnished his position further by citing the same group of cases as the Illinois court.[143] Finally, he declared that general principles of international law also supported his reading of the statute, providing further evidence of its correctness. Since Iran did not use the property for commercial activity in the U.S., the commercial use exception to the FSIA did not apply. All the antiquities in question remained immune from attachment by the plaintiffs.

Conclusions In contrast to their analyses of the FSIA standing issue, both courts reached the correct outcome here. Principles of statutory interpretation, as well as considerations of sound policy, support the view that an exception to the default rule of sovereign immunity from attachment exists only where the sovereign itself has used property for a commercial purpose. The first rule of statutory construction is to read a statute in the context of the *corpus juris* of which it is a part, giving each word its plain meaning.[144] In enacting the FSIA, Congress laid out a statutory purpose section at 28 U.S.C. § 1602 which states that international law provides that "commercial property may be levied upon for the satisfaction of judgments rendered against [foreign sovereigns] in connection with their commercial activities,"[145] and that the federal courts should decide sovereign immunity questions "in conformity with" those norms.[146] This is strong evidence that only property used commercially by a sovereign is attachable. Interpreting the commercial use exception to attachment immunity as co-extensive with the commercial use exception to suit immunity is also rational. The provisions implement the same idea: sovereign immunity should be abrogated only where the foreign state engages in commercial activity.

Another seminal code of statutory construction is the clear statement rule, which prescribes that courts should not read statutes in a way that would fundamentally change existing state or international law, absent a "clear statement" that Congress intended to do so.[147] Since the background international norm is that sovereign property has immunity from attachment, except when sovereigns themselves engage in commercial activity, a court should not override that rule without a specific congressional command. As discussed, the statutory purpose set forth at the outset of the FSIA indicates that Congress intended to codify the existing norm, not change it.[148]

In sum, the difference in language used in the two commercial use exceptions provisions of the FSIA appears to be a "distinction without a difference." Notwithstanding the failure of Congress to specify that a "commercial use" must be "by the foreign state," limiting the attachment exception to instances in which the foreign sovereign itself pursues a commercial activity is the most reasonable reading of the provision. In this way, the commercial use exception to attachment immunity is harmonized with the exception for suit immunity. Here, both district courts followed the weight of authority in reaching this sensible outcome.

C. Recovery under the Terrorism Risk Insurance Act

Soon after the terrorist attacks of 9/11, Congress enacted the Terrorism Risk Insurance Act of 2002 (TRIA).[149] Section 201 created a new way for individuals who obtained judgments against terrorist parties for acts of terrorism to collect on those judgments. Subsection (a) reads,

> Notwithstanding any other provision of law, and except as provided in subsection (b), in every case in which a person has obtained a judgment against a terrorist party on a claim based upon an act of terrorism, or for which a terrorist party is not immune under section 1605(a)(7) of title 28, United States Code, the blocked assets of that terrorist party (including the blocked assets of any agency or instrumentality of that terrorist party) shall be subject to, execution or attachment in aid of execution in order to satisfy such judgment to the extent of any compensatory damages for which such terrorist party has been adjudged liable.[150]

Subsection (b) deals with consular property and is not applicable here. Because of the relatively new mint of the statute, few courts have pronounced upon its various provisions. At issue in the Rubin litigation was whether the Persian antiquities sought by the plaintiffs fell within the definition of "blocked assets," thereby making them amenable to attachment.

Positions of the Litigants The plaintiffs first argued that, as a threshold matter, the plain language of TRIA § 201(a) revealed that it overrode the sovereign immunity provisions of the FSIA. The phrase "notwithstanding any other provision of law" is as clear a statement as Congress can make to indicate its desire to have the provision enter with full force.[151] Given the desire of Congress to ensure that terrorist states could not injure American citizens with impunity, the plaintiffs argued TRIA should be read to grant relief to individuals who obtained valid judgments based upon terrorist attacks—notwithstanding other impediments to attachment. Thus, even if the district courts thought the FSIA barred recovery, the plaintiffs ought to recover under the TRIA.

Having established that § 201 of the TRIA could provide them a remedy even where the FSIA could not, the Rubin plaintiffs further asserted that the antiquities at issue met the statutory and regulatory definitions of "blocked assets."[152] Section 201(d)(2) of the TRIA provides that "blocked assets" means "any asset seized or frozen by the United States under . . . sections 202 and 203 of the International Emergency Economic Powers Act [(IEEPA)]."[153] Under the authority of the IEEPA, Executive Order 12170 froze all assets owned by the Iranian government in the United States in 1979.[154] The plaintiffs maintained that notwithstanding Executive Order 12281, passed two years later in 1981[155] and unblocking nearly all the assets originally blocked by Executive Order 12170, the Persian antiquities held by the third-party respondents remained frozen.[156] Executive Order 12281 was implemented by the Treasury Department in 31 C.F.R. 535.215, which provides,

> [A]ll persons subject to the jurisdiction of the United States in possession of control of properties, as defined in § 535.333 of this part, not including funds and securities owned by Iran or its agencies, instrumentalities or controlled entities, are licensed, authorized, directed and compelled to transfer such properties held as of January 18, 1981 as directed after that day by the Government of Iran, acting through its authorized agent.[157]

Section 535.333, referenced therein, states, "The term properties as used in § 535.215 means all uncontested and non-contingent liabilities and property interests of the Government of Iran, its agencies, instrumentalities, or controlled entities, including debts."[158]

The Rubin plaintiffs argued that since the third-party respondents claimed they owned the antiquities at issue[159]—when, in fact, Iran did[160]—the assets were "contested" within the meaning of § 535.333 and thus remained "blocked assets" for purposes of attachment under TRIA § 201(a). The key fact for the plaintiffs is that an Iranian export restriction law passed in 1930 forbids the export of cultural property without proper governmental authority.[161] Since legal title to objects taken in violation of the law remains with Iran, so the argument went, the third-party respondents never acquired valid title to the antiquities.[162]

The third-party respondents contended that the plaintiffs' TRIA analysis was incorrect in several ways. First, they asserted the antiquities at issue were never blocked assets in the first place (and hence could not be blocked assets today), either because they were not owned by Iran or because they were not covered by the statutory grant of authority under which Executive Order 12170 was promulgated.[163] The factual issue of whether the antiquities were owned by Iran is explored further in Part III, infra. As noted above, the authority under which President Carter issued Executive Order 12170 consisted of sections 202 and 203 of the International Emergency Economic Powers Act (IEEPA). The IEEPA granted the president authority to seize or freeze a wide range of Iranian goods. Specifically excluded by a later amendment, however, were "information or informational materials,"[164] which are described as items "including but not limited to" "photographs, microfilms, microfiche, tapes, compact disks, CD ROMS, artworks, and news wire feeds."[165] Respondents referenced this nonexclusive list to show that the clear intent of Congress was to allow the import and export of items which spread knowledge about one culture to another.[166] Surely, they reasoned, that purpose would be materially enhanced by including within the category of "informational materials" the Persian antiquities at issue, which provide knowledge about the ancient culture of Persia.[167]

Second, even if the antiquities were originally blocked under Executive Order 12170, the respondents argued that Executive Order 12281 unblocked them.[168] The purpose behind Executive Order 12281 was to implement the Algiers Accords, which were signed by the United States and Iran in order to begin normalizing relations between the two countries following the overthrow of the Shah, the detention of American hostages, and the freezing of Iranian assets in the U.S.[169] Executive Order 12281 was designed to undo much of the freeze brought about by Executive Order 12170 and place Iranian and American parties "in the position they were in prior to November 14, 1979."[170] The third-party respondents argued that the exception in Executive Order 12281 for "contested or contingent liabilities and property interests" did not apply in this case for the obvious reason that ownership was not contested between the third-party respondents *and Iran*.[171] Indeed, the language of the implementing regulation provides, "property interests shall not be deemed to be contested solely because they are subject to an attachment, injunction, or other similar order."[172] The respondent parties thought the plaintiffs had put forth an absurdly literal reading of the regulations implementing Executive

Order 12281. Applying their hyper-literalist interpretation would mean any individual could assert (without proving) that a piece of property in the U.S. was owned by Iran, even though the legitimate U.S. owner was in possession, and through that assertion alone transform the property into a "blocked asset" subject to execution under the TRIA.

The Oriental Institute further argued that the Persepolis Fortification archive could not be a "blocked asset," because some of it had recently been licensed for shipment back to Iran. By allowing the Institute to transport part of the archive to Iran, the Department of Treasury necessarily concluded it was not a blocked asset, that is, "seized or frozen" under Executive Order 12170.[173]

Finally, the respondents put forth an argument based on (what they termed) simple logic.[174] They first noted that, by stipulation, the Persian antiquities at issue were owned either by the museums or Iran. If owned by the museums, they were not subject to attachment because the plaintiffs had a judgment only against Iran. If owned by Iran, they were not subject to attachment because both the Illinois and Massachusetts courts had held the FSIA barred the plaintiffs from attaching property not commercially used by Iran. Therefore, whether the museums or Iran owned the property, plaintiffs could not levy upon it and section 201 of TRIA was moot.[175]

Decision of the Illinois Court As of this writing, the litigants had not sufficiently developed their TRIA argument to the point where either Magistrate Judge Ashman or District Judge Manning was ready to rule. This was largely due to the focus on Iran's entering the proceedings.[176] Once it appeared, Iran filed a flurry of motions to assert its rights to have its sovereign property declared immune from attachment under the FSIA and be exempt from discovery under Rule 69(a). The court busied itself dealing with those motions, to the exclusion of the TRIA issue. Even if the Illinois court declared the property at issue immune under the FSIA (which looks likely), it might still decide to grant plaintiffs' plea to reach the TRIA issue.

Decision of the Massachusetts Court The district court in Massachusetts agreed with the Rubin plaintiffs that TRIA § 201 was potentially available to them, since it allowed recovery against a terrorist state's blocked assets for injuries sustained in an act of terrorism.[177] Judge O'Toole first noted it was undisputed that plaintiffs had obtained their judgment under the "terrorist act exception" to the FSIA, 28 U.S.C. § 1605(a)(7), and that Iran had been designated a "terrorist party."[178] He then turned to the question of whether the antiquities held by the MFA and Harvard could be deemed "blocked assets."

Judge O'Toole agreed with the plaintiffs' argument that only "uncontested and non-contingent" property interests of Iran had been unblocked by Executive Order 12281.[179] He then concluded that since Harvard and the MFA had "[f]rom the commencement of this action" argued that they—not Iran—owned the items in question, those items were, in fact, "contested" and therefore remained blocked assets for purposes of TRIA § 210(d)(2).[180] If plaintiffs could successfully establish that the antiquities belonged to Iran, then the assets would be subject to attachment and execution under TRIA § 201(a).[181] Only a factual hearing on the issue could determine whether Iran, in fact, owned the pieces. The third-party respondents could not extinguish the lawsuit at this preliminary stage.

After the court's decision, the MFA and Harvard motioned the court to reconsider its TRIA holding.[182] They contended that the court misinterpreted TRIA § 201 and the relevant Department of Treasury regulations. In the event the court would not reconsider, they moved it to certify the question of the proper interpretation of TRIA § 201 to the United States Court of Appeals for the First Circuit.[183] As of this writing, no action had been taken by the district judge.

Conclusions Judge O'Toole seems to have erred in his analysis of TRIA § 201. By accepting the plaintiffs' reading, he swept into the category of "blocked assets" property Congress likely had never considered would be labeled as such. In essence, Judge O'Toole held that an asset owned by a U.S. citizen could become a "blocked asset," and hence liable for attachment to satisfy a judgment against Iran, if the judgment creditors could make a plausible claim of Iranian ownership. No actual proof of Iranian ownership was required. In this case, for example, the plaintiffs merely alleged "upon information and belief" that objects in Harvard's and the MFA's collection were owned by Iran. This allegation was sufficient to allow the plaintiffs to continue conducting depositions and discovery proceedings, as well as to obtain an evidentiary hearing with witnesses and experts. The upshot, of course, is that the longer the case drags on, the more incentive the museums have to reach a settlement, thereby saving legal fees and eliminating the risk of an unfavorable trial result.

The Massachusetts judge was wrong for three main reasons. First, it is likely the Persian antiquities at issue could not be "blocked assets" under the International Emergency Economic Powers Act (IEEPA). Although originally enacted in 1976, the IEEPA was amended in 1994 to create an important exception to the types of property that could be deemed "blocked assets." As the Illinois third-party respondents noted, Congress specifically excluded from the President's grant of authority to block assets "any information or informational materials."[184] The nonexclusive list following that description of the category included photographs, artworks, and publications.[185] There is a strong argument that the Persian antiquities at issue in this litigation should be deemed "information materials."[186]

Congress clearly intended the list of items mentioned in the statute to be nonexclusive. It evidenced this intent by using the phrase "including but not limited to."[187] Thus, even if the Persepolis Fortification archive, the Chogha Mish materials, and the objects housed at Harvard and the MFA were not deemed "artworks," they could still be considered part of the unenumerated list of "informational materials."[188] One of the defining characteristics of cultural property is its ability to convey information about a past culture.[189] Persian governmental seals, painted pottery shards, and sculptures are valuable precisely because they provide insight into the way people in that society lived. If the objects were excavated in an archaeologically precise manner (as the Persepolis and Chogha Mish collections were), they can tell even more about how a civilization evolved over time. Since the intent of Congress in enacting the list of exclusions to the IEEPA was to preserve the free flow of information across cultures,[190] the antiquities fit squarely within it.

The Department of Treasury's regulations and practices implementing the IEEPA also lend support to the idea that the Persian antiquities are not "blocked assets." Within the Department, the Office of Foreign Assets Control determines whether certain assets fit within the restricted class and publishes guidance to help U.S. nationals comply with its orders.[191] In 2004, the OFAC issued a ruling which clarified that "transactions relating to [Iranian] informational materials that are reproduced, translated (including both literal and idiomatic translation) or dubbed by U.S. persons for dissemination within the United States are exempt transactions"[192] for purposes of the IEEPA.[193] Using this ruling, the museums would again have a strong argument that the Persian antiquities in their collections, used for study and publication for an American audience, would be exempt as "informational materials."

Second, even if the antiquities were at one time blocked under the IEEPA and Executive Order 12170, they were later unblocked by Executive Order 12281. Although the plaintiffs contended that ownership of the objects was "contested," and therefore the objects were never unblocked, this argument should be rejected. The simple reason is that ownership was never contested by Iran. The plaintiffs' alternative reading of the regulations, adopted by the Massachusetts court, is not the most reasonable interpretation. Section 535.33 of C.F.R. part 31, which declared that only "uncontested and non-contingent liabilities and property interests of the Government of Iran" were unblocked and amenable to return to Iran, was intended to protect American interests in contested property.[194] Where both U.S. and Iranian parties claimed ownership of an asset, the U.S. parties were not forced to accede to Iran's claims; they could continue to dispute the matter. By adopting the plaintiffs' reading, Judge O'Toole turned this regulation on its head: instead of protecting the putative American owner's interest in contested property, it opened up the property to claims by even more parties. That is, instead of simply battling Iran for possession, the putative owner would have to battle unknown judgment creditors of Iran as well.

It is, of course, entirely possible Congress intended this outcome when it passed the TRIA in 2002. Congress's goal seemingly was to make additional, appropriate assets available to satisfy judgments against terrorist parties such as Iran. In section 201(b)(2), for example, Congress allowed for the collection of judgments against certain diplomatic properties owned by terrorist states in the United States "that ha[ve] been used by the United States for any nondiplomatic purpose."[195] Yet, common sense dictates that Iran's judgment creditors should only recover against assets over which Iran has actual or claimed title. If Iran has never claimed ownership of an asset, it is unclear how its ownership could be deemed "contested." The salutary goal of allowing judgment creditors to vindicate their claims would be contorted out of shape by plaintiffs' construction of 31 C.F.R. § 535.333. Allowing a third party to create a controversy over ownership would create ruinous litigation, especially for museums and other entities that possess Persian antiquities with incomplete provenances.

Finally, the third-party respondents' construction of the regulations at issue is supported by the weight of authority. In a recent Second Circuit opinion interpreting TRIA § 201, the court disagreed with the argument that Congress had "appropriated" all blocked assets in the United States for the use of satisfying judgments obtained against terrorist states.[196] It rejected an expansive reading of the statute and held "we do not believe that TRIA § 201 is an appropriation."[197] The court instead read the statute to allow attachment only in certain limited situations. Even earlier, in a case arising shortly after the issuance of the regulations at issue and interpreting their scope for the first time, the Fifth Circuit held that "we reject [plaintiffs'] attempt to create artificial distinctions as not in keeping with the purpose of the [Algerian] Declarations."[198] The general purpose of the Algiers Accords, of course, was to put all American and Iranian parties in the same position they were before Iranian assets had been frozen in the United States in 1979. In this case, that previous position was one of uncontested ownership of all the Persian antiquities by the respective museums, with the exception of the Persepolis Fortification archive which was uncontestedly owned by the National Museum of Iran.

In sum, the plaintiffs' TRIA argument fails for three reasons. First, the statutory scheme which governs Iranian "blocked assets" specifically excludes "informational materials." This likely includes Persian antiquities that help spread knowledge about the cultural history of the Iranian people. Second, the regulatory provisions that implemented Executive Order 12281 unblocked all nonfinancial assets of Iran that were "uncontested and noncontingent." Since ownership of the Persian antiquities has never been contested as between the museums and Iran, they are not "blocked assets." Finally, the statutes and regulations controlling Iranian assets in the United States must be read in conjunction with the Algiers Accords and international law norms. Under a comprehensive analysis, the policy goals animating the "blocked assets" provisions support an outcome whereby Persian antiquities in the United States since the 1930s should remain with their current owners.

Part III. The Factual Issue: Who Owns the Persian Antiquities?

Nearly all of the litigants' preliminary motions focused on the legal issues discussed in Part II, supra. During that time, both sides assumed *arguendo* that the antiquities were owned by Iran. This put the legal issues to the foreground, allowing the contested factual matter of actual ownership to be postponed for a later date. The third-party respondents pursued this strategy with the hope that they could end the litigation based solely on legal grounds. That outcome would avoid the litigation of factual matters, which might reach conclusion only after a lengthy evidentiary hearing. Unfortunately for the third-party respondents, neither the Illinois court nor the Massachusetts court was prepared to dispose of the case on purely legal grounds. Therefore, the factual question would almost certainly require extensive briefing and, perhaps, a hearing or trial.

As of this writing, neither court had yet ordered extensive briefing on the factual issues. By carefully examining the litigants' papers, however, the key issues which would likely need resolution can be deciphered. The first issue would likely be determining who had standing to assert Iran's ownership interest in the antiquities. The second would center on the proper application of the choice of law rules and related procedural matters. For the courts could only reach the actual question of ownership after they knew the controlling legal framework. These issues will be discussed in sequence.

A. Standing to Assert Iranian Ownership

A threshold question for any court is whether the parties before it have standing to assert their various claims. "In essence the question of standing is whether the litigant is entitled to have the court decide the merits of the dispute or of particular issues."[199] Thus, although the issue of standing to assert sovereign immunity under the FSIA was discussed in Part II.A, supra, a new inquiry must be undertaken to determine whether the Rubin plaintiffs could raise a claim that Iran owns the Persian antiquities in question.

Positions of the Litigants Since the factual issue of Iranian ownership was not yet before either the Illinois or Massachusetts courts, the plaintiffs had not yet fully briefed the issue. If pressed, however, their biggest hurdle would likely be overcoming the notion that they were barred by the "general prohibition on a litigant's raising another person's legal rights."[200]

The plaintiffs' best strategy might focus on an analogy to the law of fraudulent conveyances. A fraudulent conveyance is "[a] transfer of property for little or no consideration, made for the purpose of hindering or delaying a creditor by putting the property beyond the creditor's reach."[201] Judgment creditors typically have standing to make a claim that certain assets have been disposed of by the judgment debtor simply to avoid their payment to the rightful taker—the judgment creditor.[202] Using this doctrinal hook, the Rubin plaintiffs might claim that Iran's decision to not vigorously pursue its claims against the museums *at this point in time*, was done simply to keep the plaintiffs' rightfully owned assets from falling into their hands. Thus, the plaintiffs should have standing to protect their creditor rights to the Iranian-owned property.

Sensing the fight to come, the third-party respondents had begun questioning quite early the plaintiffs' ability to assert Iranian ownership of the antiquities. Their first argument was unsurprising: Only Iran can assert Iran's rights.[203] Article III of the U.S. Constitution presents a vague standing limitation by forcing a plaintiff to show he or she has a valid case or controversy against the defendant.[204] This has subsequently been construed to require that a "federal court act only to redress injury that fairly can be traced to the challenged action of the defendant, and not injury that results from the independent action of some third party not before the court."[205]

This Article III standing requirement could be used by the museums in two ways. First, they could argue that the Rubin plaintiffs are not challenging the museums' actions, but the actions of Iran in failing to assert its rights to the antiquities. Since Iran's actions are those of a "third party not before the court," the issue cannot reach proper resolution. Relatedly, the museums could argue that only Iran is hurt by any potentially culpable behavior by the museums in purchasing, receiving, and displaying the Persian antiquities. [206] That is, the plaintiffs should not stand in the shoes of Iran to attack the museums' activities, for there is a real possibility that if the plaintiffs lose, Iran's claims could be barred by the related doctrines of res judicata and collateral estoppel.[207] To avoid prejudicing the absent party, only Iran should assert Iran's claims.

Decisions of the Illinois and Massachusetts Courts Neither court has yet addressed this preliminary wrinkle to the factual question of ownership of the antiquities. Both have attempted to dispose of the litigation on purely legal grounds. It is unclear how either judge would rule on this important standing issue.

Conclusions The plaintiffs' request that the Massachusetts and Illinois courts allow them to assert, as a factual matter, that Iran owns the Persian antiquities at issue should be denied. In this situation, the federal courts should not—and, perhaps, may not—exercise any jurisdictional authority.

The standing limitations prescribed by the U.S. Constitution govern this case. Article III's "cases and controversies" requirement is an important safeguard, because it ensures that only actual disputes between two parties with sufficient incentives will be litigated in the federal courts. Our judicial system works best when both sides of an issue are adequately presented to a court before the court makes a final determination. Additionally, the cases and controversies requirement protects the rights of absent third parties by not allowing other litigants to assert those third parties' valuable, personal rights.

In addition to this constitutional dimension of standing, there is a further judge-made limitation on the ability of litigants to bring issues into federal court. This limitation has been termed "prudential standing."[208] In its most recent exposition on the topic, the Supreme Court attempted to elucidate the doctrine:

> Although we have not exhaustively defined the prudential dimensions of the standing doctrine, we have explained that prudential standing encompasses "the general prohibition on a litigant's raising another person's legal rights, the rule barring adjudication of generalized grievances more appropriately addressed in the representative branches, and the requirement that a plaintiff's complaint fall within the zone of interests protected by the law invoked."[209]

This case squarely presents all three of the issues that trigger the concerns of prudential standing. First, as noted above, Iran might be prejudiced by allowing the Rubin plaintiffs to assert its rights of ownership. For whatever reason, Iran has not asserted any claims against the museums. It might be barred from doing so in the future, if the Rubin plaintiffs are allowed to do so now. Second, Iranian governmental assets in the United States have been subject to extensive regulation by Congress and the president over the past thirty years. Numerous statutes, executive orders, and administrative regulations have been issued to prescribe the rights and responsibilities of U.S. individuals who have relations with Iran.[210] For that reason, courts should not intervene in a dispute thought "more appropriately addressed in the representative branches."[211] Finally, to the extent the plaintiffs are relying upon a 1930 Iranian statute that forbids export of Iranian cultural objects without governmental permission, they are likely outside the "zone of interests protected by the law invoked." The only parties protected by that law are the Iranian government and Iranian people who have sought to preserve their cultural heritage from export.[212]

In sum, for both Article III and prudential standing reasons, the courts should find that the Rubin plaintiffs lack standing to argue that Iran owns the Persian antiquities held by the third-party respondent museums.[213] This outcome would preserve Iran's rights to those arguments, as well as remove from the federal courts issues they do not properly have authority to decide.

B. Other Procedural Issues

Besides the standing issue, questions surrounding the proper choice of law, burden of proof, and statute of limitations would likely arise. Since none of these have been more than cursorily argued by the litigants, it is too early to speculate about the claims that would likely emerge. The only thing that can be said for sure is that the burden of proof argument will be one of the most contentious and important. As respondents noted, the fact of Iranian ownership is one which has been "taken as true at this [preliminary] stage of the litigation and which Plaintiffs must establish in order to prevail at judgment."[214]

The Supreme Court has held that the appropriate burden of proof shifts over the course of litigation:

> At the pleading stage, general factual allegations of injury resulting from the defendant's conduct may suffice . . . . In response to a summary judgment motion, however, the plaintiff can no longer rest on such "mere allegations," but must "set forth" by affidavit or other evidence "specific facts," . . . . And at the final stage, those facts (if controverted) must be "supported adequately by the evidence adduced at trial."[215]

This exposition serves as a roadmap for the increasing burden of proof that must be met by the Rubin plaintiffs to prevail in this case.

C. Reaching the Merits

In the highly unlikely event that the courts do not resolve the litigation on either the legal issues presented by the FSIA and the TRIA or the procedural issues just discussed, some kind of factual hearing would commence. A fact finder would be called upon to adjudicate, under the appropriate legal framework, whether Iran or the museums actually owned the antiquities in question.

The case of the Persepolis Fortification archive and the Chogha Mish collections would be different, of course. Both Iran and the Oriental Institute have agreed that the collections are owned by an instrumentality of Iran, either the National Museum of Iran or the Iranian Cultural Heritage Organization.[216] They have stipulated that the Persepolis Fortification collection is on long-term loan from the 1930s. The Institute is obligated to return, and has in fact returned some portions of, the collection to these Iranian entities. Likewise, the Chogha Mish collection has been on long-term loan since the 1960s and must ultimately be returned to Iran.[217]

Thus, the factual issue of ownership need only be resolved regarding the Field Museum's Herzfeld Collection and Harvard's and the MFA's more sprawling Persian antiquities collections. A key issue would likely be the applicability and scope of an Iranian law from 1930 that regulates the export of national antiquities. It is entitled "Law concerning the preservation of national antiquities" and covers "[a]ll works of art and movable and immovable creations which have been produced in Iran, as well as all historical sites."[218]

Positions of the Litigants The 1930 law is a powerful weapon for the plaintiffs. Its clear object is to protect and preserve for Iran all "national antiquities," which is defined very broadly.[219] Several of the specific provisions may well have been violated by Dr. Herzfeld or other archaeologists working in Iran after 1930. Article 13, for example, provides, "Excavations on land belonging to private individuals may be undertaken only with the authorization of the State and the consent of the owner."[220] Similarly, Article 17 prescribes, "Persons wishing to trade in antiquities must obtain a State license. A State license is also required to export antiquities." As record keeping at that time was weak and the Iranian government's bureaucracy fledgling,[221] it could be extremely difficult to ascertain whether these provisions were adhered to.

Pointing to these provisions and others, the plaintiffs would likely have a strong case that individuals who removed "national antiquities" after the law's passage did so illegally. In that case, those objects would remain "under the protection and control of the State."[222]

The third-party respondents might contest the law's applicability in several ways. First, they might argue that all the objects in their collection were excavated from Iran before 1930. Harvard has already argued, for example, that certain Persian reliefs in its collection were donated to it by Grenville L. Winthrop on his death in 1937.[223] It might also have evidence that Mr. Winthrop did not collect during the last seven years of his life. Similarly, the Field Museum may argue that Dr. Herzfeld, from whom it purchased the Herzfeld Collection, acquired his objects before the law went into effect.

The museums might also argue that even if the objects were excavated and exported after 1930, the law's requirements were complied with. It is up to the plaintiffs, they would argue, to prove that the collectors did not obtain the proper governmental permits.[224] The fact that Iran has never contested ownership of the property would further support the museums' claims. Indeed, it is conceivable that Iran possesses copies of the appropriate records or has some particularized knowledge of the collectors' actions. If no documents were discovered, the burden of proof would be important. Whoever needed to carry the burden would have a difficult time doing so.

A third argument would be that once the objects left Iran, they were no longer governed by Iranian law. It was up to the Iranian customs agents to stop the objects' export if that export violated Iranian law. Once the objects were outside of Iran, the importing nation's border agents had no obligation to enforce Iranian law.[225] Although it is true under American law that "a thief cannot pass good title,"[226] the collectors are not thieves unless U.S. law imposes a penalty for those who break foreign export laws.[227]

Decisions of the Illinois and Massachusetts Courts Neither court has adjudicated the merits of Iran's potential ownership of the antiquities. Applying the Iranian export law of 1930 would be an interesting endeavor for a federal district court, as no American court has yet to do so. Doctrines of private international law would serve as the touchstone for the courts.[228]

Conclusions The ultimate determination of whether Iran ever held title to the Persian antiquities is dependent on (1) when the antiquities at issue were removed from the country and (2) whether the 1930 law vests title of antiquities in Iran. More information would undoubtedly be produced concerning the original excavation and exportation of the antiquities from Iran. It is doubtful any individuals who participated would still be alive to testify about the events surrounding the excavations, which took place in the early part of the 20th century. The outcome would, therefore, more likely turn on contemporaneously written notes in journals and the examination of any relevant Iranian export licenses. Iran's assistance in searching its archives would clarify the facts underlying claims.

The museums' first two potential arguments—that the objects were exported before 1930 and/or in conformity with the law of 1930—might prove persuasive. It is likely that if the museums could produce evidence of a general nature that indicated much of their collection came from certain excavations that took place prior to 1930, or from excavations conducted thereafter with the consent of the government, a fact finder would rule in their favor. They would not have to establish in detail the provenance of every item in their Persian collections. The burden of attempting that nearly impossible feat would seem too much.

The third potential argument—that Iran's export laws do not apply outside of its sovereign territory—would almost certainly carry the day for the museums. International law is quite clear that importing nations are under no obligation to enforce the export laws of foreign nations.[229] Although a UNESCO treaty from 1970[230] and subsequent Congressional legislation[231] have taken the edge off this hard rule, neither was in effect when the museums were collecting their Persian antiquities. Quite simply, the museums were under no obligation to refrain from purchasing the objects, even if they were illegally exported.[232]

This final argument showcases the gulf that sometimes exists between moral intuitions and the realities of international law. It seems wrong *morally* for the museums to argue that a rich country like America should not help enforce the export laws of a poorer nation like Iran. One can forcefully argue that Americans should not turn a blind eye to the unlawful pillaging of Persian heritage. Yet *legally* there is no such duty. International law—especially before the 1970 UNESCO treaty—creates no obligation to enforce the cultural property export laws of foreign nations. Even after the passage of the UNESCO and other treaties, enforcement of foreign export law has been usually a matter of bilateral negotiations.[233]

Part IV. Conclusion

The legal and factual issues presented by the Rubin litigation are novel, interesting, and complex. It should be no surprise, then, that the Illinois case has been pending since December 29, 2003, and the Massachusetts litigation since February 10, 2005. As of this writing, neither has reached conclusion at the district court level. Moreover, once Judge Manning in Illinois and Judge O'Toole in Massachusetts issue their final decisions, respectively, the parties will undoubtedly continue their struggle for several more years in the federal courts of appeals. As discussed above,[234] there is considerable reason to believe that certain legal holdings of each judge could be overturned in those appeals.

The implications of these decisions are likely to spread quite quickly through the rest of the antiquities world. Dealers, private collectors, museums, auction houses, and even nation-states have an interest in the Rubin litigation, as the fate of these important Persian antiquities could be a harbinger of things to come. A final outcome in which the Rubin plaintiffs are free to assert Iranian ownership of the museums' objects, attach them in a court of law, and order their auction to the highest bidder would have profound consequences for all cultural property located in the United States. That outcome—highly unlikely under the correct application of U.S. and international law—would be especially shocking to those who think "cultural property" should be treated differently than other kinds of assets.

Cultural property has been defined as "property that has some special relationship with a particular culture or nation state."[235] A more detailed attempt describes it as "object[s] that embody the culture—principally archaeological, ethnographical and historical works of art, and architecture."[236] The proper way to think about cultural property has been hotly debated in the modern era since at least the time of Napoleon.[237] The issue has surfaced most recently with respect to claims stemming from Nazi art seizures during World War II[238] and Italy's efforts to recover antiquities looted during the last century.[239] The debate over the "specialness" of cultural property rages between two main camps:

those in favor of its free movement and those in favor of its tight control.[240] In the context of the Rubin litigation, those favoring free trade in antiquities would likely argue that the Persian collections should be treated like all other assets. If found to be owned by Iran, they should be immediately made available to the plaintiffs to execute upon in satisfaction of their judgment. This would lead to the salutary outcomes of plaintiffs–judgment creditors receiving funds owed them and antiquities being transferred to whoever values them the most (as judged by purchase price). For the free traders, it wouldn't matter whether the purchaser were a private collector or a museum.

Those in favor of more control over antiquities would feel affronted by the sale of the historically significant objects on the open market. While they might think it bad enough that American museums own the objects without verifiable provenances, a sale would be even worse. The collections could be split and scattered around the globe, they could be damaged or lost during shipment, and they would almost certainly never make their way back to Iran. By selling the Persian antiquities at auction, the group ownership and moral connections embodied within them would be rudely ignored.

There is no right answer to the debate between the free traders and the group preservationists. Cultural property undoubtedly has a unique place in many people's minds; whether it warrants special treatment in American courts of law is much less clear. The courts that must decide the fate of the Persian antiquities in the Rubin litigation are unlikely to wade deeply into the debate, though. There are sufficient legal and factual grounds upon which they can hold that the antiquities should remain precisely where they are—in the hands of the museums. Yet even if the museums win this round, they will likely face more litigation in the future.[241] Sympathetic, innocent plaintiffs like those involved in this litigation can make a strong case that their rights to recovery, whether because of terrorist acts or previous thefts, should trump any more nebulous, sociological ownership claims. *Rubin v. Islamic Republic of Iran* may be only the opening salvo in a new round of litigation concerning rightful ownership—both moral and legal—of antiquities in the United States.

Notes

1. *Campuzano v. Islamic Republic of Iran,* 281 F.Supp.2d 258, 261 (D.D.C. 2003).
2. *Id.* at 261.
3. *Id.* at 266 (description of injuries of Daniel Miller).
4. *Id.* (description of injuries of Abraham Mendelson).

5. *Id.* at 267 (description of injuries of Noam Rozenman).
6. *Id.* at 262.
7. *Id.* at 261; see also News in Brief, *The Jerusalem Post,* Sept. 10, 1999, at A2.
8. See *Rubin v. Hamas—Islamic Resistance Movement,* No. 02-0975, 2004 WL 2216489 (D.D.C. Sept. 27, 2004). The Rubin plaintiffs brought suit and obtained a final judgment against Hamas *after* obtaining judgment against Iran.
9. Campuzano, 281 F.Supp.2d at 261.
10. *Id.*
11. *Id.* at 258.
12. *Id.* at 261. The lead plaintiff in the second civil action, Diana Campuzano, supplied the name for the consolidated case.
13. *Id.* at 262 (testimony of Dr. Bruce Tefft and Dr. Patrick Clawson).
14. *Id.* Iran's MOIS is analogous to the United States's CIA. It is an enigmatic organization about which hard facts are difficult to ascertain. See, e.g., Neil MacKay, Iran's Spies, *The Sunday Herald,* Dec. 24, 2006, at 39.
15. Campuzano, 281 F.Supp.2d at 262.
16. *Id.* (expert Yigal Pressler testified, "Until his death in November 2001, Hamas operative Mahmoud Abu Hanoud organized, planned, and executed a large number of deadly terrorist bombings, including the bombing at issue here.").
17. For the earliest exposition of the law surrounding sovereign immunity in the United States, see *Schooner Exchange v. McFaddon,* 11 U.S. (7 Cranch) 116 (1812) (opinion of Marshall, C.J.). For more recent decisions, see *Kimel v. Fla. Bd. of Regents,* 528 U.S. 62 (2000); *Verlinden B.V. v. Cent. Bank of Nigeria,* 461 U.S. 480 (1983).
18. See, e.g., *Republic of Austria v. Altmann,* 541 U.S. 677, 689 (2004).
19. *Id.*
20. *Id.* at 691. See also H. R. Rep. No. 94-1487 (1976); S. Rep. No. 94-1310 (1976).
21. See 28 U.S.C. §§ 1602 through 1611.
22. 28 U.S.C. § 1604.
23. See Letter from Jack B. Tate, Acting Legal Adviser, U.S. Dept. of State, to Acting U.S. Attorney General Philip B. Perlman (May 19, 1952), reprinted in 26 Dept. State Bull. 984–85 (1952), and in *Alfred Dunhill of London, Inc. v. Republic of Cuba,* 425 U.S. 682, 711–15 (1976) (App. 2 to opinion of the Court).
24. 28 U.S.C. § 1602 (implementing the position of the Tate Memorandum).
25. See 28 U.S.C. § 1605(a)(7); *Peterson v. Islamic Republic of Iran,* 264 F.Supp.2d 46, 59–62 (D.D.C. 2003).
26. Campuzano, 281 F.Supp.2d at 270; see also Peterson, 264 F.Supp.2d at 60 (citing *Flatow v. Islamic Republic of Iran,* 999 F.Supp. 1, 18 (1998)).
27. Campuzano, 281 F.Supp.2d at 262; see also 49 Fed. Reg. 2836-02 (Jan. 23, 1984).

28. Campuzano, 281 F.Supp.2d at 270. The plaintiffs also argued the Iranian defendants were liable based on the common law torts of battery, assault, and intentional infliction of emotional distress. The court upheld these causes of action as well. *Id.* at 270–71 & n.5.
29. *Id.* at 274–77.
30. *Id.* at 278.
31. *Id.* Interestingly, courts are not allowed to levy punitive damages directly against foreign sovereigns or in favor of plaintiffs not suffering a "direct harm." Thus, the punitive damages in this case were levied jointly and severally against all defendants, except Iran, for the benefit of the five Rubin plaintiffs present at the bombing. See *Id.* at 278–79 (citing *Stern v. Islamic Republic of Iran,* 271 F.Supp.2d 286, 301–02 (D.D.C. 2003)).
32. *Rubin v. Islamic Republic of Iran,* No. 01-1655, 2005 WL 670770, at *1 (D.D.C. March 23, 2005). The two accounts were held in the name of the "Consulate General of the Islamic Republic of Iran in Chicago" and the "Consulate General Iran." Parties to the litigation referred to them as the Third Account and Fourth Account, respectively.
33. *Id.* at *1.
34. *Id.* at *4. Accord *Weinstein v. The Islamic Republic of Iran,* 274 F.Supp.2d 53, 61–62 (D.D.C. 2003). For further exploration of the TRIA § 201, see Part II, infra.
35. See *Rubin v. Islamic Republic of Iran,* U.S. Dist. Ct. for the N. Dist. of Ill. (East. Div.), No. 03-CV-9370 [hereinafter "Ill. Lit."], Pls.' Consol. Mem. of Law (Docket #105), at 5.
36. *Bank of New York v. Rubin,* No. 05-4926, 2006 WL 633315, at *2 (S.D.N.Y. March 15, 2006), *aff'd* in part and vacated in part by *Bank of New York v. Rubin,* 484 F.3d 149 (2d Cir. 2007). More accurately, the procedural framework of the case was an interpleader action brought by the Bank of New York to resolve competing claims to the Iranian accounts. The analysis would have been identical had the *Rubin* plaintiffs brought a coercive action first.
37. *Id.* at *8 (finding that the accounts were not "blocked assets" and therefore not attachable under TRIA § 201(a)) (citing *Weinstein v. Islamic Republic of Iran,* 299 F.Supp.2d 63 (E.D.N.Y. 2004)).
38. Ill. Lit., Pls.' Consol. Mem. of Law (Docket #105), at 5 & nn.3, 4.
39. See *Hegna v. Islamic Republic of Iran,* 376 F.3d 485, 489 n.14 (5th Cir. 2004).
40. Ill. Lit., Pls.' Consol. Mem. of Law (Docket #105), at 5 & nn.3, 4.
41. See, e.g., Museum Security Network Mailing List, available at http://msn-list.te.verweg.com/2006-March/004754.html (last visited Nov. 18, 2007).
42. See, e.g., Ehsan Tabesh, Legal Disputes Against Harvard and the University of Chicago over Persian Artifacts Continue, Aug. 11, 2006, available at http://www.niacouncil.org (last visited Nov. 18, 2007) (predicting the cases will ultimately be

decided by the United States Supreme Court); Brian Boucher, Terrorism Victims Sue for Museum Artifacts, 94 *Art in America* 39 (Sept. 1, 2006); Robin Pogrebin, An Unlikely Suit Linking Iran and a U.S. Museum Moves Forward, *N.Y. Times,* July 18, 2006, at E1.

43. For example, the Institute has the largest collection of Iranian painted pottery shards in the United States. See Peggy Horton Grant, The Oriental Institute News and Notes, No. 142, "Iranian Pottery in the Oriental Institute," (Summer 1994), available at http://oi.uchicago.edu/research/pubs/nn/sum94_grant.html (last visited Nov. 18. 2007).
44. The Oriental Institute, "Research at the Oriental Institute," http://oi.uchicago.edu/research/ (last visited Nov. 18, 2007).
45. *Id.*
46. The Oriental Institute, "Highlights from the Collection: Iran," http://oi.uchicago.edu/museum/highlights/iran.html (last visited Nov. 18, 2007).
47. Mark B. Garrison & Margaret Cool Root, *Seals on the Persepolis Fortification Tablets, Volume I: Images of Heroic Encounter* (2001), at 1, 3. Many of the tablets can be more specifically attributed to the period 509–494 B.C., during the reign of Darius I.
48. *Id.*
49. See Ill. Lit., Cit. Resp'ts. Mem. of Law in Supp. of Mot. to Declare Prop. Imm. from Citation and Execution (Docket #22), at 5.
50. *Id.*
51. *Id.*
52. The Oriental Institute, "The Chogha Mish Project," http://oi.uchicago.edu/research/projects/cho/ (last visited Nov. 18, 2007). The project was terminated only because of the increasingly unstable political situation in Iran. In 1995, a book was published covering the first five digs (conducted between 1961and 1971). A second book (covering the years 1972–78) is being prepared for publication. See generally Helene Kantour and P. Delougaz, *Chogha Mish, Volume 1: The First Five Seasons, 1961–1971,* (Abbas Alizadeh ed. 2001).
53. Abbas Alizadeh, The Oriental Institute News and Notes, No. 153, "Excavations at Chogha Bonut: The Earliest Village in Susiana, Iran." (Spring 1997), available at http://oi.uchicago.edu/research/pubs/nn/spr97_alizadeh.html (last visited Nov. 18, 2007).
54. See Ill. Lit., Pls.' Consol. Mem. of Law (Docket #105), at 5.
55. See Ill. Lit., Cit. Resp'ts. Mem. of Law in Supp. of Mot. to Declare Prop. Imm. from Citation and Execution (Docket #22), at 5–6.
56. The Field Museum, "Research & Collections," http://www.fieldmuseum.org/research_collections (last visited Nov. 18, 2007).

57. Ill. Lit., Aff. of Bennet Bronson, Attach. A (letter by Professor Ernst Herzfeld to Orr Goodson, dated 7/18/44).
58. *Id.*
59. The Harvard parties involved in the litigation were Harvard University, the President and Fellows of Harvard College, Harvard University Art Museums, the Busch-Reisinger Museum, the Fogg Art Museum, the Sackler Museum, the Semitic Museum, and the Peabody Museum. Harvard's attorneys asserted the only legal entity capable of being made a party to the litigation was the President and Fellows of Harvard College. See Rubin v. Islamic Republic of Iran, U.S. Dist. Ct. for the Dist. of Mass., No. 1:06-cv-11053 [hereinafter "Mass. Lit."], Mem. of Law of Harvard Parties in Supp. of Mot. to Quash Summons and to Diss. Attach. by Trustee Process (Docket #17), at 1 & n.1.
60. The Harvard Guide, The Early History of Harvard University, http://www.news.harvard.edu/guide/intro/index.html (last visited Nov. 18, 2007).
61. The Harvard Guide, The University Art Museums, http://www.news.harvard.edu/guide/to_do/to_do4.html (last visited Nov. 18, 2007).
62. The Museum of Fine Arts, Mission Statement, available at http://www.mfa.org (last visited Nov. 18, 2007).
63. The Museum of Fine Arts, Art of the Ancient World, http://www.mfa.org/collections (last visited Nov. 18, 2007).
64. Upon investigation, the author has concluded the six pieces described by the plaintiffs are located in the Near East room at the Sackler Museum. There, the far wall boasts six limestone reliefs averaging approximately two feet in height and one foot in width that date to the fifth century B.C. They were found at the same site in Iran as the Oriental Institute's Persepolis Fortification archive. Their placards show they were donated by Grenville L. Winthrop and came into the museum's collection in 1943.
65. See Mass Lit., Mem. of Law in Supp. of Pls.' Mot. for Order of Attach. by Trustee Process (Docket #3), at 3–4.
66. See Mass Lit., Mem. of Law of Harvard Parties in Supp. of Mot. to Quash Summons and to Diss. Attach. by Trustee Process (Docket #17), at 2.
67. *Id.*
68. See 28 U.S.C. § 1963 ("A judgment in an action for the recovery of money or property entered in any court of appeals, district court, bankruptcy court, or in the Court of International Trade may be registered by filing a certified copy of the judgment in any other district . . . when the judgment has become final by appeal or expiration of the time for appeal or when ordered by the court that entered the judgment for good cause shown. . . . A judgment so registered shall have the same effect as a judgment of the district court of the district where registered and may be enforced in like manner").

69. See, e.g., *U.S.I. Properties Corp. v. M.D. Constr. Co.*, 230 F.3d 489, 496–98 (1st Cir. 2000) ("Where a post-judgment proceeding presents an attempt simply to collect a judgment duly rendered by a federal court, even if chasing after the assets of the judgment debtor now in the hands of a third party, the residual jurisdiction stemming from the court's authority to render that judgment is sufficient to provide for federal jurisdiction over the post-judgment claim").
70. Fed. R. Civ. Proc. 69(a).
71. 28 U.S.C. § 1609; see also Part I, supra, notes 17–24 and accompanying text.
72. Section 1610 deals with the commercial use exception, while § 1611 implements immunity provided for by the International Organizations Immunities Act.
73. See H. R. Rep. No. 94-1487, at 17 (1976).
74. See *Verlinden B.V. v. Cent. Bank of Nigeria*, 461 U.S. 480, 494 n.20 (1983).
75. See Ill. Lit., Mem. and Order of 6/22/06 (Docket #163), available at Rubin, 436 F.Supp.2d at 941–43.
76. See *Id.*
77. Magistrate judges may issue a "report and recommendation" on issues under the authority of 28 U.S.C. § 636(b)(1). A district court judge reviews these "R&Rs" de novo. See 28 U.S.C. § 636(b)(1); Fed. R. Civ. Proc. 72(b).
78. See Ill. Lit., Mem. and Order of 6/22/06 (Docket #163), available at Rubin, 436 F.Supp.2d at 942.
79. *Id.*
80. See generally *Powers v. Ohio*, 499 U.S. 400 (1991).
81. See Ill. Lit., Mem. and Order of 6/22/06 (Docket #163), available at Rubin, 436 F.Supp.2d at 943 (citing Powers, 499 U.S. at 411).
82. *Id.*
83. *Id.*
84. See Ill. Lit., Mem. and Order of 6/22/06 (Docket #163), available at Rubin, 436 F.Supp.2d at 944.
85. *Id.* (citing six recent cases).
86. See Mass. Lit., Mem. and Order of 9/30/06 (Docket #70), available at Rubin, 456 F.Supp.2d at 232–34.
87. Mass. Lit., Mem. and Order of 9/30/06 (Docket #70), available at Rubin, 456 F.Supp.2d at 230–31 (citing 28 U.S.C. § 1963; *U.S.I. Props. Corp. v. M.D. Constr. Co.*, 230 F.3d 489 (1st Cir. 2000)).
88. Mass. Lit., Mem. and Order of 9/30/06 (Docket #70), available at Rubin, 456 F.Supp.2d at 232 n.3.
89. Mass. Lit., Mem. and Order of 9/30/06 (Docket #70), available at Rubin, 456 F.Supp.2d at 231–33.
90. 28 U.S.C. § 1609.

91. Mass. Lit., Mem. and Order of 9/30/06 (Docket #70), available at Rubin, 456 F.Supp.2d at 232 (citing *Walker Int'l Holdings Ltd. v. Republic of Congo*, 395 F.3d 229, 233 (5th Cir. 2004)).
92. *Id.*
93. *Id.*(citing Mass. Gen. Laws ch. 223, § 42; *Toomey v. Toomey*, 1997 Mass. App. Div. 181 (Mass. App. Div. 1997)).
94. See *Lyon v. Agusta S.P.A.*, 252 F.3d 1078, 1082 (9th Cir. 2001), cert. denied, 534 U.S. 1079 (2002).
95. U.S. Const. art. III, § 1 states, "The judicial power of the United States, shall be vested in one Supreme Court, and in such inferior courts as the Congress may from time to time ordain and establish." Section 2 continues, "In all the other cases before mentioned, the Supreme Court shall have appellate jurisdiction, both as to law and fact, with such exceptions, and under such regulations as the Congress shall make." See also *Marbury v. Madison*, 5 U.S. (1 Cranch) 147 (1803) ("Congress have not power to give original jurisdiction to the supreme court in other cases than those described in the constitution.").
96. E.g., *Duke Power Co. v. Carolina Environmental Study Group, Inc.*, 438 U.S. 59, 68–69 (1978); *Liberty Mutual Ins. Co. v. Wetzel*, 424 U.S. 737, 740 (1976).
97. *Id.*
98. *Duke Power Co.*, 438 U.S. at 68.
99. See, *supra*, notes 95–98 and accompanying text.
100. *Verlinden B.V. v. Cent. Bank of Nigeria*, 461 U.S. 480, 494 n.20 (1983).
101. See 28 U.S.C. § 1610(c).
102. Ill. Lit., Mem. and Order of 6/22/06 (Docket #163), available at Rubin, 436 F.Supp.2d at 945.
103. Mass. Lit., Mem. and Order of 9/30/06 (Docket #70), available at Rubin, 456 F.Supp.2d at 230–31.
104. See 28 U.S.C. § 1602.
105. See generally *FG Hemisphere Associates, LLC v. Republique du Congo*, 455 F.3d 575 (5th Cir. 2006).
106. Mass. Lit., Mem. and Order of 9/30/06 (Docket #70), available at Rubin, 456 F.Supp.2d at 230–231.
107. See *U.S.I. Props. Corp. v. M.D. Constr. Co.*, 230 F.3d 489, 497 (1st Cir. 2000).
108. *Id.* at 496.
109. See, e.g., 28 U.S.C. § 1602 (Congress's findings and declaration of purposes for the FSIA).
110. Ill. Lit., Pls.' Consol. Mem. in Opp. to Iran's Mots. for Summ. Judg. and for a Protect. Order (Docket #222), at 11–21.

111. Compare 28 U.S.C. § 1610(a)(7) ("[property] used for a commercial activity in the United States") with *Id.* § 1605(a)(2) ("commercial activity carried on in the United States by the foreign state").
112. Ill. Lit., Pls.' Consol. Mem. in Opp. to Iran's Mots. for Summ. Judg. and for a Protect. Order (Docket #222), at 16 n.11.
113. Mass. Lit., Mem. and Order of 9/30/06 (Docket #70), available at Rubin, 456 F.Supp.2d at 234 n.5 (discussing *Sesostris, S.A.E. v. Transportes Navales, S.A.*, 727 F.Supp. 737 (D. Mass. 1989)).
114. See Part I, *supra*, at note 52.
115. See 28 U.S.C. § 1603(d).
116. See, e.g., *Sun v. Taiwan*, 201 F.3d 1105, 1109 (9th Cir. 2000).
117. See *Malewicz v. City of Amsterdam*, 362 F.Supp.2d 298, 314 (D.D.C. 2005).
118. Ill. Lit., Pls.' Consol. Mem. in Opp. to Iran's Mots. for Summ. Judg. and for a Protect. Order (Docket #222), at 11–21.
119. *Id.* at 19.
120. *Id.* (citing Exhibit C).
121. *Id.* (citing Exhibit E).
122. Ill. Lit., Cit. Resp'ts. Mem. of Law in Supp. of Mot. to Decl. Prop. Imm. from Citation and Execution (Docket #22), at 6; Mass. Lit., Mem. of Law of Harvard Parties in Supp. of Mot. to Quash Summons and to Diss. Attach. by Trustee Process (Docket #17), at 5.
123. Ill. Lit., Cit. Resp'ts. Mem. of Law in Supp. of Mot. to Decl. Prop. Imm. from Citation and Execution (Docket #22), at 8 (citing *Republic of Argentina v. Weltover*, 504 U.S. 607, 613 (1992)).
124. *Id.* at 11; Mass. Lit., Mem. of Law of Harvard Parties in Supp. of Mot. to Quash Summons and to Diss. Attach. by Trustee Process (Docket #17), at 5.
125. Ill. Lit., Cit. Resp'ts. Mem. of Law in Supp. of Mot. to Decl. Prop. Imm. from Citation and Execution (Docket #22), at 11.
126. *Id.* at 22.
127. Black's Law Dictionary 151–52 (8th ed. 2004).
128. Mass. Lit., Mem. of Law of Harvard Parties in Supp. of Mot. to Quash Summons and to Diss. Attach. by Trustee Process (Docket #17), at 17.
129. *Id.*
130. See supra notes 77–85.
131. Ill. Lit., Att'y Appear. for Def., The Islamic Rep. of Iran, by Michael D. McCormick (Docket #169), at 1 and The Islamic Rep. of Iran's Mem. in Supp. of its Mot. for a Protect. Order (Docket #182), at 2–3.
132. Ill. Lit., The Islamic Rep. of Iran's Mem. in Supp. of its Mot. for a Protect. Order (Docket #182), at 6.
133. *Id.* at 6–7.

134. Ill. Lit., The Islamic Rep. of Iran's Mem. in Supp. of its Renewed Mot. to Decl. Prop. Exempt (Docket #199), at 4.
135. The commercial use issue was actually litigated twice in the Illinois court: first, to determine the appropriate scope of any discovery proceedings and second, to determine whether Iran and the third-party respondents were entitled to summary judgment. This duplication was necessary because the order issued during discovery was not binding for the case as a whole.
136. See Ill. Lit., Mem. Op. and Order of 12/01/04 (Docket #32), available at Rubin, 349 F.Supp.2d 1108, 1109 (N.D. Ill. 2004); Ill. Lit., Statement of 3/18/05 (Docket #46), available at Rubin, No. 03-9370, 2005 WL 783057, at *1 (N.D. Ill. Mar. 18, 2005).
137. *Conn. Bank of Comm. v. Rep. of Congo,* 309 F.3d 240, 257 n.5 (5th Cir. 2002); *Flatow v. Islamic Rep. of Iran,* 76 F.Supp.2d 16, 23 (D.D.C. 1999).
138. *Id.*
139. See *Conn. Bank,* 309 F.3d at 252; H. R. Rep. No. 94-1487, reprinted in 1976 U.S.C.C.A.N. at 6626.
140. Mass. Lit., Mem. and Order of 9/30/06 (Docket #70), available at Rubin, 456 F.Supp.2d at 233–34.
141. Mass. Lit., Mem. and Order of 9/30/06 (Docket #70), available at Rubin, 456 F.Supp.2d at 234.
142. Mass. Lit., Mem. and Order of 9/30/06 (Docket #70), available at Rubin, 456 F.Supp.2d at 234 n.5.
143. Mass. Lit., Mem. and Order of 9/30/06 (Docket #70), available at Rubin, 456 F.Supp.2d at 234 (citing *Conn. Bank,* 309 F.3d at 251–60; *Flatow,* 76 F.Supp.2d at 21–24; *De Letelier v. Republic of Chile,* 748 F.2d 790, 795–98 (2d Cir. 1984)).
144. See, e.g., *Branch v. Smith,* 538 U.S. 254, 281 (2003).
145. 28 U.S.C. § 1602.
146. *Id.*
147. See generally *Spector v. Norwegian Cruise Line Ltd.,* 545 U.S. 119 (2005).
148. 28 U.S.C. § 1602.
149. Pub. L. No. 107-297, 116 Stat. 2322.
150. TRIA § 201(a).
151. Ill. Lit., Pls.' Consol. Mem. of Law (Docket #105), at 4 (quoting *Hill v. Republic of Iraq,* No. 99-3346, 2003 WL 21057173, at *2 (D.D.C. Mar. 11, 2003)).
152. *Id.* at 6.
153. *Id.* (quoting TRIA § 201(d)(2)).
154. 44 Fed. Reg. 65729 (Nov. 14, 1979); *Hegna v. Islamic Republic of Iran,* 376 F.3d 485, 488 n.8, 493 n.32 (5th Cir. 2004).
155. 46 Fed. Reg. 7923 (January 19, 1981). Exec. Order No. 12281 was designed to unfreeze most assets blocked by Exec. Order No. 12170 (financial assets owned

by Iran, for example, were specifically excluded). It flowed directly out of the Declarations of the Government of the Democratic and Popular Republic of Algeria dated January 19, 1981 ("Algiers Accords"). The Algiers Accords called for the creation of an Iran-U.S. Claims Tribunal to arbitrate outstanding issues that had arisen since 1979 between the two nations and citizens thereof. For the text of the Algiers Accords, see 20 Int'l L. Mat. 224 (1981), also available at www.iusct.org/general-declaration.pdf.

156. 46 Fed. Reg. 7923, at 7 (Jan. 19, 1981).
157. 31 C.F.R. 535.215(a).
158. 31 C.F.R. 535.333.
159. University of Chicago's Oriental Institute is the only third-party respondent that concedes Iran has some ownership interest in the property. Even the Institute's antiquities fall into the "contested" category, however, because it has maintained Iran does not have full ownership, but rather only partial title. See 31 C.F.R. § 535.333(c). The Field Museum, MFA, and Harvard all assert that they have complete ownership of the antiquities.
160. This is a contested factual issue between the Rubin plaintiffs and the third-party respondents. For purposes of preliminary discovery motions, however, the third-party respondents assumed *arguendo* that Iran had ownership. See Part IV, infra, for an analysis of the factual determination of who owns the antiquities in question.
161. Ill. Lit., Pls.' Consol. Mem. of Law (Docket #105), at 10 ("In sum, if (as plaintiffs intend to prove) the properties at issue do in fact belong to Iran, then those properties will [be] subject to attachment and execution by plaintiffs in satisfaction of their judgment under § 201 of TRIA."); see also Law Concerning the Preservation of Nat. Antiquities, Approved on 3 Nov. 1930 (Iran) [hereinafter "Iranian Export Law of 1930"], reprinted in UNESCO, The Protection of Movable Cultural Property, Collection of Legislative Texts: Iran (1988).
162. Iranian Export Law of 1930, art. 1; see also Part III, infra.
163. Ill. Lit., Field Museum's Reply in Supp. of its Mot. for Entry of Protect. Order (Docket #110), at 4–5; Ill. Lit., Cit. Resp'ts. Mem. of Law in Supp. of Mot. to Decl. Prop. Imm. from Citation and Execution (Docket #22), at 19.
164. Ill. Lit., Cit. Resp'ts. Mem. of Law in Supp. of Mot. to Decl. Prop. Imm. from Citation and Execution (Docket #22), at 19 (quoting 50 U.S.C. § 1702(b)(3)). The 1994 amendments can be found at Pub. L. 103-236, Title V, § 525(c)(1), 108 Stat. 474. For additional analysis, see notes 184–93 and accompanying text.
165. Ill. Lit., Cit. Resp'ts. Mem. of Law in Supp. of Mot. to Decl. Prop. Imm. from Citation and Execution (Docket #22), at 19–21.
166. *Id.* at 19–21. For legislative history on the 1994 amendments, see S. R. No. 103-107, H. Conf. R. No. 103-482, and 1994 U.S.C.C.A.N. 302.
167. *Id.* at 21 ("The exchange of these informational materials has allowed U.S. scholars to gain an expertise in Elamite unmatched in the world, and has provided consid-

erable information about important aspects of the operation of the ancient Persian empire, and thus about the earliest forms of organization of human civilization.").

168. *Id.*
169. *Id.*
170. *Id.*
171. Ill. Lit., Field Museum's Reply in Supp. of its Mot. for Entry of Protect. Order (Docket #110), at 6–8; Mass. Lit., Mem. of Law of Trustee Process Resp'ts. in Supp. of their Mot. for Recons. (Docket #73), at 3–6; Ill. Lit., The Islamic Rep. of Iran's Renewed Mot. to Declare Prop. Imm. (Docket #199), at 8–10.
172. 31 C.F.R. § 535.333(d) (quoted in Mass. Lit., Mem. of Law of Trustee Process Resp'ts. in Supp. of their Mot. for Recons. (Docket #73), at 11 n.7).
173. Ill. Lit., Cit. Resp'ts. Mem. of Law in Supp. of Mot. to Decl. Prop. Imm. from Citation and Execution (Docket #22), at 17–19. The Respondents note an important distinction between the Iranian "Blocking Regulations" promulgated in connection with Exec. Order No. 12170 (1979) and the Iranian "Transactions Regulations" promulgated under Exec. Order No. 12613 (1987). The Transactions Regulations imposed an import embargo on Iranian goods and services because of Iran's support of terrorism. The Blocking Regulations, on the other hand, made certain assets located in the United States "seized or frozen" for an indefinite period of time. Thus, while the Blocking Regulations created blocked assets which were seized or frozen, the Transactions Regulations only required that goods traveling into or out of Iran be licensed.
174. Mass. Lit., Mem. of Law of Trustee Process Resp'ts. in Supp. of their Mot. for Recons. (Docket #73), at 6.
175. *Id.*
176. See, *supra*, note 131 and accompanying text.
177. Mass. Lit., Mem. and Order of 9/30/06 (Docket #70), available at Rubin, 456 F.Supp.2d at 235.
178. *Id.*
179. *Id.*
180. Mass. Lit., Mem. and Order of 9/30/06 (Docket #70), available at Rubin, 456 F.Supp.2d at 235–36.
181. *Id.*
182. See Mass. Lit., Mem. of Law of Trustee Process Resp'ts. in Supp. of their Mot. for Recons. (Docket #73).
183. See *Id.* at 13–19 (arguing the court's order involved a "controlling question of law," "substantial ground for difference of opinion about the legal question at issue existed," and "immediate appeal from the order may materially advance the ultimate termination of the litigation").
184. See 50 U.S.C. § 1702(b)(3). This amendment came into effect under the Foreign Relations Authorization Act, Pub. L. 103-236, 108 Stat. 382 (1994).

185. *Id.*
186. This position is not universally held. In a criminal case dating back to 2003, the Department of Justice took the position that antiquities did not fit into the "informational materials" exception. The Department was prosecuting Hicham Aboutaam, a prominent art dealer, for illegally importing an Iranian antiquity. Aboutaam had claimed a Syrian origin for an Iranian silver rhyton. Because Aboutaam entered into a plea agreement, however, the court never reached the merits of the issue. See *United States v. Aboutaam*, No. 04-562 (S.D.N.Y. June 14, 2004) (Information filed as to Hicham Aboutaam by the United States); Barry Meier, Art Dealer Pleads Guilty in Import Case, N.Y. Times, June 24, 2004.
187. See *Id.*
188. See generally Ill. Lit., Cit. Resp'ts. Mem. of Law in Supp. of Mot. to Decl. Prop. Imm. from Citation and Execution (Docket #22), at 19–21.
189. See, e.g., Eric A. Posner, The International Protection of Cultural Property: Some Skeptical Observations, Univ. of Chicago Pub. Law Working Paper No. 141 (2006), available at http://ssrn.com/abstract=946778 (last visited Nov. 18, 2007).
190. See, e.g., H. Conf. R. No. 103-482, reprinted in 1994 U.S.C.C.A.N. 398, 482 ("The provisions of [the Act] seek to protect the constitutional rights of Americans to educate themselves about the world by communicating with peoples of other countries in a variety of ways, such as by sharing information and ideas with persons around the world, traveling abroad, and engaging in education, cultural and other exchanges with persons from around the world.").
191. See U.S. Dept. of Treasury, Office of Foreign Assets Control, Interpretive Rulings, http://www.treas.gov/offices/enforcement/ofac/rulings/index.shtml (last visited Nov. 18, 2007).
192. Office of Foreign Assets Control, Interpretive Ruling 040706-FARCL-IA-16, available at http://www.treas.gov/offices/enforcement/ofac/rulings/ia070604.pdf (last visited Nov. 18, 2007).
193. Although the opinion was discussing an exemption to the Iranian Transactions Regulations, 31 C.F.R. 560, the same language is used in the Iranian Blocking Regulations promulgated under the authority of the IEEPA.
194. Indeed, this provision later became an issue at the United States-Iran Claims Tribunal. Iran claimed the provision protected American interests too much and that more property should be returned to Iran. The issue was eventually adjudicated in Iran's favor.
195. TRIA § 201(b)(2), Pub. L. No. 107-297, 116 Stat. 2322.
196. *Smith ex rel. Estate of Smith v. Federal Reserve Bank of New York,* 346 F.3d 264, 270 (2d Cir. 2003).
197. *Id.*
198. *Gulf Ports Crating Co. v. Ministry of Roads and Transp.,* 674 F.2d 318, 319–20 (5th Cir. 1982).

199. *Warth v. Seldin*, 422 U.S. 490, 498 (1975).
200. See *Elk Grove Unified Sch. Dist. v. Newdow*, 542 U.S. 1, 12 (2004) (quoting *Allen v. Wright*, 468 U.S. 737, 751 (1984) and citing *Sec. of State of Md. v. Joseph H. Munson Co.*, 467 U.S. 947, 955–56 (1984)).
201. Black's Law Dictionary 687 (8th ed. 2004).
202. See Ill. Code of Civ. Proc. § 2-1402.
203. See, e.g., Ill. Lit., Field Museum's Reply in Supp. of its Mot. for Entry of Protect. Order (Docket #110), at 9 ("Plaintiffs are improperly attempting to use a supplementary proceeding as a means to adjudicate some unpled claim that the Field Museum did not acquire valid title to the Herzfeld Collection.").
204. U.S. Const., art. III.
205. *Simon v. Eastern Ky. Welfare Rights Org.*, 426 U.S. 26, 41–42 (1976) (quoted in *Lujan v. Defenders of Wildlife*, 504 U.S. 555, 560–61 (1992)).
206. Cf. *Warth v. Seldin*, 422 U.S. at 498–99 (noting that "the standing question is whether the plaintiff has alleged such a personal stake in the outcome of the controversy as to warrant his invocation of federal-court jurisdiction and to justify exercise of the court's remedial powers on his behalf" (citation omitted)).
207. Cf. *San Remo Hotel, L.P. v. City and County of San Francisco*, 545 U.S. 323, 336 n.16 (2005) ("Under res judicata, a final judgment on the merits of an action precludes the parties or their privies from relitigating issues that were or could have been raised in that action. Under collateral estoppel, once a court has decided an issue of fact or law necessary to its judgment, that decision may preclude relitigation of the issue in a suit on a different cause of action involving a party to the first case.").
208. E.g., *Elk Grove Unified Sch. Dist. v. Newdow*, 542 U.S. 1, 12 (2004).
209. *Id.*
210. See, e.g., TRIA § 201; IEEPA §§ 202 & 203; Exec. Order Nos. 12170 and 12281; 31 C.F.R. §§ 525.215 and 525.333.
211. Indeed, the United States has intervened in the Illinois litigation to introduce two Statements of Interest. See Ill. Lit., Statement of Int. of the United States of Am. (Docket #20); Second Statement of Int. of the United States of Am. (Docket #145).
212. See, infra, notes 219–227 and accompanying text.
213. Admittedly, this conclusion may be in some tension with the rights of creditors in other areas of the law. For example, commercial law typically allows a judgment creditor to step into the shoes of his debtor to assert rights to the debtor's property. See, e.g., *City of Arkansas City v. Anderson*, 749 P.2d 505, 511 (Kan. Ct. App. 1988) ("[T]he plaintiffs were entitled under the charging order to certain accountings and the opportunity to step into the shoes of the debtor partner so far as distributions and withdrawal of the partnership funds were concerned.") Further, there is some authority in trust law for a judgment creditor of a trust beneficiary to assert whatever rights the beneficiary has to the trust property. See

Restatement (Third) of Trusts § 59 (2003) ("The interest of a beneficiary in a valid spendthrift trust can be reached in satisfaction of an enforceable claim against the beneficiary for (a) support of a child, spouse, or former spouse; or (b) services or supplies provided for necessities or for the protection of the beneficiary's interest in the trust."). But cf. *Scheffel v. Krueger* (N.H. 2001) (holding that spendthrift trusts bar recovery by all third-party creditors against beneficiary's trust assets, except if trust was self-settled or amounts to fraudulent conveyance).

214. Mass. Lit., Reply Mem. of Law of Trustee Process Resp'ts. in Supp. of their Mot. for Recons. (Docket #79), at 5.
215. *Lujan v. Defenders of Wildlife,* 504 U.S. 555, 561 (1992).
216. Ill. Lit., The Islamic Rep. of Iran's Mem. in Supp. of its Mot. for a Protect. Order (Docket #182), at 1–2.
217. *Id.*
218. Iranian Export Law of 1930, supra note 161.
219. *Id.*
220. *Id.*, art. 13.
221. Reza Khan (more commonly known as Reza Shah) took power following a military coup in 1921.
222. Iranian Export Law of 1930, supra note 161, art. 1.
223. See, supra, note 66; see also Mass. Lit., Mem. of Law of Harvard Parties in Supp. of Mot. to Quash Summons and to Diss. Attach. by Trustee Process (Docket #17), at 2.
224. See Ill. Lit., Field Museum's Reply in Supp. of its Mot. for Entry of Protect. Order (Docket #110), at 9 ("If the Plaintiffs believe that they have some claim to the Herzfeld Collection, they must identify the basis for that claim. They must then carry the burden of proving that claim, whatever it may be.").
225. Cf. Posner, supra note 189 (arguing that only exporting nations can enforce their export restrictions, as importing nations will not bother).
226. E.g., *Hammer v. Thompson,* 129 P.3d 609, 613 (Kan. Ct. App. 2006); *Cochran v. Jones,* 707 So.2d 791, 793 (Fla. Ct. App. 1998); *Mattson v. Commercial Credit Business,* 723 P.2d 996, 998–99 (Ore. 1986).
227. See, e.g., Paul M. Bator, An Essay on the International Trade in Art, 34 Stan. L. Rev. 275, 287 (1982) (arguing that "[t]he fact that an art object has been illegally exported does not in itself bar it from lawful importation into the United States . . . .").
228. See generally 44B Am. Jur. 2d International Law § 1 (2007).
229. See generally Bator, supra note 227, at 287.
230. UNESCO Convention on the Means of Prohibiting and Preventing the Illicit Import, Export and Transfer of Ownership of Cultural Property, Nov. 14, 1970, 823 U.N.T.S. 231 (1972), 10 Int'l Legal Materials 289 (1971).

231. Convention on Cultural Property Implementation Act, 19 U.S.C. §§ 2601 through 2613 (1982), Pub. L. No. 97-446, 96 Stat. 2329, approved January 12, 1983; as amended by Pub. L. No. 100-204, 101 Stat. 1331, approved December 22, 1987.
232. The high court for England and Wales seems to have reached this conclusion while interpreting the 1930 Iranian law in a recent case. See *Iran v. Barakat Galleries Ltd,* [2007] EWHC 705 (March 29, 2007), available at 2007 WL 919380 (QBD) (holding Iran had failed to demonstrate its ownership interest, under Iranian law, in several Persian antiquities illegally exported from the country).
233. E.g., Importation of Pre-Columbian Monumental or Architectural Sculpture or Murals, Pub. L. No. 92-587, 66 Stat. 1296 (codified at 19 U.S.C. §§ 2091–2095 (1976)).
234. See Part II, supra.
235. Posner, supra note 189, at 1.
236. John Henry Merryman, The Public Interest in Cultural Property, 77 Cal. L. Rev. 339, 341 (1989). For an even more detailed definition, see UNESCO Convention on the Means of Prohibiting and Preventing the Illicit Import, Export and Transfer of Ownership of Cultural Property, Nov. 14, 1970, 823 U.N.T.S. 231, 234–36 and B. Burnham, The Protection of Cultural Property: Handbook of National Legislation (B. Burnham ed. 1974).
237. See John Henry Merryman, The Free International Movement of Cultural Property, 31 N.Y.U. J. Int'l L. & Pol. 1, 1 (1998).
238. See, e.g., Carol Kino, Stolen Artworks and the Lawyers Who Reclaim Them, N.Y. Times, Mar. 28, 2007, at H28 (describing several recent Nazi-restitution cases); Nicholas Glass, Paintings from the Goudstikker Collection, Looted by the Nazis, are Finally Being Returned to Their Rightful Owners—And Dutch Museums are Feeling Their Loss, Financial Times, Nov. 25, 2006, at 42 (describing the return of the Goudstikker Collection, worth $300 million, to various heirs); Talya Halkin, New Web Site to Help Heirs, Museums Identify Art Looted by the Nazis, The Jerusalem Post, June 5, 2006, at 4 (describing the Swift-Find Looted Art Project).
239. See, e.g., Elisabetta Povoledo, Italy Recovers Rare Marbles, N.Y. Times, Jan. 25, 2007, at E2 (describing the recovery of 12 marble panels); Peter Popham, U.S. Museum Returns Looted Antiquities as Italians Stand up for Lost Heritage and Pride, The Independent, Oct. 1, 2006, at N15 (describing return of 13 looted pieces by Boston's MFA); Tracy Wilkinson, et al., Getty to Return Artworks to Italy, L.A. Times, June 22, 2006, at A1 (describing deal between J. Paul Getty Museum and Italy for the return of "a number of very significant pieces"); Elisabetta Povoledo, Italy and U.S. Sign Antiquities Accord, N.Y. Times, Feb. 22, 2006, at E1 (describing return to Italy of the Euphronios krater); Tracy Wilkin-

son, Getty Curator's Trial is Delayed, L.A. Times, July 19, 2005, at E1 (describing Italian prosecution of former-Getty curator for antiquities, Marion True).

240. Professor Merryman describes "discourses" from the international free traders, the acquisitors, the cultural internationalists, the source nations, and the archaeologists. See Merryman, supra note 237, at 9–13.

241. See, e.g., Rebecca Mead, Den of Antiquity: The Met Defends Its Treasures, The New Yorker, Apr. 9, 2007, at 52–61 (showing that Carlos Picón, the Met's curator of the Greek and Roman Department, was more interested in justifying the provenance of items in his sprawling collection than discussing the new wing that housed them).

Law School Update

Special Focus on Teaching

• • •

Michael Scherzer

The 2007 *Yearbook of Cultural Property Law* published a summary of a survey that asked some general questions about the courses taught by professors around the country (a full recap of the data will appear on the LCCHP website). As a follow-up to that study, we have asked several professors to discuss their courses a little more in-depth. We asked four professors at law schools around the country to provide a copy of their syllabus and to discuss the goals of their course. As their responses indicate, cultural property law may be approached from a variety of backgrounds, from the academic to private practice. Courses may highlight theoretical questions of what it means to "own" culture or rigorously prepare students entering the world of museum management. Educators currently teaching a version of cultural property law or those considering how they might create their own program will find their perspectives enlightening and encouraging.

Stephen K. Urice, University of Miami School of Law

Professor Urice is an Associate Professor of Law at U. Miami School of Law. He also serves as Director of the Project for Cultural Heritage Law & Policy, which he founded in 2003 to promote the teaching of cultural heritage issues in law schools, schools of public policy, and departments of art history, anthropology, archaeology, and related fields. He has served for many years on the faculty of the American Law Institute-American Bar Association's annual course of study "Legal Issues in Museum Administration." Professor Urice has practiced trusts and estates at Milbank, Tweed, Hadley & McCloy, LLP in New York and at Irell & Manella in Los Angeles. His primary interests are in international movement, repatriation, museum law, and estate planning for artists. At Miami he teaches a course he developed called Cultural Heritage Law and Policy, a seminar on museum law, as well as a course on art law.

He developed "Cultural Heritage Law and Policy" at the University of Pennsylvania School of Law, where he taught prior to Miami. The course emphasizes that, at its core, cultural property law seeks to protect cultural heritage, which can be used and appropriated as property, but which is also very much alive and dynamic at the same time. The course is built around five major themes: defining cultural heritage, possessing cultural heritage, using cultural heritage, preserving cultural heritage, and destroying cultural heritage. Several lectures under each theme follow chapters in a class textbook covering, for example, ownership, control, trade regulation, theft, intellectual property, and war.

Marilyn Phelan, Texas Tech University School of Law

Professor Phelan is a Paul Whitfield Horn Professor of Law and Professor of Museum Science at Texas Tech University School of Law and serves as Director of the Tax Clinic at the School of Law. She is a member of American Law Institute and is a Texas Commissioner to the National Conference on Uniform State Laws. She has served as Chair of the International Cultural Property Committee and the International Taxation Committee for the American Bar Association Section of International Law and Practice. She currently serves as Vice-Chair of the International Cultural Property Committee. Professor Phelan also serves as a member of the Legal Affairs and Properties Committee to the Executive Council of the International Council of Museums (ICOM). Professor Phelan teaches Art and Museum Law, Nonprofit Organizations, Taxation of Business Enterprises, and a clinical course in tax procedure. She is interested in cultural property law as a means to protect the world's cultural heritage, which has "suffered severely because of plunder, pillage, and neglect."

She developed the syllabus for her course "Art and Museum Law" at Texas Tech University. Her course focuses more on museum law than Professor

Urice's overview course. Bringing to bear her background in tax, her course prepares students for the legal regime governing charitable and nonprofit cultural institutions. A student interested in working in a museum's general counsel's office would be well-advised to attend her course. The subject is divided into a series of focused sessions, such as organizational structure, accounting, fundraising, commercial activities, and tort liability; duties and responsibilities of institutional directors; museum loans, purchases and acquisitions; artists' rights; and the protection of cultural property and natural resources.

One interesting feature of her course is that she supplements the textbook reading assignments with a fulsome set of exam-style questions tied to each class, requiring students to analyze problems according to textbook readings and case law. Here is a sample problem from the session on art forgeries:

> Art Museum purchased a painting listed in an auction catalogue as a work of Claude Monet. The museum paid $1 million for the painting. The auction catalogue described "conditions of sale," which included a disclaimer of warranty as to genuineness or authorship. Its director later discovered the painting is a forgery. The museum director wants to sue the art gallery for return of the purchase price. The owner of the art gallery contends he is not liable.
>
> 1. Is there an "express" warranty that the work was a Monet?
> 2. Does the "conditions of sale" negate any warranty?
> 3. Is the art gallery liable to the museum?
>
> See *Weisz v. Parke-Bernet Galleries, Inc.*, 325 N.Y.S.2d 576 (Civ. Ct. N.Y. 1971) and 351 N.Y.S.2D 911 (1974), and *Balog v. Center Art Gallery*, 745 F. Supp. 1556 (D. Haw. 1990).

Here is a sample question from the session on laws protecting natural heritage:

> A native Alaskan hunts whales. He uses the whale meat for food, and he makes artifacts for sale to a local museum from hides and other parts of the whales. A native Hawaiian takes green sea turtles and an Hawaiian monk seal. He is indicted under the Marine Mammal Protection Act.
>
> 1. May the museum legally display the artifacts it purchased from the native Alaskan?
> 2. May either a native Alaskan or a native Hawaiian be convicted under the Marine Mammal Protection Act?
>
> See Marine Mammal Protection Act, 16 U.S.C. §§ 1361-1407, and *U.S. v. Nuesca*, 945 F.2d 254 (9th 1991).

Jennifer A. Kreder, Northern Kentucky University Salmon P. Chase College of Law

Professor Kreder is an Associate Professor of Law at the Salmon P. Chase College of Law. She serves as the elected Vice Chair of the Art & Cultural Heritage Committee of the ABA Section of International Law. Prior to entering academia, Professor Kreder was a Litigation Associate with Milbank, Tweed, Hadley & McCloy in New York, where she concentrated on Holocaust era intergovernmental negotiation and litigation issues and art disputes. Professor Kreder approaches cultural property law from a multi-faceted set of interests: Nazi-looted art, ethical questions at galleries and museums, choices between criminal and civil remedies, and problems in international procedure. At Chase she teaches civil procedure, remedies, art law, and cultural property law.

Professor Kreder created her course "Law & Social Problems: The Art Repatriation Movement" at the Chase College of Law. The course "explores the legal and moral arguments in favor of various repatriation requests, as well as the legal, moral, and practical arguments commonly raised by those on the receiving end of repatriation requests." Like the other courses reviewed here, Professor Kreder's course begins with the definition of cultural property. She also spends some time describing the problem of and players involved in the legal and illegal trade of cultural property. The course moves next into an overview of international and domestic legal protections. The remainder of the course focuses on the special problems encountered during wartime, exploring the legal, moral, and ethical questions of what to do with Nazi-looted art and with property lost during the recent Iraq War.

Professor Kreder has designed her course to maximize active student participation in and out of the classroom. Professor Kreder brings archaeologists and anthropologists into her class and brings students on two field trips to the Cincinnati Art Museum. In addition, students may elect to write a 15–20 page research paper. Professor Kreder encourages students to "get out of the library" and get in direct contact with "artists, dealers, museum employees, collectors or others (administrators, legislators) to learn more about the case or problem or activity or institution or proposal and to get authentic, experience-based ideas about the problem and its workable resolution." Students writing such a paper in Professor Kreder's course are required to make two 10–15 minute "colloquia" presentations on their topic before their classmates. The purpose of the first colloquium is to assist the student in fleshing out his or her thesis. The purpose of the second is for the student to present his or her nearly finished work "to show how the student solidified and strengthened his or her thesis and addressed counterarguments."

Sarah K. Harding, Illinois Institute of Technology Chicago-Kent College of Law

Professor Harding teaches at the Chicago-Kent College of Law and serves as Associate Dean for Faculty Development, where she teaches torts, property, legal philosophy, and comparative constitutional law. In 1989 she was awarded a Rhodes Scholarship and went on to obtain a B.C.L. from Oxford University and an LL.M. from Yale Law School, where she was submissions editor for the *Yale Journal of Law and the Humanities*. Professor Harding is interested in exploring the theoretical foundations of cultural property law and its broader issues relating to indigenous people and cultural rights. At Chicago-Kent she teaches a course she developed called Property Rights and Social Conflict, as well as property, comparative law, international intellectual property, and comparative constitutional law

Professor Harding's course *Property Rights and Social Conflict* was developed at Chicago-Kent. The course explores the role of property rights in resolving current social conflicts. About a quarter of the class focuses on conflicts relating to culture and cultural heritage. After establishing the theoretical groundwork for the basis of property rights, the course examines various constitutional approaches to property protection. Finally, the course examines how property rights resolve conflicts in several areas: the environment and conservation, the human body and intellectual property, and cultural property and traditional knowledge. Professor Kreder assigns readings from a textbook and her own course supplement that draw liberally from legal opinions, philosophy, international and comparative materials, and political and economic theory. Her course serves as a great counterpoint to the more practice-oriented approach of Professor Phelan. Comparing their syllabi indicates the wide variety of source material educators may draw from in teaching cultural property (see below).

Conclusion

Getting a new course approved at most law schools involves developing a syllabus and submitting it to the administration and/or faculty for review. Professor Phelan advises aspiring professors to submit a proposal for the course, suggesting that "Most law schools will welcome such an innovative, interesting, and concededly—at this point in time—relevant elective course. Students will appreciate having the opportunity to take such a course and learn about laws protecting cultural property." The greatest challenge at the early stages in creating a course is often a matter of promoting interest among students. Professor Urice advises new educators not to be discouraged by low initial turnout. When he started as a lecturer, he had fourteen students. Enrollment has since grown to seventy. Professor Kreder recommends that new professors "think creatively about guest speakers who can make the subject come alive for the students and provide insight into the practical application of the law." Fortunately, the tendency of cultural property law to overlap with other areas makes it easy to develop a broad audience. Get in touch with faculty teaching copyright, federal courts, advanced civil procedure, litigation clinics, nonprofit organizations, art law, and international law to see about cross-promoting opportunities. For example, Professor Phelan stresses that cultural property law has taken on greater international legal significance in recent years: "The collective efforts of all nations and peoples are required to protect and preserve the cultural heritage of humanity."

Review of Books, Articles, and Other Resources

• • •

Compiled by Gary Nurkin

The Yearbook *seeks to keep readers informed on the growing body of scholarship in the diverse field of cultural property law. The list below is not intended to be exhaustive. Articles may reflect a diversity of viewpoints. The editors invite information on new items as they are published, past items of ongoing value to readers, as well as information on new websites and in film.*

Selected Bibliography of Recent Books and Articles

Books

A.R.B. Amerasinghe, THE PROTECTION OF CULTURE, CULTURAL HISTORY AND CULTURAL PROPERTY (Colombo: National Trust Sri Lanka, 2006).

Janet Blake, COMMENTARY ON THE UNESCO 2003 CONVENTION ON THE SAFEGUARDING OF THE INTANGIBLE CULTURAL HERITAGE (Institute of Art and Law, UK 2006).

Ben Boer and Graeme Wiffen, HERITAGE LAW IN AUSTRALIA (Oxford University Press UK 2006).

Lisa Breglia, MONUMENTAL AMBIVALENCE: THE POLITICS OF HERITAGE (University of Texas Press, 2006).

Council of Europe, COUNCIL OF EUROPE FRAMEWORK CONVENTION ON THE VALUE OF CULTURAL HERITAGE FOR SOCIETY: FARO, 27 X 2005 (Strassbourg FR 2006).

Jessica L. Darraby, ART, ARTIFACT AND ARCHITECTURE LAW (Clark Boardman Callaghan, 2007).

Graham Fairclough, Rodney Harrison, John Schofield, Jr., John H. Jameson (eds.), HERITAGE READER (Routledge, 2007).

Francesco Francioni, 1972 WORLD HERITAGE CONVENTION (Oxford University Press, UK 2008).

David Freestone, Richard Barnes and David M. Ong, THE LAW OF THE SEA: PROGRESS AND PROSPECTS (Oxford University Press, UK 2006).

Derek Gillman, THE IDEA OF CULTURAL HERITAGE (Institute of Art and Law, UK 2006).

James F. Goode, NEGOTIATION FOR THE PAST: ARCHAEOLOGY, NATIONALISM, AND DIPLOMACY IN THE MIDDLE EAST (1919–1941) (University of Texas Press, 2007).

Great Britain, House of Commons, GOVERNMENT RESPONSE TO THE CULTURE, MEDIA, AND SPORT COMMITTEE REPORT ON PROTECTING AND PRESERVING OUR HERITAGE, THIRD REPORT OF SESSION 2005–2006 (Stationery office, UK 2006).

Yannis Hamilatis and Philip Duke, ARCHAEOLOGY & CAPITALISM (Left Coast Press, 2007).

David Harmon, Francis P. McManamon and Dwight T. Pitcaithley (eds.), THE ANTIQUITIES ACT: A CENTURY OF AMERICAN ARCHAEOLOGY, HISTORIC PRESERVATION, AND NATURE CONSERVATION (University of Arizona Press, 2006).

Sherry Hutt and David Tarler (eds.), YEARBOOK OF CULTURAL PROPERTY LAW (Left Coast Press 2007).

Jordan E. Kerber, CROSS CULTURAL COLLABORATION: NATIVE PEOPLE AND ARCHAEOLOGY IN THE NORTHEASTERN UNITED STATES (University of Nebraska Press, 2006).

David Le Vere, LOOTING SPIRO MOUNDS: AN AMERICAN'S KING TUT TOMB (University of Oklahoma Press, 2007).

David Lowenthal, Kenneth Olwig (eds.), THE NATURE OF CULTURAL HERITAGE, AND THE CULTURE OF NATURAL HERITAGE (Routledge, 2006).

Travis McDade: THE BOOK THIEF: THE TRUE CRIMES OF DANIEL SPIEGELMAN (Praeger Publications, 2006).

John Henry Merryman, IMPERIALISM, ART AND RESTITUTION (Cambridge University Press, UK 2006).

John Henry Merryman, Albert E. Eisen and Stephen K. Urice (eds.), LAW, ETHICS AND THE VISUAL ARTS (Fifth Edition) (Kluwer Law Aspen Publications, 2007).

Patrick J. O'Keefe, COMMENTARY ON THE UNESCO CONVENTION (Second Edition) (Institute of Art and Law, UK 2007).

Roger O'Keefe, THE PROTECTION OF CULTURAL PROPERTY IN ARMED CONFLICT (Cambridge University Press, UK 2007).

Lyndel V, Prot (ed.), FINISHING THE INTERRUPTED VOYAGE, Papers of the UNESCO Asia-Pacific Workshop on the 2001 Convention on the Protection of the Underwater Cultural Heritage (Institute of Art and Law, UK 2006).

Eleanor Robson, Luke Treaswell & Chris Gosden (eds.), WHO OWNS OBJECTS?: THE ETHICS AND POLITICS OF COLLECTING CULTURAL ARTIFACTS (Oxford University Press, UK 2006).

Lawrence Rothfield, Antiquities Under Siege: Cultural Heritage Protection after the Iraq War (Altamira Press, 2008).

Wayne Sandholtz, Prohibiting Plunder: How Norms Change (Oxford University Press, UK 2007).

Chris Scarre and Geoffrey Scarre (eds.), The Ethics of Archaeology: Philosophical Perspectives on Archaeological Practice (Cambridge University Press, UK 2006).

Gunnar Schnabel and Monika Tatzkow, Nazi Looted Art: Handbuch Kunstrestitution Weltweit (Propreitas-Verlag, Berlin 2007).

Laurajane Smith (ed..), Cultural Heritage: Critical Concepts in Media and Cultural Studies (Routledge, 2006).

Mark Staniforth & Michael Nash, Maritime Archaeology: Australian Approaches (Springer, 2006).

Karen D. Vitelli and Chip Colwell-Chanthaphonh (eds.), Archaeological Ethics (Alta Mira Press, 2006).

Gillian Wallace, Duckworth Debates in Archaeology: Globalism and Archaeology (Duckworth, UK 2007).

Joe Watkins, Sacred Sites and Repatriation (Chelsea House Publishers, 2006).

James O. Young, Cultural Appropriations and the Arts (Blackwell Publications, 2007).

Articles

Andrew Adler, *Expanding the Scope of Museums' Ethical Obligations With Respect to Nazi-Looted Art: Incorporating Restitution Claims Based on Private Sales Made as a Direct Result of Persecution*, 14 Int'l. J. Cultural Prop. 57 (2007).

William Anderson, *Commodifying Culture: Ownership of Cambodia's Archaeological Heritage*, 13 Limina 103 (2007).

David J. Bederman, *Current Development: Congress Enacts Increased Protections for Sunken Military Craft*, 100 A.J. I. L. 649 (2006).

Shoshana Berman, *Protection of Cultural Objects on Loan: The Israeli Perspective*, 12 Art, Antiquity & Law 113 (2007).

Venus Bivar, *History for Sale: The International Art Market and the Nation State*, 13 Int'l J. Cultural Prop. 259 (2006).

Corrine Brenner, *Cultural Property Law: Reflecting on the Bamiyan Buddha's Destruction*, 29 Suffolk Transnat'l. L. Rev. 237 (2006).

Aaron Kyle Briggs, *Symposium: Islamic Business and Commercial Law: Consequences of the Met-Italy Accord for the International Restitution of Cultural Property*, 7 Chi. J. Int'l. L. 623 (2007).

Neil Brodie and Colin Renfrew, *Looting and the World's Archaeological Heritage: The Inadequate Response*, 34 Annu. Rev. Anthropol. 343 (2005).

Susan B. Bruning, *Complex Legal Legacies: The Native American Graves Protection and Repatriation Act, Scientific Study, and Kennewick Man*, 71 American Antiquity 501 (2006).

Bruce W. Burton, *In Search of John Constable's The White Horse: A Case Study in Tortured Provenance and Proposal for a Torrens-Like System of Title Registration for Artwork*, 59 FLA. L. REV. 531 (2007).

Charlene A. Caprio, *Artwork, Cultural Heritage Property and the Foreign Sovereignty Immunities*, Act, 13 INT'L. J. CULTURAL PROP. 285 (2006).

David N. Chang, *Stealing Beauty: Stopping the Madness of Illicit Art Trafficking*, 28 HOUST J. INT'L. L. 829 (2006).

Elizabeth Dillinger, *Note, Mutilating Picasso: the case for amending the Visual Artist Rights Act to provide protection of moral rights after death*, 75 UMKC L. REV. 897 (2007).

Justin S. DuClos, *A conceptual wreck: Salvaging the Law of Finds*, 38 J. MAR. L & COM 25 (2007).

Heather J.H. Edgar, Edward A. Jolie, Joseph F. Powell and Joe E. Watkins, *Contextual issues in Palaeoindian repatriation*, 7 JOURNAL OF SOCIAL ARCHAEOLOGY 101 (2007).

Timothy J. Famulare, *Has Sandoval Doomed The Private Right of Action Under The National Historic Preservation Act?*, 16 B. U. PUB. INT. L. J. 73 (2006).

Derek Fincham, *Why US Federal Criminal Penalties for Dealing in Illicit Cultural Property are Ineffective, and a Pragmatic Alternative*, 25 CARDOZO ARTS & ENT. L.J. 597 (2007).

Derek Fincham, *Rejecting Renvoi for Movable Cultural Property: The Islamic Republic of Iran v. Denyse Berend*, 14 INT'L J. CULTURAL PROP. 111 (2007).

Raymond Fisman and Shang-Jin Wei, *The Smuggling of Art, and the Art of Smuggling: Uncovering the Illicit Trade in Cultural Property and Antiques*, NBER Working Paper No. W13466 found at http://www.nber.org/papers/w13446.

Craig J. S. Forest, *The Doctrine of Military Necessity and the Protection of Cultural Property During Armed Conflicts*, 37 CAL. W. INT'L. L. J. 177 (2007).

Marion P. Forsyth, *Article: Symposium: Antiquities Law: International Cultural Property Trusts: One Response to Burden of Proof Challenges in Stolen Antiquities Litigation*, 8 CHI. J. INT'L. L. 197 (2007).

Micaela Frulli, *Advancing the Protection of Cultural Property Through the Implementation of Individual Criminal Responsibility: the Case-Law of the International Criminal Tribunal for the Former Yugoslavia*, 15 ITALIAN YEARBOOK OF INT'L. LAW 195 (2006).

Patty Gerstenblith, *Article: Symposium: Antiquities Law: Controlling the International Market in Antiquities: Reducing the Harm, Preserving the Past*, 8 CHI. J. INT'L. L. 169 (2007).

Patty Gerstenblith, *Cultural Heritage Legal Summary*, 32 JOURNAL OF FIELD ARCHAEOLOGY 83 (2007).

Patty Gerstenblith and Lucille Roussin, *Art and Cultural Heritage Law Committee*, 41 INT'L LAW. 613 (2007).

David Gill and Christopher Chippindale, *From Malibu to Rome: Further Developments on the Return of Antiquities*, 14 INT'L J. CULTURAL PROP. 205 (2007).

David Gill and Christopher Chippindale, *Review Article, The Illicit Antiquities Scandal: What It Has Done to Classical Archaeology Collections*, 111 AMERICAN JOURNAL OF ARCHAEOLOGY 571 (2007).

David Gill and Christopher Chippindale, *From Boston to Rome: Reflections on Returning Antiquities*, 13 INT'L. J. CULTURAL PROP. 311 (2006).

Christine L. Green, *Comment: Antiquities Trafficking in Modern Times: How Italian Skullduggery Will Affect United States Museums*, 14 VILL. SPORTS & ENT. L. J. 35 (2007).

Graham Green, *Recent Development: Evaluating the Application of the National Stolen Property Act to Art Trafficking Cases*, 44 HARV. J. ON LEGIS. 251 (2007).

Eliza Hall, *Student Article. The French exception: why the resale royalty works in France and why it matters to the U.S.*, 1 J. INT'L MEDIA & ENT. L. 142 (2007).

Paul Hallwood and Thomas J. Micell, *Murky Waters: The Law and Economics of Salvaging Historic Shipwrecks*, 35 J. LEGAL STUDIES 285 (2006).

Marja van Heese, *The Fight against Illicit Traffic in Cultural Goods: The Dutch Approach*, 11 ART, ANTIQUITY & LAW 85 (2006).

Allison B. Hornstein, *Note. A strange case of Holocaust art; the historical and cultural property debate over who "owns" Bruno Schulz*, 1 COLUM J. E. EUR. L. 142 (2007).

Katherine Jane Hurst, *The Empty(ing) Museum: Why a 2001 Agreement between the United States and Italy is Ineffective in Balancing the Interests of the Source Nation with the Benefits of Museum Display*, 11 ART, ANTIQUITY & LAW 55 (2006).

Sherry Hutt, *Federal Preservation Laws Protecting Archaeological Sites and Native American Cultural Resources*, American Law Institute-American Bar Association Continuing Legal Education, ALI-ABA Course of Study April 26–27, 2007, SM056 ALI-ABA 357 (2007).

Craig W. Jerome, *Balancing Authority and Responsibility: The Forbes Cave Collection, NAGPRA, Hawai'i*, 29 U. HAW. L. REV. 103 (2006).

John C. Johnson, *Under New Management: The Obligation to Protect Cultural Property During Armed Conflict*, 190/191 MIL. L. REV. 111 (2006 - 2007).

Sophia Kelly, *Developing and Implementing Archaeological Site Steward Programs*, 22 NPS Archaeological Program Technical Brief (2007).

Christina K. Knox, *Note: They've Lost Their Marbles: 2002 Universal Museums Declaration, The Elgin Marbles and the Future of the Repatriation Movement*, 29 SUFFOLK TRANSNAT'L L. REV. 315 (2006).

Elizabeth M. Koehler, *Repatriation of Cultural Objects to Indigenous Peoples: A Comparative Analysis of U. S. and Canadian Law*, 41 INT'L. LAW. 103 (2007).

Jenifer Anglim Kreder, *Reconciling Individual and Group Justice with the Need for Repose in Nazi-Looted Art Disputes: Creation of an International Tribunal*, 73 BROOK. L. REV. 153 (2007).

Jenifer Anglim Kreder, *A Nazi Looted Art Tribunal*, 1 WORLD ARBITRATION AND MEDIATION REVIEW (2007).

Michael Kremer and Thomas Wilkening, *Antiquities: Long-Term Leases as an Alternative to Export Bans* (2007), American Law & Economics Association Annual Meetings, American Law & Economics Association 17th Annual Meeting Working Paper 15 at http://law.bepress.com/alea/17th/art15.

Lawrence R. Kueter and Christopher S. Jensen, *Conservation Easements: An Undeveloped Tool to Protect Cultural Resources*, 83 DENV. U. L. REV. 1057 (2006).

Frank Kuitenbrouwer, *The Darker Side of Museum Art: Acquisition and Restitution of Cultural Objects with a Dubious Provenance*, 13 EUROPEAN REVIEW 597 (2005).

Paul Kuruk, *Goading a Reluctant Dinosaur: Mutual Recognition Agreements as a Policy Response to the Misappropriation of Foreign Traditional Knowledge to the United States*, 34 PEPP. L. REV. 629 (2007).

Paul Kuruk, *The Role of Customary Law Under Sui Generis Frameworks of Intellectual Property Rights in Traditional and Indigenous Knowledge*, 17 IND. INT'L & COMP. L. REV. 67 (2007).

Paul Lagarde, *La restitution internationale des biens culturels en dehors de la Convention de l'UNESCO de 1970 et de la Convention d'Unidroit de 1995*, 11 UNIFORM LAW REVIEW 83 (2006).

Katherine Newman Lewis, *Hunters, Oil, Native Americans and archaeologists: Can Conflicting Interests Co-exist on the "Most Significant Archaeological find in North America in 50 Years,"* 26 J. LAND RESOURCES & ENVTL. L. 447 (2006).

Tolina Loulanski, *Revising the Concept for Cultural Heritage: The Argument for a Functional Approach*, 13 INT'L. J. CULTURAL PROP. 207 (2006).

Christina Luke, *Diplomats, Banana Cowboys, and Archaeologists in Western Honduras: A History of the Trade in Pre-Columbian Materials*, 13 INT'L. J. CULTURAL PROP. 25 (2006).

Simon MacKenzie, *Psychosocial Balance Sheets: Illicit Purchase Decisions in the Antiquities Market*, 18 CURRENT ISSUES IN CRIMINAL JUSTICE 231 (2006–2007).

Jana Magnuson, *Glacial Bay And Alaska v. United States: Who Owns Submerged Lands in Federal Reserves?*, 12 OCEAN & COASTAL L. J. 161 (2006).

Harmony A. Mappes, *Note: National Parks: For Use and "Enjoyment" or "Preservation"? And the Role of the National Park Service Management Policies in That Determination*, 92 IOWA L. REV. 601 (2007).

Kelly Mauceri, *Note: Of Fakes and Frauds: An Analysis of Native American Intangible Cultural Property Protection*, 5 GEO J.L. & PUB. POL'Y 263 (2007).

Martin E. McAllister, *Archaeological Resource Damage Assessment: Legal Basis and Methods*, 20 NPS ARCHAEOLOGICAL PROGRAM TECHNICAL BRIEF (2007).

Molly L. McIntosh, *Exploring Machu Picchu: An Analysis of the Legal and Ethical Issues Surrounding the Repatriation of Cultural Property*, 17 DUKE J. COMP. & INT'L. L. 199 (2006).

John Henry Merryman, UNESCO, Art and the Antiquities Market, American Law Institute-American Bar Association Continuing Legal Education, ALI-ABA Course of Study April 26–27, 2007, SM056-ALI-ABA 481.

John Henry Merryman, *The Good Faith Acquisition of Stolen Art*, found at http://ssrn.com/abstract=1025515 (October 2007).

Amy Miller, *The Looting of Iraqi Art: Occupiers and Collectors Turn Away Leisurely from the Disaster*, 37 CASE W. RES. J. INT'L 49 (2005).

Marian Leigh Miller, *Underwater Cultural Heritage: Is the Titantic Still in Peril as Courts Battle over the Future of the Historical Vessel*, 20 EMORY INT'L L. REV. 345 (2006).

Jessica Eve Morrow, *Sharpening The Cutting Edge of International Human Rights Law: Unresolved Issues of War Crimes Tribunals: Note: The National Stolen Property Act and the Return of Stolen Cultural Property to Its Rightful Foreign Owners*, 30 B.C. INT'L. & COMP. L. REV. 249 (2007).

James A. R. Nafziger, *Article: Symposium: Antiquities Law: The Principles for Cooperation in the Mutual Protection and Transfer of Cultural Property*, 8 CHI. J. INT'L. L. 147 (2007).

James A. R. Nafziger, *Panel: Protecting the Cultural Heritage in War and Peace*, 5 SANTA CLARA J. INT'L. L. 486 (2007).

Patrick J. O'Keefe, *Protection and International Collaboration: The Legal Framework of the UNESCO Convention on the Protection of Underwater Cultural Heritage 2001*, 11 ART, ANTIQUITY & LAW 167 (2006).

Robert K. Patterson, *Recent Legislation Comment: Totems and Teapots: The Royal British Columbia Museum Corporation*, 40 U. B. C. L. REV. 421 (2007).

Kirsten E. Petersen, *Note: Cultural Apocalypse Now: The Loss of the Iraq Museum and a New Proposal for the Wartime Protection of Museums*, 16 MINN. J. INT'L. L. 163 (2007).

Mark J. Petr, *Note: Trading Places: Illicit Antiquities, Foreign Cultural Patrimony Laws, and the U.S. National Stolen Property Act after United States v. Schultz*, 28 HASTINGS INT'L & COMP. L. REV. 503 (2005).

Benjamin E. Pollock, *Out of the Night and Fog: Permitting Litigation to Prompt an International Resolution to Nazi-Looted Art Claims*, 43 HOUST. L. REV. 193 (2006).

Eric A. Posner, *Article: Symposium: Antiquities Law: The International Protection of Cultural Property: Some Skeptical Observations*, 8 CHI. J. INT'L. L. 213 (2007).

Timothy Potts, *Combating Illicit Trade: An Assessment*, 11 ART, ANTIQUITY & LAW 131 (2006).

Lyndel V. Prott, *The Dja Dja Wurrung Bark Etchings Case*, 13 INT'L. J. CULTURAL PROP. 241 (2006).

Peter Prows, *Tough Love: The Dramatic Birth and Looming Demise of UNCLOS Property Law (and What Is to Be Done About It)*, 42 TEX. INT'L L. J, *241* (2007).

Anna Przyborowska-Klimczak, *The International Protection of the Intangible Cultural Heritage*, 27 POLISH YEARBOOK OF INTERNATIONAL LAW; 59 (2006).

Rob Regan, *Sovereign Immunity and the Lost Ships of Canada's Historic Merchant Fleet*, 64 U. T. FAC. L. REV. 1 (2006).

Charles Rennick, *The National Historic Preservation Act: San Carlos Apache Tribe v. United States and the Administrative Roadblock to Preserving Native American Culture*, 41 NEW ENGLAND L. REV. 67 (2006).

Marc-Andre Renold, *An Important Swiss Decision Relating to the International Transfer of Cultural Goods: The Swiss Supreme Court's Decision on the Giant Antique Mogul Gold Coins*, 13 INT'L. J. CULTURAL PROP. 361 (2006).

Anne-Marie Rhodes, *On Art Theft, Tax and Time: Triangulating Ownership Disputes Through the Tax Code*, 43 SAN DIEGO L. REV. 495 (2006).

Ryan M. Seidemann, *The Reason Behind the Rules: The Archaeological Resource Protection Act of 1979 and Scientific Study*, 13 B. U. J. SCI. & TECH. L. 193 (2007).

Richard West Sellars, *A Very Large Array: Early Federal Historic Preservation–The Antiquities Act, Mesa Verde and the National Park Service Act*, 47 NAT. RESOURCES J. 267 (2007).

Susan Shearing, *One Step Forward? Recent Developments in Australian State and Territory Indigenous Cultural Heritage Laws*, 3 MQ. J.C.I.E.L. 35 (2006).

Carolyn Shelbourn, *Protecting Archaeological Resources in the United States: Some Lessons in Law and Practice for England?*, 12 ART, ANTIQUITY & LAW 259 (2007).

Carolyn Shelbourn, *Bringing skeletons out of the closet? The law and human remains in art, archaeology and museum collections*, 11 ART, ANTIQUITY & LAW 179 (2006).

Erin K. Slattery, Lead Article: *Preserving the United States' Intangible Cultural Heritage: An Evaluation of the 2003 UNESCO Convention for the Safeguarding of the Intangible Cultural Heritage as a Means to Overcome the Problems Posed by Intellectual Property Law*, 16 DEPAUL-LCA J. ARTS & ENT. L. 201 (2006).

Kim TallBear, *Narratives of Race and Indigeneity in the Geonographic Project*, 35 J. L. MED & ETHICS 412 (2007).

Jason M. Taylor, *The Rape and Return of China's Cultural Property: How Can Bilateral Agreements Stem the Bleeding of China's Cultural Heritage in a Flawed System?*, 3 LOY. INT'L. L. REV. 233 (2006).

Erica J. Techera, *Protection of Cultural Heritage in Times of Armed Conflict: The International Legal Framework Revisited*, 4 MQ. J.C.I.E.L. 1 (2007).

Rebecca Tsossie, *Cultural Challenges to Biotechnology: Native American Genetical Resources and the Concept of Cultural Harm*, 35 J. L. MED. & ETHICS 35 (2007).

Ian Upjohn, *The Protection of Iraqi Cultural Heritage in Australian Domestic Law*, 11 ART, ANTIQUITY & LAW 93 (2006).

Spyriden Vrellis, *The New Act No. 3028/2002 on the Protection of the Antiquities and the Cultural Heritage in General*, FESTSCHRIFT FÜR APOSTOLOS GEORGIADES ZUM 70. GEBURTSTAG (2006).

Marc Weber, *Iran v. Berend - Renvoi for Movable Property*, 12 ART, ANTIQUITY & LAW 103 (2007).

Marc Weber, *New Swiss Law on Cultural Property*, 13 INT'L. J. CULTURAL PROP. 99 (2006).

Leah J. Weiss, *Note: The Role of Museums in Sustaining the Illicit Trade in Cultural Property*, 25 CARDOZO ARTS & ENT. L. J. 837 (2007).

Matthias Weller, *Iran v. Barakat: Some Observations on the Application of Foreign Public Law by Domestic Courts from a Comparative Perspective*, 12 ART, ANTIQUITY & LAW 279 (2007).

Peter T. Wendel, *Protecting Newly Discovered Antiquities: Thinking Outside the "Fee Simple" Box*, 76 FORDHAM L. REV. 1015 (2007).

Jennifer L. Williams, *Review of Selected 2007 California Legislation: Public Resource: Grave Disturbances: Been Digging Lately?*, 38 MCGEORGE L. REV. 299 (2007).

Burt R. Willie, *Kennewick Man Mission Accomplished?*, 43 IDAHO L. REV. 301 (2006).

Lindsay E. Willis, *Note: Looting in Ancient Mesopotamia: A Legislative Scheme for the Protection of Iraq's Cultural Heritage*, 34 GA. J. INT'L & COMP. L. 221 (2005).

Nacy H. Yeide, *NUREMBERG: The Plunder of Art as a War Crime: The Art Looting Investigation Unit Reports and the Hermann Goering Art Collection*, 8 RUTGERS J. LAW & RELIG. 13 (2007).

Ashley Young, Lead Article: Continuing an American Legacy of Racial and Cultural Injustice: A Critical Look at Bonnichson v. United States, 17 Depaul-LCA J. Art & Ent. L. 1 (2006).

James O. Young, *Cultures and Cultural Property*, 24 JOURNAL OF APPLIED PHILOSOPHY 11 (2007).

Other Resources

Additional Readings

Andrew Adler, *The Case Against the Extension of the Archaeological Resource Protection Act to Foreign Lands*, (2006) at http://ssrn.com/abstract=995641.

Kimberly Alderman, *The Ethical Trade in Cultural Property: Ethics and Law in the Antiquity Auction Industry*, found at http://works.bepress.com/kimberly_alderman/1/.

Evan Barr, *From Open-Air Bazaar to Buyer Beware: Evolution of the Antiquities Trade*, 85 MUSEUM NEWS 48 (2006).

Susan Breitkopf, *Lost: The Looting of Iraq's Antiquities*, 86 MUSEUM NEWS 44 (2007).

Tatiana Flessas, *The Repatriation Debate and the Discourse on the Commons*, LSE Legal Studies Working Paper No. 10.2007 found at http://papers.ssrn.com/sol3/papers.cfm?abstract_id=1021205.

Patrick Raden Keefe, *The Idol Thief: Inside One of the Biggest Antiquities-Smuggling Rings in History*, THE NEW YORKER, MAY 7, 2007.

Jenifer Anglim Kreder, *U.S. Museums' Use of Declaratory Judgment Actions in Nazi-Looted Art Disputes, Art Cultural Institutions and Heritage Law Committee e-bulletin* (August 2007) found at: http://papers.ssrn.com/sol3/papers.cfm?abstract_id=999666.

Jennifer Kreder, *Undoing the Native American Graves and Repatriation Act* (2006), at http://law.bepress.com/expresso/eps/1702.

Simon Mackenzie and Penny Green, *Criminalizing the Market in Illicit Antiquities: An Evaluation of the Dealing in Cultural Objects (Offences) Act 2003*, at http://papers.ssrn.com/sol3/papers.cfm?abstract_id=1004267.

Heather Pringle, *Insider: Profiteers on the High Seas*, 60 Archaeology (July/August 2007) at http://www.archaeology.org/0707/etc/insider.html.

Lauren F. Redman, *The Foreign Sovereign Immunities Act: Using A "Shield" Statute as a "Sword" for Obtaining Federal Jurisdiction in Art and Antiquity Cases* (2007), at http://works.bepress.com/lauren_redman/1/.

James Wawrzyniak, *Rubin v. The Islamic Republic of Iran: a Struggle for Control of Persian Antiquities in America* (2007), at http://lsr.nellco.org/harvard/students/papers/17.

Sandra B. Zellmer and Jessica Harder, *Unbundling Property in Water* (2008), http://works.bepress.com/sandi_zellmer/1/.

New Web Sites

The Art Newspaper found at: http://www.theartnewspaper.com/.

Association of Art Museum Directors found at: http://www.aamd.org/papers/.

IFAR.org found at http://www.ifar.org/index.htm.

Lawyer's Committee for Cultural Heritage Protection found at: http://www.cultural-heritage.org.

Museum Security Network found at: http://www.museum-security.org/.

SAA Professional Standards for the Determination of Archaeological Value December 22, 2003: www.saa.org/goverment/ARPAstandards.pdf.

Saving Antiquities for Everyone found at: http://www.savingantiquities.org/.

Blogs

Archaeoblog found at: http://illicit-cultural-property.blogspot.com/search?q= .

Archaeonews found at: http://archaeonews.blogspot.com/search?q=..

Art Hostage found at: http://arthostage.blogspot.com/.

The Assemblage found at: http://politicalarchaeology.wordpress.com/.

Cultural Heritage News found at: http://culturalheritagenews.blogspot.com/.

Cultural Heritage in Danger found at: http://safecorner.savingantiquities.org/search?q=.

Friends of American Past found at: http://www.friendsofpast.org/kennewick-man/.

Illicit Cultural Property Blog found at: http://illicit-cultural-property.blogspot.com/search?q=.

Looting Matters Blog found at: http://lootingmatters.blogspot.com/search?updated-min=2007-01-01T00%3A00%3A00Z&updated-max=2008-01-01T00%3A00%3A00Z&max-results=14.

News Input found at: http://www.law.harvard.edu/faculty/martin/art_law/art_law_news.php.

Recognizing Career Achievements in Cultural Resource Protection

• • •

The *Yearbook of Cultural Property Law* is dedicated to keeping cultural resource practitioners up to date with legal developments in the field and with placing milestones into context. The *Yearbook* editors enjoy recognizing individuals who have made lasting contributions to the field. This year we recognize two brilliant individuals—one a lawyer—whose names are known around the world for their contributions to the development of two important museums: the Iraq Museum in Baghdad and the National Museum of the American Indian in Washington, D.C. While both men have now gone on to other endeavors, each faced incredible challenges in the last few years of their careers; one in keeping a museum collection intact in the midst of war, and the other founding a huge new museum that stands as a monument to the greatness of Native American culture. Each is recognized here by a museum lawyer who has had the privilege to work with them and support their efforts.

Dr. Donny George Youkhanna: Museum Director in Transition

By Patty Gerstenblith

Dr. Donny George Youkhanna became known to the world of cultural heritage professionals during the U.S. invasion of Iraq and the looting of the Iraq Museum in Baghdad between April 8 and 10, 2003. Since that time, Dr. George has been the face and, more importantly, the voice for the rescue and preservation of Iraq's cultural heritage—its ancient Mesopotamian culture and its later, equally illustrious, Islamic past. The Director General of Research and Studies for the Iraq State Board of Antiquities and Heritage (SBAH) at the time of the U.S. invasion, Dr. George became, in quick succession, the Director General of the Iraqi Museums from November 2003 until August 2005 and then, for a year, the Chairman of the State Board before his retirement and move to the United States, where he is currently a visiting professor at the State University of New York at Stony Brook.

Dr. George was born in Habbania in al-Anbar province and was educated in Baghdad, where he received a B.A. in Ancient Archaeology and his M.A. and Ph.D. degrees in Prehistoric Archaeology, all at the University of Baghdad. Both latter degrees focused on the archaeology of the sixth-millennium B.C. site of Tell Es-Sawwan. Over a period of thirty years, he held numerous positions with the SBAH and the Iraq Museum. At the museum, he worked in registration and was the director of its Documentation Center and later assistant director general for technical affairs. He also directed archaeological field projects for the Babylon Restoration Project, the Bekhma Dam Archaeological rescue project, the Neo-Assyrian site of Nineveh and the Early Dynastic Sumerian site of Um Al-Agareb and served as the Head of the Technical Committee, which supervises the authentication and receipt of accidentally discovered antiquities that are brought to the Iraq Museum.

As Director General of the Iraqi Museums, he supervised all fifteen Iraqi museums, including collections management, restoration laboratories, postgraduate students and scholars, and international relations with other museums in the world. As chairman of the SBAH, he supervised all archaeological and architectural heritage activities in the country. During this time, Dr. George also taught in the Departments of Archaeology and of Architecture at the University of Baghdad and at the College of Babylon for Philosophy and Theology. He has had numerous publications in both Arabic and English concerning Mesopotamian archaeology and was a member of the Iraqi Science Academy, Department of Syriac Language, for which he translated Syriac literature.

His life and career took a dramatic turn with the U.S. invasion in the spring of 2003 and the looting of the Iraq Museum in April of that year. He quickly assumed the role of indefatigable advocate for the recovery and conservation of the museum's collections and for the preservation of sites in Iraq, whose looting has taken on massive proportions since the mid-1990s. He has lectured throughout the world, including Germany, Britain, Spain, Italy, Sweden,

Belgium, Denmark, Japan, and Syria, concerning Iraq's looted antiquities. In 2007 alone, he has given eleven lectures in the United States on the subject of the Iraq Museum and the efforts to recover the looted antiquities and to protect the sites in southern Iraq. He serves on several international committees that are devoted to law enforcement efforts to recover looted antiquities, including the Iraq Cultural Committee of UNESCO, the International Regional Committee of Interpol, and the Iraqi National Committee for Education, Science, and Culture in Iraq. He has also attended and spoken at numerous conferences devoted to Mesopotamian archaeology and the looting problem, including the Rencontres assyriologique in London and in Munster, Germany, and conferences in Istanbul, Amman, Seoul, Boston, Washington, and Paris. In recognition of his efforts, he has been made a corresponding member of the German Archaeological Institute and an Honorary Member of the Archaeological Institute of America. Most importantly, he has spoken tirelessly to the press and to the public to make the case for the preservation of Iraq's heritage, even in the face of the most daunting circumstances.

In August 2006, Dr. George fled Baghdad after he and his family, who are Assyrian Christians, received death threats. He arrived in the United States a few months later and took up his teaching position at SUNY Stony Brook. As the extensive list of his publications and lectures shows, Iraq's cultural heritage has remained at the center of Dr. George's life and work. Although he was cast into the role of museum director under the most adverse circumstances, he has devoted his professional life to the Iraq Museum in the many different positions he held there over the course of thirty years and continues to do so now from afar. Throughout these difficulties he has retained a sense of calm and acts as kind advisor and inspiration to many who work in the cultural heritage field. His life is now truly in transition—but also clearly one that will remain dedicated to the preservation of Iraq's cultural heritage.

W. Richard West, Jr.: Founding Director of the National Museum of the American Indian

By Lauryn H. Guttenplan

W. Richard West, Jr. retired at the end of 2007 as the founding director of the Smithsonian Institution's National Museum of the American Indian after seventeen years as a visionary and tireless leader of that Museum. Rick West, a citizen of the Cheyenne and Arapaho Tribes of Oklahoma and a Peace Chief of the Southern Cheyenne, joined the Museum as its first director soon after Congress enacted the National Museum of the American Indian Act in November, 1989. Rick, a successful attorney, expert in Indian law, and advocate for Native people throughout his life, was the perfect choice to carry out the congressional mandate to create a museum of living cultures dedicated to the life, languages, literature, history, and arts of the Native peoples of the Western Hemisphere.

From the Museum's inception, Rick articulated a vision of a "museum different"—a museum that would not depict objects as static symbols of a lost people, but rather would showcase Native people and their culture as alive and vibrant. In every facet of planning, constructing, and operating the Museum's three facilities—The Museum on the National Mall, the George Gustav Heye Center in New York City, and the Cultural Resources Center in Suitland, Maryland—Rick's commitment is evident, from exhibitions, presentations, and public programs that are presented in Native voice, to an award-winning café featuring Native cuisine, to the National Pow Wow that has brought thousands of Native people to the nation's capital to celebrate their culture. At every step of the way, Rick West has been there inspiring, guiding, and challenging museum professionals and the public to discard obsolete views about Native people as "cultural relics" and recognize them as a dynamic people flourishing in the present yet with deep ties to the past. There have been countless successful examples of Rick's vision, but perhaps none more profound and indelible than the Museum's opening ceremonies in September 2004, when thousands of Native people, many dressed in Native regalia, gathered on the National Mall for several days of celebration.

None of these accomplishments and countless others would come as a surprise to anyone who has had the good fortune to know Rick and work with him. Rick grew up in Muskogee, Oklahoma, the son of an American Indian master artist, the late Walter Richard West, Sr., and Maribelle McCrea West. He graduated from the University of Redlands in California in 1965 with a degree in American history and received a Master's Degree in American History from Harvard University in 1968. He graduated from Stanford University School of Law with a jurisprudence degree in 1971 and it was during law school that he met his wife, Mary Beth. They have two grown children, Amy and Ben.

Prior to becoming director of the Museum, Rick enjoyed a long and successful legal career as a partner in the Washington D.C. law firm of Fried, Frank, Harris, Shriver & Jacobson and, subsequently, in the Indian-owned Albuquerque law firm of Gover, Stetson, Williams & West, P.C. Throughout his legal career, Rick represented the interests of numerous tribes and Native organizations in federal, state, and tribal courts, various federal agencies, and the Congress.

During his tenure as director of the Museum, Rick served the museum profession with distinction as chair of the American Association of Museums and in numerous other capacities. He is currently serving as vice chair of the American Association of Museums/International Council of Museums, which represents the interests of American museums in the international museum community. In addition to his museum service, Rick serves on several charitable and educational boards.

On a personal note, Rick and I first met in 1990 soon after he became director of the Museum. I had been working on the Museum project since the mid-1980s when the Smithsonian commenced discussions with the Museum of the American Indian, Heye Foundation, to transfer the Museum and its collection of 800,000 objects to the Smithsonian. Rick, as an attorney, made an effort in his earliest days to introduce himself and he quickly became one of my favorite clients. Over the years, we worked closely on a wide range of legal matters ranging from interpretations of the enabling statute that created the Museum to requests for repatriation of Native American sacred and patrimonial objects. Though he often referred to himself as a "lapsed lawyer," Rick simply couldn't help himself when an interesting legal issue arose, often "relapsing" into his lawyer mode as we discussed and sometimes even engaged in heated debate over esoteric legal issues. He liked to joke about it and we shared many laughs over the years, but I always welcomed his analysis, insight, and incredible intelligence. I often told Rick that it made my job easier having an attorney as a client—well, at least most of the time! Because of his legal background, he appreciated and valued lawyers, inviting me to many meetings of his Board and staff, which enabled me to better counsel the Museum. At those countless meetings, I witnessed first hand the admiration and respect he earned from everyone associated with the Museum and the larger museum and Native community. Rick always appreciated my advice even when we sometimes disagreed and even when the outcome may not have been what he wanted to hear. It has been an honor and a privilege to serve as an attorney for the National Museum of the American Indian, and I have learned a great deal from my valued client, Rick West. But it is not just our professional relationship that I have come to cherish; after seventeen years of our working together, I am proud and honored to call Rick a good friend and I will miss him as will the entire Smithsonian community.

Table of Cases

Yearbook 2008 Contributors and Editorial Board

Caroline M. Blanco, Editorial Board, Marine Environment Practice Area, Board member LCCHP, is coauthor of HERITAGE RESOURCES LAW (1999), and CULTURAL PROPERTY LAW (2004). She is the Assistant General Counsel for the Environment at the National Science Foundation, where she provides advice on the environmental and cultural resources laws implicated by the Foundation's mission in promoting cutting edge science. Prior to assuming her current position, she served as a trial attorney in the Natural Resources Section of the Environment and National Resources Division of the United States Department of Justice where, from 1991 to 2007, she specialized in heritage resources law and, in particular, historic shipwreck litigation. Ms. Blanco, twice a recipient of the Attorney General's Award for Distinguished Service, frequently lectures in the field of heritage resources law at law schools and government training seminars throughout the country. In recognition of her work in cultural resource preservation and outstanding contributions to the legal protection of submerged cultural resources during her tenure at the Department of Justice, she was recently presented with A Legacy of Excellence in Submerged Resource Preservation award by the Submerged Resources Center of the National Park Service. In addition, Ms. Blanco serves on the faculty of American University's Washington College of Law as a Professorial Lecturer on cultural property law. Prior to her government service, Ms. Blanco was a litigation associate at the law firm of McCutchen Doyle Brown & Enersen, San Jose, California.

L. Eden Burgess is an associate in the Washington, D.C., office of Andrews Kurth LLP, where she focuses on general litigation matters including art recovery and cultural property cases and has written and spoken on these subjects. She received her J.D. from George Washington University Law School, with honors.

Trinidad Contreras is a first-year law student at the University of Arizona Rogers College of Law. In 2003, he completed his undergraduate degree at the University of California at Berkeley in Native American Studies. In May 2007 he also obtained his Master's Degree in American Indian Studies with an emphasis in Law and Policy, at the University of Arizona. He is an enrolled member of the Santa Ysabel Band of Diegueno Indians.

Ildikó P. DeAngelis serves as the Director of the Museum Studies Program at The George Washington University where she has taught Collections Management, Legal and Ethical Issues since 1997. Prior to joining GW, Professor DeAngelis was primary legal advisor on collections issues to the Smithsonian Museums for more than a decade. She has published and taught numerous workshops on legal/ethical topics relevant to museum operations, including stolen art, old loans, tax implications of gifts, information laws, and appraisals. She has served for many years on the Steering Committee (and as faculty) of the American Law Institute/American Bar Association annual course of study, Legal Problems of Museum Administration. In addition to a law degree (1980 magna cum laude), Professor DeAngelis holds a Certificate in Museum Administration (1976) from the Smithsonian, a Master of Arts in Art History (1974), and gained practical collections management experience as contract Registrar at the National Collection of Fine Arts (now known as the Smithsonian American Art Museum) (1976).

Kelly Yasaitis Fanizzo, editorial board member of the State and Local Practice Area, is a historic preservation specialist with the Advisory Council on Historic Preservation (ACHP). She currently works with a number of federal property management agencies in their section 106 compliance. She holds a J.D., magna cum laude, from American University, Washington College of Law, and a Graduate Certificate in Museum Studies from George Washington University, Columbian College of Arts and Sciences.

Elise Foster is an attorney with the U.S. Department of Agriculture, Office of the General Counsel, in Ogden, Utah. Since 1997 she has been active in the development of ARPA civil penalty prosecutions. Elise has handled many ARPA civil penalty cases, collecting thousands of dollars which have been used for restoration and repair of archaeological resources on National

Forest System lands. She has provided training on the subject of ARPA civil penalty prosecution to a wide range of federal attorneys and government land managers. She is also the author of USING ARPA CIVIL PENALTIES TO PROTECT ARCHEOLOGICAL RESOURCES ON PUBLIC AND INDIAN LANDS, a guide to civil ARPA prosecution, published cooperatively by the Forest Service and the National Park Service in 2007.

Patty Gerstenblith, Editorial Board, International Practice Area, President of Board LCCHP, is a professor of law at DePaul University College of Law, where she is Director of DePaul's program in art and cultural heritage law. She served as Editor-in-Chief of the INTERNATIONAL JOURNAL OF CULTURAL PROPERTY from1995 to 2002, as a public representative on the President's Cultural Property Advisory Committee in the U.S. Department of State from 2000 to 2003, and as Co-Chair of the American Bar Association's International Cultural Property Committee from 2002 to 2006. Her most recent books include ART, CULTURAL HERITAGE, AND THE LAW and IRAQ BEYOND THE HEADLINES: HISTORY, ARCHAEOLOGY, AND WAR (coauthored with Benjamin R. Foster and Karen Polinger Foster). She received her J.D. from Northwestern University and a Ph.D. from Harvard University in Fine Art and Anthropology.

Lauryn H. Guttenplan is an Associate General Counsel for the Smithsonian Institution, where she has served as an attorney since 1985. She has focused on issues of Native American repatriation, intellectual property, contracts, nonprofit tax, and various legal matters related to the establishment of the National Museum of the American Indian. She has been the chair and a regular faculty member of the annual conference on Legal Issues in Museum Administration sponsored by the Smithsonian Institution, the American Association of Museums, and the American Law Institute/American Bar Association. Prior to joining the Smithsonian Institution, she worked for four years in private law practice. She received her J.D. in 1980 from Georgetown University Law Center, where she served as an editor of TAX LAW JOURNAL, and her B.A. in history from Cornell University (magna cum laude) in 1977.

Sherry Hutt, Senior Editor, Board member LCCHP, is the program manager for the National NAGPRA program, in the Department of the Interior, formerly a Superior Court Judge in Arizona, an assistant United States Attorney assigned to ARPA cases, and trustee of the Heard Museum. She is the coauthor of CULTURAL PROPERTY LAW (2004), HERITAGE RESOURCES LAW (1999), ARCHEOLOGICAL RESOURCE PROTECTION (1992), and co-editor of PRESENTING ARCHAEOLOGY IN COURT (2006). In addition to the J.D., she holds a Ph.D. in forestry.

Thomas R. Kline, Editorial Board, Art Market Practice Area, Board member LCCHP, is a partner in the Washington, D.C., office of Andrews Kurth LLP, has represented governments, museums, churches, foundations, and families, including Holocaust survivors and heirs, in recovering stolen art appearing in the United States. He has also represented a major American museum in responding to a Holocaust claim. Mr. Kline co-teaches a seminar, Stolen and Illegally Imported Art and Cultural Property, in the George Washington University Museum Studies Program. Mr. Kline writes and speaks on the subject of restitution of stolen art, and appeared before the Presidential Advisory Commission on Holocaust Assets in the United States. He is a member, Editorial Board, KUNST UND RECHT (Art and Law), www.kur-journal.de.

Gary Nurkin was an Assistant District Attorney in Nassau County, where he handled environmental crimes, among others, was a trial attorney in the Appeals Bureau, and then chief of the Environmental and Frauds Bureau. Gary joined the EPA in 1989 as a Regional Enforcement Counsel, became Assistant Regional Counsel, and, for two years, was a Special Assistant United States Attorney handling environmental cases. A graduate of Chicago-Kent College of Law, Gary has also been an adjunct faculty member at Seton Hall University School of Law and Pace University School of Law, where he taught cultural property law. His undergraduate and graduate degrees are in anthropology.

Lucille A. Roussin, Editorial Board, Museum Practice Area, Board Member LCCHP, is an advisor to SAFE, Saving Antiquities for Everyone. She is the founder and director of the Holocaust Restitution Claims Practicum at the Benjamin N. Cardozo School of Law in New York City, where she teaches a seminar, Remedies for Wartime Confiscation. She also teaches a course, Art, the Law and Professional Ethics, at the School of Graduate Studies at the Fashion Institute of Technology. She is an associate with the firm of McCallion & Associates and earned her law degree in 1996 from the Benjamin N. Cardozo School of Law, where she was a Belkin Scholar. She was Deputy Research Director of the Art and Cultural Property Team of the Presidential Commission on Holocaust Assets and was an associate in the Art and International Law Practice Group at Herrick, Feinstein LLP in New York City. In 2001, she negotiated the first restitution of a rare Jewish ritual object to a private family in the United States.

Michael Scherzer is an associate at Latham & Watkins, LLP in Washington, D.C., where he has worked in the energy and transactional practices as well as with housing and historic preservation issues. He received a degree in history from Yale College, graduating magna cum laude, and a J.D. from the Georgetown University Law Center where he graduated cum laude.

Rob Roy Smith, Editor, Tribes, Tribal Lands, and Indian Arts, is counsel with the Indian Law Group of the law firm Ater Wynne, LLP in Seattle, Washington. He received a J.D., cum laude, with a certificate in natural resources and environmental law from Northwestern School of Law of Lewis and Clark College. He has extensive experience advising Indian tribal clients and those doing business in Indian Country on all aspects of federal Indian law, including economic development, cultural resource protection, taxation, tribal sovereignty, and Indian gaming.

David Tarler, Assistant Editor and Editor, Enforcement Practice Area, Board member LCCHP, is a Near Eastern archaeologist and an attorney. From 1978 to 1990 he was a senior staff member of the City of David excavation project, in Jerusalem, Israel. After completing his legal studies, in 1993, he served as a consultant to the Archeology Program and the Native American Graves Protection and Repatriation Act Program of the National Park Service, in Washington, D.C. In 2006, he became the enforcement and training coordinator for the National NAGPRA Program. During 2001–2002, he provided assistance to staff at the United States Sentencing Commission working on Federal Sentencing Guideline 2B1.5, which applies to crimes involving cultural heritage resources. He was a contributing editor for Hutt, Blanco & Varmer, HERITAGE RESOURCES LAW (1999), and PRESENTING ARCHAEOLOGY IN COURT (2006).

James Van Ness, Editorial Board, Editor, Federal Land Management, Board member LCCHP, is the acting Deputy General Counsel (Environment & Installations), Department of Defense. In this capacity, he is responsible for advising senior DoD officials on legal matters related to natural and cultural resources management, environmental planning, and consultation with indigenous peoples. Mr. Van Ness earned an LL.M. from the University of Washington; a J.D. from the University of Iowa; and a B.S. from Iowa State University. He is a member of the adjunct faculty at The George Washington University School of Law.

James A. Wawrzyniak, Jr. is currently a law clerk for Judge Timothy M. Tymkovich of the United States Court of Appeals for the Tenth Circuit in Denver, Colorado. He is a graduate of Georgetown University and Harvard Law School.

Index